Oxford Studies in Soci
General Editor: Keith

C000101512

The Crimes of W
Early Modern Germany

The Crimes of Women
in Early Modern Germany

ULINKA RUBLACK

CLARENDON PRESS · OXFORD

OXFORD
UNIVERSITY PRESS

Great Clarendon Street, Oxford OX2 6DP

Oxford University Press is a department of the University of Oxford.
It furthers the University's objective of excellence in research, scholarship,
and education by publishing worldwide in

Oxford New York

Athens Auckland Bangkok Bogotá Buenos Aires Calcutta
Cape Town Chennai Dar es Salaam Delhi Florence Hong Kong Istanbul
Karachi Kuala Lumpur Madrid Melbourne Mexico City Mumbai
Nairobi Paris São Paulo Shangai Singapore Taipei Tokyo Toronto Warsaw

with associated companies in Berlin Ibadan

Oxford is a registered trade mark of Oxford University Press
in the UK and in certain other countries

Published in the United States
by Oxford University Press Inc., New York

British Library Cataloguing in Publication Data
Data available

Library of Congress Cataloging in Publication Data
Data applied for

ISBN 0-19-820637-2 (hbk)
ISBN 0-19-820886-3 (pbk)

1 3 5 7 9 10 8 6 4 2

Typeset in Garamond
by J&L Composition Ltd, Filey, North Yorkshire
Printed in Great Britain
on acid-free paper by
Biddles Ltd., Guildford and King's Lynn

ACKNOWLEDGEMENTS

My first debt is to Bob Scribner, for his expert guidance and full support for this project from beginning to its end as a Cambridge Ph.D. thesis. His recent premature death has deprived early modern German studies of one of its most distinguished and innovative scholars. This book can only be a small tribute to his memory and vision of history. Throughout the writing, Lyndal Roper's work, commitment, and generosity were invaluable. Olwen Hufton, Sheilagh Ogilvie, Keith Thomas, and Keith Wrightson read my thesis and made helpful suggestions; Heide Wunder gave generous advice and encouragement at early stages of the work. Renate Dürr and Wolfgang Zimmermann guided me on sources in Schwäbisch Hall and Constance. Many friends and colleagues provided me with references, discussed findings, or gave moral support. Daniela Hacke deserves special thanks, and so does my family, who supported me with inexhaustible interest and love. To Vic Gatrell I owe an equally personal debt of gratitude for giving me both a respect for narrative and a vivid sense of the past as seen through the history of crime and punishment. This work has benefited enormously from discussions with him, and from his careful reading of the manuscript.

U. R.

NOTE

A shortened version of this book in German was published in March 1998 by Fischer: *Magd, Metz' oder Mörderin: Frauen vor frühneuzeitlichen Gerichten.*

CONTENTS

LIST OF FIGURES

ABBREVIATIONS

ARG	*Archiv für Reformationsgeschichte*
GWU	*Geschichte in Wissenschaft und Unterricht*
HA	*Historische Anthropologie*
HStASt	Hauptstaatsarchiv Stuttgart
HWJ	*History Workshop Journal*
HZ	*Historische Zeitschrift*
JIH	*Journal of Interdisciplinary History*
JSH	*Journal of Social History*
MedGG	*Medizin, Geschichte und Gesellschaft*
ÖZG	*Österreichische Zeitschrift für Geschichtswissenschaften*
P&P	*Past and Present*
SCJ	*Sixteenth Century Journal*
StABh	Stadtarchiv Besigheim
StABM	Stadtarchiv Bad Mergentheim
StAE	Stadtarchiv Esslingen
StAFr	Stadtarchiv Freiburg im Breisgau
StAH	Stadtarchiv Schwäbisch Hall
StAKN	Stadtarchiv Konstanz
StAL	Staatsarchiv Ludwigsburg
StAMM	Stadtarchiv Memmingen
VSWG	*Vierteljahresschrift für Sozial- und Wirtschaftsgeschichte*
ZfWLG	*Zeitschrift für württembergische Landesgeschichte*
ZHF	*Zeitschrift für historische Forschung*
ZRG Germ. Abt.	*Zeitschrift für Rechtsgeschichte, Germanische Abteilung*

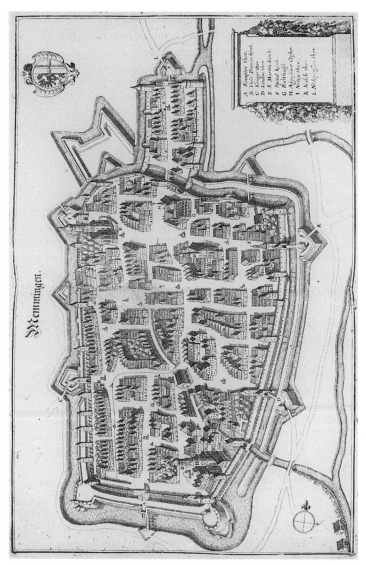

Fɪɢ. ɪ. Merian's View of Memmingen

Introduction

MATTHÄUS MERIAN's topographies have left a lasting impression of seventeenth-century German towns. We still look at his engravings with pleasure. One of his views, of Memmingen, shows the size, boundaries, gates, markets, streets, and important buildings of this upper Swabian Imperial city (Fig. 1, opposite). In this case there is next to no record of natural forms; what vegetation there is is cultivated for display rather than use. The brook that curves through Memmingen is narrow and disciplined; it serves the paper-makers, dyers, tanners, and other crafts. The city is empty, however. We see neither humans nor animals; no pigs, goats, cows, or hens. Outside the fortified walls, nobody moves on the paths; the environs are empty. Nothing indicates how the land is used. We see no peasants, out-burghers, tradesmen, or wanderers. Instead our gaze is directed to the houses and religious and communal buildings in the town itself. Mainly represented in side-view, they seem spacious, and some are larger than others. Even so, if Merian's engraving were our only source, it would be difficult to guess where rich and poor lived in Memmingen. Questions about rich and poor are not raised. This is one reason why Merian's *Städteansichten* are nowadays framed to decorate bourgeois livingrooms. They affirm an image of pre-modern times which displays order and a limited and humanly mastered world.

How might we put some life into this town? A small story will help. One July morning in 1608 all those empty Memmingen streets were filled as the innkeepers assembled in the town hall. A new ale ordinance was to be read out to them, and they would have to swear to obey it. Among the assembled people was Anna, the wife of the innkeeper Michel Müller. When she left the town hall with three of the men she was in a fine temper. 'All your hands should be cut off', she fumed: 'you stood in there as if frozen. It's the same as in court, no one is allowed to say a word!' One of the innkeepers asked what was annoying her so much: the lords' demands had to be obeyed, after all. Anna, he said, was 'always cleverer than everyone else. My lords will soon have to fill the

council with women.' Shortly afterwards, Anna was arrested for her
'immodest speech', and witnesses were summoned to testify to her
insolence.[1]

Never mind that we do not know what happened to her after that.
The point is that quarrels like these allow us to glimpse the relationships which brought communities to life. For it can be said that what is
common to any community is not so much 'shared values or common
understanding' as the fact that members are 'engaged in the same
argument'. Communities are held together by what divides them, and
by the business of threshing out 'alternative strategies, misunderstand-
ings, conflicting goals and values'.[2] Yet, in the early modern period (as
now) the chances of making claims in this argument were not equally
distributed. Status mattered, and so did gender. There were limits to
what could be said. And anyone who challenged the notion of community itself could be forcefully silenced; communal speech and
argument were regulated. The law was an important instrument in
regulating such conflict. It affirmed order, and decided about the
social exclusion of wrongdoers, sometimes their life or death.

This study is concerned with how gender shaped conflicts in early
modern German communities, and with the lives of women on the
social margins of society; it is also, consequently, about the ways in
which women experienced the law. Our way into this world is
through an imaginative engagement with the stories of women
who were gossiped about, accused, and punished. Look at that
map again. Inscribed with a *G* is the town hall. This was where
Anna angrily heard the ordinance and was arrested. Presumably she
was admonished and released after a couple of hours. Would she
have known 'better' in future? We cannot always say; none the less,
interrogations like hers, recognizances, and dossiers of criminal
cases all give insights into early modern lives which would otherwise be unknown. They fascinate because they speak to us of
people's thoughts, feelings, and fantasies.[3] Of course what we
hear from and about these people is mediated by the interrogators'
interests, scribes' framing of the protocol, and offenders' excuse

---

[1] StAMM, A 135/8, 10 July 1608.
[2] D. Sabean, *Power in the Blood: Popular Culture and Village Discourse in Early Modern
Germany* (Cambridge, 1984), 29. Objections are raised in L. Roper, '"The Common
Man", "the Common Good", "Common Women": Gender and Meaning in the German
Reformation Commune', *Social History*, 12 (1987), 8.
[3] See C. Ginzburg, *The Cheese and the Worms: The Cosmos of a Sixteenth-Century Miller*
(Harmondsworth, 1992), p. xi; a seminal manifesto for approaching court records in
this way.

strategies, not to mention the mortal fear of those tried for capital crimes. But for all their shortcomings and probable distortions of truths, it is nevertheless necessary to trust court records and to respond to them empathically, if we are to engage with the experiences of the humble people, which can be heard only in this source, and with the narratives culturally available to them in order to make sense of violence, power, pleasure, and transgression.[4]

Let us return to Anna and to Memmingen. On leaving the town hall Anna would step into a bustling town of around 5,000 inhabitants. Nearly half of them would be children, playing together in groups, having their own arguments. Older children looked after younger siblings after school, or helped their parents. Boys herded cows in meadows outside town, girls cut grass. They assisted their parents by selling merchandise, fetching things, delivering to customers. Children also ran cheap messenger services: Michel Müller would probably have heard about his wife's arrest through children who had picked up the news from the innkeepers outside the town hall. What would Müller have thought of his wife's behaviour? Had he sent her to the town hall alone because he was ill? Or did he himself not want to swear obedience? Artisans' wives were allowed to stand in for their husbands at such assemblies. They were respected for managing household workshops along with their husbands. But they enjoyed no public rights like voting, speaking, or making oaths. Like all other women, they had to know their place and swallow ridicule of the kind Anna had to, when she was told that the Memmingen council would soon have to be filled with women.

There were many crafts in Memmingen, but weaving predominated. Over 200 weaving masters operated in those streets. Everywhere you would hear the sound of shuttles. It was small workshop production; around 1590 nobody owned more than one or two looms.[5] Cart-loads

---

[4] 'Narratives of litigation' are interestingly explored in L. Gowing, *Domestic Dangers: Women, Words, and Sex in Early Modern London* (Oxford, 1996), ch. 7; M. Chaytor, 'Husband(ry): Narratives of Rape in the Seventeenth Century', *Gender & History*, 7 (1995), 378–407; G. Walker, 'Rereading Rape and Sexual Violence in Early Modern England', *Gender & History* (forthcoming); the construction of judicial texts in M. Mommertz, '"Ich, Lisa Thielen": Text als Handlung und sprachliche Struktur—ein methodischer Vorschlag', *HA* 3 (1996), 303–29; the dynamics of torture and confession in L. Roper, *Oedipus and the Devil: Witchcraft, Sexuality and Religion in Early Modern Europe* (London, 1994), ch. 10; the attempt to establish 'truth' in trials in C. Ginzburg, *Il guidice e lo storico: Considerazioni in margine al processo Sofri* (Turin, 1991).

[5] T. M. Safley, 'Production, Transaction, and Proletarianization: The Textile Industry in Upper Swabia, 1580–1660', in id. and L. N. Rosenband (eds.), *The Workplace before the Factory: Artisans and Proletarians, 1500–1800* (Ithaca, NY, 1993), 128.

of flax came into the city for spinners to transform it into yarn. Spinning was women's work, and every woman would devote most of her free time to it. It was an occupation which always kept her busy, but was not particularly skilled. It designated women's place in society. The phrase most frequently used to rebuke women who spoke out politically was to tell them to go back to their spinning wheels. Berthold of Regensburg proclaimed that 'men shall fight and women spin', and Argula von Grumbach, one of the few female Reformation pamphleteers, was reprimanded by a student writer: 'So put an end to your boldness and haughtiness, and spin at your wheel instead, or knit caps and weave lace. A woman should never parade God's words and teach men; rather, she should listen to them, as Mary Magdalen did.'[6]

Some women contested this view, however. In 1682, for example, several Memmingen wives sent an anonymous libel complaining about their husbands to the mayor. The men, they said, sat in inns all night gaming their money away, when not a 'drop of dripping or a loaf of bread' remained to feed the family. In the morning the women had to cope with hung-over husbands. One councillor responded that the women should get back to their spinning wheels. They retorted that if only their husbands earned enough to bring them flax they would happily do so.[7] These women were making their protest within the confines of a dominant understanding: man was provider and woman the protector of the home. Even so, they exploited its logic ingeniously. Their argument makes us aware of their highly audible roles in everyday life and their part in the politics and economy of the household.

Artisans' wives were respected members of communities. The women we will meet in this book, by contrast, spoke mainly from the margins of society. In the Memmingen court books we find, for example, the confession of Katharina Hertz, a thief arrested in 1609. Katharina had been whipped out of at least three other towns in the region. This time she had stolen money and bread, but mainly cloth, belts, and caps. Textiles were in high demand. There was a flourishing second-hand trade, and women thieves could easily

---

[6] 'So stell ab dein Muet und guet Dunckel und spinn dafuer an einer Kunckel Oder strick hauben und wirck Borten. Ein Weyb solt nit mit Gottes worten stoltzieren und die Männer leren sonder mit Madalen zu hoeren', cited in C. Ulbricht, 'Unartige Weiber: Präsenz und Renitenz von Frauen im frühneuzeitlichen Deutschland', in R. v. Dülmen (ed.), *Arbeit, Frömmigkeit und Eigensinn* (Frankfurt on Main, 1990), 18.   [7] StAMM, A 140/2, 27 Feb. 1682.

dispose of their stolen wares. Katharina Hertz was unlucky, though. On Memmingen market, near the Augustinerkloster, the hangman put her in the pillory, cut her ears off, and banished her from the Niedergassentor. The city-scribe made a drawing in the court book next to Katharina's confession (Fig. 2). What prompted city-scribes to draw these images of punishment? The practice was common. Other drawings from the Memmingen score-books are reproduced throughout this study. Were they functional, a visual index of offenders and their punishments? Or did they result from the need somehow to assimilate and tame the witnessing of such violence? Either way, in this case the hangman's name was noted as 'Master Franz'. His stretched-out tongue may denote his pleasure in the punishment and the panache with which he executed it. Hertz's hands were bound together, her face small and expressionless. It is left to us to imagine her pain.

The histories of several thousand women who were protagonists in court cases and criminal trials survive fragmentarily in the court records of south-west Germany for the period 1500–1700. These allow us to analyse the assumptions about gender upon which early modern justice was built, and to understand the social context of crimes and accusations. We examine women tried in Protestant Württemberg (the largest territory in the south-west, with a population of 300,000–450,000 inhabitants), three Protestant Imperial cities (Memmingen, Esslingen, and Schwäbisch Hall, each with c.5,000 inhabitants), and Catholic Constance. The crimes include all major ones—mainly sexual crimes, infanticide, and property crime. Witchcraft is omitted, however. This is partly because it is already the subject of a large number of excellent studies,[8] and partly because it was regarded as a *crimen exceptum,* and therefore treated exceptionally. (Stronger tortures could be used against witches than against other transgressors, for example.) Another reason for omitting it is that it has been too widely assumed that the history of early modern crime is subsumed in the history of witchcraft. This has distorted our view of ordinary early modern trial procedure, and also the experiences of a vast number of women tried for crimes other than witchcraft.[9] Recent

[8] An overview of research on witchcraft in German speaking lands is given in R. Briggs's superb *Witches and Neighbours: The Social and Cultural Context of European Witchcraft* (London, 1996), with a bibliographical note on pp. 435 ff. For the area studied here see in particular H. C. E. Midelfort, *Witch-Hunting in Southwestern Germany, 1562–1684: The Social and Intellectual Foundations* (Stanford, Calif., 1972).

[9] My omission of this subject is not to deny that this extraordinary historical phenomenon, which in the core century of the witch craze, 1561–1670, cost at least 3,200 people's lives in the south-west of Germany alone, gives us important clues

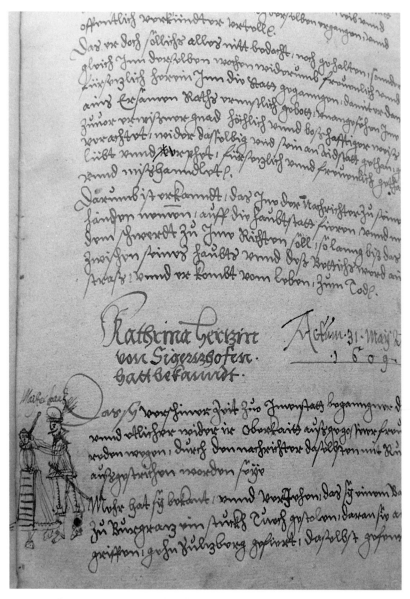

FIG. 2. Katharina Hertz is punished for theft

studies have begun to redress that balance,[10] but we still lack substantial studies of how laws regarding female crime were communally enforced, of accusation patterns, and the treatment of 'ordinarily' criminal and deviant women over a long time period. We also, surprisingly, have much to learn about the ways in which communities were governed between 1500 and 1700; if only to understand why people could be fined for drunkenness and imprisoned for premarital sex. These centuries witnessed a highly organized attempt to make an entire population conform to a narrow moral code of behaviour. It is this that is distinct about the period. The values of the code were Christian. They centred on the prohibition of swearing, cursing, gaming, luxury, the profanation of the Sabbath, immodest behaviour like dancing, and sexual licentiousness. From the late Middle Ages onwards secular authorities increasingly took over the enforcement of these values from the Church. They claimed that peace and prosperity could be secured only if people lived together in neighbourly harmony, obeyed God's laws, and respected the 'common good'. Otherwise war and dearth would threaten, God's punishment for sin. This renewed moralism was at first an urban phenomenon. It fed into movements for religious reform led by Martin Luther. Protestants wanted to abolish convents and a celibate priesthood, to prohibit prostitution, and generally strengthen the institutions of marriage and the Christian household.[11] Wherever the Reformation was successfully 'domesticated', it catalysed reform policies of these kinds. Then, as territorial rulers fastened their grip on lands and subjects in the second half of the sixteenth century, moral legislation, combined with a collective confessional sternness, expanded

about anxieties and tensions in that society; figure in Midelfort, *Witch-Hunting*, 72; on the nature of such anxieties see especially Briggs, *Witches and Neighbours*; Roper, *Oedipus and the Devil*; D. Purkiss, *The Witch in History: Early Modern and Twentieth-Century Representations* (London, 1996).

[10] For research overviews see R. Jütte, 'Geschlechtsspezifische Kriminalität im späten Mittelalter und in der frühen Neuzeit', *ZRG Germ. Abt.* 108 (1991), 86–116, and O. Ulbricht, 'Einleitung', in id. (ed.), *Von Huren und Rabenmüttern: Weibliche Kriminalität in der frühen Neuzeit* (Cologne, 1995); the articles in the Ulbricht volume all deal with female crime in early modern Germany; for England see J. Kermode and G. Walker (eds.), *Women, Crime and the Courts in Early Modern England* (London, 1994); on France see J. R. Farr's excellent study, *Authority and Sexuality in Early Modern Burgundy (1550–1730)* (New York, 1995); on Spain M. E. Perry, *Gender and Disorder in Early Modern Seville* (Princeton, 1990).

[11] See L. Roper's seminal study, *The Holy Household: Women and Morals in Reformation Augsburg* (Oxford, 1989).

everywhere.[12] It tied in with rulers' ambition to raise taxation levels. Unsuitable marriages, early marriages (if there was no money to feed children), and spendthriftness in drinking and feasting were all prohibited in order to stabilize household economies and to guarantee the tax money to be gained from them. These shared views soon made Lutheran, Catholic, and Calvinist territorial moral policies look very similar indeed.[13]

The central location of the kind of social order envisaged here was households governed by husbands. As men, they had a natural ability to think and act rationally, and hence to control drives and be reliable moral beings. Like rulers, their duty was to provide peace, protection, nourishment, and wise disciplining. Wives, children, and servants owed them obedience. In 1602, the Bavarian ducal secretary Aegidius Albertinus compared life in the ordered household to a 'cloister', and the Lutheran Cyriacus Spangenberg viewed it as a 'divine service'.[14] Albertinus warned that if members of a household followed their own heads, the house was 'to be deemed a hell'.[15] A husband's misrule, however, did not legitimize women's resistance. All humans were to some degree weak, and any precipitate reversal of roles between husband and wife would only increase misery. Magistrates and rulers were, however, more and more determined to interfere in the household sphere and restore order themselves. A wife could therefore accuse a manifestly spendthrift or violent husband before the magistrates, and he would be imprisoned for not feeding and protecting her. But she could not question marriage itself and demand a divorce from a bad or violent husband. Similarly, a maidservant might accuse her master of withholding her wages. It was understood that the unpunished meanness of masters caused servants to steal. But a decision on her part to work without a master would be disapproved of. Thus, the ideal of the household endorsed a hierarchical order based on mutual obligation.

During the sixteenth and seventeenth centuries, however, this

---

[12] P. Münch, 'The Growth of the Modern State', in B. Scribner (ed.), *Germany: A New Social and Economic History* (London, 1996).

[13] R. Po-Chia Hsia, *Social Discipline in the Reformation: Central Europe 1550–1750* (London, 1989); J. F. Harrington, *Reordering Marriage and Society in Reformation Germany* (Cambridge, 1995); on Counter-Reformation France see Farr, *Authority and Sexuality.*

[14] H. Smolinsky, 'Ehespiegel im Konfessionalisierungsprozeβ', in W. Reinhard and H. Schilling (eds.), *Die katholische Konfessionalisierung* (Gütersloh, 1995), 323; R. Dürr, *Mägde in der Stadt: Das Beispiel Schwäbisch Hall in der frühen Neuzeit* (Frankfurt on Main, 1995), 64.   [15] Smolinsky, 'Ehespiegel', 332.

model of social order came under considerable pressure. Most obviously, an order based on the enforcement of rules of behaviour within households was ill-equipped to deal with people living outside the household. And the number of 'masterless' people seemed to be growing. Élite anxieties about rapid economic change and an overturning of a society of ranks grew, and about the 'low' instincts and desires of ignorant people, whose 'destructive potential' seventeenth-century German political writers, for example, systematically overrated.[16] Prostitutes and beggars were the first social group in regard to whom attitudes became harsher in the course of the sixteenth century: prostitutes were no longer seen as a 'necessary evil' but as thoroughly immoral and threatening,[17] and beggars no longer as unfortunates, but as needlessly idle and dishonest people, burdening society. By the end of the century nearly all civic brothels were closed, and male beggars and vagrants were being forced into public labour or banished to Venice to man the galleys against the Turks.[18] Mobility in itself was the great enemy of a society based on household control. 'Nothing is more incompatible with the character of social and civil life', the seventeenth-century philosopher Pufendorf explained in his chapter on the duties of marriage, 'than a casual and vagabond way of life, with no fixed abode and no settled property.'[19] Independent and mobile labour was therefore commonly associated with a sexually free lifestyle. This view crops up in a Württemberg mercantile mandate from 1645. Pedlars and second-hand dealers were criticized not only for selling goods across borders which later had to be bought more expensively, but also for

all sorts of sinful, shameful and bad behaviour, in that men, women, widows and single lads hop around indiscriminately in chambers, rooms and stables,

---

[16] W. Weber, *Prudentia gubernatoria: Studien zur Herrschaftslehre in der deutschen politischen Wissenschaft des 17. Jahrhunderts* (Tübingen, 1992), 357. This process has, of course, been observed elsewhere, see K. Wrightson and D. Levine, *Poverty and Piety in an English Village: Terling, 1525–1700* (2nd edn. Oxford, 1995). The social history of 17th-cent. Germany is still very much an open field, especially for the time after the Thirty Years War; my study points to the centrality of this period for our understanding of early modern social change; see also T. Robisheaux, *Rural Society and the Search for Order in Early Modern Germany* (Cambridge, 1989).

[17] B. Schuster, *Die freien Frauen: Dirnen und Frauenhäuser im 15. und 16. Jahrhundert* (Frankfurt on Main, 1995). [18] See Ch. 2 n. 1.

[19] S. Pufendorf, *On the Duty of Man and Citizen According to Natural Law*, ed. J. Tully, trans. M. Silverthorne (Cambridge, 1991), 121.

behaving offensively in words and deeds, and growing up in an almost wild barbarous way, greatly despising sermons.[20]

Lazy, pagan, sexually driven, resisting rationality, morals, authority, and thus betraying their country, order, civilization, and religion— this was how poor, mobile groups were represented. Hence over-mobile servants began to be targeted too. The household order was threatened when they moved on every couple of months, not least because they created a high demand for labour and favourable conditions for their own demands. Maidservants were increasingly portrayed as 'enemies within the home': unreliable, idle, vain, cheating, stealing, and bringing the household into disrepute by gossip.[21] There were also fears about a growing number of women who worked as spinners and seamstresses in centres of textiles production: they seemed to be hopelessly beyond control. Anxieties about the unruliness of youth intensified, too, one main concern (familiar to us nowadays) being that young people were fashion addicts, and blew all their money on clothes.[22]

Such perceptions were intensified by social and economic crisis. In the late sixteenth century, population increase and bad harvests forced more people into casual work, begging, or vagrancy; journeymen had fewer chances of progressing from apprenticeship to mastership and marriage; village communities became more markedly stratified. The seventeenth century brought additional strains. Governments began to threaten masters and mistresses with fines if they did not report lewd servants. Sentences got harsher, thanks to the late sixteenth-century sense that laws and deterrent punishment had little effect on intemperance and disobedience. The most influential political theorists began to stress constancy as a guiding principle for rulers. Rulers were to act energetically (and not always paternalistically) in the interest of the common good against disorder. Next, the Thirty Years War (1618–48) increased the territories' financial needs, so that mercantile policies had to be more strongly implemented and

---

[20] A. L. Reyscher (ed.), *Vollständige, historisch und kritisch bearbeitete Sammlung der württembergischen Gesetze* (19 vols., Stuttgart and Tübingen, 1828–51), xiii. 47, 'Verordnung, den Handel ins Ausland betreffend', 4 June 1645.

[21] Dürr, *Mägde in der Stadt*, ch. 1.

[22] See, for example, the 1629 broadsheet 'Amsterdamischer Gesundbrunn, Denen Zerrütten Gemüther der Kinder unfehlbar dienlich', in W. Harms (ed.), *Deutsche illustrierte Flugblätter des 16. und 17. Jahrhunderts* (Tübingen, 1987), iv. 51. Similar anxieties in England are explored in P. Griffiths, *Youth and Authority: Formative Experiences in England, 1560–1640* (Oxford, 1996).

control over spending widened. This in turn extended the State's control over the economy and social life in the interest of the 'common weal'. Population losses, destruction, and the breakdown of confessional tolerance deepened anxieties about God's condemnation of sin and social upheaval. In these conditions, princes issued a flood of harsh laws against premarital sexuality and fornication, and rigorously prosecuted illegitimate sexual unions, single mothers, and women who committed infanticide. All these offences were thought to subvert marriage and the family as the proper loci of fertility and education, and to undermine the religious view that children were God-given to bless a union.

It is not surprising in view of these changing expectations that during the first half of the seventeenth century a legally trained bureaucracy developed in most territories.[23] Military discipline became an important part of upper-class education. When the war ended, the philosopher Justus Lipsius' neo-stoical doctrine of the *prudentia civilis* or *politica* was disseminated through universities, Jesuit colleges, Protestant and Calvinist grammar schools, and the academies for the sons of noblemen. This doctrine 'stressed obedience and discipline as necessary conditions for well-ordered government, and created the climate for the institutional reforms in town and country'. Moreover, it taught the 'individual to control his own life by mastering his emotions and to subordinate himself politically without resistance'.[24] 'Will, reason, and discipline' as well as 'activity and perseverance' became dominant values for the educated and upper classes,[25] and corporate models of society less influential.[26] Natural physical functions and expressiveness were increasingly restrained and 'civilized'—a change being advocated, as it were, from belching and brawling to stiff smiles and polite conversation. As the upper classes' self-fashioning proceeded, social gulfs seemed to widen—intensifying irritation at peasants' ignorance of how to shoot, march, or follow commands when called upon to defend their

[23] For Württemberg see J. A. Vann, *The Making of a State: Württemberg 1593–1793* (Ithaca, NY, 1984).
[24] G. Oestreich, '"Police" and Prudentia Civilis in the Seventeenth Century', in id., *Neostoicism and the Early Modern State*, trans. D. McLintock (Cambridge, 1982), 164; W. Schulze, 'Gerhard Oestreichs Begriff "Sozialdisziplinierung" in der frühen Neuzeit', *ZHF* 14 (1987), 265–302.
[25] G. Oestreich, 'The Political Intent in Neostoic Philosophy', in id., *Neostoicism*, 35.
[26] W. Schulze, 'Vom Gemeinnutz zum Eigennutz: Über den Normenwandel in der ständischen Gesellschaft der frühen Neuzeit', *HZ* 243 (1986), 619.

villages against the French.[27] Seventeenth-century Württemberg officials began obsessively to use the formulae *cum* or *salva venia* (I beg
your pardon) in their reports to the duke when refering to sexual
matters, the body, low occupations, dung, or even socks![28] Leibniz's
definition in 1688 of what 'separates the common man from those
whom Prometheus has formed out of more noble clay' is characteristic of the deepened self-esteem and contemptuous language of
seventeenth-century élites. Common people, Leibniz wrote,

cannot occupy themselves with a thought other than about their food, and
never try to fly higher, and have as little conception of the desire to know or
of the pleasure of thinking as a deaf and dumb person can appreciate a
wonderful concert. . . . They live from day to day in this world and pace
their movements like animals.[29]

According to Leibniz, only those who listened to stories and journey
descriptions, or who read books and listened to scholars, could raise
themselves above this 'stupid lot'. The more numerous such people
were, the more civilized a nation became. People of this kind would
not rebel against the authorities or follow the 'passionate impulses of
the mob', but gladly accept orders from their superiors. We are
reminded here of the Memmingen innkeeper who regarded obedience to town councillors as his natural duty. Altogether, then, disorder of this kind was dissociated from social injustices or the
failures of the governors. The sources of any kind of disorder (and
not just revolt) resided primarily in the lower orders' disobedience,
greed, and blindness to the consequences of their actions and their
own limitations. The philosopher Lipsius drew up his own lengthy
list of the 'rude multitude's' negative qualities in the fourth book of
his Politics, describing them as unstable, as 'voyd of reason' and
'light of beliefe', quick of speech, but slow of spirit.[30] Once more the
seventeenth century marks a period when firmness and constancy
were actively called for to govern subjects of this nature.

[27] B. Wunder, *Frankreich, Württemberg und der schwäbische Kreis während der Auseinandersetzungen über die Reunionen (1679–97): Ein Beitrag zur Deutschlandpolitik Ludwig XIV.*
(Stuttgart, 1971), 138 n. 294.
[28] D. W. Sabean, 'Soziale Distanzierungen: Ritualisierte Gestik in deutscher bürokratischer Prosa der frühen Neuzeit', *HA* 2 (1996), 216–33.
[29] G. F. W. Leibniz, 'Ermahnung an die Teutsche, ihren Verstand und Sprache
beßer zu üben, sammt beygefügten vorschlag einer Teutsch gesinnten Gesellschaft',
in O. Klopp (ed.), *Die Werke von Leibniz. Erste Reihe: Historisch-politische und staatswissenschaftliche Schriften* (Hanover, 1872), vi. 196f.
[30] J. Lipsius, *Sixe Bookes of Politickes or Civil Doctrine*, trans. W. Iones (London, 1594,
repr. Amsterdam, 1970), 68–70.

In this discussion we seem to have come a long way from the history of 'criminal' women. Yet these large cultural, ideological, and social shifts conditioned women's experiences intimately. Constancy and firmness, for example, were highly gendered terms, for women embodied immoderateness, inconsistency, and uninformed speech most strongly. More generally, we witness in the cultural changes outlined above the accentuation of a long-standing dichotomy between a superior culture and nature, which had to be mastered and managed, and subjugated by the forces of reason and civilization.[31] Needless to say, there were different ways of comprehending nature in the early modern period: it could be seen as a divine creation to be cherished. But it was also described ambivalently, as nurturing mother and destructive fury, for example. In descriptions of the human state, references to 'nature' usually designated areas of eruptive, selfish, and self-destructive passions, above all of lust. Hence, to contemporaries, the 'natural' self could be the worst self imaginable. Reason had to be harnessed to control desire. This was exactly the point which put women in the sight-lines. Along with peasants and savages, women were those most constantly linked to nature. As cultured manhood was associated positively with rationality and self-control, the opposite and less desirable characteristics were projected onto 'female nature'. The female was regarded as fickle, morally and rational ignorant, unreliable, and lecherous. Moreover, women were understood to be uniquely dangerous because they could seduce men, and because their imagination and desires were so easily aroused. Commenting on women's dangerous imagination, Montaigne could for example lament the 'great harm' done by 'those graffiti of enormous genitals which boys scatter over the corridors and staircases of our royal palaces!'[32] The desirous woman was dangerous because she tested and exhausted virility, and the one organ which, Montaigne thought, made a man 'more properly a man' than any other.[33] In Montaigne's essay we encounter men's anxieties about being made a fool of by women. The reverse of such anxieties was a contemptuous fantasy that men controlled women by giving them what they most wanted. We find this expressed, for example, in a mid-seventeenth-century broadsheet entitled 'Mr Wifemaster', which exclaimed:

---

[31] K. Thomas, *Man and the Natural World: Changing Attitudes in England, 1500–1800* (Harmondsworth, 1984), esp. ch. 1.

[32] M. de Montaigne, *The Complete Essays*, trans. M. A. Screech (Harmondsworth, 1991), 971.   [33] Ibid. 1004.

All men must gain victory,
All women on the bottom be;
And if they raise a fray,
It's only in the day.
No one has ever yet
Heard any woman fret
That her husband in the night
Made marriage a bitter plight.

You women be good servants,
and do as here you're told,
And you'll have happy daytimes
and nights of purest gold.[34]

Even though in real life women were often experienced quite differently, as autonomous and in some cases even as equal beings, this perception of women as the desirous and subordinate sex underlay the model of social order and shaped male and female identities.

The law took up such notions and reinforced gender hierarchies rooted in distinctions between 'nature' and 'culture', passion and reason. Sixteenth- and seventeenth-century trials clearly turned on the view that women's weaker moral nature and stronger sexual desire were principal causes of social disorder. Legal references to accused women would endorse the proverbs 'long dresses, short minds', or 'if there were no whores, there would be no bad boys'.[35] The rape of an adult woman seemed inconceivable.[36] Similarly, in incest cases the notion that women might be victims of abuse in the family hardly entered judges' minds. They were punished just as severely as the abusing men.[37] Many women were beheaded for 'crimes' such as infanticide, incest, bigamy, and even adultery, or banished from their home town or territory for ever. Their punishment was exemplary; the sight of a young, wandering woman with a bastard child was meant to be a warning to all other women.

So, taken together, there is our programme. Clearly, this study moves on several levels. It is, primarily, a study of female deviance and its treatment. It aims to connect us with the concrete, lived

---

[34] 'Herr Weiberherr', cited in J. Wiltenburg, *Disorderly Women and Female Power in the Street Literature of Early Modern England and Germany* (Charlottesville, Va., 1992), 148.
[35] See Ch. 4.
[36] M. Lorenz, 'Da der anfängliche Schmerz in Liebeshitze übergehen kann: Das Delikt der "Nothzucht" im gerichtsmedizinischen Diskurs des 18. Jahrhunderts', *ÖZG* 3 (1994), 328–57.   [37] See Ch. 7.

realities of those past times: with the textures of female living and transgression.

Next, it observes the changing cultural, confessional, and political attitudes which determined how that transgression was regarded: the history of prosecution, trial, and punishment is understood in these broadest contexts. Finally, the book aims to record the large social consequences of the perception of femininity as embodiment of unruly desire. The view of femininity explored here, of course, collapsed in the eighteenth century. It turned into its opposite, so that femininity came to be predominantly associated with sensitivity, a positive softness in nature, and sexual passivity. This fundamental transition cannot fully be understood without attending to the construction in European culture of the 'dangerous female', and to how this representation of femininity was reproduced by the law and by common men and women in their daily lives.

I

Gossip, Silence, or Accusation

A CENTRAL paradox of early modern government was the disjunction between an ever-widening programme of moral policing and the lack of corresponding investments in preventive measures and police officals. This made authorities highly dependent on communal cooperation in the prosecution of crime. In order to understand which women and which crimes were most likely to end up before the court we need to identify those who preferred out-of-court settlements, how gossip could alert authorities to crime, and the conditions under which policing could operate. We begin by attending to three concrete cases to show how typical female offences—fornication, infanticide, and adultery respectively—were talked about in urban communities.

In 1561 the Memmingen citizen Georg Meurer initiated a unique investigation into a rumour. Meurer had held the office of a city-scribe for twenty-five years, enjoying a powerful political position until he was mysteriously dismissed in 1549.[1] Twelve years later someone started the rumour that his daughter had concealed a pregnancy and had been sent to Speyer to deliver the child. He wanted to know who had said this first. More than fifty citizens were required to relate where, from whom, and in whose presence they had heard this news and to whom they themselves had then mentioned it. This inquiry provides us with the first case we shall analyse. It shows how a powerful man like Meurer could defend his family's honour by trying to ensure that evidence was given the status of a lie. Those interrogated were presumably careful in what they admitted about their past conversations; but we can still gain a plausible picture of the dynamics of their gossiping. Our second case reflects a situation which typically ensued on accusations of infanticide. The woman under suspicion was socially vulnerable, and her

---

[1] P. Frieß, *Die Außenpolitik der Reichsstadt Memmingen in der Reformationszeit 1517–1555* (Memmingen, 1993), 243.

growing belly was referred to as a visible proof of her subsequent planned offence. Gossip spread the suspicion, and the baby's corpse merely affirmed what had become a shared expectation. The suspect's arrest and decapitation followed quickly. For our third example we turn to another social milieu and examine a case of adultery among the Constance nobility.

MADLENA'S PREGNANCY

In the winter of 1561, women remembered two events when they were interrogated about the Memmingen case. The first event was the fine wedding of *Stadtamtmann* Lehlin's daughter with *Stadtamtmann* Besserer's son; the second was the strange departure of the former city-scribe's daughter Madlena Meurer.[2] Memmingen was a medium-sized Imperial city. During the fifteenth century it had been an important centre of trade with Switzerland and Italy. Merchant families like the Besserers and the Lehlins had moved in, and they soon came to dominate not only the cloth trade but politics as well. In 1561 the news of Madlena Meurer's concealed pregnancy seemed like a counterpoint to the honourable wedding which had united wealth and rank in a time of economic decline. The meanings ascribed to the pregnancy differed according to age, rank, and sex. The upper classes knew that Madlena and her family would lose status. Ordinary citizens saw her case as emblematic of the shame that followed any loss of female chastity. Single women were excited by the sense that Madlena had transgressed a law they themselves found so hard to obey. Illegitimate pregnancies were tolerable only if the begetter agreed to marry a woman instantly. Madlena's situation was worse. She concealed her pregnancy and the begetter was unknown.

These circumstances and her strange departure gave rise to gossip. Four questions are of interest to us. Where did people gossip? What conventions ruled their gossip? Who forbade whom to gossip? And who brought additional evidence to reveal the truth of Madlena's case?

---

[2] On Kaspar Besserer and the Lehlins see R. Eirich, *Memmingens Wirtschaft und Patriziat von 1347 bis 1557: Eine wirtschafts- und sozialgeschichtliche Untersuchung über das Memminger Patriziat während der Zunftverfassung* (Ottobeuren, 1971), 220, 223, 290.

The Locations of Gossip

Visiting her sister-in-law for 'business', the widow Dorothea Meier heard the rumour that the ex-scribe's daughter was pregnant. Meier was urged to tell her daughter about it, so that she would 'behave cautiously' and 'meet no shame'. Meier forbade her daughter to tell anyone else about it. The message was far too exciting, though. A little later her daughter Dorothea ran into the house of *Stadtamtmann* Lehlin. In its back room young women sat sewing for Katharina's wedding, thus taking part in the virgin's ritual transition to a wife. Dorothea told the news to the bride's younger sister (also called Madlena) and the cook. Instantly, Madlena reported it to the women in the back room. She kept telling others, until her father heard about it and forbade her to say more.

Typically, the news was not broadcast to a group of people. Usually two people talked about it confidentially. Then each of them would tell one or two further people. The unemployed Augsburg cousin of the widow Stein, for example, heard about it in another woman's living-room. He told his cousin, with whom he was staying, and she told Pfefferlin's maidservant. Thus, the news spread slowly but surely. When Pfefferlin's maidservant was waiting for an old laundress together with the seamstress Anna Bugg, they began to talk about two other illegitimately pregnant women. Then Pfefferlin's maidservant said: 'I know about a fat one, who is also quick with a child.' She reported that when all single women had gathered at the Lonsers' for a spinning-bee, Madlena's dress had only been tied loosely, so as to hide her belly. They had all pointed at her. Anna Bugg again heard about Madlena's pregnancy when she walked into a workshop to cut cloth. Seamstresses frequently picked up news and disseminated it, because they entered many houses. This could turn out to be profitable. When Bugg was at Frau Dr Bartholome's, the latter promised her half a loaf of bread for any further information. This special gift probably was to do with the fact that most of Frau Dr Bartholome's upper-class friends were *Junker innen*. If the Meurers' rank declined, her position might rise.

Gossip took place most frequently in living-rooms, streets, in front of houses, where two people briefly talked about daily events. News was rapidly discussed in families during meals. In *Junker* Albanus Wolfhart's pharmacy, established by his father in 1500, his young daughters and an apprentice served customers, and news circulated among cooks and maidservants of wealthier households; while men

gossiped in inns and during their business.[3] Upper-class women
kept to themselves in rooms and avoided gossiping in public. Private
meetings in their houses provided occasions to chat, but more
frequently they gossiped in church, or, as they would add hastily,
on their way out, on the church-steps, or actually only in the church
yard. A heightened sensibility about gossip among the upper classes
is also conveyed by the fact that the brother of a *Junkerin* whispered
the news only into her ears at a dinner! Affluent women immediately
stopped gossiping if a maidservant entered the room. Other groups
did not feel disturbed by servants, journeymen, children, or relatives,
but a conversation between two people was regarded as confiden-
tial and ended if another person joined it.

How They Talked About It

Older women often spun together with friends. While one was
spinning, as the old steward's wife did with Frau Buff, the other
would talk 'about all sort of things, especially pain and worries', or
'want and pain', as Buff put it. Buff's mother had told her about
Madlena's pregnancy, whereas the steward's wife knew about it
from her cook. 'Something about the old city-scribe's daughter has
been heard, which I am truly sorry about,' she said. Frau Buff
responded that she had heard about it and felt sorry for her as
well. Both merely indicated their knowledge and concern. Conversations typically began with such a reference to gossip: 'it was said'
something had happened. Gossip had to be anonymous, because
this protected everyone from the accusation of having started it.[4]
Some people interpreted the news as a sign of a general moral
decline. 'It is going badly', the wife of the merchant Ludwig Stern-
haber told her sister in church; 'it is said that Madlena is pregnant.'
Times were difficult, dearth being only one sign of a wider economic
crisis. Last year's discipline ordinance had urged citizens to avoid
God's punishment by living a less sinful life.[5] Still, people spent less
energy thinking about God's anger at a concealed pregnancy than
they did about Madlena's diminished social status.

At first, conversations would begin by referring to two other
illegitimately pregnant women known at that time. After Madlena
had left, they would explicitly comment on her departure, such as

---

[3] On Wolfhart see Eirich, *Memmingens Wirtschaft*, 310.
[4] R. Schulte, *The Village in Court: Arson, Infanticide and Poaching in the Court Records of
Upper Bavaria, 1848–1910*, trans. B. Selman (Cambridge, 1994), 111–18.
[5] StAMM, A 265/2.

'well, that Madlena went away so quickly', Frau Dr Bartholome then suggesting that she had no choice. But generally no further speculations followed. Conversations principally affirmed both parties' knowledge.

The indirect manner in which everyone steered towards the real issue allowed the other person to signal her or his willingness to gossip. One woman said that the midwife had started to talk about it 'without having been asked', thus criticizing her directness. Hence she had raised doubts: 'maybe it was not true.' The negotiations involved were delicate. Curiosity was rebuked or punished. When a belt-maker's daughter asked a maidservant 'whether it was true', she was answered that she had also heard about Madlena's story. When the belt-maker's daughter mentioned it at home during dinner, her father forbade any gossip. Young, single women's spontaneous gossip was checked because it was likely to be mischievous. Pharmacist Wolfhart's cook was also forbidden to gossip, so that both his maidservants remained ignorant of the current news. Frau Brenner told her daughters to keep quiet, after having told them about Madlena as a warning example. The authority of the source of information was checked before news was spread. People were extremely aware of the danger of being told mere rumour.[6] Upper-class women faced the difficult task of presenting their lower-class informants as convincing. One *Junkerin* said to her friend, 'a *Mensch* had truthfully told her' about Madlena. Frau Dr Bartholome said the rumour was spread 'by a woman of the Kemptnerstreet, who went in and out of her house'. The pharmacist's wife knew 'a distinguished person had said it' who would only be prepared to withdraw the accusation after Madlena had been examined by midwives. This made her friends more sceptical.

Knowing the Truth

Only people who knew Madlena, or knew others who knew her, could make firm judgements about the accusation based on their own first- or second-hand knowledge. Truth was ascribed to the visible rather than to hearsay. The only invention was that single

---

[6] 'From whom did she know about it?', Lienhart Dochtermann's wife wanted to know from Peter Knopf's unmarried daughter when she told her about Madlena. Because she had only heard this from another single woman, she was told to keep quiet. Maurerin, a married woman, had told her earlier that it was unlikely to be true. Zieglerin's unmarried daughter knew from her mother, and her mother had heard the news at *Stadtamtmann* Lehlin's house.

women had pointed with their fingers at Madlena. Counter-evidence was produced next. Otmar Bregenzer had recently ridden to Speyer with Madlena and her family without noticing the slightest sign of a pregnancy. A friend of Madlena had weighed apples at the market with her only a fortnight ago, and she had not noticed anything either. At Frau Dietmann's wedding, Anna Bienger asserted, 'things had been with Madlena as with a virgin'. And *Junkerin* Brenger told Frau Dr Bartholome to her face that she thought the news was a lie. She herself had been to a dinner with Madlena last week at which Madlena had not eaten any fish, just like a virgin. (Fish could symbolize fertility, which is why here it was first eaten during pregnancy).[7]

But then suspicious signs accumulated. *Junker* Brenger's wife became more sceptical when she heard that there had been a lot of noise in the city-scribe's house. Someone had gathered that Doctor Berman and Madlena's father were in favour of her departure, while her mother was not. It seemed curious anyway that she should leave Memmingen with the doctor during winter. *Junker* Lynsen's wife had seen them riding away and asked Madlena's mother later on the street why she had let her daughter go away during winter, and she had replied that she did not like it, but that her husband and the doctor had wanted it. Then news spread about the delivery. *Stadtamtmann* Besserer's maidservant Appel had been told by a laundress that Madlena was in childbed in Augsburg. The information David von Dettigkofen had received from his nurse-maid seemed to be more trustworthy. Her sister served at Doctor Berman's in Speyer and confirmed the delivery. Networks of communication were already widespread. Lehlin's son-in-law said that people in Munich were already talking about the birth.

Rumours multiplied with Madlena's departure, and by the ensuing inquisition into the gossip. The local notabilities waited for a clear statement and were annoyed by prolonged interrogations. 'Good God, when is it going to end?', Albanus Wolfhart's wife admitted saying when her maidservants returned from the interrogation. No information had been leaked by the city-scribe's servants. Likewise Madlena remained invisible throughout. The inquisition did not bring clarity. It was impossible to find out who had started the gossip.

---

[7] Cf. H. Bächtold-Stäubli, *Handwörterbuch des deutschen Aberglaubens*, vol. ii (Berlin, 1929–30), cols. 1528–31.

The Meanings of Gossip

Let us sum up the results so far. Concealed information nurtured gossip. Order relied on wide access to all information which influenced a person's honour. Status was tied to a family's wealth and rank, which were relatively fixed, and to the family's honourable moral behaviour in everyday life, and here status was flexible. Gossip transferred symbolic capital, which in turn determined the quality of a future marriage, trust in social transactions, and respectability. In Madlena's case, upper-class men most readily admitted to having talked about the matter, and seemed to search for clarity. As long as the truth remained murky, they were insecure in their dealings with the city-scribe's family. The pious women of the upper and middling classes regarded the case as a deplorable sign of the decline of morals in general and the endangered state of virginity in particular. Frau Dr Bartholome was the only woman who welcomed the news. Single women constituted another group directly affected by it. Norms had been transgressed which they had to obey, and it would have been unfair to them if a member of the upper classes could conceal that she had yielded to temptation.

On the whole we can see that gossip was not gender specific. How people gossiped was determined by their rank and intimacy. Nobody wallowed in gossip. News was exchanged quickly, or, when it was clear that most people had the information, people merely reasserted their awareness of the case. Gossip about delinquency was distinct from gossip about less important matters. There was a high potential for ill will among social groups. Suspicion spread quickly and threatened suspects' honour. Speech conventions therefore sought to limit the dangers by forestalling gossip based on self-interest and prejudice, to prevent people being brought into ill repute solely at the will of the gossiper. Gossip could not create its own truths, because the accuser had to prove his or her claims. It was not explicitly judgemental or accusatory, but collectively registered possible delinquency and altered status positions. Everyone remained watchful until clear evidence existed.

MARIA'S SWOLLEN BELLY

Our second case concerns Maria Späth in Urach in 1630. Maria was likewise suspected of concealing her pregnancy, but her position was for several reasons worse than Madlena's had been. As a maidservant she daily went to the market, fetched water, worked in fields, gathered wood, cut grass, and sat in the back church pews on Sundays. She had no choice but to be publicly visible. Maria was still new to Urach, a district town of about 2,000 inhabitants in the Swabian Alps. She had come from Laichingen and only recently gone into service at her aunt's, after her father had died. Her aunt was widowed. No male member of the family provided protection. Maria was over 30 years old and still unmarried. Many saw how her belly had swollen. She told everyone who wanted to know that she suffered from dropsy. Over the next four months suspicion grew. One woman said to a neighbour of the Späths that something was not right in that house. Still, truth would 'creep out' some time. The mayor's wife told Maria right away that she thought she was pregnant. Meanwhile she was nicknamed 'fat Maria'. Despite such pressure, Maria kept defending herself. She called a young woman a fool who had passed by and snootily asked Maria whether it was true that a Laichingen weaver had made her pregnant. She tried to convince women that she was a victim of gossip, which had now also spread to Laichingen, a proto-industrial weaving town with c.1,200 inhabitants on the trade route between Urach and Ulm. Maria complained about the gossip to a young married woman, pushed her own apron aside, and asked the Laichingen woman to touch her belly.

Maria concealed the pregnancy because she was going to get her father's inheritance after her aunt had died. Presumably she feared losing it by a premarital pregnancy or by marrying a weaver. However, when Maria finally gave birth, she was in such poor health that her aunt overcame her anxiety about further gossip and called in neighbouring women. Neighbours and midwives trooped into the house on this and the following day in order to examine or warn Maria. Two days later two men dug out the dead baby behind a barn.[8]

Maria's assumption that she would be able to stay in Urach, walking around visibly with her growing belly while concealing her pregnancy at home, had been unrealistic. But she had no choice: a departure would have caused her aunt's suspicion. As we have seen in Madlena's case, families often sent a woman out of town if they supported her. This had no consequences if she returned and it only happened once. Likewise in Maria's case and despite people's clear suspicion, everyone had waited for the birth. Another factor

[8] HStASt, A 209, Bü. 1968, 16 Aug. 1630.

weakening Maria's defence was that some regarded her aunt as a 'bad woman', one of the neighbours being particularly hostile towards her. This neighbour joined the group of women around Maria's bed without having been invited, took a light, and searched for suspicious signs. Later she publicly pretended to have seen the birth. It would have been easy to alarm the junior bailiff, whose house was off the market square, presumably just some streets away from the Späths'. But neither she nor anyone else did report Maria to the authorities. Boundaries between suspicion, gossip, and an accusation were thus suprisingly clear cut. A 70-year-old Urach woman nevertheless warned Maria: 'They will chop off your head.' She had grabbed her breasts and felt how soft they were. And so it was: Maria was beheaded. The whole of Urach watched her die.

ADULTERY IN CONSTANCE

Our third and final case took place thirty years later in Constance. A married noblewoman, Maria Anna Barbara Atzenholtz, was suspected of adultery with a *Junker* and building-master, the son of a council member.[9] His mother finally accused her of adultery. Maria Anna and her husband furiously denied the charge. Her husband demanded the enormous sum of 6,000 florins as compensation and declared that they were prepared 'to lose all . . . property, yes life itself, . . . rather than to carry such stain upon our name'. In contrast to the Memmingen city-scribe and despite their rank they did not live in a house which guaranteed privacy. From the back premises the garden-house was visible. 'Bad people's envious ears' and tongues were sharpened through close proximity. An embroideress who lived in the back premises testified that even though she had not herself heard the son calling his mother a whore, a pedlar had heard it and told her. Whenever Maria Anna's husband rode away for business the alleged lover entered the house twice a day through the back door. They would eat, drink, and laugh in the garden-house. Another woman in the back premises had been assured by the cow-girl that as soon as he arrived, there was 'nothing but serving food, drink, pastry, and other things, and the mistress sells the new wine, keeps the old wine, and orders it to be delivered to the garden-house'.

In this case, gossip was the weapon of former and present staff

---

[9] StAKN, K 51, 21 July 1660.

objecting to unfair treatment.[10] The cook, for example, never stayed up as late as her mistress did at night. To feed her mistress, she put fish, meat, and asparagus into the glowing ash, and grapes on the table. Such luxury, however, incited the cook's anger, because of the basic food the servants got. Adultery provided an opportunity to turn anger against a mistress. However, only one maidservant had direct evidence of wrongdoing. She had found Maria Anna and her lover in bed, 'their faces turned towards each other like a married couple'. A maidservant from Feldkirch, who had served there the year before, supplied further details. On one occasion the lover had stayed until three o'clock in the morning. Whenever he came, the children were immediately swept out of the living-room. The best wine and confectionery was fetched. Next, the bed was made in the very best manner, with two big cushions propped up proudly. Sure enough, she had seen that the bed was untidy by morning. Lastly, she had to take letters to him, all tied with nice ribbons. Up to this point, it seems, servants were loyal, not least because they had promised silence.

Their attitude changed when their mistress's behaviour became unusual. Once, after she had publicly called her husband an old devil 'with whom it was a shame to lie together', people told her that such speech caused anger. Then she replied that there were princes and 'many other people of even higher rank in hell' with a much thinner skin than she herself. If they were able to endure hell, she would be too. Beside such blasphemy she had once shown her maidservant a powder which prevented ageing. For the servants this explained why a younger man should be attracted to her rather than to her daughter.

The final act began when Anna Maria was taken into custody. The whole neighbourhood witnessed her indecent behaviour. She did not even look at the council's decree that she was to be imprisoned, but threw it out of the window instead. Worse still, she threatened to attack the constable with a knife when he came to apprehend her. Only several watchmen could force her into prison. She stayed in prison for a night and half a day, which was as long as it took the elite's petitions her husband had set in motion to take effect. Terrified of the mockery that awaited her, she only went home at night. Her subsequent attempts to convince the council that the story had

---

[10] On the typicality of such behaviour in England see L. Stone, *Road to Divorce: England 1530–1987* (Oxford, 1990), 211–30.

been 'real street-rumour and women's gossip' failed. Her final fate is unrecorded.

THE LOGIC OF TALK

These examples have shown that gossip spread more easily, and was more judgemental, if delinquent behaviour was open and visible. Gossip heightened people's attention and created prejudices, which could persist for a very long time. In a first phase people typically exchanged their knowledge about suspicious behaviour. Scepticism about the accusation could be voiced as well. In this sense gossip can be adequately described as a process of opinion-making.[11] Only first-hand knowledge took gossip to a second phase. An accusation depended on clear evidence and was a condition of manifest damage, not of rumour in itself.

Gossip was a collective process of gathering and exchanging information. It tried to assess the likelihood of someone's delinquent behaviour and was far from being uncontrolled. Conventions determined who would talk to whom, when, and in which way, according to rank, the nature of leisure, work, and individual relationships. Gender hardly made any difference, despite the persistent cliché of female gossip (although it is apparent that except for family and kin, gossip took place in gender-differentiated groups). The term 'female gossip' served as a negative stereotype to outlaw loose, uncontrolled, and socially unwise talk, against which all conventions, shared by men and women, were directed.[12] Gossip was closely tied to the social meaning of its subject, and in regard to criminal accusations people knew all too well that they could be talking about someone's life or death.

How credible suspicions were depended finally on a number of factors. The alleged offender's reputation and that of friends and kin were important. The absence of male kin who could step in and protect a women from bad talk increased her vulnerability. The social, economic, and political climate provided further categories for the framework in which cases became meaningful. People inside communities who had not committed a major crime were likely to be accused only for an agglomeration of reasons, for example if they

---

[11] J. B. Haviland, *Gossip, Reputation and Knowledge in Zinacantan* (Chicago, 1977), 4.
[12] N. Schindler and P. Holenstein, 'Geschwätzgeschichte(n): Ein kulturhistorisches Plädoyer für die Rehabilitierung der unkontrollierten Rede', in R. v. Dülmen (ed.), *Dynamik der Tradition* (Frankfurt on Main, 1992).

either depended on alms or lived in luxury, *and* were additionally unchaste, blasphemous, behaved untypically for their age, were unneighbourly, or were deviant in some other sense.[13] Gossip did not always indicate morally grounded notions of what would or would not be tolerated. Spatial and social closeness made gossip inevitable; even while it also gave rise to the rule that being nosy about other people's affairs was bad. The authorities failed to understand this latter rule when they assumed that familiarity and knowledge would facilitate denunciations and produce the kind of moral order they envisaged.

SETTLEMENTS

This reluctance to denounce others is one reason why recorded crime in the early modern period has to be understood as the tip of the iceberg of real delinquency. Just how large the 'dark' figure of crimes 'really' committed is, is usually impossible to guess. The capacity to detect or the inclination to report different kinds of crime was hugely varied. A crime like incest usually led to an accusation only if the abused woman became pregnant, so the dark figure must have been very large. Premarital sex, on the other hand, was easily detected when a pregnancy followed a wedding too closely; but those who had sex only a few times, or who successfully practised contraception, or who failed to become pregnant, would escape detection. In regard to infanticide, women might easily hide a baby, move away quickly, and remain undetected; but again nothing can be said for sure. For all these reasons it may be more useful simply to reconstruct the situations when victims and outsiders settled cases in or out of court, leaving intact the basic premiss that justice systems were used infrequently in relation to the numbers of law-breaking acts actually committed.[14]

---

[13] E. Labouvie, *Zauberei und Hexenwerk: Ländlicher Hexenglaube in der frühen Neuzeit* (Frankfurt on Main, 1991), 201.
[14] J. A. Sharpe, 'Enforcing the Law in the Seventeenth-Century Village', in V. A. C. Gatrell, B. Lenman and G. Parker (eds.), *Crime and the Law: The Social History of Crime in Western Europe since 1500* (London, 1980); N. Castan, 'The Arbitration of Disputes under the Ancien Régime', in J. Bossy (ed.), *Disputes and Settlements: Law and Human Relations in the West* (Cambridge, 1983); C. Herrup, *The Common Peace: Participation and the Criminal Law in Seventeenth-Century England* (Cambridge, 1987); R. Shoemaker, *Prosecution and Punishment: Petty Crime and the Law in London and Rural Middlesex, c.1660–1725* (Cambridge, 1991).

Property Offences

Theft offers a good opportunity to understand why it was that courts were only used as a last resort and how people normally responded to crime.[15] If a thief was still within reach, people would be sent after her.[16] If she could be caught people thought it easiest to take back the goods and beat her, especially in rural areas (and it may be useful to remind ourselves here that 80 per cent of the early modern population lived in the countryside). This made her return unlikely.[17] Women did not carry weapons, and therefore such confrontations were not dangerous. Thieves often themselves offered to return the goods or money in order to be let off.[18] Thus the victim was 'recompensed', and the only reason to take such an offender to court would have been to make a public example of her and warn others. But even inside towns the mere business of apprehending a thief, taking her to a mayor or junior bailiff, and describing the accusation were complicated and time-consuming undertakings; and reduced working hours meant reduced earnings. Also, people did not see sufficient returns. Petty theft by mobile people was punished with short imprisonment, public shaming, or sometimes banishment, and these sentences were not seen as particularly deterrent for people who moved on anyway. They were only effective if thieves were resident, and if further local thefts had to be prevented.

It hardly made sense to turn to the authorities if there was no suspect. Searches only targeted gangs of professional thieves. Most victims thus had to detect offenders independently, if they had no clear knowledge of who had committed the crime. This was bound to be an almost impossible undertaking. However, surprising attempts were made to regain goods, since 'petty theft' was not

---

[15] P. Wettmann-Jungblut, '"Stelen inn rechter hungersnodtt": Diebstahl, Eigentumsschutz und strafrechtliche Kontrolle im vorindustriellen Baden 1600–1850', in R. v. Dülmen (ed.), *Verbrechen, Strafen und soziale Kontrolle* (Frankfurt on Main, 1990).

[16] In 1571, Agnes Knab confessed that she had been caught twice by maidservants and given away all stolen goods: StAKN, HIX F. 33, 14 Mar. 1571.

[17] The vagrant Anna Knecht, for example, had broken into a peasant's house outside Hall and stolen meat, bread, eggs, and milk. She was caught in a field and, despite her baby, given 'a good thrashing', StAH, 4/480, 4 Sept. 1574, fo. 211[r]. One thief was beaten so hard by the Memmingen weaver from whom she had stolen yarn that she asserted years later, 'she would not forget [it] for the rest of her life': StAMM, A 44c, 7 Feb. 1564, Margaretha Riechler.

[18] When in 1693 a bread-carrier from the Thurgau was found out to have stolen money from her Constance supplier, she returned the money and was slapped in the face by the baker's daughter: StAKN, K 67, 1 Apr. 1693, Magdalena Biedmann.

regarded as a small crime by the large percentage of the population who owned little. In 1694, for example, a Nürtingen innkeeper had lost a pair of brown woollen socks and heard that a thief had sold them 6 miles away in the Neckartailfingen market the next day. He went there and caught her.[19] Others guessed that their goods were on the way to the next market and went there instantly.[20] Through the intimate knowledge of the few possessions people owned, clothes which had been altered and mended a hundred times, battered kettles and jugs, victims retained the hope that they would recognize them for a long time—just as we keep looking for stolen bikes. In towns, retailers and second-hand dealers were checked to see whether the goods had been sold.[21]

Even magic seemed to do better than policing officials. A common practice involved spells, which were transmitted over generations, in oral verse or on paper.[22] Seers were consulted. Protestant authorities prosecuted this 'superstitious' habit harshly, which undermined the authority of institutionalized justice. In 1676, for example, the Hall magistrates heard about a midwife who had visited a fortune-teller in Elpershofen, and judged that such 'superstitious rule is not in the least becoming for a sworn midwife'; she was not only imprisoned for some hours but also lost her job.[23] Two months later a married woman was banished from the territory because a wandering fortune-teller had tried to locate something she had lost as a maid-servant by gazing into 'pieces of mirror and glass'.[24]

Most of these efforts were lost causes, and money or goods were most likely to be regained if they had been stolen by someone inside

---

[19] HStASt, A 209, Bü. 1735, 31 Oct. 1694, Catharina Rotter.

[20] In 1696 the Cannstatt schoolmaster and his wife went 5 miles to the Zuffenhausen market, where they found the woman who had stolen 'women's clothes' in their house during church-time: HStASt, A 209, Bü. 1251, 24 Sept. 1696, Catharina Lonsinger.

[21] In 1699, for example, a Constance woman accused another of having sold some of her possessions: StAKN, BI 178, RP 1699, fos. 122ʳ, 206ʳ. Accidentally, in 1698 a Constance woman was invited to buy a devotional object which her own sister had once donated to the church of St Joß, StAKN, K 65, 15 Jan. 1698, Anna Kolb.

[22] E. Schubert, *Arme Leute, Bettler und Gauner im Franken des 18. Jahrhunderts* (Neustadt, 1983), 258; for spells against thieves see T. Hoffmann, 'Zaubersprüche aus dem 17. Jahrhundert', *Volkskunde=Blätter aus Württemberg und Hohenzollern*, 1 (1911), 6ff.

[23] StAH, 4/484, 4 Aug. 1676, fo. 49ʳ, Maria Kress.

[24] StAH, 4/484, 15 Nov. 1676, fos. 51ᵛ-52ʳ, Eva, Phillip Küstner's wife, from Eselbach. This case corresponds with that of a man near Memmingen, who had lost a hammer and an axe in the forest. Salt-sellers advised his wife to visit a soothsayer. He told her to utter three times the 'Ave Maria, Lord's prayer and confession of faith'. As a result she was banished from the district during the daytime: StAMM, RP 12 Feb. 1672–13 Feb. 1674, fo. 90ᵛ.

the household, especially by servants. Female servants were so easily suspected of theft that if they bought expensive goods at markets, or paid with valuable coins, they would immediately be reported to their master.[25] Stolen goods could be regained, because maidservants usually wanted to keep them as part of their dowry in their trunks.[26] During the seventeenth century authorities began to call for the deterrent public punishment of disloyal maidservants, and took much of the initiative from the enforcement of justice away from householders themselves. But few masters and mistresses were willing to report their servants. If thefts fell into the usual range of food, wine, clothes, or small goods, they thought it sufficient to cut the servants' salaries, to beat or dismiss them.[27] Thus in 1697, the maidservant Ursula Geiger confessed she had stolen nine florins from her former master, a saddler, and been discharged even though she had returned the money. She had been equally unlucky when she had served the Constance chancellery administrator's wife. When her mistress had been in town she had broken into the cellar, 'which was poorly locked and could easily be opened with a fork'. She had taken out wine and 'caroused with the other maid, using meat and bread with it'. Her mistress took a stolen apron from her, cut her salary by one florin, and dismissed her. She was only prosecuted after she had stolen money from her next master.[28] Informal punishment shortened the procedure and re-established the master's authority in the face of such disobedience directly within the household. Since the household was defined as a public

[25] In 1689 a female shoemaker apprentice and a maidservant in Asperg stole silver coins and ducats while their master was at a wedding and his wife drunk. When they wanted to buy clothes at a market, they were asked where the money came from and later apprehended: HStASt, A 209, Bü. 67, 5 July 1689, Anna Schwan, Barbara Mayer.

[26] In 1689 a Constance tin-maker's wife felt that her money kept disappearing. Her maidservant was a day-labourer's daughter from the Black Forest, and she had always trusted her. But when she opened her trunk she found embroidery and silver which the maidservant had bought with stolen money, and seven florins she had kept: StAKN, K 63, 27 July 1696, Anna Hilg.

[27] P. King, 'Crime, Law and Society in Essex, 1740–1820', (Ph.D. thesis, Cambridge, 1984), 100; Maria Isler was 'paid with a thrashing' when her master caught her with several pairs of socks: StAKN, K 44, 15 Oct. 1697. Another maidservant from Neckarembs miscarried after her master hit her for having stolen grass seeds: HStASt, A 209, Bü. 2058, 12 Oct. 1680. The habit of cutting maidservants' salaries was even used by some masters as a preventive measure. In 1687 the wife and daughter of a Hall grain-measurer complained about a Gelbingen parson who took a florin off any maidservant's salary in case she had stolen! The mother demanded furiously that he should get one single witness to prove that her daughter had stolen bread or milk, lights or soap: StAH, 4/553, Einungergerichtsprotokoll 1685–7, 10 May 1687, fos. 250–4[r].

[28] StAKN, K 65, 4 May 1697.

realm, the punishment was not understood to be simply of private significance either. As in the case of Ursula Geiger, only maidservants who appeared to be notorious thieves were usually likely to face an accusation by a master who thought tougher punishment was a necessary means of achieving discipline.

Denunciation and Moral Disciplining

Victims of property offences experienced manifest damage and were interested in an independent or official prosecution and in compensation. In regard to moral offences the situation was different, especially if no outside victim was involved. Responses were layered and drawn out. Domestic disputes are a case in point. Warnings were the dominant kind of outside intervention. Neighbours tended to report conflicts between couples only after a long period of intolerable behaviour, unsuccessful attempts to settle the dispute, frequent warnings, and a final dramatic and disturbing event: if a woman was once more badly beaten and all hope gone that the husband might change; or if husband and wife both notoriously drank, and it was feared that if they dropped a candle at night fire would break out. Up to then the neighbours' interest (if they got involved at all) was to reconcile opposing parties; and so they would talk to them, give women protection in their houses, and lend money and food until nothing seemed to help.[29] People who reported internal family quarrels before long negotiations of these kinds were treated with hostility for what seemed to be the accuser's mean or moralistic motives.[30]

Drinking, swearing, and dancing were likewise not reported until they became habitual and seemed to endanger the community. This was not changed by the authorities' attempts to stimulate secret denunciation. During the first half of the sixteenth century the problem had already become apparent in Protestant attempts to establish moral discipline. In Constance, for example, paid informers were continually threatened with violence and insults from 1526 onwards. In 1531 the council therefore stipulated that all citizens were to rotate as informers. But the eagerness prevalent in the first years of the Reformation to create a godly town, as envisaged by the charismatic reformers Blarer and Zwick, had quickly evaporated. Whereas in 1532, 94 informers had reported 344 offences to the discipline lords, in 1547, a year before the defeat of Protestantism

---

[29] See Ch. 5.   [30] StAKN, HIX F. 62, 30 Oct. 1581.

in Constance, 100 informers merely reported 172 offences. Eighty-one people were interrogated, but only nine further inquiries were made. The bulk of offences concerned swearing (41), dancing (41), and drinking (38), and were treated with fines; 25 people were admonished for their deviant sexual behaviour. Whereas from the viewpoint of a reformer like Zwick, this scheme was vital to withstand the Catholic threat, people themselves continued to regard denunciation for common offences like drinking as unneighbourly behaviour. The office of a discipline lord was thus disliked by council members themselves.[31] In Esslingen similar intentions were frustrated from the very beginning because the population brought only few voluntary accusations. The 1532 discipline ordinance was based on the Constance ordinance and co-written by the reformer Blarer, but it was so little obeyed that a new ordinance had to be issued in 1598. It revoked the earlier order to report anyone who behaved in a disorderly fashion, and said that such people should first be warned and reported only when their bad behaviour was repeated.[32]

A similar setback occurred in Württemberg. According to the 'Ordinance on political censorship' of 1559, annual district courts had to choose twelve informers. In 1567 the territorial ordinance withdrew the order because the informers' identities were, of course, quickly known.[33] The job was turned over to council members and judges, as well as 'each and every town and village official, such as beadles, guards, gate guards, field guards and wine guards'.[34] During the Thirty Years War, however, the 1642 'Mandate, concerning the punishment of blasphemy and crimes of the flesh', influenced by the pietist Johann Valentin Andreae, again tried to press people to report others.[35] Those who refused to report blasphemy, cursing, and

[31] W. Dobras, *Ratsregiment, Sittenpolizei und Kirchenzucht in der Reichsstadt Konstanz 1531–1548: Ein Beitrag zur Geschichte der oberdeutsch-schweizerischen Reformation* (Gütersloh, 1993), 165–217, table 1. The Counter-Reformation's efforts to revive discipline courts failed as well; see StAKN, K III, F. 14, for a badly kept and short *Zuchtbuch*. I owe this reference to Wolfgang Zimmermann.

[32] T. Schröder, *Das Kirchenregiment der Reichsstadt Esslingen: Grundlagen–Geschichte— Organisation* (Esslingen, 1987), 297–300.

[33] H. Schnabel-Schüle, 'Calvinistische Kirchenzucht in Württemberg? Zur Theorie und Praxis der württembergischen Kirchenkonvente', *ZfWLG* 49 (1990), 180.

[34] The example of Wildberg shows that in some towns this model worked well: see S. C. Oglivie, 'Coming of Age in a Corporate Society: Capitalism, Pietism and Family Authority in Rural Württemberg, 1590–1740', *Continuity and Change*, 1 (1986), 279–332.

[35] M. Brecht, *Kirchenordnung und Kirchenzucht in Württemberg vom 16. bis zum 18. Jahrhundert* (Stuttgart, 1967), 73.

swearing were to be punished. The ordinance then argued that 'accusations do not, as it is commonly assumed, diminish honour', but show 'good Christian eagerness to maintain God's honour and to save one's neighbour from eternal damnation'.[36] Junior bailiffs now also had to appoint secret informers, who were to 'attend all places often and eagerly and get information'. They had to report blasphemy and other offences to the junior bailiff, and were rewarded with one-third of the fine.[37] The success of such measures is once more doubtful. Pietist norms and beliefs were not shared by a large part of the population. Swearing and cursing were knitted into everyday language. Most people's tolerance snapped only when someone cursed others continually and maliciously. People did not regard reporting as positive purification,[38] but as the disturbing instrument of a few individuals with selfish and malicious motives. As the authorities encouraged secret denunciation and financed rewards through higher fines, this attitude was probably accentuated rather than altered.

Of course this does not mean that communities did not frown upon certain kinds of behaviour. Out-of-court responses to delinquent and criminal behaviour entailed a whole range of reactions similar to those of the legal system. As already mentioned, offenders were admonished to behave better in future, threatened if they kept misbehaving, and told to show repentance. If these measures did not succeed, shaming rituals and mocking customs could dishonour offenders and cause them to change their behaviour.[39] Mockery was usually delivered by groups of young people, otherwise unable to accuse persons of higher standing. Songs against fornicators and adulterers were typical. They could respond to routine out-of-court settlements achieved by those who could afford to do so: in 1574, for example, single men in Hall put a cradle on Jos Virnhaber's doorstep, and a fiddler played a lullaby. Virnhaber was a wealthy citizen who had already impregnated three maidservants. Other citizens had not reported or prosecuted him for this because he was too powerful. As for the maidservants, he presumably compensated

[36] A. L. Reyscher (ed.), *Vollständige, historisch und kritisch bearbeitete Sammlung der württembergischen Gesetze* (19 vols., Stuttgart and Tübingen, 1828–51), v. 423.
[37] Ibid. 424.
[38] e.g. for the creation of a pure *Abendmahlsgemeinde*, as in Emden, see R. Po-Chia Hsia, *Social Discipline in the Reformation: Central Europe 1550–1750* (London, 1989), 124–6.
[39] K.-S. Kramer, *Grundriß einer rechtlichen Volkskunde* (Göttingen, 1974), 70–82; M. Scharfe, 'Zum Rügebrauch', *Hessische Blätter für Volkskunde*, 61 (1970), 45–68.

them more than they would have got from an in-court settlement, and they thus escaped punishment for lewdness too.[40] Sexual offences often remained unreported by women whom we nowadays see as 'victims' because early modern judges simply saw them as lecherous. As the chapter on incest will show, families and others who knew about the case often continued to live with sexual abuse. A mother would know, for example, that if the stepfather was prosecuted, her abused daughter was likely to receive exactly the same punishment as her abuser, namely banishment; in order to earn a living and maintain her family's reputation she had to withhold or prevent an accusation. In all these instances people knew that the courts' imperative to punish did not necessarily 'settle' or solve conflicts for them, but could create new ones. And so they preferred their own disciplinary devices. Children, women, servants, and other social inferiors could be disciplined by physical violence. Light beating served to humiliate, whereas thrashings punished habitual or severe offenders. Village communities could banish offenders or marginalized people, masters could eject servants from their household. Thus there existed a pattern of measured responses which was analogous to judicial punishments: admonishments were followed by mild punishment and threats, more or less publicly executed shaming and physical punishment, and finally the implicit or explicit exclusion from the community. The logic behind these communal punishments should be familiar by now: they were motivated less by belief in an abstract moral law than by anxiety about the damage done to the norms vital to peaceful coexistence.

In Germany it seems as if most arbitration was attempted by family, kin, neighbours, and friends. Hence courts chiefly dealt with cases in which such arbitration or informal punishment failed because the offender was stubborn, or an outsider anyway. No official like the justice of the peace in England or the *seigneur* in France existed in German states to do this job. There are some hints that mayors fulfilled this role for people within the community, or that local judges, the parson, and parents got local men to marry the

---

[40] StAH, 4/480, 6 May 1574, fo. 187ʳ, Zacharias Deuber. This seems to have been a common habit; in 1644, for example, the Wildberg maidservant Anna Pfullinger was given twenty florins by her mistress after the master had impregnated her. She then had to leave Wildberg and promise not to accuse him, HStASt, A 573, Bü. 18, Rechtstagsprotokoll, 18 Mar. 1644, fos. 111ᵛ-112ʳ. For examples of shaming songs in Constance see StAKN, HIX F. 32, 20 June 1561; F. 38, 27 Aug. 1584; F. 48, 15 Feb. 1603; BI 155, RP 1675, 18 Feb. 1675, fo. 117ʳ.

local women they had impregnated. Then the punishment would be for premarital sex and not for fornication; it might be mitigated to a fine or even not imposed at all.[41] But such transactions usually remained unrecorded. The authorities' growing preference for prosecution and thus punishment of sins meant that institutionalized processes of arbitration were unlikely to be approved of.

Two Concepts of Order

In conclusion we can say that common people hesitated to report offences for four main reasons. It was clearly a delicate social matter to accuse someone of a serious crime if that person was rooted in a community, and even more so if there was no undeniable proof of the offence. Those who accused others of less serious immoral behaviour were often regarded as troublemakers, resisted, and exposed. It was equally difficult to accuse mobile outsiders, because they often escaped after the offence. Moreover, the effort of alerting the authorities was often deemed too large in relation to the benefits of punishment. Secular authorities had not yet established a monopoly of justice, and with it the notion that all offences had to be publicly punished in the interest of the common weal. There was a clear sense that disorder within the household, for example, should be punished by the master, husband, or father whose authority and property had been attacked most directly. Also the threat of punishment could be deemed disproportionate to the crime. The death sentence must have been a chief reason why rape was so dramatically underreported, and in regard to offences like incest the joint punishment of both parties likewise hindered accusations. The law was, moreover, experienced as hegemonic if authorities prosecuted common offences like poaching or swearing. The divide between the 'two concepts of order' could be deep.[42] The need to prosecute and punish murder, professional property crime, and outside or notorious offenders was, however, uncontested. And it was in regard to such offences and offenders that communities cooperated with the prosecution process.

---

[41] Magistrates are sometimes recorded to have arbitrated disputes between two opposing parties without formally accusing them: see StAH, 4/479, fo. 32^r; StAH, 4/480, 11 Dec. 1573, fo. 165^r. The commonness of the arbitration of disputes is demonstrated for France by Castan, 'The Arbitration of Disputes under the Ancien Régime'.

[42] K. Wrightson, 'Two Concepts of Order: Justices, Constables and Jurymen in Seventeenth-Century England', in J. Brewer and J. Styles (eds.), *An Ungovernable People: The English and their Law in the Seventeenth and Eighteenth Centuries* (London, 1980), 24.

PROSECUTION BY THE AUTHORITIES

Why this cooperation should have been so crucial is easy to see. A large territory like Württemberg, for example, was split into about forty districts. Each district had a district town of about 600–1,000 inhabitants. One ducal official resided in every district town and oversaw all major government business in the district. The junior bailiff's tasks included not only policing, but also collecting taxes, which made him unpopular. He was helped only by one or two constables.[43] The efficiency of such lower officials in policing functions was severely hampered by the fact that they had a low basic income, little authority, and too many tasks. Leonberg, for example, a district town with a population of about 1,000 inhabitants around 1600, employed one constable and two watchmen. Whereas constables could make a living out of their salary, being a watchmen was an odd job for people who received alms and had little authority.[44] Magistrates had no illusions about the zeal of such officials. In order to increase their effort and decrease their susceptibility to bribery they were usually exempt from taxes, and received provisions for the apprehension and imprisonment of offenders and special salaries for a number of tasks.[45] But this did not solve the problem—which existed in exactly the same form in the larger Imperial cities. In 1685, for example, the four Hall officials (*Graben-*

---

[43] Musketeers could be called in to apprehend serious offenders, and citizens were expected to help in apprehending offenders and always told to report 'strange, sneaking vagrants'. The Essingen village ordinance for example prescribed that 'if someone, be it a man or a woman, is taken into custody and resists, so that the beadle is not strong enough to hold them, subjects are obliged to help the beadle, otherwise they will be fined two florins and twenty Kreuzer': *Gemeindeordnung* 1554 and 1648, see F. Wintterlin, *Württembergische ländliche Rechtsquellen* (6 vols., Stuttgart, 1910–55), ii. 522. In 1510, a Justingen district ordinance had already made it a duty to apprehend suspicious wandering people or unemployed outsiders hanging around in inns: ibid. 563. During the 17th cent. there were recurrent attempts to establish voluntary night-watches in villages, see StAH 4/495, *Dekret* 14 Dec. 1691.

[44] V. Trugenberger, *Zwischen Schloß und Vorstadt: Sozialgeschichte der Stadt Leonberg im 16. Jahrhundert* (Vaihingen, 1984), 130, table 19.

[45] A 1699 query of the Kirchheim constables provides a telling example. They asked the Württemberg supreme council to comment on the fact that the imprisonment of people sentenced for fornication or premarital sex was often mitigated into a fine, so that they were deprived of their extra pay for imprisoning offenders. They said that in Herrenberg offenders had to compensate the constable with money or grain, and that the Böblingen constable received two *Scheffel* of spelt and rye: HStASt, A 209, Bü. 1377, 8 Feb. 1699. On the *Schloßgeld* in Hall see H. Nordhoff-Behne, *Gerichtsbarkeit und Strafrechtspflege in der Reichsstadt Schwäbisch-Hall seit dem 15. Jahrhundert* (Sigmaringen, 1971), 88.

reiter) were accused of 'laziness'. Their main function was to police the Hall territory, one of the largest in the south-west. They had twenty-two tasks, ranging from guarding the borders to banishing offenders or vagrants. In the absence of district courts they were also supposed to prosecute offences within the large territory and report suspects to the magistrates. Common people were probably not inclined to support their efforts, since they also had to oversee weddings, dances, disorderly behaviour, and church attendance.[46] In Hall itself two constables and one beadle had to fulfil these tasks.[47] Additional watchmen were hired only for fairs, such as in Esslingen for the annual Michaelsmarket, to apprehend vagrants, cutpurses, and thieves.[48]

In Memmingen, routine policing was chiefly the duty of the overseer of the poor, for he had to banish vagrants and to report those who worked during sermons, drank, gambled, had too many wedding-guests, opened inns for too long, violated sumptuary laws, or committed fornication.[49] In a town of this size this was an overwhelming task, and he therefore chose the easiest strategy. Instead of inquiring about fornication, he mainly patrolled the town during sermons and went to weddings and inns. Some miscreants could always be spotted, whose names he would then pass on to the beadle or the town council. The disadvantage was that the fines for these offences were low, and so therefore was the percentage of the fine the official recieved in addition to his meagre fixed salary. In 1674, for example, twenty *Kreuzer* was the usual fine for opening shops during sermons or inns too long at night. In one week, an innkeeper's wife was fined twenty *Kreuzer* for threshing during the

---

[46] A 1699 query of the Kirchheim constables provides a telling example. They asked the Württemberg supreme council to comment on the fact that the imprisonment of people sentenced for fornication or premarital sex was often mitigated into a fine, so that they were deprived of their extra pay for imprisoning offenders. They said that in Herrenberg offenders had to compensate the constable with money or grain, and that the Böblingen constable received two *Scheffel* of spelt and rye: HStASt, A 209, Bü. 1377, 8 Feb. 1699. On the *Schloßgeld* in Hall see H. Nordhoff-Behne, *Gerichtsbarkeit und Strafrechtspflege in der Reichsstadt Schwäbisch-Hall seit dem 15. Jahrhundert* (Sigmaringen, 1971), 56. [47] StAH, 4/495, 1 July 1685, fos. 154–9ʳ. [48] StAE, A Reichsstadt, F. 42. In 17th-cent. Freiburg special patrols were made in the evening during fairs. The four inns of the Wiehre were controlled by the junior bailiff, who had to enter them every night with four pages and a pike and look for suspects. Each innkeeper had to give them a *Maß* of wine and bread for four pennies: 'they shall drink it while standing and then continue their work', said the order: U. Huggle, *Johann Simler: Kupferschmid und Rat zu Freiburg im 17. Jahrhundert* (Freiburg im Breisgau, 1989), 64. Simler held the office 1630–6. [49] StAMM, D 169/2b, *Dekrete* 17 Jan. 1673 and 22 Nov. 1680.

sermon, and five days later the postmaster's wife was fined for doing
her washing. 'Kyri's wife' was hit harder. The overseer of the poor
had found out that spinning-bees took place in her house at night.[50]
Instead of punishing her with a fine the *Kastenknecht* threatened to
discontinue her poor relief, and this deprived the overseer of the
poor of his percentage.[51]

A further strategy of policing officals was to keep a firm eye on
local 'outcasts', who could be easily blamed for an offence. In Memmingen, in the 1670s, a woman called 'Boozy Barbelin' belonged to
this group. Because she drank from morning to night she was thrown
out of the poorhouse in 1672, and a little later taken into custody. She
protested that the overseer of the poor had suspected her of stealing a
tin plate after she had exchanged this tin plate for an old hat. Her life
was disorderly and her behaviour loose, but first it was decided to
give her poor-relief: a loaf of bread once a week.[52]

Policing small or medium-sized towns could therefore be financially rewarding only if officials had good contacts with the population and were informed about offences which were punished with
higher fines. Their low status made this unlikely. For they were
disregarded not only because of their small incomes and willingness
to denounce others, but also because their work involved encounters with serious offenders; people believing it to be dishonouring to
touch someone who was going to be executed or banished.[53]

Special Controls

To resolve the problem of mobilizing cooperation, intensive temporary controls were used in some towns to uncover deviance. These
strike us as extraordinary attempts to enforce social and religious
discipline. In March 1672, for example, a house-to-house search took
place in all four quarters of Memmingen, because not enough people
went to sermons.[54] The discipline ordinance commanded that at least

---

[50] The 1630 discipline ordinance had forbidden all spinning-bees: StAMM, A 265/2,
fo. 17ᵛ.
[51] StAMM, RP 12 Feb. 1672–13 Feb. 1674, fo. 119ʳ, and 13 Nov. 1672, fo. 129ʳ.
[52] StAMM, RP 12 Feb. 1672–13 Feb. 1674, 19 July 1672, fo. 71ᵛ.
[53] This is vividly conveyed in a Lauffen case from 1646, when no one applied for the
job of constable. The junior bailiff decided to call in all fourteen new citizens. Two
were drawn by lot to be excused service, and each of the remaining twelve ordered to
be constable for a month with a salary of seven florins. Even though the condition was
that none of them would have to touch serious criminals or announce their sentence,
five citizens protested, were imprisoned, and petitioned to the supreme council. They
said that this kind of labour quickly destroyed one's honour: HStASt, A 206, Bü. 3055.
[54] StAMM, RP 12 Feb. 1672–13 Feb. 1674, 22 Mar. 1672, fo. 23ʳ.

one member of each household had to attend any sermon, and the search aimed to expose those who broke this rule. In September a further inquisition followed, because too many outsiders were given shelter.[55] These searches took some time, so that we can easily imagine that most people knew what to say by the time the interrogators appeared on their doorsteps. A more effective measure was to summon guilds before the council, remind all members of their duty to report offences, allude to the difficulties of the times and God's punishments, and then start questioning them. This was done after the Memmingen preachers had claimed in 1652 that not enough people attended sermons and morals were low. All reported offenders were noted, and an ombudsman proceeded to inquire into them. Again accusations mainly focused on people who notoriously drank too much alcohol or couples who never stopped quarrelling. This is a typical minute from the *Lodner* guild (whose trade was to process coarse woollen cloth): Jonas Maier's wife should go to church more often; Mathes Hermes ought to make sure that the people to whom he has rented his house in the Kalch do not hold spinning-bees; Hans Dirr, called Hans the Sausage, and his wife ought to visit church more often and 'should be more friendly with each other, avoid quarrelling and swearing, and also Hans Dirr's wife should not curse her children, give them bad names like fool and the like'. Finally one artisan thought that Jerg Miller, the pigherd, should stop drinking and swearing 'and live more peacefully with his wife and be a better householder'.[56]

Such inquisitions remained rare. Police personnel was lacking and offenders often refused to pay fines or even to appear before the court. In 1623, the Wildberg constable complained that if he told an offender to present himself before the magistrates, 'two or three men' finally had to go and get him.[57] People further effectively resisted by plaguing council and court until fines were reduced. Those who were unable to pay fines had to be imprisoned, but towns tried to avoid such costs and also had only limited prison space. The ensuing problem of enforcing widespread discipline becomes apparent if we look at the Hall lower court minutes from 1687/8, when it was attempted to push through sumptuary legislation for the first time. In towns of this size it was impossible to follow the magistrates in the small Swiss town of Wil, who in 1684 published an

---

[55] StAMM, RP 12 Feb. 1672–13 Feb. 1674, 23 Sept. 1672, fo. 96ᵛ.
[56] StAMM, A 265/2, 23 May 1653.   [57] HStASt, A 582, Bü. 86, 8 June 1623.

ordinance listing all citizens and the clothes they were allowed to wear![58] In Hall, the constable and his wife tried to spot on the streets which people seemed to indulge in luxury and pretence. Women's defiance was impressive. When, for example, the constable forbade an innkeeper's wife to walk around in expensive clothes on Sunday, she boldly replied: 'now she wanted to wear them all the more and see who would keep her from doing so, because her husband was not only an innkeeper, but also a doctor.'[59] She was told to appear before the court within eight days. But women's excuses and defences did not end there. Each and any velvet or taffeta cap and headband suddenly appeared to be shoddy and hardly worth mentioning, had not been purchased by the accused herself, or was only a help against toothache. Then requests for a mitigation of fines followed, like that of a council servant's widow who said she had been wearing her velvet cap for eight or nine years, that it was torn, and she did not know that she had behaved wrongly. Relentlessly she was fined ten *Schilling*, but she appeared again and said that the velvet cap had been a gift from her deceased husband. The fine was cut by two-thirds.[60] Because of the women's inventive resistance the authorities' zeal collapsed within less than a year. Time and again authorities had to realize that their means of control were limited and citizens' stubbornness massive.

Inquisition and Prosecution

Let us finally turn to the ways authorities might apprehend more serious offenders. Here, the prosecution posed two main problems, even if suspects had already been identified: first, the prevention of their escape, and second, the collection of information which would justify imprisonment. Junior bailiffs were often given instructions to inquire 'discreetly' about suspects before they were imprisoned. An inquiry, on the other hand, only had to be completed within eight days, which left informed offenders enough time to escape.[61] We shall see that in incest cases, for example, escapes by men were extremely common. There was then a considerable tension between the goal of securing offenders and the desire not to imprison anyone

---

[58] N. Bulst, 'Kleidung als sozialer Konfliktstoff: Probleme kleidergesetzlicher Normierungen im sozialen Gefüge', *Saeculum*, 44 (1993), 32–46.

[59] StAH, 4/554, 10 Jan. 1688, fo. 43[v].   [60] StAH, 4/553, 8 Aug. 1687, fo. 295[r].

[61] HStASt, A 209, Bü. 547, 3 Aug. 1631, Agnes Kaufmann. Late accusations that enabled the offender to escape were punished with high fines: StAMM, RP 12 Feb. 1672–13 Feb. 1674, 21 Feb. 1672, fo. 8[rv].

on unfair charges. Württemberg mandates repeatedly warned junior bailiffs that evidence had not 'in each case been weighed sufficiently', that inquiries had been 'made on the basis of guesses', and that the accused had been held a 'long time in prison before the first interrogation'.[62] After an escape, postillions, musketeers, constables, or similar officials would sometimes be sent out to pursue an offender, but their efforts were limited by time. The search could continue only through warrants for arrest. These were issued only for robbers and gangs of thieves and gave detailed descriptions of some of them. It is not clear whether such warrants for arrests ever led to the apprehension of offenders.[63] What is clear is that those who escaped for other than notorious property crimes usually escaped for good.

However, if a suspect could be apprehended, authorities were able to work much more effectively. In most cases which led to a criminal trial clear evidence existed, of the kind the *Carolina*, the 1532 Imperial law code of Charles V, described in articles 33–44 in order to prevent accusations which were based merely on suspicion and someone's bad name. Clear evidence was constituted by stolen goods which were sold, or forged money which had been circulated. Goldsmiths and bell-founders often gave evidence about people who had offered them melted metals. Shoplifting was detected. Pharmacists named suspect murderers who had purchased poison. Fornication, adultery, incest, and premarital sex could be identified through the woman's pregnancy or the observation that men visited a house frequently. A previous marriage certificate proved bigamy. Sometimes an offender who had been banished and who returned without permission was identified and immediately apprehended, in which case an interrogation and harsh punishment would follow without a further trial.

If a resident was suspected of a crime, people with possible inside knowledge, in particular neighbours and employers, would be interrogated first. Apart from relatives, the impartiality of witnesses was never assessed during the inquisition. Sometimes houses were searched. Gossip was useful for the authorities now. Every sign of suspicious behaviour which had been registered was examined. If people felt that an offence violated their moral norms, they often

---

[62] Reyscher, *Gesetze*, v. 404, 'General=Rescript, das Verfahren in Strafsachen betreffend', 23 Nov. 1629. The claims were repeated throughout the 17th cent.
[63] In Memmingen, however, several warrants were issued for adulterers who had escaped: StAMM, A 344/1, 16 Sept. 1574.

supported the authorities, apprehended offenders, and produced evidence against them. Additional offences from years ago would be remembered if an offender had a bad reputation and the community wanted to exclude him or her.[64]

DEFINING IMMORALITY

Our survey of attitudes towards crime and delinquency has opened a window into the struggle 'over basic definitions of morality and power' between early modern authorities and communities.[65] Regardless of whether it was extended to others grudgingly or generously, there was a much higher tolerance of deviant and delinquent behaviour inside communities than the authorities liked to see. The crux was that low financial rewards for too few officials with little authority made the authorities depend on communal cooperation to obtain information about suspects and prosecute offenders.[66] The zealous and godly with an interest in widespread moral reform being few, communities were usually able to limit the scope of the prosecution of offenders to what fitted their interest. Whether or not informal settlements were preferred after a concrete offence depended on how personal the relationship between victim and offender was, the nature of the offence, and the presumed effectiveness of the authorities' punishment. For women and men alike four factors—mobility, poverty, low social capital, and single status (and, as a consequence, youth)—dramatically increased the threat of being labelled and accused. Such people were hardly in a position to object to accusations and sentences. They constituted the group of 'marginal'[67] and vulnerable people who were usually accused of serious crime. In the following chapter we shall therefore be mainly concerned with their experiences during a trial.

---

[64] Moreover, women who had once been suspected of concealing a pregnancy locally were remembered whenever a decayed baby corpse was found: HStASt, A 209, Bü. 40, 8 June 1687, Agatha Glaser; A 309, Bü. 172, 1615, Barbara Schweitzer.

[65] Herrup, *Common Peace*, 1.

[66] J. K. Brackett, *Criminal Justice and Crime in Late Renaissance Florence, 1537–1609* (Cambridge, 1992), 139–43.

[67] See B. Geremek's seminal book on this theme, *The Margins of Society in Late Medieval Paris* (Cambridge, 1987).

2

Trial and Punishment

THE early modern criminal process has long been associated with the terrors of torture and gibbeted bodies. Instruments of torture are preserved in museums, and in towns like Schwäbisch Hall surviving street-names like 'Gallows Hill' or 'Blood-path' can still make us shudder. There, in the clay where the gallows once stood, the bones of the executed are still buried.

The death sentence remained a visible political reality for many centuries. In Prussia and other German states it was only in and after the late eighteenth century that the range of capital offences was limited. Executions were replaced by sentences of lifelong imprisonment and hard labour. From the mid-nineteenth century onwards executions were hidden behind prison walls.[1] Whether these changes spoke for advances in humanity seems doubtful. Foucault's *Discipline and Punish*, published in 1975, famously holds that the early modern onslaught on the offender's body was merely replaced by a modern attack on the offender's mind and soul. Since the late eighteenth century, Foucault writes,

judgement is also passed on the passions, instincts, anomalies, infirmities, maladjustments, effects of environment or heredity; acts of aggression are punished, so also, through them, is aggressivity; rape, but at the same time perversions; murders, but also drives and desires.[2]

In the modern state, a growing number of experts—doctors, psychiatrists, and criminologists—began to produce knowledge about asocial and perverse people's characters, making it possible to judge something that is 'not juridically codifiable: the knowledge of the criminal, one's estimation of him, what is known about the relation

[1] See the magisterial studies by V. A. C. Gatrell, *The Hanging Tree: Execution and the English People 1770–1868* (Oxford, 1994), and R. J. Evans, *Rituals of Retribution: Capital Punishment in Germany 1600–1987* (Oxford, 1996).

[2] M. Foucault, *Discipline and Punish: The Birth of the Prison*, trans. A. Sheridan (London, 1977), 17.

between him, his past and his crime, and what might be expected of him in future.'[3] Nothing demonstrates this more clearly than the dossier about the murderer Pierre Rivière, which Foucault had edited two years earlier.[4]

How can this viewpoint about the purpose of early modern justice being an attack on the 'body' rather than an offender's 'soul' be related to recent studies of the early modern legal system? The death sentence was an exemplary punishment. Its whole purpose was to deter others, so that in theory it only rarely had to be executed. Large cities and centres of trade like Frankfurt, Munich, and Augsburg saw on average only three executions per year during the sixteenth century; Constance saw thirty-three during the whole seventeenth century; and in some Württemberg district towns gallows simply rotted away. Robbers and murderers were the largest group of executed offenders. Their deaths moved few people to tears; but even in these cases capital trials did not only aim at retribution or deterrence. They also passed judgement on the personality and its 'passions', drawing boundaries between nature and culture. Desirous, greedy, bestial, and perverse behaviour was invariably compared with civilized, reasonable, and thus desirable behaviour. No one, however, explained 'perverted passions' in individualized ways, as they were to do in the nineteenth century; biblical references defined immorality in a relatively standardized fashion.

In regard to most crimes, three factors determined sentencing: the gravity of the offence, the political necessity of public punishment, and mitigating circumstances, the last of these assessed in terms of the degree of intent, the probable social consequences of punishment, and the accused's reputation. In seventeenth-century Württemberg this reconstruction of an offender's reputation was undertaken with increasing precision. Bailiffs wrote to all previous places of residence and the place of birth in order to track down former indictments; a profile of the offender's character as a youth might also be requested. Trials centred around the question of whether the offender would be likely to behave better in future, and how wicked he or she really was. Penitence was crucial. During the seventeenth century women's gestures and facial expressions were observed with increasing care and sometimes given evidential status

---

[3] Ibid. 18.
[4] Id. (ed.), *I, Pierre Rivière, Having Slaughtered my Mother, my Sister and my Brother . . .: A Case of Parricide in the Nineteenth Century*, trans. A. Sheridan (Harmondsworth, 1978).

in regard to the question of how much guilt they felt, or how good or bad their nature was. Since it was well known that women's feelings dominated their reason, experiments were conducted to determine the amount of their guilt according to their 'spontaneous' physical reactions to shock. All this rather undermines the Foucaultian claim that the offender's body rather than his or her character or 'soul' were at the centre of early modern punishment, or that repentance and the internalization of guilt are exclusively modern penal devices. The 'onslaught' on the offender's mind had a long history, in short. What is true, however, is that long-term imprisonment or the psychiatric treatment of offenders were unthought-of in south-west Germany until the eighteenth century. No one proposed prison workhouses; death and banishment were cheaper and more efficient punishments. Communities either got rid of seriously threatening offenders once and for all, or ejected them into neighbouring territories. In our period these practices were never contested.

Before we turn to punishments and their consequences, this chapter will discuss the practices of mercy, a subject which has not as yet received due attention from early modern historians of crime in Germany.[5] The early modern judicial system was characterized by the fact that before and after every judgement petitions from friends, relatives, clerics, and communities could be considered. The persistence of this practice illuminates the human bonds that were important in early modern society, and also how punishment was experienced. Once more we note change, however. As we shall see, from the mid-sixteenth century onwards, the right to claim mercy for condemned offenders was restricted. Principles of judicial equality began to undermine the Christian tradition of forgiveness. In regard to banishment, mitigation increasingly had to be earned through good behaviour. References which showed that the person had worked somewhere for a number of years and behaved well became a condition of re-entry into towns or countries. Only Catholic clerics seem to have held on to an older view of redemption; in Constance, for example, they vehemently tried to influence sentencing processes. Their Protestant colleagues usually left such decisions to the secular authorities, as the doctrine of the two empires required. Catholic clerics, however, did not enjoy much success with

---

[5] For France cf. N. Z. Davis, *Fiction in the Archives: Pardon Tales and their Tellers in Sixteenth-Century France* (Princeton, 1988); C. Gauvard, '*De grâce especiale': Crime, état et société au France à la fin du Moyen Âge* (2 vols., Paris, 1991).

their petitioning either. Petitions from the offender's family and community had the most effect, for their support better indicated whether or not the offender's reintegration was possible. It was equally clear that those for whom no one petitioned had scant chances of reintegration.

DECISION-MAKING PROCESSES

Village and District Courts

Our first questions must be how offenders lost, acquired, or cultivated protection; and also about the ways in which courts worked on the local level. In Württemberg villages, a local *Rüggericht* was held quarterly and a *Vogtrüggericht* annually or biannually in the presence of the junior bailiff. In the case of minor offences the decision-making of the six judges was speedy. During the local quarter sessions no one bothered to consider contradictory evidence or to interrogate witnesses. Rather, fines were decided upon swiftly, without much room for defence by the accused. Offences such as drunkenness, wood-theft, and disorderliness were punished on the basis of witnesses' reports. Slander cases and brawls were more complicated to rule upon, since it was usually difficult to decide who had started them. Decisions were then made with reference either to factual evidence or to the reputation of the accused; alternatively, both parties were punished with the same fine. These fines were unrecorded. Until the end of the seventeenth century fines were used to buy drinks for the judges.[6]

This suggests that some kind of reconciliation with those who had broken the peace was achieved. The fragility of this intra-communal regulation of enmity became apparent in regard to notorious offenders, to those who refused reconciliation, or to outsiders. Such people could be reported at the *Vogtgericht* or taken directly to the junior bailiff in the district town. Junior bailiffs were employed by the duke, they represented the 'State' in the localities, belonged to office-holding élite families, and had to have some legal training. The nature of their power in the district was highly conflictual and their understanding of it traditional rather than bureaucratic.[7] A

---

[6] K. and M. Schumm (eds.), *Hohenlohische Dorfordnungen* (Stuttgart, 1985), 54, village ordinance of Eichenau in the Schwäbisch Hall territory.

[7] These aspects are explored in detail in my article 'Frühneuzeitliche Staatlichkeit und lokale Herrschaftspraxis in Württemberg', *ZHF* 3 (1997).

reliable junior bailiff visited villages in his district once or twice a year to hold the *Vogtgericht*. The junior bailiff and his scribe were expected to call in the commune, take oaths, hear bills, read ordinances, supervise elections, listen to grievances, and ask all male citizens, their sons, male servants, and sometimes widows whether they knew about any offences. A junior bailiff would typically deal with five violent quarrels,[8] through fines fixed in district court ordinances. On most visits, only one or two serious offences would usually be reported. The decision-making process which ensued remains unclear. It seems as if decisions rested on the junior bailiff's personal view of the offender's reputation, the weight of an offence, and the consequences of a sentence for the accused. From about 1660 onwards, church consistories, held by the parson, mayor, and councillors, often acted as intermediary courts.[9] Sentences in district courts or church consistories were no minor events. They affected people's reputations and were remembered later in life, constituting a criminal record which could affect later sentences.[10]

Women were allowed to bring accusations only through their husbands or guardians, unless they were widowed. In 1656, for example, a widow accused the former mayor of Engelhard of having 'embraced her and forced his tongue into her mouth'. She confessed that she had been too ashamed to report this to the junior bailiff, and had only reported that the man wanted illegitimate sex with her. The mayor denied the charge and insulted her as a whore. Upon further questioning, the junior bailiff decided in her favour, mainly because she had not contradicted herself, had remained 'persistent', and seemed too 'honest' either to invent an accusation of this kind or to provoke lewd behaviour.[11] Bailiffs thus decided on the basis of short interrogations and inquiries about the reputation of the accused. For those of bad reputation it made no sense to bring charges, especially if the person they wanted to accuse was more powerful than they.

---

[8] HStASt, A 237a, Bü. 522, 523, 531, 542, registers of fines for several districts, 1618–28. Conflicts with mobile outsiders had to be settled informally before they went away. In 1567, the Gröningen junior bailiff thus urged the community to report every conflict to him as quickly as possible. He would sentence the offender immediately, because 'in this big commune, with wandering journeymen . . . and people from all places, a lot of offences occur daily': HStASt, A 206, Bü. 141, 10 Feb. 1567.

[9] Too little is known about their functions within late 17th-cent. communities; useful insights for the 18th-cent. are provided by D. W. Sabean, *Property, Production, and Family in Neckarhausen, 1700–1870* (Cambridge, 1990).

[10] HStASt, A 209, Bü. 790; HStASt A 209, Bü. 1064.   [11] HStASt, A 214, Bü. 683.

Women were rarely prosecuted for minor offences before such courts. In the Württemberg registers of fines from 1630 onwards, hardly any female offenders are listed. Perhaps, therefore, conflicts involving village women were usually settled out of court, or simply had to be lived with. This situation changed only if a woman transgressed the boundary of broadly tolerable behaviour, became notorious, and did not have the power to hinder an accusation.[12]

The situation in the territorial district towns was different. Courts of censure were held between twice and four times a year and presided over by the junior bailiff. In regard to accusations of more serious offences, interrogations of witnesses would usually be conducted after court sessions—as when in Wildberg, for example, a hat-maker told the session of 1621 that 'Jerg Beren's wife was so indecent and the neighbours so disgusted by her' that he thought it necessary to accuse her.[13] Junior bailiffs or mayors took up such cases and questioned neighbours. They tried to get a sense of how often a particular offence had been committed, and then decided on procedure and punishment. Once more, a plausible promise of improvement often settled the case. When, for example, Daniel Sittich and his wife were accused of laziness and infrequent church attendance in 1635, Sittich assured the junior bailiff that he had suffered from fever all winter and wanted to be more industrious in future. This satisfied the junior bailiff.[14] Such decisions are interesting. They show us that church and state responses to delinquency did not differ necessarily fundamentally. It was not the case that the Church admonished and the State punished.[15] Young people were often similarly treated with warnings, because youth was characterized by a lack of understanding, modesty, and temperance.[16] Apart from admonishing or sentencing, councils responded with social measures, as in the Memmingen case of 'Boozy Barbelin', or in Wildberg in 1624, when Hans Maier's wife was reported for not attending

---

[12] On the question of women's low representation in courts see S. Burghartz, *Leib, Ehre und Gut: Delinquenz in Zürich am Ende des 14. Jahrhunderts* (Zurich, 1990), and id., 'Kein Ort für Frauen? Städtische Gerichte im Spätmittelalter', in B. Lundt (ed.), *Auf der Suche nach der Frau im Mittelalter: Fragen, Quellen, Antworten* (Munich, 1991).

[13] HStASt, A 582, Bü. 86, 1621.   [14] HStASt, A 582, Bü. 86, 3 Mar. 1625.

[15] As implied by H. Schilling, '"History of Crime" or "History of Sin"? Some Reflections on the Social History of Early Modern Church Discipline', in E. Kouri and T. Scott (eds.), *Politics and Society in Reformation Europe* (London, 1987).

[16] Thus, in 1629, a Wildberg girl who had cursed her parents merely received a 'strong warning': HStASt, A 582, Bü. 86, 3 Aug. 1629.

church. When she replied that she had no clothes to wear for church, her husband was told to do his duty and 'clothe her'.[17]

Serious Offences

In Württemberg, sentences for more serious offenders who were prosecuted during the year were decided by junior bailiffs independently of a court and without any control unless it was assumed that serious offences like theft, fornication, or prostitution had been repeated so often that they constituted a capital crime. We do not know whether or not contradictory evidence was ever examined in cases decided by junior bailiffs, or how closely witnesses and offenders were interrogated. It seems as if the accused were almost unprotected in such cases and the power of junior bailiffs huge.[18] Judgements about these offences were often determined by the threat they constituted at a given time. If a certain type of offence seemed too common, harsher punishments were chosen. In times of crisis their rise was interpreted as a sign of the moral decline manifested in economic, military, social, and cosmic developments. Decisions were also once more determined by a suspect's previous sentences, age, and reputation; this last turned on whether he or she was known to be notoriously quarrelsome and a nuisance to others. The authorities would also assess whether the laws had been transgressed wilfully, in full knowledge of the meaning of the offence and its possible punishment. The ducal supreme council repeatedly emphasized the need to reduce the length of imprisonment and costs, and thus clearly favoured quick impressionistic decisions over a careful assessment of each case. The duke's concern was that too many imprisoned subjects were unable to pay for their maintenance. Decisions could be influenced only through petitions, bribery, and attempts to present oneself as honest and trustworthy. Suspects who had neither money nor friends were excluded from all three ways of mitigating their sentences. It was difficult to make a good impression if you belonged to a social group associated with disorderly behaviour. Mobile people, poor and single women, and widows without strong social contacts were vulnerable to such 'labelling'. Because these groups did not have a local dependent family, the social consequences of their punishment were of no

---

[17] HStASt, A 582, Bü. 86, 19 Nov. 1624.
[18] In Wildberg, in 1630, one woman accused of blasphemy, of buying stolen goods, and of disorderliness was banished from the town even though she firmly denied the charge, HStASt, A 582, Bü. 86, 16 Aug. 1630.

importance to the authorities; no poor remaining families had to be cared for. In Imperial cities these decision-making processes were more controlled. Two magistrate's deputies would usually interrogate witnesses and suspects. Their testimonies were reported to the council, which then decided upon the sentence or the necessity of further interrogation. Junior bailiffs in the Hall territory did not decide independently either, but had to report offences to the Hall magistrates, who decided either to hear the accused themselves or to punish him or her instantly. They therefore had to spell out criteria for each decision and reach a consensus on them. This could, however, also mean that magistrates transgressed the law collectively. It is clear that in Hall only very few criminal trials were initiated, but torture was used nevertheless. When in 1678 the vagrant Anna Seidler was apprehended because she had distributed her husband's forged coins, she was, for example, first questioned in prison, and a magistrate reported back to the council what she had said. After two deputies had unsuccessfully searched for a baby she claimed to have left behind in the territory, the council concluded that she could only be lewd and ought to be treated 'with greater seriousness and master Andrew', the executioner. In a further interrogation she denied having been a forger at all. Despite her bad health, the council decided to interrogate her again with the executioner's help, and to ask other authorities to search for her husband. After this failed, she had to stand in the pillory and then be banished.[19] The fact that no criminal trial had been initiated in this case had the advantage for the council that the procedure was quicker and the amount of work smaller. It also meant that the accused had no rights to defend herself, while, on the other hand, she was protected from the death sentence, which had to be preceded by a criminal trial.[20]

---

[19] StAH, 4/484, 9 Mar. 1678, fo. 65^r; RP 1678, fos. 98^r, 103^r, 131^r; for another interesting example see StAH, 4/485, 28 Sept. 1674, fo. 30^r, Jörg Trescher's wife.

[20] There was, nevertheless, a sense of the tolerable limits of such procedure. In 1677, council member Schragmüller said that if a woman accused of adultery, who had been imprisoned for some time already and been interrogated harshly, were to be questioned any further, 'a real criminal trial had to be arranged'. In order to avoid costs and effort, she was banished a little later: StAH, RP 1677, fos. 490^r–491^v, Maria Barbara Lautten.

CRIMINAL TRIALS

Judges, Trials, and their Supervision

Criminal trials were arranged for capital offences. They usually used torture unless the offender confessed to the gravest possible crime in the first interrogation. Capital offences were either repeated serious crimes, such as adultery which had been committed three times, or crimes which had been committed once but were intolerable, like incest, forgery, or murder. In Württemberg judgements were passed by the junior bailiff and the twelve judges who formed the local criminal court. The trial took place in the usual council session room in the town hall. Before it began a special bell, the *Malefizglocke*, was rung to dramatize the possibility that someone might lose his or her life.

Judges had the highest civic office. They had to be of mature age, that is at least 25 years old. In Leonberg, which offers a typical example for the composition of criminal courts, most judges had formerly been in the council for years and the average age of entry into the court was 43 years.[21] Only the sons of former long-standing judges, ducal officials, or very rich citizens could be elected earlier. Judges had to be pious, unrelated to each other, and fair in their judgements about rich and poor, weak and strong suspects. Offices were confirmed annually, but judges changed rarely, and were mostly only replaced after their death. Juridically trained judges were rare in Württemberg. Judges came from the local élite, the *Ehrbarkeit*. The Württemberg *Ehrbarkeit* was comprised of three groups: a top group of those employed at the ducal court and their relatives, a middling group of civic and ecclesiastic authorities, and a lower group of merchants, doctors, lawyers, and those with civic offices.[22] Courts were primarily constituted by members of the lower group. In Leonberg their average income was twice as high as that of all citizens together. In the most important families the office was inherited over generations. As the example of Leonberg further

---

[21] Forty-three years was also the age of entry to the Hall council 1487–1803. Forty-four per cent of those elected were related to other members by blood-kinship, 15% being a son- or brother-in-law. The number of artisans in the council decreased steadily: there were thirty-eight 1512–99, thirty during the 17th cent., and four during the 18th cent.: see G. Wunder, *Die Bürger von Hall: Sozialgeschichte einer Reichsstadt 1216–1802* (Sigmaringen, 1980), 78.

[22] H.-M. Decker-Hauff, 'Die Entstehung der altwürttembergischen Ehrbarkeit, 1250–1534', (D.Phil. thesis, University of Vienna, 1946), 28–36, 57–60.

demonstrates, artisans who had earned themselves a high reputation were occasionally also elected. But they were unable to pass the office on to their sons or sons-in-law.[23] In order to counteract judges' lack of training, ducal control of criminal trials was extraordinarily tight in Württemberg. The duke also sought to prevent different judicial policies from developing in each district independently of his ordinances. From 1577 onwards the junior bailiff therefore had to report to the supreme council whenever a criminal trial had begun. From 1629 onwards he was also obliged to add the minutes of the first interrogation of the accused. He had to get permission to use torture, and in difficult cases he had to commission one or several legal references from the Tübingen law faculty. The questions for the interrogation of suspects were also often pre-formulated by the supreme council or the Tübingen lawyers. Sentences almost always followed the lawyers' recommendations. However, the junior bailiff still had to ask for permission from the supreme council to execute them. Since the junior bailiff was the accusing party in most cases and therefore dominated trial procedure, one can only imagine that the judges' influence was very limited. This secured the duke's monopoly over criminal jurisdiction and limited the élite's ability to enforce different norms.[24] The Imperial law code of 1532 served only as a guideline in regard to basic questions of evidence, procedure, and punishment; every territory composed and updated its own law codes.[25]

In the Imperial cities criminal courts similarly consisted of twelve judges or more who belonged to the local élite and had qualified through council membership. Sometimes the court was no different from the council as a whole. The mayor acted as accusing party, and he also supervised interrogations and torture together with one to

[23] V. Trugenberger, *Zwischen Schloß und Vorstadt: Sozialgeschichte der Stadt Leonberg im 16. Jahrhundert* (Vaihingen, 1984), 95–119.

[24] For example, their lenient punishment of poachers struck at the nerve of the permanent conflict between the duke and the estates about hunts, their cost for the population, and poaching, see W. Grube, *Der Stuttgarter Landtag, 1457–1957: Von den Landständen zum demokratischen Parlament* (Stuttgart, 1957), 230; A. E. Adam, *Württembergische Landtagsakten unter Herzog Friedrich I, 1599–1608* (Stuttgart, 1911), 41; The judges' opposition to junior bailiffs and the lenient punishment in other cases were also noticed with unease, see HStASt, A 206, Bü. 1771: a woman who had committed infanticide in Dornstetten in 1556, whose dead baby was brought back by a dog after two days, had only to stand at the pillory and was banished.

[25] J. H. Langbein, *Prosecuting Crime in the Renaissance: England, Germany, France* (Cambridge, Mass., 1974) for an extensive discussion of the *Carolina* and an English translation of its most important sections.

four judges. The criminal court assembled when the delinquent's final confession, the *Urgicht*, had been written out. The mayor then read it back to the accused, the procurator and the accused commented on it and asked for a mild sentence, the judges voted on it and announced the sentence. If the vote remained undecided the mayor's vote was decisive. In some Imperial cities (as distinct from most territorial district towns) there was an advance in professionalization from the late seventeenth century onwards. Important council posts were often filled by legally trained citizens, who then came to dominate criminal trials. Between 1629 and 1798 each of the Hall *Stättmeister* had studied law.[26] Council libraries with the main legal commentaries supported their decision-making. References from law faculties were commissioned less frequently than in a territory like Württemberg, which referred most cases to Tübingen.

The Hall citizen Johann Nicolai Schragmüller (1643–1711) provides a typical example for these 'home town' careers. His father Johann Phillip was a lawyer and had been an influential council syndic in Hall. Johann Nicolai studied civil and canon law in Strasbourg, Tübingen, and Heidelberg. In 1666, aged 23, he returned to Hall 'with highest praise from Heidelberg', married the daughter of a doctor, and became a member of the inner council only three years later. He became a junior bailiff in two towns of the Hall territory, was elected to the privy council in 1687, became tax-master in 1689, and *Stättmeister* in 1703.[27] He was highly influential in all council decisions about the treatment of offenders, made registers of all judgements passed in criminal trials during the sixteenth and seventeenth centuries, and collected written legal 'considerations' about cases in order to systematize the local jurisdiction.

This development towards a professionalization of the city council was much more marked in Hall than it was, for example, in Constance or Memmingen. Yet on the whole legal subtleties were not often required during criminal trials. Mostly they dealt with sentences for robbery, murder, and theft, with evidence determining whether or not the death sentence was carried out. These decisions followed clear criteria. A death sentence was required if a living child had been killed, if a father and daughter had had intercourse, or if the suspect had stolen professionally for a long time, etc. The

---

[26] G. Wunder, 'Geschlechter und Gemeinde: Soziale Veränderungen in süddeutschen Reichsstädten zu Beginn der Neuzeit', in W. Rausch (ed.), *Die Stadt an der Schwelle zur Neuzeit: Beiträge zur Geschichte der Städte Mitteleuropas* (Linz, 1980), 49.

[27] StAH, 2/73, Todtenbuch St. Michael, fo. 543[r].

absence of a police force and poorly developed forensic tests meant that there was usually a lack of circumstantial evidence. In the case of professional thieves magistrates would usually write to some of the towns where the accused had stolen in order to verify information about previous punishments. The real weight of the offences could in most cases only be gathered through a complete confession. Even if suspects immediately confessed to an offence magistrates usually worried whether they had concealed further evidence. This was why most offenders accused in criminal trials were tortured.[28]

Torture

An offender would first realize that she was going to be tortured when the executioner showed her his tools in order to excite terror. Sometimes the offender was then 'heavily beaten'.[29] Torture itself began when big iron screws were bolted onto her thumbs. This was followed by another interrogation. Sometimes the magistrates now only pretended to go further, in which case the offender might be pulled up on a rope, but then be taken down and once more interrogated. But usually no confession followed and the offender was 'pulled up' again. Her feet were tied together and her hands bound behind her back and tied to a rope; this was linked to a drum and a wheel which the executioner turned. She could hang in the air for a long time: in 1677 Tübingen lawyers regarded fifteen minutes as minimum for a woman in poor health.[30] These measures were usually just bearable, but excruciating pain was caused next by weights hung on her feet to stretch the body in both directions. This could be repeated several times, with ever heavier weights. Every stage was followed by an interrogation, and its result determined whether or not the torture was continued. The *Carolina's* regulations about torture had been groundbreaking in 1532, because they stipulated that only clear grounds for suspicion justified torture, that two council deputies had to supervise its execution, and that a suspect had to be let off if he or she still denied the charge after having been pulled up with weights three times. These rules were always obeyed, even though it was in the nature of things that the last one could only rarely be applied.

Lawyers were, however, aware that physical pain was as likely to produce lies as it was to produce truth. Suspects often resisted by

---

[28] See J. H. Langbein, *Torture and the Law of Proof: Europe and England in the Ancien Régime* (Chicago, 1972).   [29] StAMM, A 134/2, Elsbetha Fleck.
[30] HStASt, A 209, Bü. 277, Margaretha Frank.

pointing out this paradox. When Maria Sauer was suspected of infanticide and pulled up three times in 1699, she cried out in misery and said 'she would have to lie out of pain, if she was pulled up again'. She later stated that she had given a false confession, and threatened to kill herself if she was tortured any further. This prompted the supreme council to end her trial.[31] In 1691 a seamstress shouted 'God help me', and 'I don't want to be tortured like this' in the Urach torture-chamber when the executioner, three judges, and two mayors watched her being pulled up for the second time.[32] A Stuttgart woman sent her imprisoned daughter a letter in which she encouraged her not to be frightened and to remain firm. Hence she herself was imprisoned and said that she had just heard about an innocent man who had confessed to being a thief after torture.[33] Stories like this were often heard and suspicion about tortured confessions remained widespread.[34]

Interrogations could take place only after torture. By the end of the seventeenth century, however, the behaviour of suspects during torture could be observed and interpreted. The decisive question was whether the accused was obdurate and hence cold-blooded and unable to feel guilty and penitent. Emotions were recorded for lawyers who would have to judge on the basis of a text, without a personal impression of a woman, her voice, and gestures. The case of a Swiss maid who had given birth to a dead baby in the Unter-türkheim poorhouse is typical. The fact that she had merely shouted when she had been tortured with thumbscrews, but not shed 'one tear', and kept talking firmly and clearly was taken as 'a sign of great obduracy'. Moreover, she had never been seen praying in prison (if it can be termed a prison: she was watched only by a pigherd and his wife).[35] Signs of repentance were thus monitored during a trial and now constituted a recorded part of the evidence.

[31] HStASt, A 210, Abt. II, Bü. 125.
[32] HStASt, A 209, Bü. 2009, 29 Aug. 1692, Agnes Klingenstein.
[33] HStASt, A 210, Abt. I, Bü. 128, 5 Feb. 1700, Maria Fröhlich.
[34] When the Cannstatt junior bailiff wanted to save an old woman from being tortured in 1668 he added as a rather explicit hint for the duke that this was why 'King Emanuel of Portugal deserves eternal praise, because he has told his councillors that suspects ought to be protected from torture': referring to Emanuel 'the Fortunate' (1495–1521), HStASt, A 209, Bü. 778.
[35] When she was tortured for the second time she remained silent, and later maintained that the baby had been born dead. The Tübingen lawyers decided that she could not be beheaded, but after having been imprisoned for fourteen months she died just before their reference reached Cannstatt: HStASt, A 209, Bü. 798, Maria Gainshaber.

Methods of Interrogation

We do not know much about how interrogations were conducted and how suspects were made to confess offences. It seems that the depositions they had already made were read back to them and questions about further offences added. It is, however, important to realize that the minutes of these questions and answers in trial records reflect only part of the procedure. Interrogations could begin with an intimidating warning sermon to raise a suspect's sense of guilt. In 1569, for example, the Memmingen adulteress Dorothea Jürgen was told:

> it is not for nothing that you have been brought into the honourable council's prison. You have led such a disreputable life that the whole town talks and sings about it (as the saying goes). Also, the honourable council received so much information that we could not but apprehend you. This is, in short, why we want to learn from you with whom you have kept dishonourable company.[36]

When she admitted only one affair, they told her: 'how can you be so insolent? It is known that you have not only been with Nadler, but also with Peichinger's son.'[37] She suspected that witnesses had testified maliciously against her and said that she could hardly confess to something she had not done. Relentlessly she was asked how she could pretend to be so 'nice and innocent' since there were even further accusations against her. Pulled up and hung for a long time, she cursed those who tortured her and denied the charge. She was finally let down shouting, 'devil, won't God help me?'

In this situation many suspects claimed that they wanted to 'live and die' for their previous deposition, and many others said they would not confess to anything else, even if every vein was pulled from their bodies. When in 1681 a woman accused of fornication with soldiers was asked 'whether she thought she would get away with her persistent denials', she responded piously that she wanted to 'endure all torments, whether thumbscrews or stretching, for God had commanded it and she wanted to suffer as patiently as God had; but once and for all she could not confess to something she had not done'. Immediately the magistrates tried to demolish her self-representation as martyr. They knew she had publicly cursed a soldier and told him that 'thunder and hail should silence his voice'. She was asked how long she had had this habit of

---

[36] StAMM, A 132/11, 11 Nov. 1569.   [37] Ibid.

swearing and cursing, and she replied that she had merely said it in anger and knew well it was sinful.

Interrogations were therefore cat-and-mouse games during which the accused tried to work out replies acceptable to magistrates, who in turn had to unmask them. Interrogations became circular. A woman accused of infanticide was asked in 1699 'whether she had left her child behind without help?', but she replied it would be 'unchristian if she had done something like that and God would punish her if so'.[38] This was why the interpretation of non-verbal behaviour was so important. Furthermore, leading questions were used to break through the verbal self-representation. In regard to thieves, for example, authorities always tried to find out about collaborators. When in 1564 Margaretha Riechler told the Memmingen magistrates that she had committed all thefts by herself, she was told that 'she could not have done it all by herself, and that there were proofs that she had done it with a man', even though there was no evidence for it.[39] Magistrates mercilessly tested consistency. The plausibility of depositions was repeatedly questioned. At the same time magistrates affirmed that no one would be let off easily. After Riechler had been tortured, she was for example told that 'the honourable council does not think you have told the truth, because things are not as you have said they are. You will not get away with this. This is why we now want to know the truth from you.'[40]

Those under interrogation walked a tightrope. Inconsistency was a sign of unreliability, and thought to be typical female behaviour.[41] In 1693 a Constance ferryman spelt out common knowledge when he told a woman accused of adultery that, regardless of whether she confessed to or denied the charge, no one would 'trust a woman anyway'.[42] Consistency, on the other hand, made a negative impression of obduracy. The problem for suspects was of course that the same questions were repeated over and over again, and anyone who remained mentally clear could only give the same answer. If a suspect was impatient and denied the charge she could be accused of 'scornful, contemptuous talk'.[43]

Non-factual evidence in criminal trials mainly drew on witnesses' testimonies. There was no guideline as to how many witnesses were

---

[38] HStASt, A 210, Abt. I, Bü. 125, 24 Apr. 1699, Maria Dorothea Sauer.
[39] StAMM, A 132/7, 7 Feb. 1564.   [40] Ibid.
[41] For example HStASt, A 309, Bü. 145, 2 July 1630, Katharina Lonhardt.
[42] StAKN, K 65, 4 May 1697, Ursula Geiger.
[43] HStASt, A 209, Bü. 1909, 1649, Sabina Caskarten.

to be heard apart from neighbours and victims, and their number differed with each case. Witnesses had to answer set questions and were paid costs for travelling and lodging. If more than one person was accused a second means of gathering evidence was to confront the accused parties with each other. Their aggressive reactions were observed and analysed, since they usually blamed each other. Both means often led to contradictory results.[44]

From the second half of the seventeenth century onwards we find that an interesting new method was employed not only to observe but also to produce emotional reactions in a suspect in order to gain evidence. Women accused of murder were now sometimes confronted with the dead victim. Until the early seventeenth century this would have been the set-up for an ordeal; God was expected to make the dead corpse bleed if a suspect was guilty.[45] Now the sight of the corpse was thought likely to provoke authentic feelings of love and intimacy, guilt and repentance. The scene was turned into a secularized test of a person's individual nature. In the case of Susanna Bayler, who was suspected of having killed her melancholic husband (she claimed he had committed suicide), a surgeon looked at the corpse, too. But there was no point in an examination, as the shot which killed her husband had been fired three years before. The Canstatt junior bailiff and two council deputies went to the coffin, opened it, and took away the linen cloth which had covered the corpse. There lay her dead, rotten husband, and despite the horror of this sight Bayler knew that she had to stay calm because her own life was at stake. It was necessary to censor responses whose meaning was open to contrary interpretations. She had to cry and to express horror and closeness to the deceased by touching his corpse. The choreography of emotion had to convince, and Bayler staged it well: she fell on her hands and knees, said, 'treasure, in what poor state you are', took his hands, and repeated that she had not killed him.[46]

The display of a particular repertoire of gestures and emotions was generally vital for female suspects during criminal trials. Arms were raised, women fell on their knees, and, most importantly, tears had to flow. It was, of course, assumed that women might simulate:

[44] Detailed minutes of interrogations are rarely preserved in trial records, so that it is difficult to reconstruct how judicial truth was established when in the course of the trial one track was followed intensely while others were neglected.
[45] See e.g. HstASt, A309, Bü 906, 6 Feb, 1574, Magdalena Brodtbeck.
[46] HStASt, A 209, Bü. 778.

'Die Weiber weinen offt mit Schmerzen gleich als gieng es ihn von Herzen Sie pflegen sich nur so zu stellen und können weinen wann sie wöllen', rhymed Grimmelshausen.[47] 'Crocodile tears' and hysterical behaviour were disregarded.[48] Paleness, trembling, sighs, and nervousness were taken to be signs of guilt. The crucial sign of innocence was weeping 'from the heart'—a kind of deep crying, which had to be composed and silent, but which had to be followed by verbal declamations of innocence. Anna Martha Laistler, who was accused of infanticide in 1665, is a case in point. The constable's wife put the 'slightly blue' baby into her arms before it was buried. Anna pressed the baby to her right cheek, kissed it, and said, 'Oh dear golden child, dear angel, that God the father, God the son . . .'. She then pressed it against her cheeks in silence, put it in its bed, held its hands, and repeated several times: 'Oh dear treasure, be quiet, I will soon be with you, oh holy child.' Maintaining that she had not killed it, even though she was a 'great, great sinner', she took the baby up and kissed it again and again. Those who observed her remained unconvinced, however. Even though it was agreed that the movements of her eyes and head expressed sadness, nothing could eradicate the fact that she had 'not shed one tear during the whole time'. She had merely been shocked. The junior bailiff concluded that her behaviour was a sign of terror rather than of real sadness. So she was beheaded.[49] There are many similar cases in the court records. In 1670 a junior bailiff reported of a woman accused of infanticide that she was stubborn, bad, and did not show any emotions.[50] Or again: 'this person has proven herself to be very hidden and stubborn in her gestures; she wanted to cry many times but was unable to shed a tear'—so ran the comment on a Constance thief in 1697.[51] By the end of the seventeenth century, faces in particular were understood to bear the imprints of character: one women allegedly had 'bad and lewd eyes'.[52]

Altogether, then, the body was an important site in the confession process because it unfailingly exposed women's 'true' nature. Women were forced to somatize their emotions and to display

---

[47] *Grimmelshausen: Lebensbeschreibungen der Ertzbetrügerin und Landstörtzerin Courasche*, ed. W. Bender (Tübingen, 1967; repr. of the first 1670 edn.), 68.

[48] Judges were warned of women's tears in J. Döpler, *Theatrum poenarum . . . Oder Schau-Platz derer Leibes- und Lebens-Straffen* (2 vols., Sondershausen, 1693), i. 192f.

[49] HStASt, A 210, Abt. I, Bü. 444, 4 Oct. 1665.

[50] HStASt, A 209, Bü. 1994, Anna Clas.

[51] StAKN, K 65, 4 May 1697, Ursula Geiger.

[52] HStASt, A 210, Abt. I, Bü. 128, 4 Sept. 1700, Maria Fröhlich's mother.

them on request (i.e. not just to feel sad, but actually to shed tears). The problem for judges was to get an accurate 'reading' of the reactions displayed.[53] Hence there was a relatively fixed semiology of feeling, according to which women had to perform. Their expressions of grief and despair had to be 'natural', but also controlled and readable, i.e. not 'hysterical', however much it might determine their life or death.[54]

Excuse Strategies

So far, we have seen that what was judged as good or bad behaviour in court was very much related to gender. Verbal excuse strategies were standardized accordingly. Most women demonstrated repentance and referred to their lesser intelligence and 'female weakness'. This notion was summed up in a 1660 legal reference with the saying: 'Long dresses, short minds.'[55] However, this excuse was not necessarily helpful. While women's lack of rational self-control explained why they were easily led to commit crime, it did not justify their transgressions. Their 'weakness' could thus be as much interpreted as a reason for firm treatment as it could for mild treatment.

Youth was a further basis for a claim of diminished responsibility, especially for single women. Except in the case of those under 14, however, judges often remained sceptical when youth was used as an excuse for poor moral judgement and the inability to foresee the consequences of one's behaviour. When in 1573, for example, the 16-year-old maidservant Barbara Lorentz was accused of infanticide she was considered 'old enough' to know what she had done. The Leonberg jury concluded that her lack of 'fear of God' was more likely to be the reason for the offence than her youth. She had hardly ever visited church, so that they believed God had 'let her fall'. Church attendance was rarely used in such a clear way to judge behaviour. A young woman's reputation was usually determined by the fact that she behaved 'decently' and obediently to her family and masters, was not flirtatious but modest in words, deeds, and dress. Like every woman in her situation, Barbara Lorentz could only

---

[53] L. Hunt, 'The Many Bodies of Marie Antoinette: Political Pornography and the Problem of the Feminine in the French Revolution', in ead. (ed.), *Eroticism and the Body Politic* (Baltimore, 1991).

[54] Some of the behaviour of 19th-cent. 'hysterics' can be seen as a rebellion against similar expectations that women stage a readable, emotional body language to reveal their nature. For their behaviour, displayed before doctors and psychiatrists, like Charcot, was no longer readable and its meaning could not be fixed.

[55] StAKN, K 29, 22 Sept. 1660, Anna Zecklein.

defend herself by saying that she had behaved well in service, had attended sermons, and that her youth and female stupidity were the only reasons why she had not behaved more considerately. This was unlikely to convince the jury. Barbara Lorentz's punishment was to be drowned.[56]

Only those people who were extremely poor, had no education, lived in remote areas, and were evidently stupid had a chance of having their charges lessened on grounds of mental deficiency.[57] In 1698, Anna Specht, accused of incest, skilfully tried to create the impression that she belonged in this category. She told the jury that she was unable to 'express herself well in words' and announced that she was prepared to give 'one florin or more' if she was let off. Suspects were obviously often advised to behave like this before a trial started, because several other women offered ridiculous sums of money and also tried to pretend that they had no idea about the weight of the offence. Specht's mental capacity was then tested with prayers and quotes from the Bible. She was hardly able to repeat them and misspelt words. But since she could remember circumstances of the offence and was fit to answer questions, the jury concluded that even if she was stupid, she possessed the intelligence to realize that she had acted illegally.[58] Anna Dorner was luckier when accused in 1659 after her stepfather had impregnated her. Both civic and ecclesiastical authorities in Beilstein were questioned about her reputation; they said that she had always led a quiet life. She had been repentant and had resisted her stepfather when he had forced himself upon her a second time. The supreme council acknowledged the 'rusticity and simplicity of such people'. The consequences of her public punishment were taken into consideration. Everyone agreed that it would destroy her prospects of marriage. The evidence suggested that the offence had been a one-off mistake and that it was senseless to destroy her life, so she was banished 10 miles from the town for a year.[59]

The heinousness of an offence was partly indicated by the evidence, but judgements were also influenced by the political necessity of deterrent punishment at a given time, by an offender's behaviour during the trial, by the possibility of her or his reintegration into society, and by the social consequences of particular punishments. With the exception of clerics (who were not publicly

[56] HStASt, A 309, Bü. 90b, 6 Feb. 1574.
[57] HStASt, A 582, Bü. 5950, 3 Oct. 1687.
[58] HStASt, A 209, Bü. 1619, 28 July 1689.
[59] HStASt, A 209, Bü. 268, 7 Oct. 1659.

punished lest other denominations exploit their case), higher social status did not offer complete protection from conviction, even though it did protect high-status people from being suspected of criminal behaviour in the first place, or made their delinquency look like an isolated fall from grace. Dishonourable punishments were commonly commuted to high fines. Poverty, on the other hand, was only rarely regarded as a reason for mitigating punishment. Decisions were negatively influenced if a whole family was of ill repute. 'Her family is badly thought of, especially her mother,' went one report.[60] An 'honest family' could, on the other hand, be a cited as a reason for mitigation.[61]

The case of a Swiss female lace-maker's maid, Veronika, on the other hand, illustrates the kinds of evidence that supported an impression of incorrigibility. Veronika was 25 and came from the Pfäffikon, a highly agricultural region. Her father lived there as a widowed smallholder with six other children. Veronika had last worked at a Zurich inn and then agreed to work for the 58-year-old lace-maker. They had set off together in January 1685. In each hostel they arrived at, in Schaffhausen, Sulz, Tübingen, Herrenberg, and Wildberg, her seemingly pregnant belly aroused comment. They arrived in Tübingen at carnival time. Veronika defied all suspicion and the lace-maker's growing anger, went to the Saturday carnival dance, and afterwards could hardly be brought to bed. On the following morning, nothing could make her attend church in Reutlingen either. The lace-maker complained everywhere about her behaviour. After a couple of days, by which time they had joined a journeyman tanner who was walking to Calw, Veronika fell behind, and was later found amidst the blood of her afterbirth. Later, the junior bailiff searched her bundle and saw that she had stolen a 'nicely sown piece for a bodice and some lengths of lace' from her mistress. He wrote to the mayor of Zurich to find out about her reputation. But this was almost unnecessary. 'The apprehended woman is an experienced person (*ein erfahrenes Mensch*), whom everyone considers to have been lewd like this before,' he reported to Stuttgart. Her fate was sealed. Neither her weeping and shouting during the trial, nor her pleas for forgiveness, nor her insistence that she did not know whether the baby had been born dead or alive helped her. She was beheaded in May, just three months after she

[60] HStASt, A 209, Bü. 1940, 6 Mar. 1686, Anna Maria Bidermann.
[61] HStASt, A 209, Bü. 1331, 1644, Margreth Kreuser.

had left Zurich.[62] Why was she so clearly suspected of incorrigible lewd behaviour? First, she had no defence during the trial, because the Treaty of Tübingen ensured that only Württemberg citizens should be represented by an advocate. But more importantly her story read like a chronicle of bad behaviour: theft, dancing, disobedience, the refusal to attend church, and a concealed pregnancy to boot. That she had once served at an inn was no good certificate either. She appeared to be 'experienced', because she had left her family behind, acted independently, and decided against Christian morality to pursue pleasure. She was an outsider and alone. Her death had no consequences to bother the constable and Liebenzell magistrates, the Tübingen lawyers, or the supreme council.

Decision-making

The gravity of the offence thus influenced judgements decisively but not exclusively, even though it generally depended on the nature of the offence whether the harshest sentence was considered at all. In the last third of the seventeenth century a woman suspected of having committed infanticide was always beheaded and soldiers' whores were relentlessly banished. Tübingen lawyers could deal with a clear case of infanticide under five heads, the standardized grounds for a possible mitigation of the death sentence being: '1) Seduction by the child's father, 2) the woman's youth, 3) her stupidity, 4) her belonging to the "weaker sex", 5) and her immediate confession.'[63] When Anna Jäger from Bruch in the district of Backnang was accused in 1678, she gained little from the fact that her advocate came forward with more original arguments than those and told the court that she had been poorly educated by her parents, had been left by her husband, had had a good reputation before her pregnancy, was now repentant, and had to care for a 7-year-old child. Nor did her falling on her knees when the sentence was announced and crying out that 'she wanted to live' prevent her from being beheaded.[64]

The full rigour of the law had to be demonstrated from time to time in regard to all other crimes, too, so that nobody would think they would get away with offences by claiming that they had old

---

[62] HStASt, A 209, Bü. 1513, 14 Mar. 1685 and 15 Mar. 1685, Veronika Rick.
[63] HStASt, A 209, Bü. 1154, 31 Aug. 1679, Maria Wacker.
[64] HStASt, A 209, Bü. 104.

parents or little children to care for. In 1653, the supreme council thus reacted with indignation to a petition by a woman and her six children which begged the council not to ruin their life by punishing and banishing her husband. In this case, the supreme council concluded, 'the need to administer justice, and eradicate disorder, and deterrence' were more important than the interests of 'such private individuals'. Through harsh punishment, they explained, God's anger could better be averted from the duchy. Additionally, it was unfair that those who did not care about their family when they committed their offence should later receive milder sentences because of them. Moreover, a husband could die at any time, and this did not necessarily mean that his family had to go begging as a result.[65]

Decisions were always much more straightforward in regard to women who were professional and mobile thieves. They could hardly defend themselves by referring to their weakness, stupidity, or families. It was clear that only the death sentence would end further thefts.[66] The second harshest punishment, banishment, had no particular effect on them. Still, this was the judges' usual choice, partly because women did not commit robbery and were less dangerous than men, but also because women's property offences did not hit a moral nerve. Women's offences were perceived as a threat chiefly if they transgressed norms of motherhood and sexuality.

Among the sexual offences, bigamy and adultery between married persons allowed the largest room for individual decision-making, mainly because in both cases a marriage had to be protected.[67] It is therefore useful to re-examine closely how the evidence was weighed in an interesting case of theft, adultery, and bigamy, which also entails a remarkably detailed account of interactions in the session room. In 1666, Catharina Schnoth and a herdsman of the district of Backnang were accused of bigamy. Both were extremely poor. He had no possessions at all, whereas she owned a small house from which the junior bailiff realized nine florins to pay the costs of the trial. When asked about her reputation as a youth, the junior bailiff and parson answered that she had already

---

[65] HStASt, A 209, Bü. 1435, 25 Apr. 1654.   [66] See Ch. 3.

[67] See HStASt, A 209, Bü. 40, 8 June 1687, Agatha Glaser, for a particularly interesting case.

been punished thirteen years before (aged 20) for having an illegitimate child by a mason. She had then married a carpenter and soon had three children by him before he went away to war. She had not heard from him for nine years and assumed he had died. She had therefore slept with two other men. Seven years after her husband had left her, she had married a Catholic herdsman. Her thefts sounded serious because she had robbed cellars, but her booty had been small: bread and a chain which she had immediately sold to a miller for thirteen *Batzen* (not even one florin).

During the trial the court advocate routinely asked for leniency for a 'weak woman'. The junior bailiff elaborated on the moral meanings of adultery. She excused herself by saying that the devil had seduced her. The reply was that she had had a bad reputation since her youth. Speculations followed, which came naturally to the junior bailiff: she had probably seduced the carpenter through lewdness and driven the herdsman to a marriage through 'whoredom and seduction'. He further assumed that she had lived badly with her first husband and driven him to go to war. Closer to factual evidence, several earlier thefts were proven, and the junior bailiff saw no sign that her behaviour had improved. She confessed the gravity of her action and conceded that her 'head should be removed'. The junior bailiff exclaimed that this was exactly the punishment the *Carolina* and territorial ordinances prescribed. She asked for a short break, and two judges went with her as guards. Back in the session room she said the harsh accusation had 'pained her deeply in her heart' and asked for forgiveness. She had seen a parson, confessed and received absolution, and begged the jury to consider her youth, weakness, and pregnancy. The procurator demanded that the trial should proceed more speedily because she had already tried to hang herself with a belt, and secondly she had no money and had 'cost his honourable Majesty enough'. The junior bailiff was not moved to mercy. Sarcastically he remarked that despite her alleged weakness and youth she was no longer a 'young rabbit, but a thirty-three year old worn-out fox, who was not weak but bold'.

When the trial was resumed after several days the woman had changed her tactics and argued about the concrete evidence. She said she had bought part of the alleged booty, and that she had not known that one of the men she had slept with was married. Her advocate pointed out contradictions in the written accusation. She raised her arms and promised to improve her behaviour. A week later the Tübingen legal report arrived, recommending that she be spared the death sentence.[68]

This trial therefore supports the assumption that women did not necessarily receive lesser sentences if they brought forward the three standard arguments of youth, seduction, and stupidity. In order to receive mercy they had to show emotional despair about the sentence, submission to God and the authorities, and the promise of better behaviour in future. The threat of harsh punishment and moral condemnation were used to create, at best, a sense of guilt and repentance in the offender, or at least to teach her a lesson. We have seen that from the second half of the seventeenth century onwards the moral and criminal record of suspects was reconstructed even when they came from a different district or region. This highlights the development of more bureaucratic surveillance and control. For the Tübingen lawyers, who finally decided on sentences in Württemberg, factual evidence, the legal weight of the offence, petitions by a husband, and an indication of repentance mattered most. Suspects' statements about the evidence were crucial to their fate, and they did well to make it absolutely clear which offences they thought they had committed in ignorance of their gravity, or which ones they had not committed at all. This was not always easy, because advocates and procurators usually cooperated with the authorities, and women had to endure highly condemnatory and sometimes even speculative judgements on their behaviour.

MIGRATION AND MERCY

Money and friends [69]

Since paternal power was based on a balance of severity and of favours, sentences were never regarded as fixed. They could be negotiated through out-of-court petitioning, bribery, and formal, written petitions sent to magistrates and dukes. Widows and orphans, who were stereotypically described as 'poor, weak, and lonely', could ask for protection against the harshness of the law; so could poor mothers who had stolen bread for their children. But

---

[68] Two midwives examined whether she was pregnant but did not reach a conclusion. Four days after the reference had been sent the junior bailiff reported the sentence to the duke, and five days later the duke gave the order to execute it: HStASt, A 209, Bü. 97.

[69] This is a shortened version of a section more fully developed in the German edition of this book.

paternalism mainly worked for those who lived inside a community and knew the mayor or bailiff. Those who were poor, strange, and single were in a much worse situation. Because imprisonment or dishonouring sentences were usually mitigated into fines, those without money had no chance of asking for favours. They lacked social capital, too, in the form of connections: usually the authorities mitigated sentences only if relatives, employers, neighbours, and communities exerted pressure. Recognizances often likewise demanded considerable sureties for an offender's release, while a person who had to stand in the pillory lost honour and reputation, and would not be reintegrated into the community or even be taken back by a spouse.

Petitions were most likely to be successful if they came from married citizens, especially if they had dependent children. They were also more successful if offenders could refer to social merits, such as military and communal services and offices. Artisans could hope for support from their guilds if they argued that their guild's honour was at risk and their work valuable for communities. Women's exclusion from guilds and offices meant that they were clearly disadvantaged here, although Constance in 1664 provides a rare counter-example: a barber convicted for adultery was able to have his sentence mitigated because of his sister's 'loyal efforts' on behalf of injured soldiers during the occupation of Constance.[70] And in 1564 a Freiburg guild supported a petition for an artisan's daughter suspected of theft.[71] Female labour could be represented as invaluable if old parents, children, or a household had to be looked after, or if a harvest was imminent. Petitions also reveal strong bonds of dependency between the generations. In 1679, the parents of a Stetten women wrote that they would have to die grey-haired and with 'hunger and woe' if their imprisoned daughter did not return to them.[72]

Most petitions were highly emotional: parents wrote how they received all their 'comfort' from children, and saw them as the 'joy of their old age'.[73] The widow of a Württemberg vineyard-worker wrote in 1615 that she was a 'poor, old, and very weak woman', and that she needed her daughter, her 'sole comfort', who was about to be banished from the country.[74] Laments for the harshness of the sen-

---

[70] StAKN, RP 1664, BI 144, 20 Oct. 1664, 526ʳ.   [71] StAFr, AI XI f, U 1 Mar. 164.
[72] HStASt, A 209, Bü. 1863, 30 Apr. 1679, Maria Bestlin.
[73] On the language of petitions see Gatrell, *Hanging Tree*, ch. 16.
[74] HStASt, A 237a, Bü. 323, c.1615.

tence were movingly expressed. A Memmingen father, aged 70, wrote in 1668 that he did not have anyone except his daughter, and that he was anxious that her children should not 'decay' while she was in prison.[75] In 1678, a Hall advocate appeared four times before the magistrates to draw their attention to a petition by 'old, sick' parents on behalf of their pregnant daughter, to have her sentence mitigated to a fine.[76]

In regard to married women efforts were even stronger and dependence more marked. The Hall salt-maker Maria Lautt was imprisoned in 1677, for example, because a barber's servant had frequently visited her house 'naked, wearing only his lower garments', in order to 'play' with her. Her husband, her seven children, and her other kin and neighbours petitioned for her release and to protect her from public mockery. Her husband was willing to forgive her the adultery and seek reconciliation. Without her, after all, he faced four unpalatable alternatives: poverty, permanent dependence on kin or friends, a struggle for the annulment of the marriage and a remarriage, or following Maria into banishment. Soon after the first petition one of the *Stättmeister* reported that the husband had come to his house and had 'behaved in a desperate manner, saying that if no one helped him he would go to a place nobody knew and kill himself'. It was decided to hasten procedures. Soon Lautt mobilized his mother and siblings, a salt-worker, and other friends to plead for mercy, too. But the council was divided. On the one hand, Johann Nicolas Schragmüller said it was important that her husband should desire to have Maria back 'with all his heart', and he for one wanted to release her after a fortnight in prison. On the other hand, most other councillors still wanted her banished for life. Soon a further petition reached them, from Maria's father, pleading the council to recall his 'former services during war and hence only to confine his daughter to her home for a time'. In the event was decided to confine her to her house for a year, but only after she was imprisoned in the fool's house in the market for a couple of days, thus to shame her. Her husband, brother-in-law, children, and relatives then petitioned three more times that she be saved from such exposure—but in vain. Several months later Maria's advocate asked for her release from home confinement. She had paid half of her fine, and wanted to pay the rest once she was working at the salt-works

[75] StAMM, RP 1 July 1667–11 Aug. 1669, 12 Feb. 1668, fo. 73ʳ, Maria Magdalena Esser.
[76] StAH, RP 285/1678, fo. 479ʳ.

again. This petition did not succeed either.[77] Altogether, nine pleas for mitigation of Maria's sentence survive in the council minutes. She was sentenced to banishment again four years later; she had continued her disreputable life, been imprisoned again and again, and released only because of her 'good, pious husband, as simple-minded as he was patient'.[78]

When sentences were mitigated into fines, the amount of money to be paid either equalled payment per day of imprisonment, or related to the gravity of the offence and the offender's status. Wealthy citizens often had to face extremely high fines. In 1688, a Hall baker who had committed adultery several times and impregnated his maidservants had to pay 200 florins, was confined to his home for four months, and was dismissed from his office as a judge. If this seemed severe, the maidservant's punishment was somewhat worse. After three weeks' imprisonment she was publicly shamed and banished forever.[79]

Fines caused obvious problems for the authorities. They gave the impression that the authorities sought to profit from sentences and that they favoured wealthy people. And the mitigation of imprisonment to fines was indeed unjust, because there were those who did not mind paying such sums, and others who had to borrow the money and hardly knew how to pay it back, and yet others who did not know anyone who would give them credit. The situation of single women was very difficult here. Maidservants earned less than male servants, and were unable to save or borrow much money. Fines for a trespass (*Frevel*) were therefore lower for women; but fines for more serious offences were not. Throughout the sixteenth and seventeenth centuries there was an attempt to limit the mitigation of imprisonment into fines. But prisons were small, and the authorities were unwilling to carry the costs of feeding prisoners and of paying the constable for locking them up and releasing them. Offenders who were able to pay for their keep in prison were asked to do so, but again many would delay payment and there were not enough officials to chase them. Thus, despite the arbitrariness of the process, the practice of mitigating imprisonment into fines continued.

---

[77] StAH, 4/485, 6 July 1677, RP 1677, fos. 453^v, 456^{rv}, 470^r, 490^r–491^{rv}, 507–8$^{r–v}$, 512^v, 739^r. [78] StAH, 4/488, 9 July 1681, fo. 122$^{r–v}$.
[79] StAH, 4/486, 5 Jan. 1688, fos. 24^r–25^r.

The Decline of Forgiveness and the Bureaucratization of Mercy in Criminal Trials

In 1517 something extraordinary happened in Esslingen. Barbara Schreyer, who had killed her baby, was about to be buried alive. The procession had just begun to move from the town hall to the gallows. At that very moment a journeyman shoemaker from Leimen in the Palatinate appeared before the council. He offered to marry Barbara and promised to beg with her for the forgiveness of her sins. He said that he would be able to lead a honourable life with her. The council permitted her release. The procession stopped. A little later, at the nearby Sirnau convent, Barbara and the journeyman shoemaker promised each other marriage.[80]

This custom was called 'marrying off', *Losheiraten*. It enacted secular forgiveness because of another party's preparedness to save a stranger from execution. The idea behind this custom can perhaps be related to acceptance of the medieval principle *Amor vincit omnia*, which was sometimes interpreted to mean that love even weighed stronger than the law.[81] This was a medieval notion and we know little about its application or about the origin of customs like the *Losheiraten*. In the early modern period, however, we register their decline. Fewer and fewer exceptions were made from the principle that mercy depended on the gravity of the offence and the repentance shown. Trust in marriage as the restorer of honourable life was slowly lost. Instead, officials might begin to think about what happened to couples such as Barbara Schreyer and the journeyman shoemaker. Thus, we find the Esslingen city-scribe noting in the court book in 1553, just below Schreyer's confession, that she was still alive, but had treated her husband badly and 'not shown much gratefulness to him'. He still added the sentence, 'May God forgive her.'[82]

It was not only the custom of 'marrying off' that enabled death sentences to be mitigated. 'Pledging free', or *Freibitten*, could work to the same effect. High-status people could free offenders by asking magistrates to spare them. In Imperial cities pledges were decided upon by councils. In 1519, for example, Clara Scheu, imprisoned for life for infanticide, was released thanks to the pledge of the master of

[80] K. Maier, *Das Strafrecht der Reichsstadt Esslingen im Spätmittelalter und zu Beginn der Neuzeit* (Tübingen, 1960), 126 n. 32.

[81] M. Clanchy, 'Law and Love in the Middle Ages', in J. Bossy (ed.), *Disputes and Settlements: Law and Human Relationships in the West* (Cambridge, 1983).

[82] StAL Ludwigsburg, B 169, Bü. 119 I, fo. 84ʳ.

the Teutonic knights.[83] Thirty-five years later the duke and duchess of Zweibrücken asked for a mitigation of Barbara Schönmann's sentence for infanticide: so she was merely banished.[84] Such acts of grace were acts of power, but also of compassion. They testify to a horror of execution or of lifelong imprisonment, especially in regard to young offenders and those whose offences were not completely abhorrent. Robber-murderers were invariably excluded from such empathy; even so, the sight of their execution and corpses was generally known to cause sickness or madness.[85] Horror of the death sentence is apparent in reports such as this one about an Augsburg Anabaptist woman in 1528. A journeyman wanted to save the woman by marrying her. But she told him that she 'already had a husband, and he had told her to stay with him'. Jörg Preu, the chronicler, reports that men and women, young and old, cried pitifully when she was duly burned.[86] As late as 1621 an Augsburg woman was married off to save her from death.[87] A more typical experience by that time, however, was that of a Franconian corporal, who in 1633 asked the Constance councillors to let him marry a woman about to be beheaded for infanticide: he was dismissed instantly.[88]

Women in turn could get men's sentences mitigated through offers of marriage and petitions. During the Middle Ages, abbesses and other high office-holders also had the right to cut offenders down from the hangman's noose without the council's permission.[89] But whereas in Lucerne in 1423 a felon had been 'given' to the petitioning women with permission for them to 'do and behave with him as they liked',[90] authorities from the sixteenth century onwards tended to lay down conditions for this practice. In 1553, for example, when a Württemberg citizen was condemned for homicide, his family and 'several princesses' petitioned for him. Moreover, an Urach girl named Anna asked three times to be married to him. He was released on condition that he never forget what Anna had done

---

[83] StAH, 4/477, fo. 320[v].   [84] StAH 4/79, Fraisch- und Malefizrepertorium.
[85] I. Gierl, *Bauernleben und Bauernwallfahrt in Altbayern: Eine kulturkundliche Studie auf Grund der Tuntenhausener Mirakelbücher* (Munich, 1960), 77.
[86] *Die Chroniken der deutschen Städte vom 14. bis ins 16. Jahrhundert* (36 vols., Leipzig, 1862–1931), xxix. 42.
[87] E. Osenbrüggen, *Das alemannische Strafrecht im deutschen Mittelalter* (Schaffhausen, 1860), 192.   [88] StAKN, RB BI 115, 13 Aug. 1633, fo. 128[r], Christoph Willem.
[89] C. G. Bonnekamp, *Die Zimmersche Chronik als Quelle des Strafrechts, der Strafgerichtsbarkeit und des Strafverfahrens in Schwaben am Ausgang des Mittelalters* (Bonn, 1940), 19 f.; K. S. Bader, *Die Zimmersche Chronik als Quelle der rechtlichen Volkskunde* (Freiburg im Breisgau, 1942), 33.   [90] Osenbrüggen, *Strafrecht*, 192.

for him, that he never carry weapons, and that he abstain from drinking in company and at feasts. Six citizens promised either to pay 300 florins within a fortnight should he reoffend, or else to surrender themselves to the authorities in his place.[91] At the same time the authorities were beginning to be sceptical about the custom of marrying off felons. In 1562, for example, both the family of an apprentice sentenced to death for killing a young woman, and petitioners from the Augsburg painters' guild, failed to win a mitigation of his sentence, even though they had found an honourable and pious maiden ready to 'constrain him within marriage'.[92]

It was not only redeeming offers of marriage and the merciful expectations of honourable ladies that testified to a belief in the power of love and life over death. The pleas of pregnant women did as well. The Villingen chronicler Hug noted in 1509 that the whole community of a man who was to be beheaded for homicide arrived with 'many pregnant women' and cut him from the hangman's rope.[93] A late medieval Swiss formula to be spoken immediately before the execution asked judges to listen to married women's requests for mercy because Jesus had been born of a woman. It then referred to the pregnant women present, and asked for mercy because of the children they carried.[94] In a theology which focused on Mary rather than on Eve, women were honoured as the bearers of humanity. Childbirth and the pain it involved were regarded as an unparalleled gift to humankind, outside any logic of rational exchange. This entitled pregnant women to insist that generosity should temper retributive justice. When in 1501, for example, a woman in the Bregenz area was about to be buried alive, many virgins and pregnant women joined the rest of the community successfully to plead for mercy.[95] At executions women thus had a rare public voice on matters of justice. They were recognized as part of the political community.

However, although we do not know how common they had been in the fifteenth century, these practices were slowly eroded in the sixteenth century. In 1596, for example, 'many pregnant women'

---

[91] HStASt, A 44, U 5833, 10 July 1553, Gori Widmann.
[92] *Chroniken der deutschen Städte*, xxxiii. 154 n. 2.
[93] C. Roder (ed.), *Heinrich Hugs Villinger Chronik von 1495 bis 1533* (Tübingen, 1883), 39.   [94] Osenbrüggen, Strafrecht, 180f.
[95] C. Ulbrich, 'Unartige Weiber: Präsenz und Renitenz von Frauen im frühneuzeitlichen Deutschland', in R. v. Dülmen (ed.), *Arbeit, Frömmigkeit und Eigensinn* (Frankfurt on Main, 1990), 34.

asked Constance magistrates to spare the life of a woman about to be executed for theft, but their petition failed.[96] However, there were still pregnant women to whom the custom made sense, who felt that they could request mercy because they carried new life in them. Thus, no less than fifty-two pregnant women gathered in Constance in 1620 and begged for an offender's life.[97] As late as 1668, the brothers of a prisoner about to be executed for homicide found 'several pregnant women' to support their petition.[98]

In a territory like Württemberg only the duke had the right to mitigate sentences in criminal trials, but once his Tübingen lawyers had made their finely balanced decisions he had little interest in exercising the right. Moreover, there was no chance of petitioning in person just before the execution since every petition had to be sent to the duke in writing. This made the whole process expensive, inflexible, and unlikely to succeed. In territories, moreover, as in the Imperial cities, the view that a good penal policy depended upon predictable and deterrent punishments for serious offenders was beginning to predominate. Compassion for 'criminals' was seen as a sign of weak politics. Justus Lipsius, for example, posited in his *Six Books of Politics* in 1596 that the best government was 'severe, constant, and restrained'. Common people, he explained, would by nature only yield to fear of punishment and inflicted pain. Leniency induced contempt. 'Wholesome Severitie', Lipsius advised, 'is to be preferred before a vaine showe of Clemencie.'[99] Other political writers emphasized that the equal punishment of similar offences was the hallmark of legal justice, and likewise disregarded the paternal display of the sovereign's pardoning power. By the end of the sixteenth century, the idea that 'love' might weigh more strongly than law seemed a mere relic of old times.

Mercy and the Clergy

Secular authorities regarded 'severity' as divinely sanctioned. They argued that God, far from being moved by poor sinners, would punish towns and territories if crime went unpunished. In 1657, in the case of a woman who had committed infanticide, the well-known Tübingen lawyers Harprecht and Bachmann grimly asserted

---

[96] StAKN, RP 1596–8, BI 80, fo. 146ʳ, 19 Oct. 1596.
[97] StAKN, A 1/28a, Chronik Franz Bickels, 55.
[98] StAKN, RP 1668, BI 148, fo. 100ʳ, 16 Feb. 1668.
[99] Justus Lipsius, *Sixe Bookes of Politickes or Civil Doctrine*, trans. W. Iones (London, 1594), 79.

that 'the country cannot be reconciled to the blood shed within it except by the blood of him who shed it'.[100] As a result, petitions by the clergy were politically risky, since they tacitly challenged the notion that the secular authorities were enacting God's will. This may have been why in Hall in 1552 parsons were ordered no longer to act as defence counsel in court. When in 1678 a parson strongly opposed the banishment of a woman who had aborted a child, he was reprimanded by the council and reported to the church superintendent.[101] Hardly any petitions from Protestant ministers on criminal trials survive. Those that do merely invoke the general desirability of divine mercy for repentant sinners, without challenging the secular authorities' claim to monopolize decision-making.

In Catholic Constance, by contrast, clerical petitions could still claim to absolve a repentant offender in God's name, making the secular authorities' failure to mitigate a sentence appear unchristian. In 1700, for example, a young woman named Scholastica Weigel had been imprisoned for stealing grain. Her brothers and nephews had visited the bishop to tell him that the case had been dealt with 'rigorously' and that Scholastica would be publicly shamed if petitions were unsuccessful. Conscious of the long frictions between bishops and town authorities, the bishop wrote to the town council stressing that he did not wish to cause trouble needlessly, but that her relatives were honourable, while a deceased cousin had been parson at St Stephan's. To protect his memory, the bishop suggested, her imprisonment until now should be regarded as sufficient.[102] The combined petitioning power of all local, urban Catholic clerical institutions was impressive. In the case of Anna Barbara Weckerlin, for example, who committed theft several times in 1665, the bishop, the warden of St Anna's, and sundry friends and neighbours supported a petition, as did the chaplain of St Johann and the prelate of Salmenschwil.[103] Similarly, Peter Humel, a local citizen, but a thief and murderer, was supported by the bishop of Constance, the prioress, mother superior, and the whole convent of Zofingen: the parents, they wrote, had shown despair and sadness which outweighed the emperor's law.[104] The cathedral chapter, the prelate of Petershausen, the Franciscan Father Guardin, and two Augustinian

---

[100] HStASt, A 209, Bü. 587, 27 Oct. 1657, Margaretha Weiss.
[101] StAH, A/490, *Decretsammlung*, 4/485, 8 July 1678, fo. 70[r–v]; RP 1678, fo. 460[v].
[102] StAKN, K 75, 2 Apr. 1700.   [103] StAKN, RP 1665, BI 144, fos. 581[r], 586[r], 594[r].
[104] StAKN, K 54, n.d.

fathers requested that Humel should be let off the death sentence.[105] Again, when Maria Blumenmacher was convicted for infanticide in 1670 the cathedral chapter, the convent of Petershausen, the Jesuits, Capuchins, and Franciscans wrote on her behalf.[106] Just as in Protestant areas, however, such petitions were usually successful if not only the family and clergy petitioned, but also neighbours, communities, and guilds showed their dissent from a harsh sentence.[107] Significantly, therefore, both Catholic and Protestant rulers and magistrates did not respect clerical attempts to influence decisions on capital punishment.

SENTENCES

Prisons

Because they were only used for the most serious offences, the percentage of death sentences was small in the early modern period, while fines, imprisonment, and binding over were the most frequent punishments.[108] In Hall, for example, we find 1,288 recognizances and confessions of women between 1500 and 1700, but only eleven women were executed. The most common experience of punishment for early modern men and women apart from fines was short-term imprisonment.

Early modern prisons ranged from the 'fool's house' to civic towers for serious criminals and to makeshift prisons in small towns. Fool's houses had been established below town halls in the late Middle Ages to punish drunken or quarrelsome people. Since they were situated in the market the imprisonment was very public and offenders could often be watched through windows.[109] In the course of the sixteenth century the aim became less one of sentencing

---

[105] StAKN, RP 1668, BI 148, fo. 100ʳ, 16 Feb. 1668.

[106] StAKN, RP 1670, BI 150, fo. 671ʳ, 4 Sept. 1670.

[107] When a Reichenau ferryman was accused of fraud in 1597, for example, a petition supported by the cathedral foundation, the prelate and the chaplain of the islands of Mainau and Reichenau, the towns of Überlingen and Kreuzlingen, the foundation of St Stephan, and the Augustinians, caused the council to consider ending the criminal trial. The councillors voted 12 : 11 to continue it, a result which shows how narrow such decisions were, StAKN, BI 80, RP 1596–8, 7 May 1597.

[108] G. Schwerhoff, *Köln im Kreuzverhör: Kriminalität, Herrschaft und Gesellschaft in einer frühneuzeitlichen Stadt* (Bonn, 1991), 123–73.

[109] In 1681 a Hall woman accused of stealing wine was put into the fool's house with a wine-jar around her neck and another woman with a shaming instrument called the 'violin' (*Geige*) around her neck. This affirms the public character of the punishment: StAH, 4/487, 20 Oct. 1681, fo. 127ʳ.

foolish behaviour than of punishing damage to others and the common weal, but fool's houses were still used for short sentences intended to serve as a public deterrent. In towns which did not possess a prison of this kind, women would be put into one of the towers. There was usually a hierarchy of tower usage—the highest ones with the thickest walls being used for serious offenders. The conditions of those imprisoned during long criminal trials were very harsh. In 1688, a 60-year-old woman complained that after four weeks in the Brackenheim prison she could 'neither bend nor walk'.[110] Absolute security could be gained only if the windows were very small. Inmates quickly became ill.[111] Cold was a problem during winter; inmates often petitioned to be transferred to the constable's chamber. In 1670, better treatment was ordered in Württemberg after several prisoners had died of cold.[112] Because of these conditions, imprisonment in prison towers was itself regarded as severe punishment and was therefore deducted from the final punishment. In 1653 the duke of Württemberg ordered prisons to be built for offenders under detention; these were to replace towers at least during the inquisition procedure. He wanted them to be safe but endurable, so that prior imprisonment in them would give no grounds to mitigate sentences.[113]

Usually the constable's wife or female guards looked after con-victed women.[114] If offenders were not sentenced to bread and water, their relatives would be allowed to bring food. Prison rules were rarely fixed, and, except for criminal trials, communications with the outside world were tolerated.[115] Except in serious cases or when evidence was unclear, imprisonment tended to be for less than five days. In Hall, minor offenders were usually imprisoned over-night to enable them to work during the day. During the seventeenth century, laws began to demand that sexual crimes be punished with

---

[110] HStASt, A 209, Bü. 1064, 10 Oct. 1688, Maria Dreher.

[111] Prisoners in the Stuttgart tower commonly became ill after one or two weeks' imprisonment: HStASt, A 210, Abt. 1, Bü. 125, 23 Mar. 1557.

[112] Reyscher, *Gesetze*, v, 'General=Rescript, die bessere Behandlung Gefangener betreffend', 23/4 June 1670.

[113] Ibid. 457, 'General=Rescript, die Einrichtung von Untersuchungs=Gefängnissen betreffend', 26 Feb. 1653.

[114] In 1664 magistrates unsuccessfully tried to find a woman who would guard a woman accused of infanticide: HStASt, A 309, Bü. 120, Barbara Ricker. In 1671, an Esslingen female warder whipped a female thief through the town, LAL, B 169, Bü. 119, II, 13 Dec. 1671, Elisabetha, Hans Kocher's wife.

[115] In 1557 the second harshest Stuttgart prison had thick walls but a hole through which one could throw letters, HStASt, A 210, Abt. I, Bü. 125, 28 Dec. 1557.

long periods of imprisonment. For fornication or adultery, sentences rose to two, four, or eight weeks' imprisonment.[116] In practice, however, such long-term imprisonment was avoided because of the costs, the inmates' idleness, and, in the case of married persons, the loss of working power in families. It was out of these considerations that Württemberg introduced public labour in 1620. Vagrants especially were to be disciplined to work: from 1661 onwards they were even employed in building Duke Eberhard's Württemberg palaces.[117] Otherwise, labour assignments were a complicated business: when the Tübingen bailiff asked in 1689 whether he could employ those sentenced for fornication and premarital sex to repair the town walls, he was told to obtain the supreme council's permission for each offender's employment.[118] In Hall, however, forty-four female offenders were sentenced to around two weeks of public labour between 1681 and 1691, after convictions for fornication or premarital sex.[119] But these were relatively short-lived attempts at 'reform', and in Esslingen and Memmingen public labour was not introduced at all, presumably because it was too dificult to control.[120]

This sparing use of long-term imprisonment or work schemes as a punitive measure was at its most problematic in regard to serious offenders such as professional thieves. Upper Swabian Imperial cities, for example, must have realized that their banishment led only to further crime in the next town along the high road. However, in contrast to Netherlandish and north German towns which established houses of correction during the seventeenth century,[121] and to Nuremberg, which opened its workhouse in 1670, there was no readiness to invest financially in cooperative crime-control. Houses of correction were costly institutions,[122] and south-west German

---

[116] See Ch. 5.

[117] Reyscher, *Gesetze*, vi. 379, 'General=Rescript, die Einführung der öffentlichen Arbeit betreffend', 19 Sept. 1620; 'General=Ausschreiben, das Abverdienen der Strafe betreffend', 25 Feb. 1661.   [118] HStASt, A 209, Bü. 1944.

[119] Source: *Urfehdbuch*, StAH, 4/485.

[120] In Constance public labour was already introduced at the end of the 15th cent., but again women were excluded: see O. Feger (ed.), *Die Statutensammlung des Stadtschreibers Jörg Vögeli* (Constance, 1951), 121.

[121] P. Spierenburg, *The Prison Experience: Disciplinary Institutions and their Inmates in Early Modern Europe* (London, 1991), 36.

[122] The Württemberg houses of correction, built in Ludwigsburg in 1736, and in Stuttgart in 1760, did not meet half of the expenses, despite profits from the inmates' production: see P. Sauer, *Im Name des Königs: Strafgesetzgebung und Strafvollzug im Königreich Württemberg von 1806 bis 1871* (Stuttgart, 1984), 118f., based on a calculation for 1832/3.

authorities sought to reduce existing costs rather than to extend them. The goal remained to get rid of delinquents as quickly and cheaply as possible; habitual crime continued to be fought by exemplary punishment only.

Shaming Punishments and the Death Sentence

The most common shaming punishment for offenders was to stand either in the pillory or on a large 'burdening-stone' (*Lasterstein*) for a quarter to half an hour. Sometimes placards named the offence, but, in view of prevailing illiteracy, it was more common for stolen goods to be hung around the neck, or for symbolic signs to designate the offence (for example red boots for female adulterers).[123] This made the offender and her crime public knowledge, exposed her to mockery, and dishonoured her for life. Shaming punishments were therefore usually followed by banishment. Offenders had to walk three times across the market and to the city gate, while the constable or executioner beat a metal basin, the *Becken*. Often they also had to wear a wooden stock or stone around their neck. The stone was associated with a millstone and was very heavy, usually weighing twenty-five pounds.[124] Symbolically it 'broke an offender's neck', forcing her to hold her head low and display the body language of submission. Carrying it was a corporal punishment and an alternative to whipping: one Memmingen woman fell sick after she had carried the stone in 1667, and her father demanded that she be taken to hospital.[125]

How attentive the population was to public punishment and banishment or how often they would mock an offender or pelt her with stones remains unclear. In 1663 the Esslingen council asserted that even when the offender's confession was publicly read in the market before executions, youths would shout and there would be such buzzing in the streets 'that one can hardly if at all

---

[123] In Hall, red boots had to be worn from 1684 onwards, StAH, 4/495, 'Poena et taxa Criminum', 14 Jan. 1684.

[124] This measure is already given for 1532 in Schönaich, HStASt, A 44, U 480, Ottilia Metzger, confirmed by other sources throughout the period. The stone seems to originate from a millstone which was associated with the slave labour of a miller's maidservant, who was considered as a maid of lowest rank: see E. Künßberg, *Zur Strafe des Steintragens* (Berlin, 1926), 39 f.; hence the saying *etwas hängt wie ein Mühlstein am Hals*.

[125] StAMM, RP 1 July 1667–11 Aug. 1669, 11 Oct. 1667, fo. 29ᵛ, Anna Wiedenmann. After three petitions he was successful, with the additional help of an Erlishofen parson who had collected money for her.

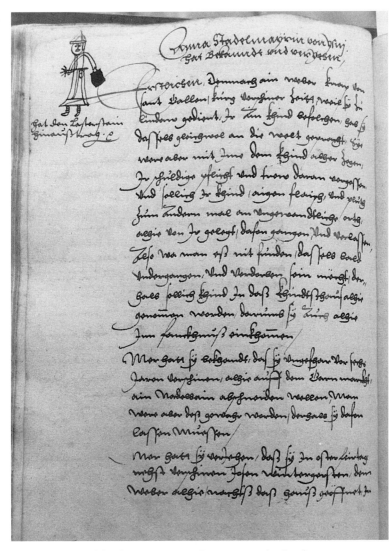

FIG. 3. Anna Stadelmayrin is sentenced to carrying the burdening-stone

understand the scribe who reads it'.[126] Publicity had the additional
disadvantage that it could also be used to mount a display of
resistance against the authorities. In 1674, for example, a Hall butcher's widow begged not to be banished and shouted that she had
been wronged, 'regardless of good, bad, or threatening words'.[127]

However, for the authorities the central problem of shaming punishments was that in some ways they were too effective. The very
touch of the constable or executioner previously in contact with
serious offenders was dishonouring. Partners often made their willingness to accept their husband or wife back home depend on
whether he or she had been touched by the executioner.[128] We
can only assume that this was why the formidable Hall pillory, built
in 1509 in the market, below the impressive steps of St Michael,
surrounded by patricians' houses and the town hall, was hardly
ever used. Such dishonouring was even publicized beyond the
town's border. In the seventeenth century most offenders in Hall,
Memmingen, and Constance thus had the alternative of being
removed quietly instead of being publicly banished. The Hall pillory
thus served as a threat rather than being the location of actual
punishment.

Cutting off limbs or branding the face or back with signs like the
gallows were the only means of marking a serious offender so that
she could be identified after banishment. It is difficult to imagine the
life of a thief without ears, but the sources say as little about this as
they do about the shrieks when such sentences were executed. In
Memmingen only women had their ears cut off, five between 1551
and 1609. Mutilation and branding became more and more an
exception. A legal report stated in 1551 that branding on the face
was forbidden by Imperial laws because mankind had been created
in God's image, while brandings on other parts of the body were
ineffective because they were hidden by clothes.[129] But still, in 1663,
two Swiss sisters apprehended for theft in Tübingen had gallows
branded onto their backs and were banished.[130] In 1680 a known
female thief from Switzerland, who had been apprehended in Hall

[126] StAL, B 169, Bü. 119, II, *Ordnung so bei Executionen von Malefikanten zu observieren*,
23 Mar. 1663.
   [127] StAH, 4/484, 10 Oct. 1674, fos. 30ᵛ–31ʳ, Catharina Weidenbacher.
   [128] In Württemberg, someone who was taken to prison by musketeers or by the
constable, or accused in a criminal trial, was dishonoured, too. People therefore often
successfully petitioned not to have the *Malefizglocke* rung: see E. Lippert, *Glockenläuten
als Rechtsbrauch* (Freiburg, 1939).   [129] HStASt, A 237a, Bü. 336, 14 Apr. 1662.
   [130] UAT, 84/16, Maria and Elisabetha Heinemann, 6 Jan. 1663, fos. 405ᵛ–408ᵛ.

once already, had one ear, already mutilated, 'cut off smoothly'.[131] And when the Catholic town of Freiburg was occupied by the French in the second half of the century, such measures were used frequently against women who had relationships with soldiers. Thus in 1685 Verena Khinderdt had to stand in the pillory for an hour for fornicating with a soldier, had both ears cut off, was beaten up, and banished.[132] In 1697, a woman who had repeatedly fornicated was whipped, burnt under her left shoulder, and had her right ear cut off.[133] There was no linear development towards more 'humane' punishments.

Death sentences for women were relatively rare in the towns I have studied (excluding witchcraft of course). In Hall we know of eleven death sentences between 1500 and 1700; in Esslingen likewise there were eleven death sentences out of 103 women tried during the same period. In Memmingen there were eleven death sentences between 1551 and 1689 out of thirty-nine women punished for serious offences (whereas sixty-one men were executed during the same period). This mainly reflected the fact that most men were executed for robbery and murder, while women were almost never accused of these offences. Female execution rates were mainly determined by the punishment for infanticide and theft. During the seventeenth century the overall rate of executions fell.[134] At the same time infanticide was prosecuted more strongly. Thus— despite the dramatic fall in witchcraft prosecutions—the proportional rate of executed women rose in many places.

Women sentenced to death were almost always beheaded. In Esslingen the last woman was drowned in 1589 (she had stolen twenty pounds of yarn and committed infanticide eighteen years before). In 1590 a professional thief was hanged. In Württemberg the last two women were drowned for infanticide in 1593. In 1615 a Heidenheim woman buried alive for killing her husband had an iron pike stuck through her heart and earth thrown upon her.[135] Württemberg women who had committed infanticide were tweaked with glowing pincers in the late seventeenth century, or their head

[131] StAH, 4/484, Catherina Camer, 31 Aug. 1678, fo. 78^r, 24 Jan. 1680, fo. 96^{r-v}.
[132] StAFr, *Urfehden*, 22 Mar. 1685.   [133] StAFr, *Urfehden*, 21 Mar. 1687.
[134] Evans, *Rituals of Retribution*, 42.
[135] HStASt, A 209, Bü. 1319, Margaretha Ferber. In 1711 the *Josephina* for Bohemia, Silesia, and Mähren still stuck to the punishment of burying alive women who had committed brutal forms of infanticide: see S. Stiassny, *Die Pfählung: Eine Form der Todesstrafe* (Vienna, 1903), 36.

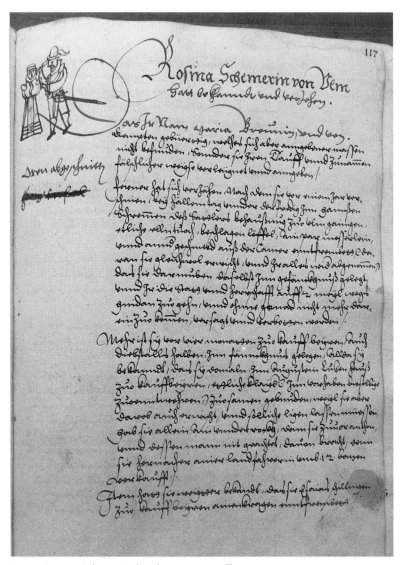

Fig. 4. Rosina Schemerin has her ears cut off

was stuck on a post. Otherwise it was stressed that simple beheading was preferred 'to avoid despair', as a legal report put it in 1687.[136] Harsh punishments, as prescribed by the *Carolina*, were usually rejected, such as drowning in a bag with animals or burying alive and sticking a post through the heart. The reason was not only compassion: these punishments were also less secure. Some women were buried alive and had resisted, some had been drowned, only to resurface and be freed.[137]

The Consequences of Punishments

In the early modern period corpses of executed offenders were valued: anatomists wanted to dissect them, and hangmen wanted to make medicine of them. By the middle of the seventeenth century eleven German universities had anatomical theatres which were in need of corpses; the Tübingen theatre had been built as early as 1536.[138] On the other hand it was generally believed that the body of the executed still contained the power of life, and could thus serve the living. The authorities however sought to draw firm boundaries between good and evil, and suppressed all magical and healing customs attached to executions. A 1663 Esslingen ordinance stipulated that musketeers were to guard hanged corpses until their burial, so that the corpses would not be used.[139] But corpses were not taken away everywhere even after a couple of days (let alone guarded). In 1648, for example, the wife of a Kirchheim mason had to live with the fact that her husband lay dead on the wheel outside the town. Her sister-in-law and two other women kept asking 'why she would not throw the wheel over or get someone to do it'. Her 9-year-old son, a cowherd, had to ward animals off his father's body. When the terror he experienced in doing so made him sick, his

[136] HStASt, A 209, Bü. 104, Anna Jäger.
[137] A. Keller, *Der Scharfrichter in der deutschen Kulturgeschichte* (2nd edn. Hildesheim, 1968), 160; V. Abegg, 'Beiträge zur Geschichte der Strafrechtspflege in Schlesien, insbesondere im fünfzehnten und sechzehnten Jahrhundert', *ZRG* 18 (1858), 447.
[138] G. Richter, *Das anatomische Theater* (Berlin, 1936), 29. In 1676, Tübingen doctors wrote to the duke to ask for a corpse, because after a period of closure they wanted to reopen the theatre with a public dissection. Four months later Eberhard Ludwig promised them the corpse of a woman who was going to be beheaded for infanticide. But her parents petitioned that her dead body should remain 'unharmed', described how their daughter had been the joy of their old days, and how they would be mocked and despised by relatives if she were dissected. Hence Eberhard Ludwig told the Tübingen doctors that they were soon to be 'gratified with another subject', HStASt, A 209, Bü. 2010, 22 Oct. 1696; 10 Jan. 1697; 13 Jan. 1697.
[139] StAL, B 169, Bü. 119, ii, 23 Mar. 1663.

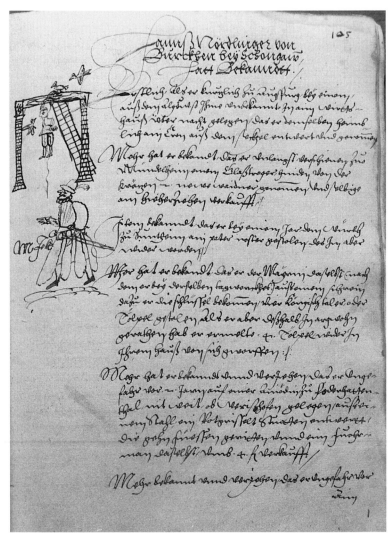

FIG. 5. Hangman and hanged

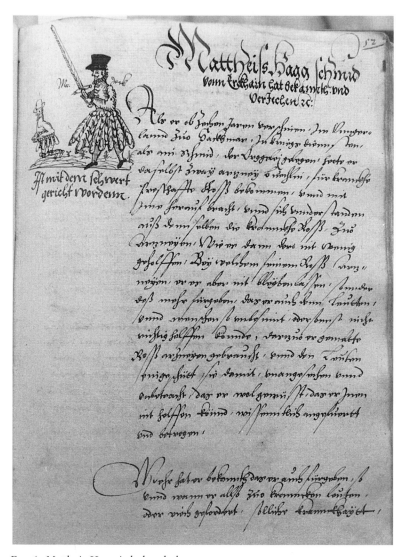

FIG. 6. Mattheis Haag is beheaded

mother asked a poor locksmith to overturn the wheel early in the morning, so that her husband could be buried.[140] Healing customs survived well into the seventeenth century. When, for example, the head of a woman fell off its stake in 1682 after nine years, an old Bottwar *Kleemeister* was ordered to bury it under the gallows. His stepson reported that he had taken it home instead and intended to sell it to a pharmacist.[141]

Even if few people would be exposed to the horror of having to look at a decaying relative, families always had to bear the brunt of the mockery and contempt which followed public punishments. Early modern people had to defend their honour daily. If conflicts surfaced, those who had been punished, or had a relative who had been punished by an executioner, always had something to answer for. In 1665 the wife of a man whose aunt was imprisoned in Esslingen told him 'now she knew into what kind of family she had married'.[142] In 1666 a man was told he was a 'fellow like his burned father'.[143] A journeyman said defiantly that 'no one had taken any of his family to the gallows yet'.[144] Defamation cases demonstrate forcefully how references to shaming punishments became part of the vocabulary of contempt. By the seventeenth century women insulted each other as 'pilloried whores', or 'lying, damned and publicly punished whores'.[145] If there was a basis for such accusations they stuck for a long time. In 1659 a Franconian peasant could matter-of-factly remember that a woman had been whipped and banished from the town forty years before.[146]

---

[140] HStASt, A 209, Bü. 1333, 10 Aug. 1648, Lucia Meyer.

[141] It turned out that the Stuttgart executioner had also dealt with the heads of two thieves, beheaded in Nürtingen. The *Kleemeister* was punished with a small fine and the head buried: HStASt A 209, Bü. 1557, 7 June 1686, Magdalena Wirn. In 1573 a Stuttgart executioner was imprisoned for a week because he had taken an executed man's skin to a tanner and made fat out of it; he sold this as a healing lotion to noblemen, HStASt, A 210, Abt. I, Bü. 263, 22 May 1573. On such practices see P. Camporesi, *Juice of Life: The Symbolic and Magic Significance of Blood*, trans. R. R. Barr (New York, 1995), 21.

[142] His father then sued her, StAE, AII, Reichsstadt, 43C/592, Stadtammansprotokoll 1665/67, 15 Sept. 1665, fo. 7[r].

[143] StAE, AII, Reichsstadt, 43C/592, 23 Oct. 1666, fo. 81[v].

[144] He was quarrelling with his mistress, StAE, AII, Reichsstadt, 43C/592, 29 May 1666, fo. 53[r].

[145] StAE, AII, Reichsstadt, 43C/592, 18 Sept. 1665, fo. 5[r]; StAMM, A 140/1, 22 May 1621, two innkeeper's wives.

[146] K.-S. Kramer, *Bauern und Bürger im nachmittelalterlichen Unterfranken: Eine Volkskunde auf Grund archivalischer Quellen* (Würzburg, 1951), 97: the peasant had to pay a fine and the costs of the trial.

For families an immediate consequence of prolonged imprisonment was of course that they had to survive without a man's or woman's salary and help.[147] Another weighty burden was imposed on families when women were sentenced to confinement at home. In 1677 the husband of one such woman complained that he was unable to cope with all his business himself. Although her sentence was mitigated, she was still not allowed to join 'honest company'. Forbidding offenders to visit taverns, weddings, baptisms, and similar occasions in this way was a frequent punishment.[148] Such punishments depended on community control. More common was physical exclusion through banishment. Banished women could try to find work as servants, pedlars, agricultural day-labourers, laundresses, or private seamstresses. While they moved around in search of work they were likely to be treated as vagrants and to be ejected from towns. In 1683 a thief wanted to be executed rather than be banished again because 'it would be worse than before, she would not be let into any town'.[149] We know little about how these women survived, how many of them became vagrants, or on the other hand managed to find work or a husband,[150] or settled as outburghers.[151] It was certainly important where and when they were banished. In towns without a territory it was possible to settle close to home and banishment counted less. Imperial cities could not always banish offenders over distant borders, such as the Rhine or Donau. In Esslingen, for example, offenders were mostly banished 10 miles from the town, whereas Hall seemed to cooperate with the duchy of Württemberg and sometimes banished offenders from the whole country. This had a strong influence on how uprooted an offender became. Many of those who had been banished tried to return once or several times. If they were apprehended, they would be sent away again without further ado, unless they had committed new offences in the meantime, in which case they were treated much more harshly. Some of those who had returned were recognized only after some elapsed time. Their chances of remaining

---

[147] Reyscher, *Gesetze*, v. 379f., 'General=Rescript, die Einführung der Strafe der öffentlichen Arbeit betreffend', 19 Sept. 1620. [148] StAH, RP 285/1687, fo. 594ʳ.
[149] HStASt, A 209, Bü. 1936, 16 Feb. 1683, Anna Maria Wörner.
[150] They then had to return to their home town in order to get their birth certificate.
[151] R. Dürr, 'Ursula Gräfin: Der Lebensweg einer Haller Magd und ledigen Mutter im 17. Jahrhundert', *Württembergisch Franken*, 76 (1992), 169–76. Gräfin was tolerated because she worked as a seamstress, had good contacts in Hall, and lived piously. When her illegitimate daughter asked for the right to be a citizen the magistrates ignored her lie that she was a legitimate child.

depended mainly on the connivance of neighbours, but then relatives could have moved house in the meantime anyway to evade hostility. Petitions imply in any case that neighbours were more sympathetic to illegal action than to broken families.

Children

Women with children had particular reasons to be anxious about banishment or a death sentence. In 1698 a woman asked for her execution to be delayed a fortnight until she had weaned her child. Her parents made it clear that their daughter's execution would leave them with two more children to care for, who would anxiously 'sigh for their mother's life'. The duke did not commute the sentence, but delayed her execution for three weeks instead.[152] If no relatives were at hand, towns might take children into orphanages. In Memmingen a woman was once especially employed to attend to one such child and received poor relief to feed it.[153]

Women with children who were banished had hardly any chance of going into service, and those with small children probably found it equally difficult to work as seamstresses or laundresses. This problem became acute when soldiers were stationed in towns during the Thirty Years War and the French wars, when the number of illegitimate mothers peaked. Soldiers could not be traced and made responsible like other fathers of illegitimate children. As a consequence of the poverty of many towns and of a feeling that the problem was worsening, illegitimate mothers began to receive harsher punishment. Women who had been impregnated by soldiers were routinely banished—no matter whether they were citizens' daughters or outsiders.[154] Illegitimately pregnant women were allowed to remain in their home towns only while they were lying in. And now they were sometimes denied even such a basic right.[155]

Some parents tried to support their daughter's attempts to find work during her exile by looking after her child. But even this was resisted by the authorities. A routine entry in the 1672 Memmingen

---

[152] HStASt, A 209, Bü. 2014, 3 Sept. 1698.
[153] StAL, B 169, Bü. 119, i, 22 Dec. 1599, fos. 272^v–277^r, Margaretha von Wachendorf; StAMM, RP 31 Oct. 1638–30 Dec. 1640, 25 Nov. 1639, fo. 119^r, Martin Schmidt's widow.
[154] See Ch. 4.
[155] In November 1668 a maidservant, made pregnant in Ulm, asked whether she could stay with her father near Memmingen until springtime, but she was allowed to live there for a month only: StAMM, RP, 1 July 1667–11 Aug. 1669, 13 Nov. 1667, fo. 51^r. In 1669, a similar request by a Memmingen woman was rejected altogether, despite strong petitions for her, ibid., fo. 73^r.

council minutes reads: 'Balthasar Rauch, corporal, asks for permission to look after his daughter's illegitimate child in his house, because she wants to go into service in Ravensburg; rejected.'[156] This was the same everywhere. In 1674, for example, the mother of a woman banished from Constance asked for permission to care for her grandchild, since her daughter would otherwise not be accepted in the town where she wanted to go into service. She was allowed to do so only during winter, and the council emphasized that her daughter had to stay away during that time, too.[157] In 1666, a father hid his banished daughter and her child until he was found out.[158] Not all parents were within easy reach, or willing to care for a grandchild. A recently widowed Memmingen woman was quite outspoken about this, complaining that one damned thing had followed another: she was old, had had sixteen children, and was now left with the baby of her accused daughter, without one night passing in which she had not been forced 'to get up and make some pap for the child'.[159] But much more audible were parents' frequent and impressive attempts to support their daughters.

During the same period it also became more difficult to return to one's home town after some years of banishment. From 1630 onwards an illegitimate mother could return to Memmingen only if she could bring good certificates about her behaviour during exile and deposited money to ensure that her child would never need poor relief.[160] Additionally she had to buy her citizenship again. In order to pay such sums either an inheritance or a lot of help was needed. In Constance, Barbara Kessinger received permission to stay at her mother's house in 1666 only because her sister, a doctor's wife, had paid a security for care of the illegitimate child in case Barbara should die.[161] Such financial resources were rare, and magistrates were generally determined to prevent the mitigation of sentences for illegitimate mothers. Incomplete households and financial demands on individual citizens and the community were never welcome.

---

[156] StAMM, RP, 12 Feb. 1672–13 Feb. 1674, 2 Aug. 1672, fo. 76[r].

[157] StAKN, RP 1674, BI 154, 19 Oct. 1674, fo. 766[r].

[158] StAKN, RP 1666, BI 146, 18 Dec. 1666, fo. 707[r], Guotmundlin's daughter.

[159] StAMM, A 143/1, 12 Oct. 1625.

[160] StAMM, RP 1 July 1667–11 Aug. 1669, 13 Jan. 1668, fo. 68[r]: Michael Engler's daughter had to pay twenty-five *Gulden* to be granted the status of a citizen again and had to pay security for her child. The need for security payments was stipulated in the 1630 discipline ordinance, StAMM, A 265/2.

[161] StAKN, RP, 1666, BI 146, 15 Dec. 1666, fo. 701[r].

This policy rendered it almost impossible to live 'honestly' during exile. Time and again illegitimate mothers were denied support.[162] Judges and magistrates knew that begging was all that was left to these women in foreign territories. This formed part of the punishment and was meant to deter others and undoubtedly did so.[163] Because of the visible misery, ordinary citizens sometimes asked whether they could shelter a woman in childbed or an illegitimate mother. But when in Constance, in 1669, Johann Kolpen's wife asked 'for permission to take a pregnant creature into her house for some time', she received a typically hostile reply: it was 'immediately rejected that this dishonourably pregnant creature shall live here'.[164]

THE FATE OF THE ACCUSED

This chapter has shown that we must regard with scepticism the assumption that women in early modern Germany were generally and as a matter of principle treated more leniently than men. If they escaped certain forms of treatment, it was usually for reasons to do with their social position, as distinct from chivalric or similarly benign reasons. Thus women were less often punished for political or quasi-political dissent because they had no political rights, and their views could easily be dismissed. Most heads of households were male and thus made responsible for debts and failure to pay taxes. Poaching was an exclusively male activity. Similarly, men were more often imprisoned for disturbing the public peace; and since women drank less often in public they rarely fought violently. These offences accounted for the bulk of prison sentences. Women's relative abstinence from drinking and violence also limited the number of homicides committed by them. All of this helps explain why fewer women were executed: offenders were mainly executed for robbery, murder-robbery, professional theft, forgery, and homicide. Since even professional female thieves did not use weapons, and never progressed into a career of murder-robbery, even their execution was rarely necessary.

Criminal trials thus clearly represented male violence and female

---

[162] In 1670 the Balingen junior bailiff wrote to the supreme council and claimed that an illegitimate mother banished 10 miles from the town was able to work as a seamstress and receive daily visits by her parents and siblings: he demanded that she be banished over the Rhine or Donau; HStASt, A 209, Bü. 163, Maria Tragner.
[163] For such explicit reasoning see HStASt, A 209, Bü. 1471, Barbara Sticker, 12 Mar. 1664.   [164] StAKN, RP 1669, BI 149, 20 July 1669, fo. 516ʳ.

desire and bad motherhood as the key threats to society. In the case of infanticide, the single violent crime which women committed in numbers greater than men and which was prosecuted with increasing vigour, the law knew little mercy, nor did it show mercy for sexual offences committed by women. Women were more harshly sentenced for adultery than men,[165] and the only reason in the end why women were not frequently banished or executed for adultery and bigamy was because marriage and the family had to be protected.[166] In Bavaria, where sexual offences had to be reported to the supreme council, women made up a third of all accused offenders in the first half of the seventeenth century.[167] By the middle of the eighteenth century, between a third and a half of all executed offenders in German towns were female.[168]

So far we have analysed the social process of how a woman was accused as an offender and how her case was dealt with. The following five chapters, by contrast, are primarily concerned with social conflicts as experienced by offenders and the textures of their everyday lives. Trial records are used to lead us into the world of the accused.

---

[165] See Ch. 6.   [166] See Ch. 7.

[167] W. Behringer, 'Mörder, Diebe, Ehebrecher: Verbrechen und Strafen in Kurbayern vom 16. bis 18. Jahrhundert', in R. v. Dülmen (ed.), *Verbrechen, Strafen und soziale Kontrolle* (Frankfurt on Main, 1990), 101 f.

[168] Evans, *Rituals of Retribution*, 42–4.

3

Women and Property Crime

FRAUD, embezzlement, smuggling, and theft were everyday crimes in early modern Germany. But although large sections of the population committed them in one way or another, it was predominantly the lower classes and marginal groups that were prosecuted. Mobile people were particularly affected by criminalizing processes, since their numbers and presumed growth intensified anxieties about the fragmentation of the social order.[1] Authorities claimed that vagrants were especially dangerous. A fundamental change in Christian solidarity supported this policy: sharp distinctions were now being made between the deserving, resident poor on the one hand and mobile beggars on the other. From the publication of the *Liber vagatorum* onwards, a steady flow of ordinances described vagrants as idle and dangerous.[2] As a result vagrants were more frequently rejected and banished than other people, and since they often reacted in revenge and by theft, fear of them came to be confirmed and self-fulfilling. Servants were likewise vulnerable to the attention of the law because of their high mobility and vagrant-like lifestyle while they were out of service. Ordinances and sermons described maidservants in particular as selfish, insolent, and disorderly.[3] Together with the generality of the poor, vagrants and servants

---

[1] B. Scribner, 'Mobility: Voluntary or Enforced? Vagrants in Württemberg in the Sixteenth Century', in G. Jaritz and A. Müller (eds.), *Migration in der Feudalgesellschaft* (Frankfurt on Main, 1988), and id., 'The Mordbrenner Fear in Sixteenth-Century Germany: Political Paranoia or the Revenge of the Outcast?', in R. J. Evans (ed.), *The German Underworld: Deviants and Outcasts in German History* (London, 1988).

[2] Forty-nine ordinances were issued against vagrants in Württemberg between 1531 and 1700, forty of these during the 17th cent. In 1562 Duke Christoph stated that everyone could survive through work, and poverty was a consequence of idleness and luxury. Young vagrants who were able to work were to be sent to galleys from 1596 onwards, and public labour for all vagrants was introduced in 1621: see A. L. Reyscher (ed.), *Vollständige, historisch und kritisch bearbeitete Sammlung der württembergischen Gesetze* (19 vols., Stuttgart and Tübingen, 1828–51), xii. 319–24.

[3] R. Dürr, *Mägde in der Stadt: Das Beispiel Schwäbisch Hall in der frühen Neuzeit* (Frankfurt on Main, 1995).

were key enemies whom the authorities targeted from the second half of the sixteenth century onwards. Order was to be based on pious, unselfish, and modest behaviour, and stable, industrious, tax-paying households.

The three groups of women who were mainly accused of property offences reflect the pattern of prosecution which ensued. Even though these groups were not responsible for all or even most serious property crime, those focused upon were predominantly mobile, professional thieves, followed secondly by maidservants, and thirdly by poor residents.[4] This chapter aims to show how criminalizing processes worked, and to reconstruct the social and economic contexts in which theft was experienced. Early modern societies were chronically needy. One- to two-thirds of the population lived close to or below the margins of subsistence. They were permanently threatened by hunger, cold, and illness, had no savings, and relied on relatives, neighbours, and friends for help. Every crisis put lives at risk.[5] Many single women and widows lived in permanent poverty.[6] Only a small part of this group, however, stole regularly. Need was a decisive motive for property crime, but not the only one.[7]

Hence the concrete experiences and lives of the accused are worth investigating. I shall attend to the textures of ordinary women's everyday lives as they tried to make ends meet, recaptur-

[4] P. Wettman-Jungblut, '"Stelen inn rechter hungersnodtt": Diebstahl, Eigentumsschutz und strafrechtliche Kontrolle im vorindustriellen Baden, 1600–1850', in R. v. Dülmen (ed.), *Verbrechen, Strafen und soziale Kontrolle* (Frankfurt on Main, 1990), 154 f.
[5] For a general definiton of poverty see O. Hufton, *The Poor of Eighteenth Century France, 1750–1789* (Oxford, 1974), 20; R. Jütte, *Poverty and Deviance in Early Modern Europe* (Cambridge, 1994); on poverty in early modern Germany see T. Fischer, *Städtische Armut und Armenfürsorge im 15. und 16. Jahrhundert* (Göttingen, 1979); B. Roeck, *Eine Stadt in Krieg und Frieden: Studien zur Geschichte der Reichsstadt Augsburg zwischen Kalenderstreit und Parität* (2 vols., Göttingen, 1989), i, ch. 3, ii, ch. 6; on women see C. Ulbrich, 'Frauenarmut in der frühen Neuzeit', *Zeitschrift für die Geschichte der Saargegend*, 40 (1992), 108–20; I. Bàtori, 'Frauen in Handel und Handwerk der Reichsstadt Nördlingen im 15. und 16. Jahrhundert', in U. Weckel and B. Vogel (eds.), *Frauen in der Ständegesellschaft: Leben und Arbeiten in der Stadt vom späten Mittelalter zur Neuzeit* (Hamburg, 1991).
[6] On women in Hall see G. Wunder, *Die Bürger von Hall: Sozialgeschichte einer Reichsstadt, 1216–1802* (Sigmaringen, 1980), 163, 191; on Memmingen P. Frieß, 'Die Steuerbücher der Reichsstadt Memmingen von 1450 und 1451', *Memminger Geschichtsblätter* (1989/90), 268, and B. Kroemer, 'Die Einführung der Reformation in Memmingen: Die Bedeutung ihrer sozialen, wirtschaftlichen und politischen Faktoren', *Memminger Geschichtsblätter* (1980), 155.
[7] It is vital to avoid depicting the lower classes as passive victims forced into crime, an impression one is likely to get from C. Kappl, *Die Not der kleinen Leute: Der Alltag der Armen im 18. Jahrhundert im Spiegel der Bamberger Malefizakten* (Bamberg, 1984).

ing the largely ordinary, sometimes spectacular, but for us always fascinating world of actions and conflicts which were important to them but have largely remained unknown to us. Trial records give us a wealth of information about the circulation of goods, leisure among maidservants, their mobility, civic female poverty, and the wit of thieves.[8] Women suspects, whom the authorities merely saw as immoral, become visible as human beings with feelings and bonds, conflicts and options, as women who searched for ways out of unsatisfying economic and social situations.[9] Their cases indicate how many people during the early modern period lived by one principle: need was the mother of invention.

THE THEFT OF NATURAL RESOURCES

Theft of natural resources was undoubtedly the property offence which was both punished most leniently and in which most people were involved. Its frequency was an expression of different social, economical, and political processes: a strong rise in population, dearth, limited common rights, conflicts about the use of common land or the distribution of individual property inside communities. We can distinguish three motives for such theft: direct need, a defence of communal rights, and conflicts between offenders and victims. Maidservants, married women, and children committed most of these offences partly because their fines were sometimes lower, but more importantly because such food-gathering activities were part of their duties within the peasant economy.[10] They cut grass, picked fruit, berries, mushrooms, acorns, nuts, gleaned, and gathered seeds.

The legitimacy of such activities on communal or foreign land

---

[8] R. Cobb, *A Sense of Place* (London, 1975), esp. 70, 134.

[9] F. Egmond, *Underworlds: Organized Crime in the Netherlands, 1650–1800* (Oxford, 1993), 15.

[10] C. Vanja, 'Frauen im Dorf: Ihre Stellung unter besonderer Berücksichtigung landgräflich-hessischer Quellen des späten Mittelalters', *Zeitschrift für Agrargeschichte und Agrarsoziologie*, 34 (1986), 147–59. On the role of women and children see J. Dünninger, 'Rügegerichte eines unterfränkischen Dorfes im 19. Jahrhundert', in P. Assion (ed.), *Ländliche Kulturformen im deutschen Südwesten: Festschrift für Heiner Heimberger* (Stuttgart, 1971); P. King, 'Gleaners and Farmers and the Failure of Legal Sanctions in England, 1750–1850', *P&P* 125 (1989), 116–50; D. W. Sabean, *Property, Production, and Family in Neckarhausen, 1700–1870* (Cambridge, 1990), 151; W. R. Lee, 'Women's Work and the Family: Some Demographic Implications of Gender-Specific Rural Work Patterns in Nineteenth-Century Germany', in id. and P. Hudson (eds.), *Women's Work and the Family Economy in Historical Perspective* (Manchester, 1990).

became increasingly limited. Poor people, who depended most on natural resources, were hit hardest. During the sixteenth century they were forbidden to gather wood.[11] This not only left them hungry and cold; it also deprived them of substitute income: wood was cut and sold, it was used to boil yarn, and independent laundresses needed it to boil clothes.[12] Stolen fruit could be sold in markets.[13] Grass was gathered for one's own household; the lower peasant classes often possessed one or two animals, but no land.[14] Since wealthy peasants often excluded them from the use of common land during crises, landless peasants had to filch grass elsewhere. They likewise looked for grain, but in 1595, the poor in Hall were even forbidden any gleaning, since 'bold young people' took away standing wheat as well.[15] Poor habitual offenders were sometimes severely punished.[16]

There is, however, clear evidence that not only the poor, but also other sections of the population were involved in stealing natural resources. This is revealed by ordinances such as one passed in 1568 in Obersschneidheim against the cutting of corn: 'Since *our* women, daughters, and maidservants have behaved in an indecent manner and cut corn and stolen fruit, we forbid anyone to commit such offences on penalty of a fine of four Bohemian florins.'[17]

Such formulae probably resulted from experiences similar to that noted in a list of complaints by a parson in the Anabaptist village of Urbach in Württemberg in 1599: 'During summer many children and maidservants run into the forest on Sunday, missing both sermons and picking cherries, strawberries and other things. Often their

---

[11] The change can be charted in district ordinances, see F. Wintterlin, *Württembergische ländliche Rechtsquellen* (6 vols., Stuttgart, 1910–55), ii. 575, 604 for Justingen.

[12] O. Feger (ed.), *Die Statutensammlung des Stadtschreibers Jörg Vögeli* (Constance, 1951), 68, *Ordnung, wie man in den hölzern umb die statt holzen soll*, 29 Jan. 1534.

[13] In 1626 a woman who was caught with fruit in a rucksack was even banished: StAH, 4/482, 21 Jan. 1626.

[14] On the ensuing conflicts in communities see: HStASt, A 206, Bü. 1341; 1355; 1358; A 214, Bü. 351.   [15] StAH, 4/490, 6 Aug. 1595.

[16] In 1575 a Hall couple with children were banished because they had sold wood: StAH, 4/480, 7 Sept. 1575, fo. 264ʳ. Wood-theft for a poor family's own consumption was punished with one to three days' imprisonment: StAH 4/479, 20 Sept. 1565; 4/480, 7 Sept. 1575; 4/481, 27 Feb. 1629; 4 Apr. 1635. During the 1630s, those who cut corn were often punished with four days' imprisonment and bound over, and gleaning was similarly punished: StAH, 4/482, two Gerlingen widows, 14 Oct. 1635, fo. 99ʳ; two young Sautzbach women, 2 July 1636, fo. 102ʳ. In 1696, a junior bailiff reported the thief Catharina Lonsinger, who was the 'godless daughter of a godless father', because they had both stolen grain: HStASt, A 209, Bü. 1251, 24 Sept. 1696.

[17] Wintterlin, *Ländliche Rechtsquellen*, i. 118 (my emphasis).

parents go out, too. The mayor sends out his servants as well.'[18] Forests provided acorns, nuts, mushrooms, and foliage throughout the year. They were the 'most versatile resource of villages',[19] and urban households used surrounding forests with the same intensity.[20] Authorities claimed that forests wholly belonged to them and classified such activities as theft.[21]

Shortages of animal fodder resulted from the three-field economy. The fallow field was used to pasture animals; since it was ploughed in June, food shortages were common until harvest time.[22] Moreover, pastures were generally used intensively, so that there was never enough grass left to make hay for winter. Inevitably, girls were sent to other people's meadows to steal grass. For maidservants in villages and small towns in particular it was almost an admitted duty to steal grass. They had to avoid field guards and were fined at district courts, while their masters remained in the background.

This impression is confirmed by a detailed list of fines and offences which the Mergentheim mayor recorded in 1595. At the time, Mergentheim had about 1,700 inhabitants. The most important market town in the Tauber valley, it had been the seat of the German knights since 1528.[23] The mayor issued ninety-nine fines. Except for one woman who was fined for slander, and two girls who had sung 'loose and worldly songs', all offenders were punished for theft and fraud. If we leave aside one action during which nineteen men and only three women picked wild pears on a September morning, marked gender- and age-specific differences become visible. Twenty men and forty-one women were accused. Thirty-seven of

[18] G. Bossert (ed.), *Quellen zur Geschichte der Wiedertäufer* (2 vols., Leipzig, 1930), i. 748.

[19] R. Beck, *Naturale Ökonomie: Unterfinning. Bäuerliche Wirtschaft in einem oberbayerischen Dorf des frühen 18. Jahrhunderts* (Munich, 1986), ch. 3; on women's marked activity see W. Troßbach, *Bauern 1648–1806* (Munich, 1993), 105.

[20] Feger, *Statutensammlung*, 68.

[21] P. Blickle, 'Wem gehört der Wald? Konflikte zwischen Bauern und Obrigkeiten um Nutzungs- und Eigentumsansprüche', *ZfWLG* 45 (1986), 167–78; H. W. Eckardt, *Herrschaftliche Jagd, bäuerliche Not und bürgerliche Kritik: Zur Geschichte der fürstlichen und adeligen Jagdprivilegien vornehmlich im süddeutschen Raum* (Stuttgart, 1958); J. Mooser, '"Furcht bewahrt das Holz": Holzdiebstahl und sozialer Konflikt in der ländlichen Gesellschaft 1800–1850 an westfälischen Beispielen', in H. Reif (ed.), *Räuber, Volk und Obrigkeit: Studien zur Geschichte der Kriminalität in Deutschland seit dem 18. Jahrhundert* (Frankfurt on Main, 1984).

[22] P. Sauer, 'Not und Armut in den Dörfern des Mittleren Neckarraums in vorindustrieller Zeit', *ZfWLG* 41 (1982), 131–49.

[23] U. Wagner, *Tauberbischofsheim und Bad Mergentheim: Eine Analyse der Raumbeziehungen zweier Städte in der frühen Neuzeit* (Heidelberg, 1985), 137, 194.

the women were girls or maidservants who had mostly been caught cutting grass.[24] Grass was usually stolen from the so-called 'citizens' forest', 'socage meadow', or 'lords' meadow'. Common people resisted the authorities' claim that only they had the right to use these meadows. Some of those involved can be traced in a 1586 list of inhabitants. Most of them employed maidservants and journeymen: i.e. they were not poor.[25] Common people sometimes aimed at officials' personal property. The Mergentheim mayor Gaßenfaydt, for example, began his notebook by noting such an offence:

Actum Wednesday after carnival, caught Hans & Flurer Bastian Horant's daughters, who cut my gate in the meadow into pieces, and carried the wood through the Milber gate, together with several pieces they had taken from the Kalbenpflegerin.[26]

The Besigheim junior bailiff became impatient with citizens in 1659. Seedlings had just been stolen from his field, and theft of this kind was so common that it was impossible that nobody knew who the offenders were. After minutes of obstinate silence he finally lost his patience and denounced the citizens as 'dishonest and loose people'.[27] In 1679 the duke of Württemberg announced with indignation that wood- and field-theft had become so common in the countryside and in Stuttgart that even his garden was raided, the walls and fences surrounding his castle were climbed and destroyed almost daily, and locks, doors, and gates damaged.[28]

If communities were united against the authorities, theft within the communities could destroy trust among all the people. In 1562, the Protestant chronicler Johann Jakob Wick saw in the case of a woman who had denied stealing wood from another woman a 'gruesome and frightening example': she had sworn her innocence and then suddenly died.[29] In 1621, the Hall magistrate reprimanded a woman whose onions were stolen because of her 'unnecessary' quarrel with

---

[24] StABM, K III, No. 344, *Verwirkte Buß, vnd Nachsteur diß 95 Jahr auch welche Personen mit dem thurm vnd dem Narrenhauß sind gestraft worden ./. In dem 95 Jahr ./. Caspar Gassenfaydt der zeit Bürgermeister.* In fourteen cases women stole in groups; in ten cases more than two women acted together, as opposed to only five group actions by men.

[25] M. Biskop, 'Die Einwohnerverzeichnisse der Stadt Mergentheim aus dem 16. Jahrhundert', *ZfWLG* 44 (1985), 143–63.   [26] StABM, K III, No. 344, *Verwirkte Buß.*

[27] HStASt, A 214, Bü. 111, 24 Feb. 1659.

[28] Reyscher, *Gesetze*, vi. 62f., 2 May 1679.

[29] M. Senn (ed.), *Die Wickiana: Johann Jakob Wicks Nachrichtensammlung aus dem 16. Jahrhundert* (Zürich, 1975), 138.

a neighbour about it.[30] Theft caused repeated tensions inside communities.[31] In 1626, a young Wildberg women dug up and stole 'several carts' of linseed, and in February 1627, a man reported that Basti Steeren's daughter had knocked down and burnt his fence after the first snow had fallen.[32] Of course, wood had to be gathered at any price. If wood was needed for heating from October onwards supplies dwindled quickly. In late autumn another Wildberg woman was reduced to stealing burning logs of wood from people's ovens,[33] while a man and his maidservants were caught carrying 'several loads of brushwood' into town in the autumn of 1626.[34] Sweet peas were mixed with grain to make bread, peas and lentils were stolen, as were nuts which had fallen from trees. Hans Mosappen's wife stole from cherry and apple trees from July onwards, and in the fields nothing was safe from her. Three widows were seen taking home wood together, and a guard had caught several women and children carrying fruit and wood into town.[35]

In Wildberg, grass was cut from the 'court-master's meadow' and the 'convent's fields', belonging to officials. But citizens' fields, meadows, ditches, and slopes were targeted also, indeed more often. Field-guard records show that most offenders owned animals and land, and so were not poor. The theft of grass expressed feuding within the community: if old Hans Jacob Memminger sent his two maidservants to Hans Roller's meadow in June, Roller's maidservant would go to Memminger's meadow in July, and Memminger would again have his oxen on Roller's ground in August.[36] Those not caught in these engagements could feel triumphant at outwitting their rivals.[37]

The examples given show how communities saw property as a social idiom. Our next theme shows the same: theft by maidservants. Obedience and loyalty were key values in the relationships between masters and servants, just as it was between the authorities and

---

[30] StAH, 4/481, 27 Aug. 1621, Margaretha Broher.

[31] In 1623, for example, a man told the court that someone had felled his mother's oak-tree. The likely offender had said she was a liar, like a witch: HStASt, A 582, Bü. 86, 8 May 1623. The Besigheim court minutes preserve many similar cases which occurred day after day: Stadtarchiv Besigheim (StABh), Gerichtsprotokolle, 01–10.

[32] HStASt, A 582, Bü. 86, 30 Oct. 1626 and 30 Feb. 1627.

[33] HStASt, A 582, Bü. 86, 16 Nov. 1627.   [34] HStASt, A 582, Bü. 86, 30 Oct. 1626.

[35] HStASt, A 582, Bü. 86, 22 July 1626.

[36] HStASt, A 573, Bü. 113, Schützenrügprotokoll, 12 Oct. 1684.

[37] In 1626 a man claimed that he was dishonoured by the fact that maidservants had cut grass in his field: HStASt, A 582, Bü. 86, 22 July 1626.

citizens. This ensured respect for differences in rank. Theft was the crime of unfaithfulness, literally *Veruntreuungen*. It was a challenge to a moral order which cemented social inequality. This, and not the material damage caused by property offences, was why the authorities punished them with such vehemence.

THEFT BY MAIDSERVANTS

It is difficult to know how frequently maidservants stole for themselves. They were quickly suspected if something went missing in a household,[38] but were rarely reported to officials. As we have seen their sentence was usually informal—either a dismissal or a cut in salary. They had good reasons not to steal. Wages were low and wage-cuts hurt. Loyalty, moreover, was often rewarded by masters. Servants who behaved well were often granted favourable conditions if they wanted to become citizens of a town,[39] while outsiders who had stolen were usually banished forever.[40] Servants were never excused for stealing out of need, since they received food and clothes from their masters. They were always severely punished. A final reason against theft could be very simple. There were many households which employed a maidservant, but had little to steal in them. The *Hausväterliteratur*, which dwelt on the theme of thieving maidservants most heavily, served as a guide for bigger farms or noble households, in which stocks and servants were both numerous and less easy to control.

Contrary factors, however, encouraged maidservants to steal. Throughout most of the early modern period there was enough demand for their services that they could afford to be dismissed.[41] Their previous record was never checked. Certificates of good conduct remained uncommon, even though the Württemberg government, for example, tried to make them obligatory in 1562.[42] Maidservants also had access to every corner of the house and were mobile. As long as they could go in and out of service as they liked, they could escape with goods which were worth more

---

[38] StAH, 4/554, 27 Aug. 1688/16; 4/482, 28 June 1630.
[39] M. E. Wiesner, *Working Women in Renaissance Germany* (New Brunswick, NJ, 1986), 19–21. In 1690, maidservants who had served in Constance for twenty years could become citizens without paying a fee: StAKN, A 1/28a, *Bickel'sche Chronik*, 93.
[40] StAKN, RP BI 147, 28 Jan. 1667, fos. 86ʳ and 107ʳ, Barbara Kessler.
[41] Even though it presumably contracted during crisis and war, but so far no detailed study of servants' employment structures is available.
[42] Wiesner, *Working Women*, 88.

than their salary. From the sixteenth century onwards towns issued ordinances which set two annual dates for servants to leave and enter service and punished with temporary banishment those who left in between.[43] But banishment was no punishment which mattered to those who wanted to move on. Regional action was needed. In 1652, the Swabian Circle therefore issued an important ordinance limiting servants' mobility and independence. The shortage of labour after the Thirty Years War caused particular problems; in 1648 several Württemberg districts complained that servants went out of service in late summer in order to work for high wages as day-labourers during the harvest.[44] It claimed that many servants

behaved in a masterless and bold manner, and if told or forbidden anything in response to their crime [sic!], they immediately became angry, and vented such hatred on animals, or destroyed plates, pans, or furniture, or even injured their masters' and mistresses' children.[45]

The ordinance was part of a wider moral campaign to affirm order in a post-war society by asserting patriarchal ideals. The difference from former campaigns was that masters were now expected to cooperate with the authorities rather than discipline and punish informally. Small offences by servants were represented as grave attacks on hierarchies of rank which had to be publicly punished in the interest of the common weal.

A year before the ordinance, for example, the Esslingen superintendent Tobias Wagner had published a sermon (*Regentenpredigt*) calling on the authorities to take their action against disobedient maidservants' prodigality, carelessness, and theft. In many households, Wagner argued, they left 'no money in the chest no corn in the attic no wine in the cellar no food in the kitchen and bowls no bedlinen in the chamber yea, sometimes no feathers in the duvets'.[46] Driven by vanity, they used stolen goods to appear richer than they were. Maidservants had to obey their masters and mistresses, accept

[43] Feger, *Statutensammlung*, 7 Feb. 1536, 164.
[44] A. Maisch, *Notdürftiger Unterhalt und gehörige Schranken: Lebensbedingungen und Lebensstile in württembergischen Dörfern der frühen Neuzeit* (Stuttgart, 1992), 48.
[45] Reyscher, *Gesetze*, xiii,. 114–23, 'Fürstlicher Befehl in Betreff der durch den Schwäbischen Kreis festgesetzten Taxen und Regeln für Dienstboten und Handwerker', 15 May 1652.
[46] T. Wagner, *Siebenfältiger Ehehalten-Teuffel / Das ist, Ein ernsthaffter Sermon / von überhandnemmender Boßheit der Ehehalten und Dienstbotten jetziger Zeit* (Esslingen, 1651), 10.

punishment, be loyal, and not waste their possessions.[47] Only so, Wagner promised, would they please God as much as the 'most learned theologian'.[48] The precondition for servants' good behaviour was firm but fair treatment by masters and mistresses. Servants revealed how well governed a household was.[49] Masters and mistresses had to provide maidservants with food, drink, and their salary, and care for them during illness.[50]

Wagner's admonishments followed the rhetorical structure of admonitory sermons: the lower social orders were accused of immoral behaviour, but it was described as a reflection of bad rule. The sermon urged masters and mistresses to provide a better example to servants, and told magistrates to diminish servants' disobedience. The effect of this call for Christian household discipline can be charted in Esslingen itself, where even trivial theft by maidservants came to be punished like a major crime if it was reported, with shaming punishments being used to deter others. In 1659, a maidservant had to stand in the pillory for half an hour and was banished 10 miles away from Esslingen, for having behaved in an 'unfaithful, disobedient, defiant, and negligent' manner, just as, the court book added, 'sadly enough many servants do nowadays'.[51] Swiss maidservants, the daughters of poor peasants who frequently sought work in Swabia, were increasingly suspected because of their mobility, poverty, and rootlessness. In 1662, a servant from Simmern near Bern was banished from Esslingen for 'unfaithfulness'. All she had done was to steal wine and drink it with young men.[52] The long-standing attack against luxurious dress showed its effects, too. In 1663, the magistrate punished two girls and a maidservant for their 'stinking vanity and flirtatiousness'. They had taken wine, cake, silk, and textiles, and had been seeing journeymen tailors. They had to stand in the pillory for half an hour, were whipped, and forever banished 10 miles from Esslingen.[53] Curiously, male servants and journeymen were never accused of such behaviour, partly because their collective revenge was more threatening, but also because their flamboyance was more accepted. Also they were allowed more

[47] T. Wagner, *Siebenfältiger Ehehalten-Teuffel / Das ist, Ein ernsthaffter Sermon / von uberhandnemmender Boßheit der Ehehalten und Dienstbotten jetziger Zeit* (Esslingen, 1651), 44f. [48] Ibid. 46.

[49] Ibid. 36.   [50] Ibid. 37–40.

[51] StAL, B 169, Bü. 119 II, fo. 94[r–v], 30 Apr. 1659.

[52] StAL, B 169, Bü. 119 II, fos. 100[v], 101[r], 29 Jan. 1662.

[53] StAL, B 169, Bü. 119 II, fos. 104[v]–105[v], 25 Feb. 1663, Anna Maria Bauer, Anna Catherina Diel, Anna Maria Mayer.

leisure, whereas maidservants were expected to be busy all the time
and to learn how to become a good wife. This meant internalizing
the importance of frugality, modesty, and contentment as the only
way to avert poverty in a society of need.

Maidservants none the less often experienced the obstacles
Wagner had mentioned: they were not given sufficient food and
clothing, or might never receive their salary.[54] It was difficult for
them to claim their rights. When in 1632, for example, the former
maidservant of a Besigheim smith accused him of not paying her
salary of more than four florins, three-quarters of a pair of shoes, and
several leather patches, he argued that she had 'spoilt' some of his
goods and used medicine he had bought for her.[55] In the same year
a Hall maidservant was imprisoned for hiding her master's tools after
he had kept her clothes and salary.[56] Whether or not a maidservant
had wasted or spoilt her master's goods could often not be defined
objectively. Maidservants needed their salary to save what they
could in order to contribute to their portion. Property, rather than
their social background, decided the quality of a marriage-match.[57]
According to the 1579 Württemberg *Taxordnung*, even the best
female servant earned less than the worst-paid male servant, a boy
who could handle a horse and plough. Lower maidservants received
as much cloth as boys did, while the best of them received no more
than a lower male servant.[58] Woman servants therefore had to spend
more money on clothes even though they earned less than their
male counterparts. They could not pay for drinks and dances. Anything better than cheap, brown, and coarse clothes was either a gift
from a generous mistress or a high investment. Because of their low
income, maidservants had difficulties in borrowing money.[59] The
consequence of all this was limited independence.

Theft offered a way of circumventing restrictions.[60] Maidservants
stole food and ate it together with friends, or stole money to buy

[54] On how frequently the *Lidlohn* (annual salary) was not paid see M. Reiling,
*Bevölkerung und Sozialtopographie Freiburgs im Breisgau im 17. und 18. Jahrhundert: Famil-
ien, Gewerbe und sozialer Status* (Freiburg im Breisgau, 1989), 37.
[55] StABh, 05, 2 June 1632, Thomas Reichardt's maidservant.
[56] StAH, 4/482, 23 Aug. 1632, fo. 81^v.
[57] S. Breit, *'Leichtfertigkeit' und ländliche Gesellschaft: Voreheliche Sexualität in der frühen
Neuzeit* (Munich, 1991), 66.   [58] Reyscher, *Gesetze*, xii. 423.
[59] H. Rebel, *Peasant Classes: The Bureaucratization of Property and Family Relations under
Early Habsburg Absolutism, 1511–1636* (Princeton, 1983).
[60] O. Ulbricht, 'Zwischen Vergeltung und Zukunftsplanung: Hausdiebstahl von
Mägden in Schleswig-Holstein vom 16. bis zum 19. Jahrhundert', in id. (ed.), *Von Huren
und Rabenmüttern: Weibliche Kriminalität in der frühen Neuzeit* (Cologne, 1995).

beer. In 1692, a Constance servant confessed that she gave four florins from the twenty she had stolen to Benedict the soldier, before spending another two florins on food and drink, and losing the rest. The truth turned out to be that she had 'wasted the whole money with a Swiss soldier, called Franz'.[61] Theft enabled such women to reciprocate hospitality and to eat and drink as much as they wanted. At home they did not get much wine.[62] Women's meals were always smaller than men's, and they received less meat, too. Female servants and cooks who shared stolen food resisted this unequal evaluation of their work. Food and drink were the main means of rewarding someone for hard labour, and maidservants and cooks took what they thought they deserved. Besides, wine and beer made living easier and love grow. A gardener's maidservant testified in 1669 that she had sometimes taken her master's money to buy beer for herself and day-labourers, in particular for the one 'who loved her'.[63]

Stolen money was mostly used to buy clothes and gifts for lovers, to spend on or lend to friends. Mature servants told beginners how to open locks and make duplicate keys.[64] This subversive knowledge eased the burden of service. The case of a tanner's maidservant is typical. In 1697, she confessed that a Tyrol cook had first induced her to steal while they had served the Constance mayor Guldinast. The cook had access to the cellar, and they had often consumed bread, meat, and wine in the apartment of a constable's wife. Ever since, she admitted, such behaviour had become 'rooted in her so that she had continued to steal'. She was an orphan and had inherited 'some small part of a little house in Altnau'. She now planned to marry. Another servant had told her about a messenger in Constance whom she could use to send a gift to a Swiss corporal with whom she had flirted recently. Such gifts signalled wealth and advanced one's worth. Thus, while her master and mistress were in church on Sunday, she stole several florins out of a trunk.[65]

Many servants could not expect to inherit anything or receive a significant dowry. Experience told them that obedience led only to

[61] StAKN, K 66, 6 June 1692, Maria Schildknecht.
[62] In 1562 a Württemberg ordinance stipulated that they should not get any wine, even on public holidays, Wiesner, *Working Women*, 88.
[63] StAKN, K 56, 22 Aug. 1669, Magdalena Rem.
[64] G. Schwerhoff, '"Mach, daß wir nicht in Schande geraten!": Frauen in Kölner Kriminalfällen des 16. Jahrhunderts', *GWU*, 44 (1993), 453.
[65] StAKN, K 65, 4 May 1697, Ursula Geiger.

exploitation. Barbara Jäger, for example, was a daughter of Thurgau smallholders with nine other children. Her parents sent her into service in a nearby town. She became courageous and curious, and wandered to Krumbach, near Meßkirch, where she worked for a parson. He got her pregnant, gave her herbs to abort, along with money, and begged her not to confess the incident in Meßkirch because his deacon would then find out, but she should go to the Capuchins instead. He did not compensate her for the loss of her virginity; she had lost out. Her next master was a mean Überlingen cooper. She received low wages and was 'hardly able to clothe herself'. A year ago she had moved to Constance. Having lost out twice, she now felt 'seduced by the devil' when her master entrusted her with keys. She stole money and was dismissed. The master was nevertheless sorry for her and advised her to learn sewing. Later his wife re-employed her: an experienced maidservant was valuable.[66] Barbara continued to steal. Her independence had become more important to her than loyalty towards her master and mistress. She sometimes met friends for a drink in the evening. They celebrated carnival, 'drinking, eating, and playing' until one o'clock in the morning. She stole 'salt, lard, bread, flour, and sausages', met journeymen and students, and flirted with one of them. When one student had become ill she had bought meat for him, and when the other student had complained of his poverty she had given him stolen money.[67] Her motive for theft was not infidelity or selfishness, but the wish to establish her own, reciprocal friendships.

Barbara Jäger had also bought 'caps and bodices' with stolen money. This again was typical, and often motivated by need. Maidservants depended on their employers' rank and goodwill in regard to clothing.[68] Clothes and cloth were a flexible part of the salary, and often expressed the masters' or mistresses' esteem for a maidservant's labour. A mistress's former clothes created a bond between her and a maidservant. Every servant recalled who had given her which cloth or clothes.[69] Dress therefore was linked to a maidservant's sense of her past and of her value. Clothes and accessories

---

[66] Masters therefore did not always punish, see the petition of an Esslingen master for his maidservant who had stolen from him: StAL, B 169, Bü. 119 II, fo. 2ʳ⁻ᵛ, 4 Feb. 1601, Anna Hill.   [67] StAKN, K 56, 6 Mar. 1675.

[68] A Hall lace-maker who accused her young maidservant of theft said that she had promised her some cloth for a shirt, but now she would give her much less, StAH, 4/554, 27 Aug. 1688/16.

[69] StAH, 4/553, 27 Sept. 1678/2, Dorothea Wild; Anna Barbara Bühl.

which maidservants bought or made themselves, such as headbands from taffeta or earrings from tin, strengthened their sense of individuality. Those who wanted to marry had to please. Preparing for church on Sunday, they washed, ironed, and exchanged caps, necklaces, and ribbons. Clothes demonstrated their status. Slovenly women were called 'dirty *Schlutten*', after women's work jackets.[70] Women who wanted to marry had to demonstrate publicly that they were clean and orderly, faithful and pretty, or maybe even something better: that they were not just common peasant-maids, for example, but that they had once served in a patrician household. All sumptuary legislation sought to undermine these differences. The 1660 Württemberg police ordinance, for example, treated all maidservants, seamstresses, knitters, and ruffle-makers alike. They were even forbidden to wear red socks. All ranks were ordered to wear the 'old, German, honourable *Tracht*' and to abstain from all French and Spanish influences.[71] Servants were told to wear only 'common, rural cloth and poor fabrics', 'humbler women's shoes', not soft and lined but coarse and blackened.[72] Sumptuary legislation wanted to freeze hierarchies of rank.[73] They were challenged if maidservants bought good clothes or stole money for them. There were scandalous cases, such as that of a Göppingen maidservant aged 33 who had spent 100 florins from her master on clothes in 1690.[74] But it was unusual for such sums of money to be spent on clothes. Like Margaretha Kurz in 1580, most servant women had little more than a petticoat made for themselves, or slippers and boots from a journeyman shoemaker.

Margaretha also used theft to increase her portion. She was proud that a journeyman carpenter, who had 'walked about like a nobleman', had promised to marry her. Admittedly he had returned to his home town, but this was the kind of marriage she hoped for. In her mind she was already preparing 'table and bed'. Her mistress found 'plunder and spices' in her trunk: muscat, nails, silk, sheets, cloth, and money. Part of the money she had lent to a maidservant from her home region, the Allgäu.[75] Young people who shared the same

---

[70] H. Fischer, *Schwäbisches Wörterbuch* (5 vols., Tübingen, 1904–36), v, col. 966.
[71] Reyscher, Gesetze, xii. 423 f.
[72] Ibid., xiii, Fürstlicher *Befehl der durch den Schwäbischen Kreis festgesetzten Taxen und Regeln für Dienstboten und Handwerker*, 15 May 1652.
[73] K. Simon-Muscheid, '"Und ob sie schon einen Dienst finden, so sind sie nit bekleidet dennoch": Die Kleidung städtischer Unterschichten zwischen Projektion und Realität im Spätmittelalter und in der frühen Neuzeit', *Saeculum*, 44 (1993), 47–64.
[74] HStASt, A 209, Bü. 939, 1 Aug. 1690, Katharina Fritz.
[75] StAKN, HIX F. 62, 6 Sept. 1580.

local background often supported each other wherever they met. They knew that they would live back home again in the near future, when they had married and had their own household. Goods for a portion formed an important capital. A Memmingen maidservant had gathered 'two pounds of soap, several pieces of linen clothes, and cloth', one 'tablecloth, three napkins, twelve handkerchiefs, five caps', and forty florins in a bag with her master's trademark on it.[76] Even if a future household did not exactly need three napkins, they lent a certain tone to a portion. Wardrobes and desk-drawers were frequently searched by maidservants for textiles, money, rosaries, and religious gems. Distinctions were clear: cheap rosaries were made of bones or wood and had twenty-five pearls, while expensive rosaries, which thieves wanted, were made from amber or corals and had fifty pearls. Worn as necklaces they immediately indicated wealth.[77]

It is easy to imagine how most maidservants would be astonished at the amount of stock, cash, and possessions in wealthy households, and would think that theft could do no harm. None the less theft by maidservants usually remained petty. They knew that their heads were at risk. Agatha Flohschütz, for example, beheaded in Constance in 1692, had been stealing for five years. She had first sold a skin from her master, an Ulm tanner, and bought a journeyman tanner ribbons for his breeches. Next, she had served an Augsburg spice-dealer and stolen money from him, with which she bought white cloth. Then she became bolder. During her six-month service with an Augsburg bookkeeper she stole 140 florins Bohemian and half *Batzen*. She used 'a small barrel' to send some money and clothes she had bought home to Kempten. The bookkeeper had become suspicious and followed her. Instead of going home she went to Speyer, where she served a doctor. Noticing that he never took his clothes into the bedchamber at night, she took keys from his pockets, opened two 'money-drawers', and stole. The doctor became suspicious, and started taking his trousers into the bedchamber, but he found no evidence against her: the money was hidden in his cellar. Next Agatha moved south. In Constance, a tailor made her a skirt, and she lent some money to him and another woman. Then she was caught.[78]

---

[76] StAMM, A 44d, 11 May 1575.
[77] H. Maurer, *Geschichte der Stadt Konstanz im Mittelalter* (2 vols., Constance, 1989), ii. 170. [78] StAKN, RP, BI 79, fos. 392^r-439^r, 5 June 1599.

Kempten, Ulm, Augsburg, Speyer, and Constance: she had travelled far. She had also chosen to work in wealthy households in bigger towns headed by single men or widowers, men who would hardly spend much of their leisure controlling servants. Theft by maidservants was a threat for such wealthy households—of merchants, civic pastors, propertied artisans, and scholars (and not surprisingly these people were responsible for many hostile ordinances against servants). Still, perhaps some masters were generous, giving their servants wine and beer, just as a mistress sometimes rewarded a good servant with a nice piece of cloth. Theft was usually described as a 'removal' (*Abtrag*) of goods, and usually it amounted to no more than some wine and bread for rare nightly gatherings. Nothing else was at stake in most cases than that young people were having a good time together or that maidservants played with the idea of buying a blue or a red ribbon for a lad they fancied. The most striking feature of these offences is their triviality, and the ordinary purposes to which stolen goods were put.

THE ART OF SURVIVAL: PROPERTY OFFENCES BY RESIDENT WOMEN

Resident women had several opportunities to steal or commit fraud: at their workplace, while buying or selling, and they could steal or receive stolen goods from relatives, neighbours, or strangers. They were mostly charged with embezzlement and fraud at their workplace. Those who worked in civic institutions like hospitals were most easily suspected and severely punished.[79] They usually stole food or bedlinen. Hospitals had much of both, so that theft might appear both harmless and difficult to detect. The victim was abstract: not a master or mistress, but the community. Women employed in hospitals and the like tended to be cooks or maidservants. The latter often cared for children or nursed sick and old people. Even though

---

[79] In 1530, a Göppingen maidservant in the hospital was punished for taking flour and bread; in 1549 a maidservant in the Sulz hospital was banished because she took food for her children; in 1564 a Hall maidservant for the sick stole and committed suicide in prison; in 1588 an Esslingen cook in the hospital was banished for taking food; in 1688 a Hall maidservant in the hospital was punished, and in 1694 a woman in the hospital who had given her sister bedlinen: HStASt, A 44, U 1359, Anna Mutler, 19 Mar. 1530; HStASt, A 44, U 5359, Barbara Sieger, 10 Oct. 1540; StAH, 4/477, Margaretha Ziegler; LAL, B 169, Bü. 119 I, Hans Secklin's wife, fo. 239ᵛ, 26 Apr. 1588; StAH, 4/483, 13 Jan. 1668, Apolonia Horlacher; StAH, 4/485, fo. 79ʳ, 15 Jan. 1694; HStASt, A 44, U 6389, 27 Oct. 1561.

they earned more than privately employed maidservants,[80] their salary and status were low in relation to the nursing skills they had to have.[81] They were employed for longer periods, were usually single or widowed, and lived in poverty. Sometimes it was a condition of their employment that they remain unmarried. In 1689, for example, a 42-year-old Constance maidservant working in an orphanage had to promise that she would not marry and would serve as long as she could. Later it turned out that she had stolen the following goods for a future husband:

a couple of old cloth-pegs and lines, copper crockery, a red and a blue pair of linen children's socks, which the children did not wear anymore, three high glasses, one of them broken, crockery into which wicks are put on tables, and a light which is stuck into walls.[82]

This jumble hardly contained anything valuable. She had thought the goods were dispensable, and her future household needed such things. She probably thought that embezzlement was a fair return for low pay.[83]

Others took where there was plenty: at the ducal court 'napkins, linen, and other things' were commonly stolen.[84] In 1699 a whole Stuttgart family and their boarders lived off the food and leftovers their two children took from the duke's kitchen. A boy, aged 18, and a girl who washed plates, aged 16, stole garbage, peas, mush, meat, pastry, filled poultry, and wine. The boy asserted that everybody employed at court did the same.[85] Single mothers often needed to feed their children with less delicious leftovers. One Constance woman grew up on the lard, bread, and pap her widowed mother brought home from the hospital. Stolen sheets were used to make

---

[80] In Vaihingen the cook's maidservant in the hospital had the highest salary (six and a half florins), twice as much as a lower maidservant, and three times as much as a privately employed maidservant (two florins): see K.-O. Bull, 'Zur Wirtschafts- und Sozialgeschichte der württembergischen Amtsstadt Vaihingen an der Enz bis zum Dreißigjährigen Krieg', *ZfWLG* 38 (1979), 128.   [81] Wiesner, *Working Women*, ch. 2.

[82] StAKN, K 63, 14 Oct. 1689, Anna Fetich.

[83] The secondary literature has so far only explored this attitude for the 18th and 19th cents.; on Germany see M. Güttner, 'Unterklassenkriminalität in Hamburg: Güterberaubung im Hamburger Hafen, 1888–1923', in H. Reif, *Räuber, Volk und Obrigkeit*, 153–84.

[84] Reyscher, *Gesetze*, vi. 81, 'Verordnung, die Strafe des Hof=Diebstahls betreffend', 10 July 1684.

[85] HStASt, A 210, Abt. 1, Bü. 125, Maria Dorothea Sauer, 17 Feb. 1699 and 4 Sept. 1699. On this practice see J.-P. Aron, 'The Art of Using Leftovers: Paris, 1850–1900', in R. Forster and O. Ranum (eds.), *Food and Drink in History*, trans. E. Forster and P. M. Ranum (Baltimore, 1979).

and sell children's shirts. Now, in 1580, the daughter feared that her own husband had died during the war; for ten years she had had to cope with the Constance hunger years without any support from him. Just as her mother used to, she had stolen from the hospital, and one maidservant helped her.[86] Low office-holders who dealt with cash were frequently suspected of fraud. Many offices were held jointly by couples. Customs officers were particularly unpopular and easily suspected of fraud. In 1598 Dorothea Rosin was accused in Constance of having encouraged her husband to embezzle customs takings,[87] a situation which was represented in a 1616 broadsheet, entitled *A pleasant tale of a customs' officer and his wife: How they distribute the customs money*, published in Darmstadt. It told how every night the husband threw coins into a tin on his wife's lap, she keeping every coin which fell on her skirt for herself.[88] Gate-keepers and their wives often held the office together, too, collecting tolls and sometimes committing fraud.[89] The Constance salt-servant and his wife were another type of office-holding couple accused of fraud in 1584.[90] Salt was taxed and trade with it controlled by the authorities. In Hall journeymen salt-makers cooperated with their wives at home: they were repeatedly prosecuted for taking salt to their women, who sold or exchanged it.[91] In 1665 the daughter of the Constance salt-servant took his keys to the salt chamber, broke the money-box, and was banished.[92]

In Constance the salt chamber was part of the warehouse, located on the Lake to attract Swiss merchants and dealers. Goods were sold in chambers and stalls, or spread out on the floor. Fraud was com-

---

[86] StAKN, HIX F. 62, 23 July 1580, Margaretha Maiß.

[87] StAKN, RP BI 80, fo. 401ʳ, 18 Apr. 1598. The Geusslingen customs officer and his wife were banished from Hall in 1679, because they had forged customs signs and embezzled money: StAH, 4/483, fos. 67ᵛ-68ʳ, 5 Mar. 1670, Anna Maria and Georg Schuhmacher.

[88] W. Harms (ed.), *Die illustrierten Flugblätter des 16. und 17. Jahrhunderts* (Tübingen, 1987), iv. 82f. n. 58.

[89] In 1553 the Vaihingen gate-keepers were accused of embezzlement: HStASt, A 44, U 6347, 4 Oct. 1553, Sander Bürckle.

[90] StAKN, HIX F. 38, 9 Jan. 1584, Hans Wirth and his wife.

[91] This deprived civic authorities of the money they received for measuring salt. StAH, 4/481 Apolonia Meier bought salt directly from a journeyman salt-maker: fo. 60ʳ, 9 May 1608; 4/482, Michael Dötschmann's daughter sold salt her father had stolen: fo. 149ʳ, 18 June 1647; Ludwig Dötschmann's wife exchanged salt for lard, 25 June 1630, and a salt-maker's maidservant carried the salt he stole home: fo. 149ʳ, 18 June 1647; a journeyman salt-maker and his wife dealt in salt: fo. 182ʳ, 17 May 1652; Hans Dötschmann's widow dealt in salt and was banished: fo. 182ʳ, 21 May 1652.

[92] StAKN, K 28, 14 Nov. 1665, Barbara Wäckherlin.

mon. Catharina Zeidmann sold flour, jam, and goats there for three years, along with apples and grain her son stole.[93] In July 1580, Susanna Jos from Schaffhausen was fined one *Pfund Pfenning* because she had 'sold flour in front of the warehouse too expensively'.[94] One woman took the cream off the milk she sold,[95] and two men were fined because their wives had not weighed goods properly. The use of false weights was frequently punished. Private trade in untaxed wine was another typical offence.[96] In Vaihingen Walburga Glaser mixed wine with water after she had pressed the grapes and told her creditors it was pure wine.[97] Others were active usurers. In 1625 Peter Herzog and Catharina Pelt bought lard and fruit in villages and sold them in Wildberg for twice as much.[98] Such offences were usually met with fines and short imprisonment.[99] Only poor, notoriously fraudulent residents were severely punished.[100]

Women's involvement in such haggling and fraud expressed their difficulty in getting into profitable business or craft. Their employment opportunities were limited, and for them every penny counted. Washing, knitting, sewing, spinning, soaking yarn, nursing, and peddling were low paid, temporary, and sometimes dangerous jobs: Constance women who received alms but were able to work were forced to nurse the sick, a job not in high demand because infections could be caught easily.[101] Women were allowed only to make clothes out of used cloth, or of cloth a customer had brought them. They could not buy new cloth and compete with tailors.[102] In 1538, women were forbidden to sell salt or lard in the Constance warehouse,[103] and artisans' widows were excluded from independent trade here as everywhere. In 1578, for example, the Constance butchers' guild became anxious about a butcher's widow who sold meat to women privately and through her father- and brothers-in-law on the market.

[93] StAKN, K 65, 25 Apr. 1691.
[94] StAKN, HIX F. 62, 30 July 1580 and L 504, Einnahmbuch 1580.
[95] StAKN, HIX F. 62, 23 Mar. 1600.
[96] StAKN, HIX F. 26, 11 Mar. 1555, 16 Dec. 1555.
[97] HStASt, A 44, Bü. 6363, 21 Oct. 1549.
[98] HStASt, A 582, Bü. 86, 9 Apr. 1625. In 1642, a widow bought food on the Hall market and sold it in the territory: StAH, 4/481, fo. 125ᵛ, 2 Sept. 1642, Sybil Wolf. In 1694, Anna Koch, aged 24, and her mother, aged 60, sold grain from Constance to Überlingen: StAKN, K 68, 29 May 1694.
[99] HStASt, A 44, U 3211, 18 Apr. 1554, Margaretha Wern.
[100] For example a Hall constable's widow, who was taken to the pillory and banished by the executioner: StAH, 4/483, Magdalena Ebenbroch, 27 Aug. 1664, fo. 7ʳ.
[101] Feger, *Statutensammlung*, 23 Aug. 1536, 168.   [102] Wiesner, *Working Women*, 179.
[103] Feger, *Statutensammlung*, 28 Sept. 1538, 184.

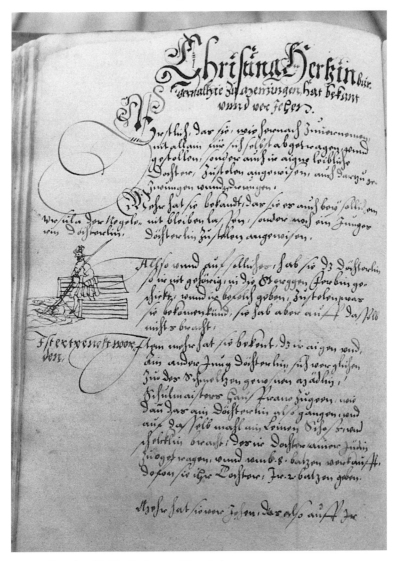

FIG. 7. Christina Herkin is drowned for theft

Her independence was deplored. 'For as long as he had been a master,' Hans Widenkeller announced, 'it had been the custom that if a widow wanted to slaughter, she had to have her own workshop and journeymen in her house.'[104] Women who became widowed, were left by their husband, or had an illegitimate child often had to find new sources of income. Those with small children presumably had to work at home. Catharina Vihllieberin, punished in Constance in 1690, had lived in Constance for thirteen years. For nine years she had worked as a postwoman between Constance and Innsbruck and 'carried her Majesty's letters without complaints'. Then her husband had died and her social decline began. For the next four years she had fed herself and two children mainly by spinning. Then she had become pregnant by a soldier and been banished. After one and a half years she had returned illegally. One day she had visited a peasant outside town to buy mutton. Nobody had answered her and the door stood open. She saw a copper pot on the wall, quickly put it into her apron, and later sold it for half a florin.[105]

Other citizens stole money and clothes inside the community or in market towns. Many stole opportunistically and without planning, like a peasant woman in 1615 who visited Thurgauer's tavern with other women after the Constance market. Slightly drunk, she stole a shoe from the front of a shop. The shoemaker followed her, retrieved the shoe, and took her to the tavern, leaving her to sleep until she was sober.[106] Thieves were only let off in this way if goods were immediately recovered or had clearly been stolen out of dire need.[107] Motives for theft were highly visible in small communities: debt, shifting employment, illness, or small dependent children.[108] Resident thieves were a tremendous threat to local inhabitants.[109]

---

[104] StAKN, HIX F. 35, 28 Oct. 1578, Georg Mayer's wife.

[105] StAKN, K 65, 28 Jan. 1690.

[106] StAKN, HIX F. 45, 16 July 1615, Ursula Lindenmann; a similar case: StAFr B 5 c 4 III, No. 7, vol. 1, fos. 197^v-198^r, 12 Oct. 1579, Barbara Spitznägelin.

[107] In 1561 a woman's sentence was mitigated because of her poverty, illness, and children, even though she had stolen thirty-one florins to pay debts and regain pawned clothes: HStASt, A 44, U 6388, 11 Oct. 1561.

[108] In 1512, the women of Aich near Nürtingen thus collectively petitioned for a woman with twelve children who had stolen flour and grain from the local mill: HStASt, A 44, U 3581, 14 Feb. 1512, Elsbeth Trigler.

[109] Artisans and market people could often hardly protect themselves from thieves because their trade was so public. A Stuttgart citizen stole everything for her daily needs: meat from butchers while they were slaughtering, bread from bakers' carts, salt, lard, candles, and other goods from grocers: HStASt, A 44, U 4313, 28 June 1525. For a detailed case involving a married woman see: StAMM, A 44e, fo. 123^{r-v}, 11 Aug. 1666; and a widow: HStASt, A 209, Bü. 591.

Textiles were stolen from bleaching-grounds.[110] Some women used opportunities such as a fire to steal,[111] or took part in soldiers' lootings,[112] or observed where citizens hid their money before the soldiers marched in.[113] Unguarded furniture was in danger whenever a single householder died.[114] Others learnt how to make duplicate keys. A sculptor's wife, for example, cast the key to her parents' house in clay and had a duplicate made by a locksmith. Then she went to her stepfather's house and returned with silverware and cloth.[115] Relatives were repeatedly the victims of theft, either because of disputes about unequal inheritance, or because trust among relatives could easily be abused.[116] The threat of regular burglars was worse. In 1686, Elisabeth Saus had become a real problem in Besigheim. She was aged 37, had two small children, and was pregnant. She was married to a Bavarian building workman who was industrious and of good reputation. Poverty drove him also to work as a grave-digger and day-labourer, and they lived next to the town wall. Seven years earlier she had broken into a shop and taken eighty-eight florins; this had led to her public punishment and banishment. Now she had stolen money from a parson. Her husband petitioned against her banishment again and was successful.[117] Councils would rather carry the burden of known burglars than that of destitute families.

Even in larger towns there would be few notorious resident thieves and burglars; they were easily recognized. But some used professional tricks to hide their activities. Having climbed through a weaver's window and stolen yarn, Margaretha Riechler of Memmingen covered her tracks by burning some of it and selling the rest over time. On another occasion she broke into Jacob Laucher's cellar to steal a bucket of lard; she burnt the bucket, and gradually sold the lard. She had sharp eyes. She spotted empty houses, open doors and windows. While Henflin Sauerbock's servants were singing in an upstairs chamber, she slipped into the open cellar and took a bucket

---

[110] One woman from Brackenheim was even banished because she had taken cloth from the bleaching-ground: HStASt, A 44, U 629, 30 July 1516.
[111] HStASt, A 44, U 4957, 5 Mar. 1529; StAH, 4/484, fo. 100ʳ, 5 July 1680.
[112] StAH, 4/482, fo. 111ʳ, 26 May 1638, three men and one woman, who were therefore banished.   [113] StAH, 4/483, fo. 19ᵛ, 2 Oct. 1665, an innkeeper's wife.
[114] StAKN, RP BI 80, fos. 146–9ʳ, 19 Oct. 1596.
[115] StAKN, K 65, 15 Dec. 1699, Moritz Husan's stepdaughter.
[116] A Hall woman stole cloth from her mother-in-law: StAH, 4/481, 30 May 1620; in 1571, a dyer's wife had taken some goods of her brother-in-law's in order to pay debts: StAMM, A 44c, 4 May 1571.   [117] HStASt, A 209, Bü. 333.

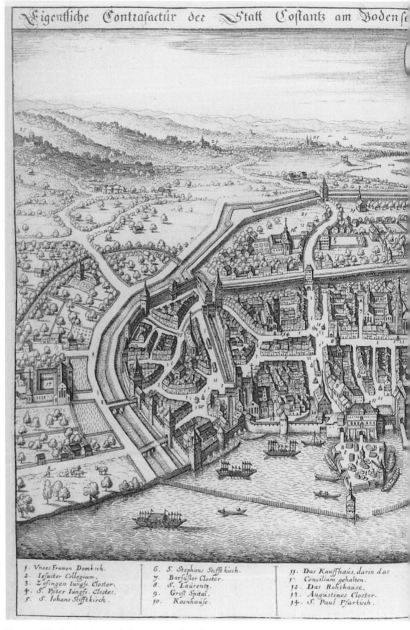

FIG. 8. Merian's view of Constance in 1633

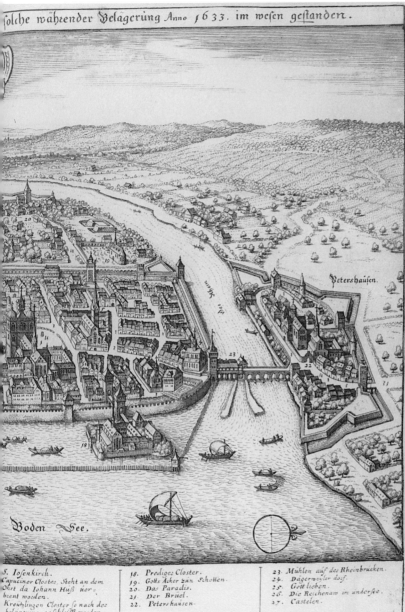

folche während er Belägerung Anno 1633. im wesen gestanden.

Petershausen

Der Rhein

Boden See.

S. Iosenkirch.
Capuciner Closter. Steht an dem
Ohrt da Iohann Huß ver=
brent worden.
Kreutzlingen Closter so nach der
belagerung geschleifft worden.

18. Prediger Closter.
19. Gotts Äcker zun Schotten.
20. Das Paradis.
21. Der Briel.
22. Petershausen.

23. Mühlen auf der Rheinbrucken.
24. Dägerweyler dorf.
25. Gottlieben.
26. Die Reichenam im andersee.
27. Castelen.

of lard and two loaves of bread. Her ears were cut off in 1564, so that everyone would know she was a thief.[118] Local thieves had to search for buyers or to sell goods on the market. Both pursuits were dangerous. They typically used local receivers. In Memmingen, most stolen goods were brought to the Jewish community. Receivers took goods to other places to sell. Then it was almost impossible for the authorities to detect goods sold outside a town or district. Furthermore, it was a basic right of citizens that they could be accused only before their local court. In 1677, the Constance innkeeper of the Star used soldiers and two middle-women to sell stolen goods in Überlingen. A suspicious woman had to go to the Überlingen mayor, who alarmed his Constance colleague, who in turn had to prosecute all participants. This was the only way in which the offence could be heard before a Constance court.[119]

Networks of receivers were based on a multiplicity of contacts. Jewish groups had a perfect division of labour: the women stayed at home and received the goods which their men sold as pedlars.[120] Independent women had to organize themselves otherwise. Many took goods elsewhere as pedlars, carriers, messengers, day-labourers, or market-women.[121] Innkeepers sold goods directly to customers or got them to sell the goods elsewhere. Together with the female innkeeper of the Star, a whole group of women received stolen goods in Constance at the end of the seventeenth century. The French War had boosted their trade. War legitimized looting, and hence many goods circulated. In 1689, a Swiss corporal's wife lived near the tavern Red Bird at the end of the *Neue Gasse* in Constance. She dealt in white and blue yarn, necklaces, and other goods.[122] A soldier's wife had moved from Saxony to Constance, and she confessed to selling to a baker's wife goods she obtained from soldiers.[123] Many soldiers ate or slept in private homes, which they often turned into a base for undercover trade. In 1699 a vine-grower's wife bought a great number of sleeves, laces, and other textiles from a soldier who stayed with her, and sold them in town.[124] This offence was less serious than theft itself. The women

---

[118] StAMM, A 44c, 7 Feb. 1562.   [119] StAKN, K 56, 11 Oct. 1677.
[120] Egmond, *Underworlds*, ch. 3.
[121] For cases involving pedlars see: StAKN, RP BI 80, 1 Oct. 1596; K 65, 15 Mar. 1690.
[122] StAKN, K 65, 15 Jan. 1698, Anna Kölpin.
[123] StAKN, K 65, 18 Feb. 1695, Catharina Fuchs.
[124] StAKN, K 65, 4 Apr. 1699, Catharina Gall.

probably regarded it as an extension of pawnbroking and second-hand trading.

Surprise at the survival of women when typically they received insufficient alms and made up two-thirds of urban poor-relief lists[125] may be lessened by looking at receivers of stolen goods. A woman like the Constance widow Catharina Müller in 1693 tried to manage 'as well as possible by sewing and washing'. Apart from that, she cooked stolen meat for the soldier who stayed with her, and bought some goods from him. This was risky for her: historians have rarely noted the pressures placed upon the urban poor by the threat that if they behaved criminally they would be denied alms. However, illegal activities provided a chance of earning the additional money the poor so desperately needed. In Constance, smuggling was one such activity. In 1691 Catharina Hettleman, aged 28, was accused of smuggling goods to Switzerland, helped by a soldier. She was a seamstress who lived on the Reichenau, and had a retarded child who could not walk.[126] Single women like her had a hard life: they were unable to go into service because they had to mind their children. This limited employment to spinning and sewing. Single women with children typically rented a room in derelict houses owned by poor widows, like the 31-year-old seamstress who lived in the house of a tin-maker's widow with her two sons in 1691. Two soldiers had brought her twenty-one skins, which she had passed on to a Swiss woman to sell them in the Thurgau. She worked together with her mother, a stocking-knitter, and had previously stolen because she 'would have died of hunger' otherwise. She was convinced that God would forgive her.[127]

These cases let us glimpse what life in early modern urban 'under-worlds' must have been like. Children learnt to steal early, women had strange, often occupational nicknames, disabilities were common. In 1677, 'Turkish Michael's wife' was punished for having taught her daughter and an orphan girl how to steal.[128] In the same year, a woman called 'Einhänderin' (one-handed woman), with thirteen children, lived in Constance, too. She had taught a Swiss girl to steal, who 'had taken refuge with her because she was

---

[125] R. Jütte, *Obrigkeitliche Armenfürsorge in deutschen Reichsstädten der frühen Neuzeit: Städtisches Armenwesen in Frankfurt am Main und Köln* (Cologne, 1984), 127.

[126] StAKN, K 65, 1 Feb. 1691.

[127] StAKN, K 65, 11 Apr. 1691, Anna Acker, 19 Apr. 1691, Anna Wallthase.

[128] StAH, 4/480, 16 Apr. 1575, fo. 247ʳ; StAMM, A 44d, 22 Jan. 1581, Catherina Herk, who taught her daughter to steal and was punished by drowning.

so poor'. One of her daughters cooperated with a woman called 'Green Seamstress'. They had often eaten and drunk together, received visits from soldiers, stolen candles, lard, cheese, and money out of shops by night, sold the cheese, and 'calmed their hunger' with bread they bought with the money.[129] Single women sometimes worked together as prostitutes, but they also met for leisure, eating together, and exchanging clothes. One Constance woman started her criminal career as a girl by standing watch while her father burgled warehouses. A neighbouring woman had later taught her to cut purses. Now she worked as a maidservant and met her neighbour for drinks in the evening, 'had a good time', and joined the gatherings of other single women and men.[130]

Other women spent their daytimes waiting for stolen goods and opportunities to sell them. In 1691, Barbara Rainbüchler confessed that someone she did not know had brought her two goats she had sold in the 'Paradise', a thinly populated and badly guarded north Constance suburb. The person in question was a girl who stayed with an old hospital nurse who was responsible for the deal. Formerly Barbara had sold some tablecloths, linen sheets, and bedding for a woman called the 'fly-butcher' (Fliegenmetzgerin) who lived on top of one of the city gates. Barbara had spent her percentage on shoes and in paying some of her debts. She offered the rest to a woman who had often invited her for supper and given her a red jacket.[131] Anna Mayer from Gottlieben, a village close to Constance, stole jars in the Paradise and sold them. She used cheap, rural artisans' markets to buy new goods and sell them at a profit in the Paradise. She also stole yarn, and then spun and sold it. All this was 'so that she and her children would have enough to eat': [132] and her case illustrates how desperately income had to be found. In the Niederburg in the west of Constance a thief, aged 20, whose father had been executed, took stolen goods to a female pedlar in the Rheingasse.[133] Antoni Contamina, a dealer in silverware, lived here, too. One woman confessed that her husband had sold all the Thurgau senior bailiff's silver to Contamina. Men had once brought her a bag of copper dishes, but she had told them to go to a neighbouring female jug-maker.[134]

---

[129] StAKN, K 56, 29 Oct. 1677.
[130] StAKN, HIX F. 32, 22 Apr. 1559, Katharina Danner.
[131] StAKN, K 68, 18 Mar. 1691.   [132] StAKN, HIX F. 34, 18 Apr. 1574.
[133] StAKN, K 67, 14 Feb. 1693.   [134] StAKN, K 59, 8 Mar. 1680, Catharina Stader.

These cases of female citizens charged with property crime give a rare insight into poor people's survival strategies. They were mainly detected in urban areas. Most suspects belonged to the urban poor. One group were single women with small children, who were particularly disadvantaged on the job market. Women did generally not have many, let alone well-paid, employment opportunities, except for artisans' wives or women who were married to public officers, who shared work with their husbands. Women officers and women who worked in hospitals and the like were typically accused of embezzlement and fraud, artisans' and peasant wives of having cheated customers. Such offences were again treated differently. Petty fraud in markets and in shops was tolerated and punished with fines. Embezzlement affecting civic money and notorious theft were severely punished, with the exception of married women with innocent husbands and small children, who were usually treated leniently. The data are not full enough for us to say anything about a rise in female theft caused by dearth. The effects of war are clearer. The sources reflect the precarious economic situation of single women and widows, which the study of tax- and poor-relief lists has already established. More importantly, they tell us about the attitudes arising from this situation: the need to watch for every opportunity to save a bit of money or sell a few goods, the ubiquity of used and reused goods, the seamstresses' craft in turning one piece of clothing into many, the sending away of children to find food. Such were the bases of the common mentality of having to manage with whatever means, which kept large parts of early modern communities busy day after day.

PROFESSIONAL THIEVES

Professional thieves were distinct from the groups we have looked at so far because theft was their main source of income for longer periods. Common images of 'criminal underworlds' as wholly separated from the normal world are, however, misleading because most professional thieves went back to regular work from time to time. Women could go into service, and both men and women frequently worked as day-labourers during the harvest. Moreover, big coups were rare. Most thieves were involved in petty theft and burglary, and would typically steal some clothes, a bit of money or food. They partly survived through charity, and followed a topography whose stages were marked out by convents, churches, and civic charitable institutions.[135] Women never committed violent robbery,[136] used no weapons, and stole only small animals, such as hens and ducks. Murder *and* robbery (*Raubmord*), and the robbery of valuable sheep and horses, were a male domain. Male robbers and thieves were thus considered to be much more dangerous, and frequently punished with the death sentence.[137] Professional thieves were also characterized by their mobility. They travelled within a limited space of known regions and places. Most of their time was spent on roads and in rural areas. It was often difficult for them to enter towns, and to stay in them could be impossible. As they approached the gates, thieves would sometimes stumble on a border-stone with a carved gallows: the sign of a town's right to execute people, and of a determination to use it.[138]

Thieves had certain resting-places to which they returned regularly. Their choice was either professionally conditioned, as when they visited the annual town fairs where stealing was profitable, or it was conditioned privately, as when they stayed with hospitable relatives, lovers, and friends. Agatha Selttenreich and her partner stole during spring and autumn for nine years, worked during summer, and moved to her brother's each winter.[139] Female professional thieves had a mixed economy of urban and rural theft which corresponded to their patterns of mobility. Katharina Heu, for example, cut purses and stole expensive textiles in markets in Kernten, Ulm, and Augsburg. In villages, she broke into houses to take textiles, hemp, knives, or 'three slices of meat in a hamlet near Ottobeuren'.[140] Thieves knew how to use favourable local conditions: Memmingen had many weavers and a lot of yarn to steal, while in Constance there were many gold- and silversmiths, from whom goods could be stolen, or to whom stolen metalwork might

---

[135] For the Constance region see C. Schott, *Armenfürsorge, Bettelwesen und Vagantenbekämpfung in der Reichsabtei Salem* (Bühl, 1978).

[136] With the exception of Margareth Keck, whose husband forced her to help him with robbery and murder in forests, HStASt, A 43, Bü. 3, 18 Jan. 1526.

[137] In Memmingen, a town which turned the prosecution of theft and robbery into one of its priorities because it lay on an important trade route, forty-three men and twenty-two women had to stand in the pillory, and be whipped and banished for property crimes, but only four women as against eighty-two men (including sixteen robber-murderers) were sentenced to death for property crime. Real numbers were even higher, as the third and final court book (1615–89) was not well kept.

[138] For such border-stones see A. Deutsch (ed.), *Richter, Henker, Folterknechte: Strafjustiz im alten Hall* (Schwäbisch Hall, 1993), 35; on border-stones in general see M. Warnke, *Politische Landschaft: Zur Kunstgeschichte der Natur* (Munich, 1992), 16.

[139] StAFR, B 5 III c 4, No. 7, vol. 1, 15 June 1570.   [140] StAMM, A 44c, 1551.

be sold.[141] Whereas Memmingen had become a regional market centre during the sixteenth century and its annual fairs were no more important than weekly markets,[142] goods and customers in big market-towns like Esslingen reflected a lively international trade. Such markets and fairs attracted many thieves from far away. Thieves often sold their goods on trade routes. While they moved from the Allgäu to Upper Swabia, on to Ulm and Württemberg, they met vagrants, flying merchants, and other customers. Textiles were frequently stolen because of the vibrant trade in second-hand clothes. In 1696, the duke of Württemberg even had to issue an ordinance against some Stuttgart citizens who wore his servants' old liveries: shabby clothes were always given away or sold until they finally fell to pieces.[143] One thief wore clothes stolen from washing lines, and later sold them to vagrants, or once to a 'prostitute, called Sabina, who lived near Augsburg'.[144] This was a 'flying' trade: pears were picked and sold in the next market, as stolen goods were too.[145] The main problem was how to keep valuable goods safe: they either had to be hidden or sold quickly. There were tricks of the trade: Barbara Meyer had sewed a 'thief's bag' under her apron, into which she put goods from Esslingen market stalls, and, once, a councillor's fur.[146] But hiding-places for larger goods were hard to find,[147] and so thieves were best advised to disappear quickly. Markets could be used to get a lift on carts, for example from Constance to Schaffhausen[148] or to other places where thieves could peddle their goods.[149]

Those who stayed in one town for longer could get in touch with receivers of stolen goods—apart from Jewish communities there would always be artisans and merchants willing to accept stolen

---

[141] Until the Thirty Years War the Constance gold- and silversmiths received work from the whole Lake Constance region; then Augsburg took the lead, but the trade remained strong in Constance: see M. Burckhardt, W. Dobras and W. Zimmermann, *Konstanz in der frühen Neuzeit: Reformation. Verlust der Reichsfreiheit. Österreichische Zeit* (Constance, 1991), 211.

[142] R. Kießling, *Die Stadt und ihr Land: Umlandpolitik, Bürgerbesitz und Wirtschaftsgefüge in Oberschwaben vom 14. bis ins 16. Jahrhundert* (Cologne, 1989), 429.

[143] Reyscher, *Gesetze*, viii. 701.

[144] StAMM, A 44d, fo. 17[r–v], 17 Aug. 1589, Rosina Schemer.

[145] StAKN, RP BI 81, 1600, fos. 37[r]-41[v], Barbara Widmer.

[146] StAL, B 169, Bü. 119, fo. 91[r–v], 9 Oct. 1654.

[147] Barbara Widmer committed a burglary on a safe day, while a Constance citizen invited the entire population for a drink at the Bohnen-market. The stolen goods were later found in a tavern trunk: StAKN, RP BI 81, 1600, fos. 37[r]-41[v].

[148] StAKN, K 28, 26 Oct. 1639, Anna Meyer.

[149] StAKN, K 66, 22 Jan. 1692, Maria Hagg.

goods. Skins, for example, were usually sold to tanners.[150] In 1692, Maria Hagg sold three nails and an iron brooch to a Constance smith in the Rheingasse for three shillings. She took a stolen chandelier to a polisher's house and melted it in the chamber of a corporal's wife who lived there. She sold the metal to a bell-maker and textiles to a female tailor. Goods without obvious value were rarely stolen; but Hagg was lucky enough to sell a small model of a boat to a cook off the fish-market.[151] Such contacts were profitable and provided one reason why thieves tried to return to towns they knew well.

Esslingen provides good examples of how thieves visited important market towns regularly. Some thieves who had come from the wider region were sentenced there; they came from Stuttgart, Beuren, Ellwangen, Weikersheim, Platthardt, and Hall, and even further away—from Augsburg, Biberach, Nördlingen, Nürnberg, Ravensburg, Schaffhausen, Solothurn, Rabsweyler in the Alsace, or, in 1613, 'Elsa, who does not know her father', a thief from the Mainz area.[152] Fairs were a 'rendezvous des filous' from all over the place.[153] They stole the familiar repertoire of textiles, leather- and metalwork, food, and some extras, like a kettle or toys, or else they were specialized cutpurses or pickpockets. The loot was tempting. In 1588, Margaretha Haafen had stolen fifty-two *Batzen* from purses at the Esslingen fair.[154] Such thieves were severely punished. In 1590, the vagrant Anna Fischer was hanged in Esslingen, because she had cut purses at markets and fairs with a gang of thieves.[155] In 1592, Helena Straub and her companions lost their lives after the Martini market, as did a woman with the same name (real or invented?), along with her fellows a year later.[156] The age of some thieves was startling. A girl aged 16 was beheaded in Esslingen in 1599. She and her boyfriend had stolen hats, caps, shoes, and cloth at markets and fairs, and sold them to 'Jews or poor people'. She begged that they should both be beheaded and buried, as 'she would die more willingly if she knew that they would lie together afterwards'.[157] Most women were merely reported to be 'drunk, dishonest, and blasphemous', as, for example, Magdalena Brunner in 1653, who dealt in

---

[150] For example five calfskins and three big skins by Margarethen Blansch in 1556: StAFr, B5 IIIc 4, No. 7, vol. 1, fo. 87ᵛ.   [151] StAKN, K 66, 22 Jan. 1692.
[152] StAL, B 169, Bü. 119 II, fo. 47ᵛ, 3 Dec. 1613.
[153] Hufton, *Poor of Eighteenth Century France*, 265.
[154] StAL, B 169, Bü. 119 I, fo. 243ʳ.
[155] StAL, B 169, Bü. 119 I, fos. 253–6ʳ, 6 Oct. 1590.
[156] StAL, B 169, Bü. 119 I, fos. 256ʳ-258ʳ, 27 Oct. 1592 and 261ᵛ-263ʳ, 12 Jan. 1593.
[157] StAL, B 169, Bü. 119 I, fos. 272ᵛ-277ʳ, 22 Dec. 1599.

forged coins and travelled with 'loose, lazy, and dishonest people'—such as pipe-players, comedians, and tricksters.[158] Descriptions of that kind tell us little about how gangs operated or thought of themselves. Recent research has shown that such gangs were organized very loosely, that members usually met in subgroups for a burglary, and dispersed quickly to avoid suspicion.[159] Thieves in prison were forced to describe other members, and some reports are highly indicative of gang members' heterogeneous appearance. Anna Möring, for example, was a dyer's daughter and a vagrant's widow, who belonged to a gang of thieves caught in Esslingen in 1599. She knew what other members looked like, their nicknames, their biggest coups, sometimes a bit about their lives, and places where they often stayed. A male cutpurse was characterized like this: his name was Hans von Lachweylen, he was a 'rough, yellow' person, and had escaped after having murdered a Heidelberg relative. He had once cut a purse with fifty *Kronen* in it in Frankfurt, and usually stayed in the Heilbronn area. Lichlin, a thief who stole at night, was a piper from the Palatinate. He was 'a long, brown, strong person', who often visited the Durlach executioner, and had already been banished from Stuttgart, Leonberg, and Württemberg. Murderers were remembered (one of them had beaten a vagrant to death at a fair), as were executed relatives (brown George's father had been beheaded at Weißenhorn); and escapes from prison could be listed (crooked Anna had 'broken out of the Ulm prison'). Anna Möring described her companions as rough or thick, or as a 'small, black man', or as strong and tall, or 'stout', or young with a 'kleinfalben' beard, or with a 'twisted moustache', a 'dotted face', 'bleary eyes', or a 'reddish, broad face'. Surnames were only derived from the name of a town, maybe the home town. Disabilities were noted (a 'soldier with a crooked hand'), and different nationalities too. Clothes were sometimes described in summary fashion as 'peasant-like', but more frequently they were remembered in detail: 'black breeches and a jacket, a broad hat with a yellow badge on it'; long breeches; a 'dagger with a deer-leather

---

[158] StAL, B 169, Bü. 119 II, fos. 89ʳ-90ʳ, 10 Dec. 1653.
[159] U. Danker, *Räuberbanden im Alten Reich um 1700: Ein Beitrag zur Geschichte von Herrschaft und Kriminalität in der frühen Neuzeit* (2 vols., Frankfurt on Main, 1988); Egmond, *Underworlds*; A. Blauert, *Sackgreifer und Beutelschneider: Die Diebesbande der Alten Lisel, ihre Streifzüge um den Bodensee und ihr Prozeß 1732* (Constance, 1993); Monika Spicker-Beck, *Räuber, Mordbrenner, umschweifendes Gesind: Zur Kriminalität im 16. Jahrhundert* (Freiburg im Breisgau, 1995).

husk'; 'green socks'; a coat lined with 'knöpfflechtem' cloth; blue breeches; a leather jacket—etc. Only Afra Georg could not be described, because 'he changed his clothes'. Comments on someone's character, such as 'he was a dexterous fellow', were rare. A former trade was only noted once: 'Hans, a glazier . . . called Hans Glazier among vagrants, or just the Glazier.' Internal differences between them were noted with care: there were cutpurses, market thieves, thieves, burglars, and one 'Steigbettler', who bought stolen goods or took them forcefully if they were too expensive. Others earned their living 'through begging rather than stealing'. Endri from Augsburg 'sometimes sold spices and made false musk-buttons', while another man was 'a real thief', but had also managed to earn himself a vendor's box. There were six highwaymen, one of them equipped with dagger and pistol; another one was a soldier who 'molested wandering journeymen'. A third highwayman had two guns, but two others no weapons at all. Every robber had 'journeymen', who carried away stolen goods. A female vagrant with two thieving daughters, a female forger, and a prostitute were further mentioned.[160]

All these descriptions confirm that although there was a broad frame of membership in such gangs, members differed from each other in ambition, skill, and the use of violence. In contrast to guilds, membership was not fixed and no uniform code of behaviour imposed. Only those stood out who had managed to cheat wealthy victims and the authorities. Barbara Widmer knew about one thief who worked as a prostitute, dealt in forged coins, and had once pickpocketed thirty florins.[161] Such success stories contributed to myths about thieves' lives and helped them to forget the everyday experiences of long marches on roads, illness, the need to seek protection from treacherous companions, the threat of capture, and memories of torture, prisons, and of executed friends, whose flesh had been picked at by birds.

If a criminal trial was initiated, the partners of robbers and thieves were often accused as 'Dirnen', prostitutes. These cases confirm that women's involvement in gang-robbery varied widely. Some women hardly knew what their partners did. Maria Buoler, for example, belonged to a gang of twenty-five robbers and forgers. The men gave her free food and a bit of money, but no information about

---

[160] StAE, A Reichsstadt, F. 42, 31 Oct. 1599. [161] StAKN, RP BI 81, fos. 38ʳ-41ᵛ.

their crimes.[162] Active women, on the other hand, usually distributed stolen goods, or helped to take away stolen goods after a burglary.[163] Some would also separate from the gang temporarily to do their own business, or work independently as prostitutes.[164] In 1618 Maria Reuß was beheaded and burnt together with her male mates in Memmingen. They had forced 'poor country people' to give them money. She had also worked as a prostitute, and 'stained herself so thoroughly with whoredom, adultery, and fornication' that the judges decided not to have her confession read out aloud in the market-place in order to spare 'young people and honourable ears' such immoral details.[165] Apolonia, 'concubine of the deceased Christoff Käfer', was drowned soon after the latter had been executed in Memmingen, in 1572. Their gang had broken into peasant houses, shops, and private homes, pickpocketed drunken travellers and innkeepers at night, and stolen at fairs. Apolonia's job had been to sell the goods. Old 'women's slippers' or black and red petticoats were better sold by a woman in any case. Sometimes Apolonia would cut a coat into vests and sell them. This camouflaged theft, and it was easier to find many customers, than one for an expensive piece. Apolonia had been stealing for sixteen years. She had made her best coup ever during the last Imperial diet in Speyer. Together with thousands of other people she had watched the emperor's entry. When a man who stood nearby had pulled out his handkerchief, a ring had fallen out of his pocket. What a nice, golden ring, she thought: it had a 'beautiful stone in the middle'. She put her foot on it quickly. Although the man quickly realized the loss and asked everyone for help, Apolonia slowly pulled the ring towards her. Then she bent over as if to tie her shoe-laces, put the ring into her shoe, and later sold it to a Jew.[166]

Female thieves who did not want to travel alone often teamed up with one man, thus securing their protection, or with other women because this was less suspicious. But cooperation of this kind was not always easy. Dividing the loot caused disputes: female thieves demanded equal returns for equal labour. Agnes Knab, for example,

---

[162] StAFr, B 5 c 4 III, No. 7, vol. 1., fos. 634^v-638^v, 12 May 1604. Agatha Strölin, who travelled with an arsonist until they were apprehended in 1551, said she never knew which house he was going to burn next. When she once asked what he wanted to do with his powder and sulphur, he told her to shut up: StAFr, B5 III c 4, No. 7, vol. 1., fos.7^v–8^r, 5 Feb. 1551.   [163] StAMM, A 44d, 4 June 1585, fo. 93^{r-v}, Anna Bayr.
[164] Danker, *Räuberbanden*, i. 271 f.   [165] StAMM, A 44e, fo. 31^{r-v}, 13 Mar. 1618.
[166] StAMM, A 44c, 19 May 1572; A 133/10.

travelled with Junker Hans. She had met him in Basle in 1571, when she had still been a maidservant at the shoemakers' guild. Together with the last soldiers they moved to France. During the war they had 'taken many things like linen sheets and similar plunder, as it was customary during war'. Back in Germany stealing was less easy. Once she had broken into a shoemaker's house, and Hans only wanted to give her three of the eight *Batzen* they had earned. Another time he beat her, and did not believe that she had told him about all the profit she made.[167]

Women who travelled without men still employed temporary help to carry heavy weights. Before Afra Klein slipped into a baker's house through the back door, she had got herself a 'carrier' who had later kept most of the money. Burglary was often carefully planned. The so-called Numenschneiderin, Sichelschnidin, and Mayenmacherin were caught as a trio of female burglars and thieves in 1618. They had hired a weaver's servant to help with a burglary in Memmingen. They usually stole metalwork, especially tin, melted it, and sold it to timber-makers. The Numenschneiderin told her daughter to ask for soup or cabbage in taverns. She later melted the dishes on which her daughter brought the food.[168]

There were other tricks and specializations. In Constance, Maria Hagg worked together with Barbara Robigler, a shoemaker's daughter.[169] They stayed in inns and took feathers out of cushions and duvets. In 1690, they had travelled through Swabia for six months, and continued to perform the same trick in other regions. They used their profit to always eat and drink as much as they wanted.[170] Stolen textiles were dyed, so that they could not be recognized by owners.[171] Farms, houses, and even workshops were often empty during the day, when people were on their fields or at markets. Then money-boxes were broken into, or money-trays emptied.[172] One vagrant drilled a hole in a door early in the morning, removed the lock, and broke into the house.[173] Many garden sheds were unguarded and goods such as 'two timber Kanten' could be stolen from a doctor, or 'twenty lengths of white cloth' from a baker.[174] Burglary during church-time on Sunday was so common that citizens

---

[167] StAKN, HIX F. 33, 14 Mar. 1571.   [168] StAMM, A 44e, fo. 34^{r-v}, 31 July 1618.
[169] StAKN, K 66, 20 Mar. 1692.   [170] StAKN, K 66, 22 Jan. 1692.
[171] StAKN, K 28, 5 Aug. 1611, Elisabeth Ziegler.
[172] StAKN, RP BI 81, 1600, fos. 38^r-41^v, Barbara Widmer.
[173] StAH, 4/480, 3 May 1575, fo. 251^{r-v}.   [174] StAKN, RP BI 80, 12 Oct. 1596.

of Gumlow in Saxony said they dared not attend sermons.[175] In 1695, Anna Konder stole no less than 400 florins from a Leonberg butcher during the Sunday sermon.[176] A further trick was to forge fire-certificates (*Brandbriefe*). Citizens who were forced to live on the streets because their house had burnt down received this certificate; it described their fate and ended with their home council's appeal to grant them alms.[177] In 1697, a woman from the Upper Palatinate was banished from Hall because she had pretended to be an impoverished noblewoman with two maidservants, and had used 'false begging certificates'.[178] Church robbery was a type of crime rarely committed by women,[179] and female coiners were also unusual. Because women were not associated with such offences, they could easily distribute forged money.[180] The only real female coiner was arrested in Constance in 1596. A year earlier, Barbara Wölfflin had joined a Weinfelden man, his journeyman, and a woman who had taught her to forge coins. She had had to order the wooden moulds they used from a carpenter, telling him that she wanted to make 'badges for hats'. When she went coining in Weinfelden, Barbara gave her four children to someone else to care for. She and her gang poured hot metal into the moulds, which were pasted with egg-white and ash. She was not a fully accepted member of their 'company' yet, and had only been paid eight florins. That did not stop her being beheaded and burnt in Constance.[181]

Some thieves lived from prostitution, too. Barbara Widmer was paid with food by the young villagers who slept with her; she ate some of it and sold the rest to innkeepers. She stole money and a hat badge from one customer who had not paid her. She stole money, too, from her godparents' son; he had only wanted to give her two *Batzen*, even though he had spent the whole night with her. A man in a tavern, by contrast, offered her four florins for sex. Prostitutes were identifiable through their clothes, reputation, and body language,

---

[175] K. Pallas (ed.), *Die Registraturen der Kirchenvisitationen im ehemals sächsischen Kurkreise* (6 vols., Halle, 1906), i, 245.   [176] HStASt, A 209, Bü. 215.
[177] In 1615, Maria Bauler was accused of having 'deceived many people of low and high rank' in this manner: StAMM, A 44e, fo. 1ʳ⁻ᵛ, 24 Apr. 1615; in 1695 two women from the Lindau region were imprisoned in Hall because they used 'forged books and letters': StAH, 4/485, 4 Jan. 1696.   [178] StAH, 4/485, 26 June 1697.
[179] StAKN, K 44, 15 Oct. 1679, Maria Isler.
[180] In 1635, a Württemberg woman, caught in Hall with forged coins, said she had only just got the money. She got away with two days' imprisonment: StAH, 4/482, 8 Oct. 1635.   [181] StAKN, RP BI 80, 20 July 1596.

and because they were outsiders. Apolonia, a 'common whore', was presumably typical of many travelling prostitutes. Her clothes were too colourful and expensive for lower-class women by 1601: a 'green skirt with a red velvet fur, . . . a hat, and a black woollen jacket with velvet sleeves'.[182]

However, neither prostitution nor specialization was typical of most female thieves. What counted for more was a mixture of luck, a lot of extremely petty theft, and an occasional big coup which kept them going.[183] This, and the fact that women never used violence, made judges hesitant about executing them.

In court women tried to give the impression that they had only committed minor offences. They confessed only to petty theft, reported every incident after which stolen goods had been taken away from them and they had made no profit, or after which they had been imprisoned and punished.[184] Another common trick which helped to mitigate sentences was to provide false information about one's name and home town, so that previous offences could not be traced. Those strong enough to withstand torture could maintain that they had never stolen before. Women frequently pretended to be pregnant. Illness, such as falling sickness, was invented. As a result, female professional thieves usually had to stand in the pillory, be whipped, and banished for life. Most thieves were mobile anyway, and if they wanted to return to a town after a year or so it was highly unlikely that they would be recognized. Those who were banished from a big territory like Württemberg could safely remain in other parts of the country.[185]

Even before they were sentenced, professional thieves often managed to escape from prison. Prisons in small towns were insecure. Controls were loose and guards open to bribery. Afra Klein, for example, told the Lindau magistrates that she was pregnant and had already been imprisoned for nine weeks. She gave the constable four florins and his wife a fur, jumped on a boat, and quickly crossed over to Fussach, on the other side of Lake Constance.[186] Some 'prisons' were public: Catharina Losinger, for example, was kept

    [182] StAKN, RP BI 81, fos. 38^r-41^v.
    [183] For two good examples see StAKN, HIX F. 33, 8 Feb. 1674, Agnes Knab; RP BI 80, 12 Oct. 1596, Agnes Kolb.
    [184] StAMM, A 44d, fo. 143^{r-v}, 2 Feb. 1589, Agnes Vater; HStASt, A 209, Bü. 1737, 24 May 1696 and 11 Oct. 1700. Vengeful theft, by contrast, was almost never mentioned: HStASt, A 209, Bü. 1251, 24 Sept. 1696, Catharina Lonsinger.
    [185] HStASt, A 209, Bü. 1735, 31 Oct. 1694.
    [186] StAMM, A 44d, fo. 143^{r-v}, 2 Feb. 1589.

and exhibited in a cage on the market-place, until soldiers freed her at night.[187] Prison towers were usually built next to the town wall, and sometimes a chair was all that was needed to climb to a window which led to the top of the wall.[188] Anna Milt reported that the Weilheim prison door had been locked only with a wooden stick, and that she had always found a hole to escape through in other places. People already thought she could make herself invisible, because she had escaped so often. Not that this made life easy. In Wiesensteig, a drunk guard had tried to rape her. The second guard likewise opened her handcuffs one day and promised her a nice present if she had sex with him. Then a lot of noise told them that the earl was passing through town. The guard went out and was so excited that he left the prison door open, so that Anna, 'since it had been on a Friday, and alms were being distributed', ran after the earl's carriage with the poor and quickly got out of town. But her luck did not last. She was beheaded, aged 18.[189]

However, most female thieves escaped the death sentence for a long time.[190] They were amazingly cunning: one butcher's widow even stole a duvet from the Stuttgart junior bailiff's office. She usually stole bedding from inns, and had already been banished from five towns and from the duchy of Württemberg, in which she remained nevertheless. Once she had been apprehended, and simulated illness. She was taken into hospital, where she immediately tied sheets together and slid out of the window. She was beheaded aged 55.[191]

Old thieves who were seriously tortured after many years realized that their list of offences was already too long. Then they would finally give in and confess to everything. Anna Maria Wörner from Balingen had first broken into a neighbour's house ten years ago. She had a skeleton key and had broken into the house of a member of the Stuttgart upper council. Afterwards, her expenditure on food and drink had raised suspicion. She served a Reutlingen

---

[187] HStASt, A 209, Bü. 125, 24 Sept. 1696.
[188] HStASt, A 209, Bü. 125, 24 Sept. 1696.   [189] HStASt, A 309, Bü. 67, 1613.
[190] Anna Seybold was imprisoned for theft as a maidservant in 1663. She was sentenced to death in Biberach, but finally pardoned because of her youth. Instead, a gallows was branded on her back. She nevertheless married and raised six children. And she still used every opportunity to steal. In the Sindelfingen prison someone gave her a bed because of the cold. She had escaped and taken the duvet with her. She went to a parson to get her husband's death certificate and stole a linen sheet. In the autumn of 1683, aged 35, she was at last beheaded: HStASt, A 209, Bü. 1482, 1 Oct. 1683; A 309, Bü. 128.   [191] HStASt, A 209, Bü. 1710.

widow and put 'something of her *menstruis*' into her son's soup. This love-magic failed. Instead she got involved with a soldier and aborted the child. She said that her parents were responsible for the way she lived, because they had deprived her of her inheritance. She was deeply tired of living. She 'could not help it and had been born under a bad planet', she said: she wanted to 'pay for her many crimes with her life', and had cancer of the nose. She wanted to be beheaded, and soon began to comfort herself with psalms and prayers.[192]

This brings us back to the question of how these criminal careers had started. Some thieves had grown up with theft as a survival strategy, while others had accidentally taken to a life on the street after they had, for example, escaped abusive husbands.[193] Resentment about a withheld inheritance was common—a feeling of having lost out, having been cheated, and of being left with nothing. Theft was often connected to the loss of trust that others would treat one adequately, justly, or even generously. Life had told these people to take everything they could from others. Professional thieves predominantly belonged to the lower classes, which meant that they had more hurdles to jump as they tried to follow the usual life plan: marriage, dowry, inheritance, an independent household. Those who had saved enough for their dowry knew that they would still remain poor during their marriage. A husband's death would turn life into a battle. Many young thieves had become orphans at an early age, and had no inheritance or home to return to.[194] They could do whatever they liked. Maria Graf is one example of a girl who became adventurous as a result. She was 17 years old when arrested in Constance. Her parents and one of her sisters had died, her other sister was married to a trooper. Maria herself had served Miss Beatrix von Guldinast in Constance, a member of a patrician family. Then a vagrant woman who dealt in mirrors had knocked on the door. Maria had opened up to her, they had talked, and finally they moved to Augsburg, working together for two years.[195]

Employment opportunities for servants were not highly dependent

---

[192] HStASt, A 209, Bü. 1936, 16 Feb. 1683.
[193] StAKN, K 58, 10 Oct. 1674, Catharina Binue from Lyon; StAF, B 5 III c 4, vol. 1, fos. 448ʳ-450ʳ, 21 Mar. 1586, Catharina Schuhmacher; HStASt, A 309, Bü. 90b, 12 Oct. 1580.
[194] StAKN, K 71, 13 Apr. 1695, Catharina Müller; StAFr, B 5 III c 4, No. 7, vol. 1, fos. 50ᵛ-51ʳ, 4 Sept. 1561; fo. 56ʳ⁻ᵛ, 23 July 1562, Anna Müller.
[195] StAKN, K 65, 10 June 1697.

on status, qualification, and records of good behaviour. An orphan's life was not at all predictable. Her job situation and social relations could work out well. But, even then, the hard truth remained that a maidservant could not save much money. The future of those who did not inherit was deeply insecure. It comes as no surprise, then, that the life stories of such women who became thieves reveal a permanent tension between a search for relationships and the instinct to take something and to leave. Magdalena Rems's story is particularly interesting. Aged 12, she had stolen from a shop-keeper, and used the money to 'gamble with the other boys in the poor house'. She always helped their caretaker, an old woman who walked on sticks. This woman had always 'loved her and given her enough to eat'. Then, Magdalena had stolen money from her benefactor and another caretaker. She stole from her first mistress and other maidservants too: money to buy herself shoes, for example, because she was still barefooted. She served a tanner, and stole some of his deceased mother's clothes. She changed confessions. Magdalena was Catholic, but became 'Lutheran in an inn called *Weißgerberherberg*. The master's daughter had taught her with Luther's Bible. She had a good time; her master and mistress had 'loved her a great deal'. She had friends, too, and danced on feast-days with journeymen butchers and tanners; a journeymen saddler (temporarily) promised to marry her. But again she stole from her mistress, a male servant, a dyer, and a shoemaker.[196] Theft was linked to a knowledge inside that all relationships were unreliable. In the end, it made more sense to survive independently.

THEFT: A SOCIAL THREAT?

This chapter has sought to illustrate the contexts in which common people were confronted with or committed theft. The sources force us to concentrate on those offenders whom the authorities prosecuted. Needless to say, their bias towards marginal groups and the lower classes bore no relation to the social cost of the offences committed by such groups. Even if no more than one Württemberg treasurer had embezzled 20,000 florins and silver ware for 2,000 florins, it would have exceeded the value of what all Württemberg

[196] StAKN, K 56, 22 Aug. 1669.

thieves together got for their stolen goods across two centuries;[197] all the stolen food put together would not have exceeded the amount eaten at the ducal court in a year. Mobile groups were nevertheless depicted as a tremendous threat to society, mainly because they could evade the moral order. Their offences were usually small and satisfied basic needs. Big thefts were rare and achieved through specialization or luck. Most judges realized this when they looked at concrete cases, so that few of them voted for the execution of female thieves.

Thieves were hardly choosy about their victims: those unable to afford proper locks were in greater danger than wealthy people. Therefore theft was certainly a serious threat to most people; even petty theft did real harm in a society close to subsistence. Rising taxes and wars made large parts of the population feel short of possessions anyway. Downward mobility was a permanent threat for most. Aggression was channelled into hatred of robbers and thieves. Common people thus regarded the offences they themselves committed as something entirely different from 'criminal' behaviour.

The image of thieves as threatening others had a clear social function. Florike Egmond has demonstrated that the notion that thieves were marginal, mobile, uprooted, lazy, and immoral in every respect was continually reproduced in trials.[198] Different social and cultural identities among the accused were ignored. Retrospectively, however, we can sometimes rescue them from their anonymity, and put crime in its social context. If the authorities never tired of talking about vain and flighty maidservants, we can reconstruct their economic position and the social meaning of dress. We can see that the theft of food was linked to a longing for conviviality and plenty; that networks of receivers of stolen goods were part of an everyday culture of survival among single women and mothers; while professional thieves' stories tell us about clever tricks and constant alertness, a life without secure property, a search for protection, and a fear of betrayal.

Penal policies and the view that laziness and immorality lay

---

[197] K. Marcus, 'A Question of Corruption: The Case of Martin Nuttel, 1543–44', *German History*, 11 (1992), 127–40; in the 17th cent. Geheimrat Enzlin increased his wealth fivefold during his fifteen years in office and was executed: see W. Grube, *Der Stuttgarter Landtag, 1457–1957: Von den Landständen zum demokratischen Parlament* (Stuttgart, 1957), 276 f.; both Nuttel's and Enzlin's cases were only taken up because they were also involved in political intrigues.   [198] Egmond, *Underworlds*, 192 f.

behind property offences did not change throughout the whole period. More effective prevention was not invested in either. It continued to suffice to hang men in great numbers. Women continued to be banished, prisons remained insecure, guards and controls insufficient, and borders uncontrolled. The only visible measure against the problem was a flood of repetitive ordinances and exemplary trials.[199] Yet ordinances cannot hide the fact that the property crimes of these low orders were of little interest to dukes and magistrates. No one sought out a convincing (i.e. more expensive) solution—like higher almsgiving, better prisons, or more concerted regional crime prevention.[200] The prosecution of offenders was *ad hoc* and socially highly selective; all those who were banished or finally sentenced to death paid a high price, and that sufficed.

[199] M. Dinges, *Stadtarmut in Bordeaux 1525–1675: Alltag, Politik, Mentalitäten* (Bonn, 1988), 322f.   [200] See Ch. 2.

4

Sinful Sexualities

WHILE most people today believe that the law's chief functions are to protect life and property, the early modern state's preoccupation with and criminalization of extramarital sexual behaviour brings out the vast difference between understandings of the law's function then and now. Most western states do not regard consensual premarital sex as harmful to anyone, and do not seek to punish adulterers with imprisonment. Sexuality is defined as a private matter, and is protected as such. In the sixteenth and seventeenth centuries, by contrast, rulers and magistrates increasingly sought to regulate sexual behaviour; public order was equated with a new sexual order which allowed sex only within marriage. This early modern determination to enforce sexual morality was central to Reformation movements. Both Protestant and Catholic towns closed their brothels, prohibited raucous shouting on the streets at night, and outlawed the wild weekend dancing where girls were twirled into the air, their skirts indecently lifted.[1] Even girls' winter gatherings in spinning-bees, where they spun together to economize on wood and light, were controlled or prohibited since when young men joined them improper liaisons might be forged.[2] Marriage was to be promised in the presence of parents or guardians and with their consent to avoid the mismatches and premarital sex which might follow secret promises of marriage. Courtship rituals like nightvisiting were discouraged. Young women had to defend their chastity until marriage.[3]

---

[1] L. Roper, *The Holy Household: Women and Morals in Reformation Augsburg* (Oxford, 1989), ch. 3. The Cologne brothel closed in 1591, see G. Schwerhoff, *Köln im Kreuzverhör: Kriminalität, Herrschaft und Gesellschaft in einer frühneuzeitlichen Stadt* (Bonn, 1991), 373.

[2] H. Medick, 'Village Spinning Bees: Sexual Culture and Free Time among Rural Youths in Early Modern Germany', in id. and D. W. Sabean (eds.), *Interest and Emotion: Essays on the Study of Family and Kinship* (Cambridge, 1984).

[3] S. Burghartz, 'Jungfräulichkeit oder Reinheit? Zur Änderung von Argumentationsmustern vor dem Basler Ehegericht im 16. und 17. Jahrhundert', in R. v. Dülmen (ed.),

Laws and punishments, sermons and tracts, however, only marginally altered real behaviour. By marrying, a couple set up an independent household and soon had to feed children. The wedding date was thus determined by their prosperity: brides and grooms were aged 25 on average when they were legally married,[4] and those who had to earn their portion themselves often had to wait several years longer than that. Not surprisingly, therefore, single men and women in their twenties developed their own love rituals. Men would share the bed of their chosen bride (and often a sibling or maidservant) 'honourably', or 'without any indecencies', as they put it. Except for women considered to be 'lewd', a woman was invariably promised marriage before she was enticed into the first sexual act.[5] An exchange was sealed: the woman gave her virginity, and the man promised to restore her honour by marrying her if she became pregnant.[6] The usual method of contraception was coitus interruptus, but if the woman became pregnant the couple resorted either to abortion or to marriage. If both partners came from the same or neighbouring villages and the families knew each other, consent was likely already to have been expressed informally. Parents exerted pressure on children to avoid risks in the choice of partner or in marrying during economic crisis.[7] But young women were usually careful anyway, and only let a man have sex if he had the same social standing and life-plans as they.[8] The low percentage

Dynamik der Tradition (Frankfurt on Main, 1992); S. Cavallo and S. Cerruti, 'Female Honour and the Social Control of Reproduction in Piedmont between 1600 and 1800', in E. Muir and G. Ruggiero (eds.), *Sex and Gender in Historical Perspective* (Baltimore, 1990).

[4] There was, of course, a great deal of regional and local variation. For a summary of demographic findings see H. Wunder, *'Er ist die Sonn, sie ist der Mond': Frauen in der frühen Neuzeit* (Munich, 1992), 48.

[5] S. Breit, *'Leichtfertigkeit' und ländliche Gesellschaft: Voreheliche Sexualität in der frühen Neuzeit* (Munich, 1991).

[6] R. Beck, 'Illegitimität und voreheliche Sexualität auf dem Land: Unterfinning, 1671–1770', in R. v. Dülmen (ed.), *Kultur der einfachen Leute: Bayerisches Volksleben vom 16. bis 19. Jahrhundert* (Frankfurt on Main, 1983).

[7] Which does not mean that this necessarily became an important area in which Reformation morals were transmitted, as Thomas Robisheaux has argued. Ulrike Gleixner had shown that every relationship was not regarded as an 'isolated moral problem' by villagers, but seen in specific 'besitzständische und familienplannerische Kontexte'; see T. Robisheaux, *Rural Society and the Search for Order in Early Modern Germany* (Cambridge, 1989), 106f., and U. Gleixner, *'Das Mensch' und 'der Kerl': Die Konstruktion von Geschlecht in Unzuchtsverfahren der frühen Neuzeit (1700–1760)* (Frankfurt on Main, 1994), ch. 5.

[8] On the continuity of such behaviour see A. Gestrich, *Traditionelle Jugendkultur und Industrialisierung: Sozialgeschichte der Jugend in einer ländlichen Arbeitergemeinde Württembergs, 1800–1920* (Göttingen, 1986), 52.

of illegitimate children among all first births therefore contrasts with the high percentage of prenuptially conceived children.[9] During the seventeenth century, authorities realized that the enforcement of pre- and extramarital sexual abstinence among common people was difficult, and became disillusioned about the effectiveness of admonishments. True to the proverb that those who did not want to listen had to feel, sentences for premarital sex and fornication, as we shall see, rose dramatically; but this had less influence on sexual behaviour than on young people's attitudes towards authority, since, with the help of their parents, they now frequently had to beg or bargain for mitigation of sentences, and were interrogated about suspicious meetings.

Whereas many urban and rural communities did not regard week-long imprisonment as a proper punishment for pre- and extramarital sex (that is, for sex before marriage and outside an existing marriage), consensus on punishments for fornication (that is, sex between couples who had no intention of marrying) and single mothers was more easily achieved. The courtship practices described above were less safe for women who possessed and expected to inherit little, particularly if they lived far from home and relatives. In regard to such women, men were more likely to break their promise of marriage, because they either hoped for a better match or wanted to move on. The mobility of journeymen, apprentices, maidservants, and day-labourers was fraught with danger. Often the women realized their pregnancy only after they and their lovers had parted. Communities in the south-west were not prepared to carry the burden of what they saw as 'thoughtless' and 'frivolous' behaviour by outsiders. Unwilling to raise bastards on communal alms, they usually banished mother and child, particularly if she had no burgher rights. The response to illegitimate children could be different in other areas; it depended on regional economic structures and inheritance customs, on the mother's possessions, and her integration into a community.[10] In areas with large

---

[9] In three early modern Württemberg villages (Bondorf, Nebringen, and Mötzingen), the percentage of prenuptially conceived children remained stable at around 20%. Even though all three villages were situated at the edge of the pietist Nagoldtal, local religious influences are not discussed by Maisch. For the figures on premarital sex see A. Maisch, *Notdürftiger Unterhalt und gehörige Schranken: Lebensbedingungen und Lebensstile in württembergischen Dörfern der frühen Neuzeit* (Stuttgart, 1992), 295 f., table 5.8.1.a.; on illegitimacy rates see pp. 298 f.

[10] P. Becker, *Leben und Lieben in einem kalten Land: Sexualität im Spannungsfeld von Ökonomie und Demographie. Das Beispiel St. Lambrecht 1600–1850* (Frankfurt on Main, 1990), 273, 312.

farms and a high demand for labour, illegitimate children posed less of a social problem; they constituted a welcome reservoir of family-related and family-dependent workers.[11] The common south-west German socio-economic structure was different, however. Partible inheritance was practised and this made the 'proper' marriage of sons and daughter a matter of importance. Small families, households, landholdings, and workshops, as well as strict guild regulations, were the norm. As we have already seen in the last chapter, illegitimate children and their poor mothers had no place in this world.

The chapter describes in some detail the changes in legislation and legal practice in regard to fornication and premarital sex. Then we look at the economic and social situation of those women who were most likely to be punished for fornication, and examine how women defended 'sexual honour' or appropriated the image of the 'desirous female' to challenge male authority.

LEGISLATION AGAINST 'CRIMES OF FLESH'

The first Württemberg mandate to enforce sentences against 'crimes of the flesh' was passed in 1585. It introduced short prison sentences for couples who had premarital sex and forbade festive wedding celebrations. Fornication was punished with twelve to fourteen days' imprisonment. Most importantly, the mandate denied that a virgin of good reputation might claim that she had been seduced or raped and was innocent. She was to be punished even more severely than a 'disreputable' woman.[12] In 1630 a second mandate signalled the mounting moral panic during the Thirty Years War. It lamented that

---

[11] On the question of whether they were treated as 'bastards' or regular children see the debate between E. Shorter and W. R. Lee in regard to Bavaria: W. R. Lee, 'Bastardy and the Socioeconomic Structure of South Germany', *JIH*, 7 (1977), 403–25; E. Shorter, 'Bastardy in South Germany: A Commentary', *JIH*, 8 (1978), 459–69; W. R. Lee, 'Bastardy in South Germany: A Reply', *JIH*, 8 (1978), 471–6.

[12] A 'common disreputable wench' and her single lover were to be imprisoned for twelve days, and if the offence was repeated, both could be banished. If an unmarried man slept with a virgin of good reputation he had to spend fourteen days in prison and compensate the woman for her lost virginity. She was to be imprisoned for eight days, unless she had provoked the act by behaving in a manner without which intercourse would not have occurred. What constituted such behaviour was a matter of male interpretation: usually the absence of strong physical resistance to sex proved consent, in which case the woman was likewise imprisoned for fourteen days: A. L. Reyscher (ed.), *Vollständige, historisch und kritisch bearbeitete Sammlung der württembergischen Gesetze* (19 vols., Stuttgart and Tübingen, 1828–51), iv. 445–50 'Mandat, die Bestrafung der Fleisches=Verbrechen betreffend', 21 May 1586.

God's anger was dangerously aggravated and the power of daily repentance lessened by sexual misconduct, while confessional enemies crowed over the sinfulness of Protestants. So sentences were dramatically raised.[13]

In 1638, matters got worse upon the arrival in Stuttgart of the pietist Johann Valentin Andreae, a court preacher and consistory councillor famous for being strongly influenced by Genevan moral disciplining. Under his influence, the 1642 mandate primarily addressed magistrates, the clergy, masters, and parents. In accordance with the logic of paternalism it admonished them to prevent disorder by being a model of good behaviour for, and controlling, the lower orders. Parsons were told to deliver warning sermons. Any councillor or judge guilty of fornication had to leave office. Parents were ordered to govern their household better, because God would make them accountable in heaven. Male and female servants had to be kept apart from each other at night. Parents were told not to push their children into premature marriages and to prevent lengthy meetings between lovers.

The mandate thus tried to strengthen preventive measures. At the same time it sought to enforce the prosecution of sexual offenders and immoral masters. Bailiffs were to hold weekly meetings with judges or council-members and to 'inquire eagerly' after any in their district who behaved immodestly. Masters who let servants sleep together could be punished with two to four days' imprisonment. Next, sentences for those who promised each other marriage only after the woman was pregnant were increased. Men had to stay twenty-eight and women sixteen days in prison. If a single person was 'suspiciously visited' by the opposite sex both were to be admonished, imprisoned for six and three days, and again imprisoned and interrogated if the visits continued. In 1645, a final mandate announced that most prison sentences for sexual offences were to be doubled.[14]

---

[13] Premarital sex was punished with fourteen days' imprisonment for men and eight for women. Sentences for fornication rose from two to three weeks' imprisonment for men and from eight to twelve days' for women, see Reyscher, *Gesetze*, v. 408 f, 'General=Rescript, die Bestrafung der Fleisches=Verbrechen betreffend', 8 Dec. 1630. Men were hit hard by this change. They now had to be prepared for long weakening imprisonment, usually during winter when work was short and the cold was unbearable.

[14] Men guilty of fornication had to remain six weeks in prison, women four weeks. Premarital sex was punished with four and two weeks' imprisonment: see Reyscher, *Gesetze*, v. 440, 'General=Rescript, die Strafen der Fleisches=Verbrechen betreffend', 1/11 Nov. 1645.

Over sixty years in Württemberg the punishment for fornication and premarital sex increased by three to four times. No distinction was made between innocently seduced virgins and 'disreputable wenches': every woman was guilty who had given way to temptation. A couple accused of premarital sex was judged according to whether or not they meant to marry before they had sex, or decided to marry only after the woman realized that she was pregnant. Men were sentenced to longer imprisonment than women, suggesting that they were assumed to have a more active role in initiating intercourse, except in regard to spinners, seamstresses, and Swiss maidservants, who were represented as lewd and responsible for most illicit sex or pregnancy. The 1642 mandate commented at great length on the lewdness of *Eigenbrödlerinnen* (women earning their own bread).[15] A 1654 mandate set out that Swiss maidservants, usually daughters of poor cottagers who had emigrated to Württemberg in search of labour, commonly went into service already pregnant, thus burdening Württemberg with illegitimate children. Such 'foreign strumpets' had to be reported immediately when they entered service, or gave birth. Then they would be banished from the country.[16] Together with the 1658 mandate against infanticide, all measures in regard to the policing of illegitimately pregnant women and premarital sex were now in place.[17] A further rise in punishments was hardly thinkable. During the second half of the seventeenth century the supreme council's attention focused more on the prosecution of infanticide—the bloodiest consequence of the new shaming of illicit sexuality.

The Württemberg mandates had followed quickly upon each other from 1630 onwards, and the example of Hall shows how impressive the legislative effort was. In Hall as everywhere, the Thirty Years War had put the 'youth problem' on top of the agenda for moral reforms, even though in practice wartime business dominated the council's concerns.[18]

The first Hall mandate against fornication in 1643 stipulated relatively mildly that single persons were to be punished with ten days'

---

[15] See below, pp. 151–153.
[16] Reyscher, *Gesetze*, vi. 459, 'General=Rescript, die Bestrafung ausländischer Metzen betreffend', 15 Jan. 1654.
[17] Reyscher, *Gesetze*, viii. 320, 'General=Rescript, die Verhütung des Kindsmords betreffend', 1 Mar. 1658.
[18] H. Nordhoff-Behne, *Gerichtsbarkeit und Strafrechtspflege in der Reichsstadt Schwäbisch-Hall seit dem 15. Jahrhundert* (Sigmaringen, 1971), 52–5.

imprisonment.[19] Measures against premarital sex did not follow until 1665, when the council announced that premarital sex was to be punished as severely as fornication.[20] Instead of a church wedding the couple were to be married in the council chamber.[21] In 1671, another mandate set out harsher sentences for those who had decided to marry only when the woman had got pregnant.[22]

Most significantly in Hall, the leisure of domestic servants began to be strongly policed. Parents or masters and mistresses who failed to report illicit intercourse in their households had to pay a ten-florin fine. If domestic servants had merely lain together in one bed they also had to pay a ten-florin fine, and a five-florin fine if they had eaten together.[23] In 1680, domestic servants were forbidden to invite each other for wine,[24] and from 1682 onwards they were punished for staying out after the evening bell had rung.[25]

Sentences were finally increased and further differentiated in 1684: premarital sex was to be punished with ten days' imprisonment *and* a ten-florin fine if the couple was already engaged.[26] A single man who impregnated a virgin or widow and did not want to marry her had to compensate her according to her status and pay for the child.[27] He and the woman had to pay a fourteen-florin fine and remain in prison for fourteen days. Those who were unable to pay a fine had to do public labour. If domestic servants had invited each

---

[19] A woman who had been punished in this way was forbidden to wear a bridal wreath: StAH, 4/499, fos. 43^v–44^r.

[20] That is with ten days' imprisonment for the man and woman.

[21] StAH, 4/499, 8 Mar. 1665, fos. 81^v–84^r.

[22] If the couple had intended to marry anyway, both partners were punished with a fine of ten florins or ten days' imprisonment, while the punishment for those who decided to marry only after the woman became pregnant was increased to fourteen florins or fourteen days' imprisonment.   [23] StAH, 4/499, 13 Oct. 1671, fo. 170^r.

[24] StAH, 4/495, 3 Oct. 1680.

[25] StAH, 4/495, 26 May 1682. Klöpflinsnächte, which were part of courtship customs, had already been prohibited in Hall in 1566, and the law was repeated three times during the second half of the 17th cent.: StAH, 4/495, 22 Nov. 1566. Dances, at which 'turning and throwing' women was prohibited in 1562, were completely forbidden in 1633 and 1677; StAH, 4/492, 1562, 'Dantzordnung'; 4/494, i, 20 May 1630; iii, 10 May 1671, fo. 17^r; 4/495, 1 June 1677. Dancing was also forbidden in Memmingen during the war: in 1639 twenty journeymen and maidservants had to pay respectively two and one florins for dancing: StAMM, RP, 31 Oct. 1638–30 Dec. 1640, 20 Feb. 1639, fo. 39^v. On 26 Aug. 1639, nine men and women were punished.

[26] Those who had decided to marry late were likewise imprisoned for ten days but had to pay an additional fine of fourteen florins.

[27] If he refused to compensate the woman he would be banished.

other for a glass of wine, the male servant had to pay one florin and the maidservant fifteen *Schilling*.[28]

In this last instance the maidservant's smaller wages were taken into account, but in regard to fornication and premarital sex the Hall magistrates assumed that men and women had to be punished equally. Compared to Württemberg, however, Hall sentences remained lower even after the French wars. The rigorous attack against domestic servants' leisure activities and courtship practices in Hall was unparalleled elsewhere.

Fewer ordinances survive for Memmingen and Constance. Memmingen issued a new discipline ordinance during the Thirty Years War, in 1630.[29] Most significantly it stipulated that local and foreign 'strumpets' were to be banished with shaming rituals, because they seduced men. If a woman was illegitimately pregnant but immodest herself, the man had to compensate her with nothing but 'a pair of shoes', presumably to assist her departure into banishment. Most surprisingly, a couple who slept with each other but did not want to marry were banished.[30] If they married, they had to serve a prison sentence and pay a fine.[31] A 1648 church disciplining ordinance additionally stipulated that those punished under the civic disciplining ordinance had to undergo church penance as well. If an offence was repeated a person could be banned from church.[32] Memmingen thus also followed the principle that both partners deserved to be punished equally. A particularly harsh measure was the banishment of men and women who had had intercourse but were unwilling to marry.

Confessional differences in the treatment of sexual sins are only apparent in regard to premarital sex. The Council of Trent had broken with the long-standing tradition of accepting a couple's mutual consent as an act of marriage. This had meant that premarital sex was not sinful as long as the promise of marriage was given and

---

[28] StAH, 4/495, 14 Jan. 1684.

[29] StAMM, 265/2, 26 Nov./ 6 Dec. 1630, fos. 14^r, 17^v. Spinning-bees were prohibited, and thoughtless marriages, into which a couple entered despite the fact they would be unable to feed a family, condemned.

[30] Local offenders could, however, shorten the time of banishment through petitions and be banished into a house in Memmingen: see StAMM, RP, 1 July 1667–11 Aug. 1669, fo. 11^{r-v}, 2 Aug. 1667, Mathes Hornung's petition for his maidservant.

[31] At her wedding, the woman was allowed to wear only a veil, and the couple had to be absolved by the sexton.

[32] T. Wolf, *Reichsstädte in Kriegszeiten: Untersuchungen zur Verfassungs-, Wirtschafts- und Sozialgeschichte von Isny, Lindau, Memmingen und Ravensburg im 17. Jahrhundert* (Memmingen, 1991), 65.

held. After Trent it was seen as an offence. But at least the Constance council rarely punished premarital sex. In 1595, an ordinance criticized pregnant women and widows who celebrated their wedding just as honourable virgins did; pregnant brides now had to be led to church by a midwife on Wednesday mornings at eight o'clock; they were not allowed to wear bridal gowns or celebrate with guests afterwards.[33] The council acted most vehemently against 'thoughtless' marriages, but less in order to campaign against the decline of Christian morals than to prevent a collapse of the alms system. At the end of the 1570s the council stipulated that all those who wanted to marry had to appear before their tax-master and be interrogated about their financial situation. Like contemporary Memmingen mandates, the ordinance reflected the dearth affecting the south of Germany.[34] It stated that too many men had either not learnt a craft and were poor, or were unable to feed a family with their craft. If they married nevertheless, their thoughtlessness caused want and a burden on resources. The interrogation also checked whether or not parents or guardians had given their consent to a marriage; those who planned to marry against their parents' will were banished instantly.[35] Before a couple was finally allowed to marry in Constance they had to promise not to ask for civic alms for five years— otherwise they lost their burgher rights. Foreigners who only received burgher rights by marrying into the community were not allowed to demand alms for ten years.[36] No ordinances are preserved between 1595 and 1674, when under the influence of the French wars the council stipulated that all 'lewd strumpets' who went with soldiers were to be banished relentlessly.[37]

The Supervision of Leisure

The change which affected young people on the whole in most everyday life was the regulation of leisure activities, especially

---

[33] StAKN, A 1/28a, Franz-Bickel-Chronik, 45.

[34] StAKN, D I, F. 202, 4 Nov. 1576, fos. 733ʳ–740ʳ. On Memmingen see P. L. Kintner, 'Die Teuerungen von 1570/2 in Memmingen', *Memminger Geschichtsblätter* (1987/8), 27–76.

[35] *Winkeleben* (i.e. secret marriages) were to be punished even more harshly than they were in Protestant Hall, where they were only rarely reported and offenders had to serve one to four days in prison. In Memmingen they were punished rarely but harshly; this again indicates that confession did not necessarily determine legal policies.

[36] StAKN, D I, F. 204, fos. 41ʳ–45ʳ. The model for this mandate seems to have been an Augsburg one from 1564; see B. Roeck, *Eine Stadt in Krieg und Frieden: Studien zur Geschichte der Reichsstadt Augsburg zwischen Kalenderstreit und Parität* (2 vols., Göttingen, 1989), i. 210, 316f.   [37] StAKN, BI 154, RP 1674, 20 Oct. 1674, fo. 593ʳ.

dances and nocturnal gatherings. Some recognizances describe such offences in detail. In 1578, for example, the daughter of a Hall vine-dresser and her two girlfriends were imprisoned for eight days because they had 'danced and cavorted and sung the whole night through' at the Steinbronn church-ale.[38] In 1608, two citizens' daughters were reprimanded for dancing and staying in a male servant's room overnight,[39] and in 1647 six baker journeymen were whipped because they had stayed out on the streets too late with musicians and 'several girls'.[40] Openly lascivious behaviour, like that of a maidservant from the Upper Palatinate, was deemed even more shocking. She got drunk during the Wolpertshausen church-ale and a Hall baker had 'put a fir-cone between her legs'.[41] Usually young people were admonished or fined for such offences and no description of them is left. Resistance to such fines brought youths before the courts. In 1687 the Hall *Stadtschultheiß* reported that one maidservant had gone to a dance in the salt-works with Wilden-mann's son. When the city-page had ordered her to appear before the magistrates and be fined she had answered 'perhaps the *Stadtschultheiß* only wanted the money; what fine would she have to pay then?'[42]

Protestant and Catholic towns wholly agreed on the need to control young people's leisure. In July 1562, for example, the Constance city-page arrested apprentices who had gathered at night and then gone to Paulsgasse, where 'girls' had similarly gathered, to begin spontaneously dancing with them.[43] In 1632, Agnes Streub, a young spinster, was imprisoned because apprentices entered her parents' home day and night; she confessed that one evening she had drunk with two young men and stayed with them 'in all honour until one or two o'clock in the morning and [they] had been merry and in a good mood, one of them playing a little violin'.[44] Catharina Meussburger, aged 20, held a spinning-bee with two sons and daughters of a baker and two daughters of a dyer, with whom she drank wine until two in the morning. Afterwards she was accused of 'taking in single persons'.[45] In 1669, several boys and girls were fined

[38] StAH, 4/480, 20 Aug. 1578, fo. 58[v], Christina Clausen, Margaretha and Anna, Ulrich Haman's daughters.   [39] StAH, 4/481, 3 Sept. 1608, fo. 68[r].
[40] StAH, 4/482, 12 Jan. 1647, fo. 144[r].
[41] StAH, 4/482, 13 Oct. 1655, fos. 210[v]–211[r], Catharina Kissler.
[42] Adding 'obnoxiously' that she had already danced 'before he had become *Stadtschultheiß*, StAH, 4/553, 11 Jan. 1687, fos. 192[v]–193[r].   [43] StAKN, HIX, F. 32.
[44] StAKN, K 29, 6 May 1632.   [45] StAKN, K 4, 30 Jan. 1686.

for drinking wine at the Petershausen gate.[46] The moral was always
the same: independent meetings between the sexes, lubricated with
wine, could not but lead to fornication.

Immodest Excitements

Harmless meetings thus became tainted with the atmosphere of
possible sexual transgression, and of course more offenders were
found out, too. People were frequently interrogated on the basis of
mere suspicion that they had been lewd. On two pages from the
Memmingen council minutes in January 1668 (as a random example),
the council ordered that two single youths should be interrogated for
'meeting suspiciously', a Kalch-gate furrier was interrogated about
the rumour that he had taken a pregnant spinster to Augsburg, and a
maidservant was interrogated about abortifacients she had taken.[47] In
such matters it was always difficult for authorities to gain sufficient
evidence to prove charges—and most people would in the end
simply be admonished. Usually it needed a woman to become
pregnant to uncover 'crimes of the flesh'. Thus, in areas which
seriously prosecuted pre-marital sex, young local people made up
the largest percentage of the accused. In turn, judges were increasingly pressed by petitioning relatives or employers to mitigate sentences by substituting fines for imprisonment. Authorities lamented
these mitigations, but in Hall, for example, the council continued to
issue 'tax ordinances' which listed fines for sexual offences. Young
local people who had already married or intended to do so were
mostly protected from imprisonment or banishment. Some were
forced to marry, but most intended to do so anyway and got away
with a fine or short imprisonment. In Hall, married women accused
of premarital sex (because they had given birth too soon after the
wedding) were usually not punished at all, since they had to look
after a newborn baby. Few petitions were ever made for foreign
maidservants from outside the community who had had an affair
with a servant or journeyman. They were less likely to be able to
pay a fine and found it more difficult to borrow money. The less
their wealth, the less likely it was that the man who had slept with
them would marry them. This turned the offence into fornication,
which was punished much more severely than premarital sex.[48]

[46] StAKN, RP 1669, BI 149, 72ʳ.
[47] StAMM, RP, 1 July 1667–11 Aug. 1669, fos. 69ʳ⁻ᵛ.
[48] R. Dürr, *Mägde in der Stadt: Das Beispiel Schwäbisch Hall in der frühen Neuzeit*
(Frankfurt on Main, 1995), ch. 6.

Maidservants from outside were thus more often punished with imprisonment, public labour, and banishment than citizens' daughters. Finally, the group most at risk of receiving a shaming punishment and banishment were illegitimately pregnant women suspected of having had sex with more than one man, and women suspected of sleeping with a soldier. In such cases only forceful petitions could avert the sentence of banishment, though less and less so as the seventeenth century wore on.[49] Moreover, women in this situation were likely to live away from home. Possessing little, working as maidservants, spinners, and seamstresses, they were the easy prey of male servants, journeymen, and soldiers, and therefore equally easily suspected of immodesty. Because a relationship with a soldier was, in the authorities' eyes, clearly not aimed at marriage, such women were most frequently sentenced to a shaming punishment and banishment. When illicitly pregnant women tried to get money from the child's father, or demanded compensation for their virginity, men would usually accuse them of having slept with other men, too; and if a woman was unsupported in the community she could do little against the accusation.[50] In that case she received no money, but was additionally charged with promiscuity, and thus more harshly punished. Women belonging to this third group were on the whole most affected by the growing harshness of legal measures during the seventeenth century, they were more often banished, and with an illegitimate child they had less chance of entering towns and service.[51]

The Hall sources most clearly demonstrate the results of strict law enforcement. In 1566–76, for example, only twenty-five women were punished for fornication, of whom fourteen were banished and only one sentenced for premarital sex. In 1681–91, by contrast, 138 women were accused of fornication and thirty-one banished; seventy-six were fined or imprisoned and a further thirty-one imprisoned with

---

[49] See Ch. 3. Bailiffs who were unwilling to take formal procedures might have banished single mothers right away. A striking example is that in 1619 the Backnang junior bailiff passed on the parson's list of illegitimate mothers in the district to the mayor. He commanded the constable to banish them within a month. The Württemberg supreme council learnt about this accidentally and halted the action: HStASt, A 209, Bü. 77, 28 June 1619 and 9 Aug. 1619.

[50] On male strategies see C. Simon, *Untertanenverhalten und obrigkeitliche Moralpolitik: Studien zum Verhältnis zwischen Stadt und Land im ausgehenden 18. Jahrhundert am Beispiel Basel* (Basle, 1981), 105. Transactions about paternity claims preserved in the Tübingen University archive support this; see, for example, UAT, 84/9, 20 Mar. 1654, 269^v–272^r; 84/7, 28 July 1630, 72^v–73^r. [51] See Ch. 2.

public labour. Three women were banished for prostitution, while eleven were imprisoned for premarital sex, five doing public labour. In the years after 1665 the number who were bound over rose most dramatically, largely due to the prosecution of sexual offences. Over 40 per cent of those sentenced 1675–84 were found guilty of sexual offences (including adultery), a total of 276 men and women.[52] Clearly, times had changed. Until the last third of the seventeenth century binding-over had chiefly served to punish quarrelsome men, the politically disobedient, debtors, bad householders, and those who did not pay taxes or war contributions—as if order was assumed to depend chiefly on property, authority, and good citizenship. During the last third of the seventeenth century, however, order came to be much more strongly based on legitimate sexuality and parenthood. This became even more marked during the last years of the century: 167 women were punished for fornication between 1692 and 1700, many of them impregnated by soldiers.[53]

During 1680–1700 the main purpose of *Urfehden* in Freiburg also became the disciplining of 'lewd' women, particularly soldiers' whores. After the French had besieged Freiburg in 1677, seven to eight regiments were based in the town and the French made up half the population.[54] Fears that the original citizens might be further displaced arose when French soldiers fathered children with German or Swiss women.[55] Punishment was hard.[56]

---

[52] Dürr, *Mägde in der Stadt*, 229, table 38.

[53] Only eight women were punished for premarital sex and bound over. The French entered the Hall territory in 1688. High payments averted an occupation. The Swabian Circle put together a permanent army in 1681, and the *Kreistruppe* was based in Unterlimpurg during peace. Soldiers were now part of society, but citizens 'respected them little', writes G. Wunder, *Die Bürger von Hall: Sozialgeschichte einer Reichsstadt 1216–1802* (Sigmaringen, 1980), 161.

[54] M. Reiling, *Bevölkerung und Sozialtopographie Freiburgs im Breisgau im 17. und 18. Jahrhundert: Familien, Gewerbe und sozialer Status* (Freiburg im Breisgau, 1989), 17.

[55] In addition to members of the army or administration a further 358 French citizens had settled in Freiburg, of whom 230 were married or married in Freiburg: see F. Noak, 'Die französische Einwanderung in Freiburg im Breisgau 1677–1698', *VSWG* 23 (1930), 324–41.

[56] In 1695, for example, the council demanded that 'forty pregnant whores' be immediately apprehended and punished: see Noak, 'Einwanderung', 328. The *Urfehden* reveal that church penance had preceded any banishment from Catholic Freiburg for many years, but now shaming punishments and whipping were introduced. Foreign women had to stand in the pillory for at least an hour, then endure ten to thirty lashes, and then they were banished for three to ten years or permanently. Some women had their faces branded or their ears cut off—a retributive attack, here, on seductive, sinful, and treacherous female flesh, StAFr, *Urfehden*, 22 Mar. 1685, Verena Khindert; 21 Mar. 1687.

The French occupation had aggravated the situation in Freiburg. But here as elsewhere the focus on sexual offences and the harsh punishment of 'lewd wenches' and single mothers typified the search for a proper moral order during the second half of the seventeenth century. A quantitative analysis of the sentences passed by the Emden presbyterial court, for example, likewise shows that the punishment of single women for fornication and illegitimate pregnancies had become a main target of moral reform since the mid-seventeenth century.[57] The aim of church disciplining, Heinz Schilling finds, had shockingly changed: 'It was not the development of self-knowledge or repentance and the return of the sinner into the congregation that concerned the elders but rather the need to inflict punishment as a deterrence for others.'[58]

Distance and Mockery

The sarcasm of seventeenth-century Hall city-scribes likewise indicates the increasingly cold reception accorded sexual offenders. Couples accused of premarital sex were invariably mocked in irony or sarcasm. Barbara Korb and her husband were said to have 'looked into each other's eyes so much' before their wedding that she had become pregnant; he had to spend three nights in prison and she paid a four-florin fine.[59] In 1647, an Enßlingen couple were punished because 'they had loved each other too much and he had given her a child through amorousness'.[60] It was said of Anna Ott and Hans Rössler that their 'spooning' had made them love each other so much that her 'apron and skirt became much too short': they had to pay a three-florin fine and marry.[61] Courtship rituals were not trusted either. In 1684, an Oberspeltach maidservant and a male servant drank wine together and then 'during the night, in all honour, as they say, lay in bed together'. The councillors thought it ridiculous that a night could be spent innocently, so the couple were fined four florins and imprisoned for eight days.[62]

Many of these commentaries express the tension between the élite's disgust at the sexual vulgarity of the common people and their own curiosity and voyeurism. A judgement on a maidservant

---

[57] H. Schilling, 'Calvinism and the Making of the Modern Mind: Ecclesiastical Discipline of Public and Private Sin from the Sixteenth to the Nineteenth Century', in id., *Civic Calvinism in Northwestern Germany and the Netherlands: Sixteenth to Nineteenth Centuries* (Ann Arbor, 1991), 62 f.   [58] Ibid. 64.
[59] StAH, 4/481, 30 Oct. 1618, fo. 225ʳ.   [60] StAH, 4/482, 12 May 1647, fo. 147ʳ.
[61] StAH, 4/482, 4 Oct. 1650, fo. 170ʳ.   [62] StAH, 4/484, 23 Oct. 1684, fo. 172ʳ.

and her lover, for example, could include the information that he had not put 'his *rem* in *re*', but that they had 'tried to do it' until he ejaculated.[63] Oral sex was described too. David Klotz from Witzmannsweyler was punished for 'pulling out his *membrum virile*' and 'gliding it over his former maidservant's mouth, saying she should let him pour a rivulet into it'.[64] A month later a Geusslingen woman was sentenced to public labour because she had had a 'fur sheath' made for her husband's '*membrum virile*'.[65] In 1678 a Gründelhart widow was banished for having given young boys 'lessons in how to fornicate so that it would not make a child and other such awful business'.[66]

Unlike the male, the fertile female body exposed sexual sins and had to carry a child as a punishment for them. The mockery which often accompanied discovery spoke for satisfaction that a woman's wrongdoing could seldom be kept secret for long. In 1654, the hangman banished the pregnant Barbara Schmid from Unterlimpurg 'with her full belly' because she had slept with eleven men—including married stocking-knitters and smiths.[67] Some comments echoed the tone of civic broadsheets about peasants' spinning-bee extravaganzas. A 1667 comment on two young peasants, for example, noted that, 'as is now almost common among the peasant folk', they had several times 'gone into the spinning-bees and fallen in love , so that her belly became bigger and she soon had to apply for the midwife'. After a fine and a spell of imprisonment the couple were married in the council chamber.[68] A maidservant from Westheim accused of sex with several men had to wear a placard with the words 'shameful whore' around her neck while in the pillory before she was banished from the country to the sound of clanging on a metal basin.[69] 'Lewd shameful whore' a placard said in 1688; and 'whore's procuress', said that of a Hall labourer's wife in 1689 who had to stand before the fool's house with a shaming instrument round her neck.[70] The worst mockery was reserved for those who were poor and had entered hopeless affairs. In 1664, Catharina Näberin, a Kirchberg councillor's maidservant, was accused of having sex with a Hall journeyman cooper and letting him 'play with her underskirt'.

[63] StAH, 4/485, 19 Feb. 1686, fo. 2[r].
[64] StAH, 4/485, 16 Jan. 1686, fo. 1[r]; a similar example 4/485, 8 Aug. 1698.
[65] StAH, 4/485, 15 Mar. 1686, fo. 3[r].   [66] StAH, 4/484, 14 May 1678, fo. 68[r].
[67] StAH, 4/482, 18 Feb. 1654, fo. 195[r].   [68] StAH, 4/483, 16 Aug. 1667, fo. 37[r].
[69] StAH, 4/485, 6 Aug. 1687, fo. 21[r].
[70] StAH, 4/485, 21 Jan. 1688, fo. 26[v]; 7 July 1689, fo. 43[v].

Although this had not done her 'any harm', she wanted him to marry her, but he had refused. The council decided to banish her 'because the wench does not own much'.[71] Councillors thought that such women would use sexual intercourse or a pregnancy to make men marry them and change their subordinate status as a maidservant to that of a wife.

In conclusion, it is clear that it was difficult in most towns and districts to implement tough sentences against sexual offences; nevertheless, the atmosphere had changed. There was a new rigour in responses to illicit sexuality. In Hall punishments for premarital sex preoccupied the court during the last third of the century. Fornication by working women came to be seen as an attack on hierarchies of rank. Poor maidservants and *Eigenbrödlerinnen* were least protected from accusations and most easily suspected of lewd behaviour. Pregnant single women were regularly mocked with shaming punishments and banished. The following section examines the experiences of women who were likely to be suspected of lewdness, their social background and way of life.

SEXUAL HONOUR

The former Memmingen city-scribe's investigation into the rumour that his daughter, Madlena Meurer, had given birth to an illegitimate child has already demonstrated how any family's honour depended on the sexual behaviour of its womenfolk.[72] Madlena's status prevented her from having to answer accusations in the street, but for many other women the streets of early modern towns were the battleground where they defended their own or questioned other women's sexual honour. Historians have repeatedly stressed that by accusing each other of illicit sexual relationships women themselves actively defended norms of female sexual purity.[73] Such conflicts, however, need to be linked to two issues. First, female nature was culturally construed as being immoderate, weak, and unstable. Since, therefore, female modesty and respectability depended on a

---

[71] StAH, 4/483, 17 Jan. 1664, fo. 1ʳ.   [72] See Ch. 1.
[73] J. Farr, 'The Pure and Disciplined Body: Hierarchy, Morality, and Symbolism in France during the Catholic Reformation', *JIH* 21 (1991), 391–414; G. Cattelona, 'Control and Collaboration: The Role of Women in Regulating Female Sexual Behaviour in Early Modern Marseille', *French Historical Studies*, 18 (1993), 13–35; C. Lipp, 'Ledige Mütter, "Huren" und "Lumpenhunde": Sexualmoral und Ehrenhändel im Arbeitermilieu des 19. Jahrhunderts', in U. Jeggle et al. (eds.), *Tübinger Beiträge zur Volkskunde* (Tübingen, 1986).

woman's victory over these depraved instincts, respectable women
had to draw clear boundaries between themselves and 'truly' dishonourable women. Slander cases, in short, expressed ordinary
women's struggle for a stable social identity as honourable.[74] Secondly, especially among married women, the accusation 'whore'
served to question not only a woman's moral behaviour in general
but also her family's status which was based on the honourable
conduct of all members.[75]

Respectable people were therefore preferred targets of rumours
about illicit relationships, and the authorities took these attacks very
seriously.[76] In 1670, for example, Dr Alexander Hiltenprandt of Constance told his advocate to accuse the maidservant Afra Sauter of
insulting his aunt, who oversaw his household. Her companion, also
a maidservant, had greeted the aunt respectfully, calling her a *Jung-
frau*. But Afra had said, 'well, she is a fine virgin! If she was one, she
would come to weddings with her headdress'—instead of avoiding
weddings and hiding herself in Überlingen. The binding (or otherwise) of the hair, the nature of headdresses, and the wearing (or
otherwise) of the virgin's wreath were visible symbols of a woman's
sexual status.[77] Afra did not limit herself to allusive accusations. She
told other women while they were washing that Hiltenprandt's aunt
had an illegitimate child. And for this attack on a woman who was
protected by her wealthy and respected nephew she had to pay a
high price: she was banished with her children from Constance.[78]

Women who were most at risk of being accused of fornication or
whoredom were those with least power to defend themselves. Since
brothels had been abolished, any prostitution serving apprentices,
students, artisans, and others had to take place in private homes.
Anxious citizens and authorities had difficulties in establishing who
was a 'whore', who was fornicating, and who it was that merely
enjoyed the company of single men. Single women, widows, and
wives with absent husbands were most likely to be suspected and
accused.[79] In 1599, for example, a report on a Constance girl said that

---

[74] L. Gowing, *Domestic Dangers: Women, Words, and Sex in Early Modern London* (Oxford, 1996), ch. 3.   [75] See Ch. 6.

[76] In addition to the example of the Memmingen city-scribe see: StAH, 4/554, 24 Jan. 1688, fos. 44[r], 51[r], 61[r], the daughter of the deceased Praecept Seyboldt; 7 Feb. 1688, fo. 68[v], the city-page's widow; StABh, 01, 14 May 1599, the parson's daughter.

[77] French women would tear the headdresses off those they accused of whoring; one insult among south-west German women was that the targeted woman was a *Schappellhure*—a whore hidden under a headdress.

[78] StAKN, RP, BI 150, 12 July 1670, fo. 436[r].   [79] Roper, *Holy Household*, 130.

her father had not been in hospital for a fortnight before she started 'running around in men's clothes during carnival: she had often been like that since Christmas'; while a locksmith from Meersburg who was not a guild member slept at her mother's home. Both women were said to work so little that people wondered suspiciously how they fed themselves.[80] The consequence of such accusations was not just imprisonment. When in 1667 a daughter and her mother were said to be visited by 'clerics and secular persons', the girl was ordered to go into service immediately and her mother was struck off the alms register for three months.[81]

Because they could not marry, Catholic clerics and students were two groups traditionally suspected of a taste for illicit sex, but soldiers outnumbered them by far. Mere acquaintance with a soldier could cast a shadow on a woman's reputation. The fact that soldiers had become a perpetual feature of everyday life was not acknowledged. They lived or ate in normal people's homes, visited inns and feasts, and were present in markets and streets. Their widows and wives were part of the population, too, and inevitably mediated contacts with soldiers. One evening in June 1692, for example, a Swiss seamstress was sent to a soldier to borrow money from him. They talked until four o'clock in the morning. Then she returned to her mistress, herself a soldier's wife. By eight o'clock in the morning the council's servant had imprisoned her. She swore that nothing indecent had happened and said defiantly that 'if no other whore-thing had been committed in Constance than what she had been doing with the soldier, than there was no whore in Constance'.[82] But since a quartered soldier's night-life could hardly be controlled, only the worst was to be feared, especially if the girl was a Swiss seamstress.

Accusations of illicit sexual relationships were often vague, and not surprisingly they often misfired. In 1697, a Constance needle-maker who lived with her mother and brother was suspected of fornication because she often visited her neighbour. It turned out that she merely borrowed tools from him and was engaged to a man in Überlingen; but now she feared that the shame of the accusation might cost her her marriage.[83] A similar accusation hit Maria Conrad in Memmingen in 1626. Deserted by her husband, presumably

---

[80] StAKN, HIX, F. 42, 16 Feb. 1599, Rosina Schuller.
[81] StAKN, RP 1667, BI 147, 12 May 1667, fos. 257ʳ, 267ʳ; 23 Aug. 1667, fo. 469ʳ, Christina Ebenmann.   [82] StAKN, K 66, 6 June 1692, Maria Goblerin.
[83] StAKN, K 5, 14 May 1697, Anna Briel.

because he had many debts, her occupation was to soak yarn for weavers. It was said that many apprentices went in and out of her house and that she led a shameful life, though her neighbours could not verify this. Maria had told one of them that 'she could not feed herself anymore, however much she worked and scratched'; and she had to take in laundry. The secret of the visiting men was quickly unveiled; a next-door neighbour said that apprentices brought their laundry to her and fetched it again. Schifferlin's apprentice had only visited so frequently to see the maidservant who rented a room at Maria's; she had been 'no good' and had left Memmingen with him. This mistaken accusation had cost Maria Conrad a day in prison and a binding-over.[84]

Women who Earned their own Bread

In view of such anxieties the dilemma was that the number of masterless women grew as a result of the high male mortality of the Thirty Years war, and also, in the long run, because of economic stagnation. The responses to this were stronger restrictions on young men and on women's chances of acquiring citizen's rights to become part of a guild, or to marry.[85] The term *Eigenbrödlerin* was applied to single women who worked independently, renting their own rooms or living at their temporary employers', but almost always highly mobile. It was assumed that their independence of male control could only lead to spending on luxurious clothes, sexual lasciviousness, and the seduction of youths.[86] In proto-industrial regions, wool-spinners worked in spinning-bees day and night, mixing with local girls at night, and on Friday night men would join them.[87] This created particular anxiety about the influence of independent women on those who had to obey parents and masters. Württemberg laws first mentioned *Eigenbrödlerinnen* in a 1642 mandate. It was influenced by the pietist Valentin Andreae, who was likely to be particularly aware of such women through his previous superintendence in Calw, a district with a strong proto-industrial textile economy. During the 1630s Andreae estimated that at least

---

[84] StAMM, 144/1, 8 Aug. 1626.
[85] S. Ogilvie, *State Corporatism and Proto-industry: The Württemberg Black Forest 1586–1797* (Cambridge, 1997), chs. 3, 8, 12.
[86] On the importance of a male householder's control see HStASt, A 206, Bü. 3865a, Catharina Weylandt.
[87] See T. Meier, *Handwerk, Hauswerk, Heimarbeit: Nicht-agrarische Tätigkeiten und Erwerbsformen in einem traditionellen Ackerbaugebiet des 18. Jahrhunderts (Züricher Unterland)* (Zurich, 1986), 376.

1,200 women spinners worked in the vicinity of Calw alone.[88] The 1642 mandate cautioned that any meetings between the sexes were likely to end in illicit sex, but that the danger was higher in spinning-bees, thanks to the *Eigenbrödlerinnen*, who do not go into the light and service, or want to work, but are lazy, garrulous, and generally lewd, hiding in corners now and then, going seldom to church and public sermons, and attaching young innocent hearts to themselves and seducing them.

Moreover, *Eigenbrödlerinnen* were described as expert procuresses, and therefore all spinning-bees which took place in their rooms were prohibited.[89] Tracts about domestic servants explained that single women chose independent labour simply because they wanted individual and sexual freedom. The Hamburg parson Johann Balthasar Schupp prophesied in 1658 that if a mistress often lectures her maidservant she 'goes away rents her own little room becomes a washer-woman or seamstress the seamstress becomes a whore a whore becomes a wet-nurse'.[90]

But the truth was different. Sixteenth-century women were excluded from textile trade guilds and therefore pushed into independent and insecure labour. Spinning remained a proletarianized work no man wanted to do. Towns highly involved in textile trades needed great quantities of spun yarn and thus attracted spinners. Though artisans did not accept the women in guilds, they nevertheless wanted to control their wages and work. In 1577 Augsburg weavers were among the first to protest that they could not find enough spinners to do contract labour for them: women who came from outside the city worked independently and rented a room or lived with a family. In 1582, all non-citizens were thus forbidden to live and work independently. By 1597 the situation had not changed. The weavers complained that the *Eigenbrödlerinnen* said they would not be so stupid as to work as spinning-maids if they could earn three times as much by working independently. And because *Eigenbrödlerinnen* could determine their own work-hours, they walked about with apprentices, setting a bad example for country girls and citizens' daughters.

[88] Cited in G. Benecke, *Germany in the Thirty Years War* (London, 1978), 37.

[89] Reyscher, *Gesetze*, v. 426, 'General=Rescript, die Bestrafung der Gottes=Lästerung und der Fleisches=Verbrechen betreffend', 29 July 1642.

[90] Cited in Dürr, *Mägde in der Stadt*, 89.

Harsher ordinances duly ensued. Women from outside, along with Augsburg citizens, were forbidden to head an independent household. Women who demanded higher wages from their employers were to be banished.[91] In Lindau, in 1626, thirty to forty independent seamstresses were accused by tailors, who argued predictably that 'they alone were qualified to work as tailors by virtue of apprenticeship, journeymanship, marriage, and the performance of public duties'. The seamstresses were useful because they made house-calls, embroidered silk, and worked on low wages; but everyone agreed that they 'subverted authority by fostering pride, masterlessness, and concealment'.[92] Sheilagh Ogilvie has shown how *Eigenbrödlerinnen* in seventeenth-century Wildberg were even searched out from house to house and threatened with banishment.[93] Spinners were forced to work permanently for a master.[94] Valentin Andreae described the Calw master craftsmen as the 'stomach' on whom the whole district depended—while women spinners were a subordinate 'member' of this body politic and could be treated accordingly. He emphasized how his flock was 'second to none in praising God, in obedience to the authorities and willingness to help'. Even in the 'anarchic times' of the Thirty Years War, Andreae proudly related, sins, 'which occur all the more readily . . . and go unpunished more than is usually the case, we publicly castigate'.[95] This observance endured. In the nearby proto-industrial town of Wildberg premarital sex and fornication were both firmly punished by the church consistory introduced early in 1645. By the end of the century the names of illegitimate children were entered into the parish register upside down; just as if they would now turn the moral world itself upside down.[96]

---

[91] M. Wiesner, *Working Women in Renaissance Germany* (New Brunswick, NJ, 1986), 176 f.

[92] 'Hoffarth, Meisterlosigkeit, und Schlupfwinkhell', see J. C. Wolfart, 'Political Culture and Religion in Lindau, 1520–1628', (Ph.D. thesis, Cambridge, 1993), 334 f.

[93] S. C. Ogilvie, 'Women and Proto-industrialisation in a Corporate Society: Württemberg Woollen Weaving, 1590–1760', in W. R. Lee and P. Hudson (eds.), *Women's Work and the Family Economy in Historical Perspective* (Manchester, 1990), 86–92.

[94] Ibid. Spinners were subjected to special quality controls, their houses searched and illicit reels destroyed, for the Calw *Zeughandelscompagnie* was Württemberg's mercantile showpiece, producing only fine cloth and therefore depending, as one 1656 mandate noted, 'only on proper, good, soft thread': Reyscher, *Gesetze*, xiii. 296 f., 'Rescript, das Schneller=Spinnen betreffend', 2 June 1656.

[95] Cited in Benecke, *Germany in the Thirty Years War*, 38 f.

[96] Ogilvie, 'Women and Proto-industrialisation', 92.

The Spinner

It thus comes as no surprise that if a dead baby was found, which was not uncommon, single women were again the chief suspects. In 1608, a Memmingen silk-spinner was suspected of killing an illegitimate child, and her case very well illustrates courtship customs and common people's views of premarital relationships. The baby had been discovered when Hans Spindelin's privy was cleaned for the second time in sixty years. His household and the three neighbouring households of a widow, a tailor, and a bookbinder were interrogated. Spindelin's maidservant swore that 'she usually sat in her room and never involved herself with anything'. Spindelin's apprentice from Constance had been there only for a short while and knew nothing. Three bookbinder apprentices also claimed to know nothing. A neighbouring tailor gave longer evidence and reported that he had last employed a maidservant six years earlier. His apprentice had moved back to Biberach recently. He had often been visited by a silk-spinner who had brought her distaff and was still in service. The tailor did not think that she had had an illegitimate child with his former apprentice. The tailor's wife also remembered the silk-spinner who had come into their house, and two other silk-spinners who had become pregnant: one of them had moved away with a tailor apprentice, the other had been impregnated by a weaver. Their new apprentice had not told his master that 'he went after a woman'. The tailor explained the affair differently: Spindelin always opened his privy to peasant folk on market days, and they paid him with 'pears and berries'. He had always worried that 'one of them might have something on her, which the inhabitants of the house would have to suffer from'.

The tailor further reported that the bookbinder always employed three or four apprentices, and new ones whom nobody knew; but nothing bad could be said about them or his maidservants. The bookbinder's wife often went outdoors to sermons, weddings, baptisms, or visited women friends, staying up late with them. She and they stayed up late at night in that house, but this would be because of their business or because she was spinning with other women.

The widow was interrogated next. She had employed three maidservants over the past years, all citizens' daughters. The present maidservant knew 'several [women] who had become pregnant, but she guessed that they had taken their pregnant bellies and children away with them'. However, she remembered how a maid-servant almost five years ago had planned to hold a *Rayhen* (round dance), singing a song below a single woman's window which denied her the right to marry wearing a virgin's wreath. Nobody remembered the name of this presumably unchaste woman. Indeed, the knowledge of the fourteen witnesses was now exhausted: the only sign of a love-affair had been the frequent visits made between the silk-spinner and tailor apprentice. But no one suspected them of having had intercourse. Rather, Spindelin's open house was per-ceived as a dangerous invitation to strange, mobile women, who could have easily thrown a baby down the privy.[97]

Such depositions enable us to envisage this tiny Memmingen street with its busy bookbinding workshop, with its smaller tailor's workshop with only one single apprentice who would tell his master about a woman on his mind, with the citizens' daughters who would not leave their service until they had found the right husband in Memmingen, and likewise with the bookbinders' apprentices from cities on the trade routes from Memmingen, to which they would return and get married, and with its fear of peasants and mobile folk as carriers of filth and infection. Only the three silk-spinners did not fit well into this harmonious picture: they came from outside, but no one remembered from where. Two of them were pregnant, one had moved away, the other presumably waited to be paid by the weaver. No one could order them to do this or that: the third silk-spinner had also gone where she liked at night, admittedly with her distaff, to ensure that people thought that she and the apprentice merely worked together. Even though it was understood that this had been a 'love-affair', no suspicion developed, because no *visible* sign of immodesty was noticed.[98]

The Seamstress

However, suspicion grew as soon as a masterless woman received visits by men in her own chamber. This is clearly demonstrated by the case of Maria Meyer, which happened in Memmingen forty years later. Maria was a seamstress. The Memmingen council had stipulated in 1616 that independent seamstresses had to be citizens and had to work as apprentices for one year and as assistants for another; more-over they had to pay an annual fee to the tailors' guild.[99] Mobile

---

[97] StAMM, 135/8, 5 Feb. 1608; 8 Feb. 1608.   [98] See Ch. 1.
[99] Wiesner, *Working Women*, 178 f.

women from outside were thus excluded, and the guild's control strengthened. The fact that they were citizens made the seamstresses attractive as marriage partners for apprentices from outside the town. In 1648 Maria had been working for a number of years and rented a room in a house owned by a tailor's widow. This widow had two sons and rented two further rooms to carpenter apprentices—one from Salzburg and the other from the Emsland. Both these last worked independently in the building trade as *Eigenbrödler*, of whom there were many in Memmingen.[100] By the sixteenth century guilds had made it difficult for strangers like these to obtain membership, preferring sons of local masters and apprentices who married masters' daughters and widows.[101] During times of war, however, qualified labour was needed to rebuild houses: Memmingen lost two thirds of its own population.[102] *Eigenbrödler* were independent of a master's authority and were not tied to an apprentice wage; they could move when they wished and plan their return to any woman they fancied. They dreamed of being masters, and for this they had to be married. If they impregnated a virgin before marriage, their dream was in ruins.[103] So apprentices whose fathers did not have their own workshops courted women with citizens' rights and defended female chastity. The Salzburg journeyman therefore made a point of visiting Maria at 'honourable times'. But a tailor apprentice was bolder. He slept in Maria's room for two nights. When he visited her a third time the journeyman 'beat him out of the house' and ignored Maria from then on. But he remained jealous when the Emsland apprentice now started to visit Maria, urging their landlady to 'remove the whore from the house'. The landlady Barbara Schaup did not want to send Maria away, however—perhaps because of wartime conditions. She herself had caught the Emsland apprentice in bed with Maria, and he confessed that he 'desired and loved the seamstress'. Schaup reported that she saw Maria sitting astride him in bed, the lewdest of positions for a woman. 'Pfui! what a loose life you are leading', she had cried to Maria. When she found them in bed again, the situation exploded. Maria accused Schaup of betraying her by reporting her to the authorities; Schaup said she was a lewd whore and a worse character

---

[100] They were told to pay a weekly fee.

[101] H. Bräuer, *Gesellen im sächsischen Zunfthandwerk des 15. und 16. Jahrhunderts* (Weimar, 1989), 65.

[102] But the town was full of people: 4,700 refugees were counted in 1646, among them *c*.1,100 adult men, see W. Unhold, *Geschichte der Stadt Memmingen* (Memmingen, 1929), 243–8. [103] Bräuer, *Gesellen*, 65 n. 280.

than Maria's banished brother. The accusations against which Maria defended herself before the council revealed her landlady's envy and mistrust. There was no doubt that Maria's freedom was the main problem. In Maria the landlady saw a woman independent in her work and sexuality even if the price she paid was abortion. She had finally accused Maria of lying more often with apprentices than she had lain with her own husband by whom she had borne six children. Maria asked whether she thought she had aborted that many children. Yes, Schaup answered: there was no secret about the fact that 'she knew how to do it'.[104] Four months later, in November 1648, the people of Memmingen celebrated the Peace of Westphalia in one big joyous feast, 'as if it was Easter'.[105] How would Maria's life have changed by then?

The Desirous Woman

Cases such as this show again and again that in the last instance a woman was deemed responsible for any immodesty. If she did not live as 'withdrawn' as the maidservant in our previous case history of the silk-spinner or if she did not keep to her room, abstaining from talk and gaiety, she opened a door to immorality. The proverb that 'without whores, there would be no bad boys' ascribed to women the power to seduce men and represented them as impure. Conversely the male's position was infantilized, and he was represented as an irresponsible boy who could not resist pleasure.

The following story gives us a strong sense of how 'lewd women' were a force of disorder which had to be exiled, because they exposed men's inability to discipline lust, repudiate passion, and be loyal to their families. They were not only represented but indeed experienced as a threat to social stability. In 1653, a widowed woman called Anna Ruoder claimed that the former mayor of Hausen had slept with her but received no punishment, whereas she had been imprisoned for four weeks. Moreover, he made sure that she and her four small children were expelled from the village. In order to belittle his offence he had accused her of fornication with a *Rittmeister's* servant. The mayor was backed by the junior bailiff, who reported that the widow's mother had already been a whore and married a Catholic after banishment to the Palatinate. Her daughter

---

[104] StAMM, 145/5, 9 June 1648; 15 June 1648.
[105] J. Peters (ed.), *Ein Söldnerleben im Dreißigjährigen Krieg: Eine Quelle zur Sozialgeschichte* (Berlin, 1993), 187.

had no burgher rights, was lazy, and went begging. If she were allowed to return to Hausen someone might try to take her life or push her out. He argued that the mayor would never have sinned had she not lived in the village. The mayor even wanted to leave Hausen in case she returned. Villagers agreed: Anna Ruoder should go elsewhere.[106] For a real man the way out of the dilemma was not to succumb to female desire but to stand up to it without losing his head. But how difficult this could be was what the ducal cellar-master's son had to learn in 1666. He had accepted his friend's invitation to stay with his family over Christmas (his father was the Kirchheim administrator). On Pepperday, 28 December, single men threw things at young women until they liberated themselves by giving the men a kiss, or gifts of nuts, bacon, and liquor.[107] Some men, like the administrator's son, procured themselves the services of a maidservant. First he had slept with his father's maidservant Anna, on the *Lotterbett*, a couch near the oven. Then he had handed her over to the cellar-master's son. Between ten at night and three in the morning he had sex with her five times before telling her to go away, since 'she would be sated now'. But she had responded that 'this was not so, and that much more—mentioning a large number—would be needed'. Later she had become pregnant, but not by him, Anna thought, but by her master, notorious for his abuse of maidservants. She assumed that the cellar-master's son had not put semen in her: 'he had done it just as her master had, when he reassured her that he would be unloading before the barn', that is, was using coitus interruptus. If Anna had refused to go, it was because she was sexually unsatisfied. The cellar-master's son confessed that he always withdrew in time and that her discontent led her to talk 'shamelessly' about him in the morning.[108] He had obviously wanted to avoid having a paternity claim forced onto him by a lewd maidservant. But now that she had told everyone that he had not satisfied her, he felt dishonoured. The image of the insatiable woman thus reflected men's anxiety that they did not satisfy a woman by coitus interruptus and were vulnerable to her continuing demand for gratification. The threat was either to see one's masculinity questioned in this way, or to lose sexual freedom through the birth of a baby.

[106] HStASt, A 209, Bü. 588, Anna Maria Ruoder, widow of Weilandt Friedrich Ruoder.
[107] R. Kopf, 'Mitteilungen über volkstümliche Überlieferungen in Württemberg: Festbräuche', *Württembergisches Jahrbuch*, 2 (1906), 45–65, esp. 52.
[108] HStASt, A 209, Bü. 1345, 7 Feb. 1666, Anna Maria Vischer.

It is perfectly possible that most women were content if a man did not 'harm' them by impregnating them, but 'unloaded before the barn'. But cases like this demonstrate how men replicated the process of taming nature with the female body. A good woman was sexually domesticated and obeyed her father's or husband's will: her wild nature was pacified. Laws against sexual offences underpinned the attempt to ensure female chastity before marriage and faithful motherhood during marriage. Women who did not live under firm male control or focus their attention on one man only embodied wild and exciting desire. Projected onto them were the parts of human nature which could not be controlled by rationality. This threatened the stability of an imagined identity based on self-interested and independent decision-making. Women who were thought lewd and 'untamed' thus attracted male sexual heroics and aggression. Escapades were followed by the realization that rational control had been lost, the border between the self and the other blurred. A sense of humiliation ensued, the fearful memory that virility could lead to dependence and destruction. 'Lewd' women could thus challenge a paternal understanding of power by showing that a superior male rationality and respectability were a construct underpinning a false hierarchy between the sexes.

In the early modern period, the destructive force of desire revealed itself not least in the use of love-magic. Women particularly used magic in order to tie a man to themselves completely.[109] Love-magic was believed to be so strong that in 1667 Christina Kehrer could make a man poison his fiancée at a church-ale. He was a shepherd's son, and 19-year-old Christina had desired him for four years. He thought she had bewitched him with a glass of red wine so that 'he could only love her'. The murder cost him his life.[110] In Besigheim in 1656, a Bohemian maidservant wanted her master to marry her. A mason's wife in Steinheim advised her about love-magic, and told her: swallow nutmeg, shit it out, clean it, and give it the master to eat; or: give him one of her pubic hairs to eat; or: take a special root, bury it in a local wood, dig it out, and touch his back

---

[109] G. Ruggiero, *Binding Passions: Tales of Magic, Marriage, and Power at the End of the Renaissance* (New York, 1993); M. O'Neil, 'Magical Healing, Love Magic and the Inquisition in Late Sixteenth-Century Modena', in S. Haliczer (ed.), *Inquisition and Society in Early Modern Europe* (London, 1987); M. H. Sanchez Ortega, 'Sorcery and Eroticism in Love Magic', in M. E. Perry and A. J. Cruz (eds.), *Cultural Encounters: The Impact of the Inquisition in Spain and the New World* (Los Angeles, 1991).

[110] HStASt, A 209, Bü. 1725, 1 Aug. 1667.

with it twice; or: take his semen and give it to him in wine.[111] The body was part of all these recipes; hair, digestion, and fluids were used or the man's body touched. We know very little about the spread of knowledge about love-magic, especially in Protestant areas. But the sources clearly show that for people using love-magic, passion meant belonging to someone with body and soul, to be tied together as strongly as possible, and foremost: to destroy the chosen partner's reason. For the man, who had to be in possession of reason, it was, in short, a nightmare. This is revealed by the case of a Böblingen councillor's daughter, Rosina Pfeissinger. When husbands were away on business, their wives usually asked a younger woman friend to stay with them at night. Rosina thus kept Maria Möhrlin company several times. A vine-dresser, Leonhard, who was the son of the former mayor, joined them. Rosina and Leonhard talked dangerously about how to bind others to oneself or to destroy them, about desire and revenge for repudiation. He told her that if one broke off an oak shoot and put it into the earth in the name of the Holy Trinity, the one in whose name this was done would die. Rosina replied that a Tübingen maidservant had told her that if a woman gave a man three drops of her menstrual blood he would also die. Rosina listened carefully to other women. She also said to Leonhard that the daughter of a Böblinger judge had told her that 'a woman never liked it better than, pardon me, when it was done standing'. Leonhard felt pressed to ask whether she wanted to try it that way:

and then he had stood before her and had started such things as caused semen to run down his thighs. Rosina, unable to restrain herself, said, come here, Leonhardtle, we shall go upstairs and have some love with it; but young Leonhardt the vine-dresser was unable to move or let go of her, because he had feared she would later ridicule him, as indeed she did.

Sweating profusely, he finally entered Rosina and broke her hymen. When Maria Möhrlin saw the blood on Rosina's dress she said, 'girl, how bold you are! Are you not worried you will be with child? Take your example from the butcher's daughter.' But Rosina answered that if she became pregnant she would not keep it secret, but would marry at once, even if she were to be disinherited.[112] When they

[111] StABh, 06, 29 Mar. 1656, Ursula Brothsäckhin.
[112] HSASt, A 309, Bü. 163, 4 Apr. 1664; Bü. 164, 25 May 1664.

were accused of fornication the vine-dresser's father came before court with 'tears in his eyes': they had not been promised to each other. Rosina was herself supposed to marry a 'good, hard-working young man in the clothmaking trade'. But she tempted with passion, admired transgressiveness, and passed judgement on virility. Controlled masculinity was thrown out of balance, and with it the man's capacity to tame nature by reason.

SUSPECTS OF SIN

In the early modern period, the fantasy of the desirous woman thus constituted a threat for two reasons. She challenged an order founded on parentally approved marriages of social equals ready to form their own households. Moreover she tempted men into sin, which questioned their self-control and thus the legitimacy of male dominance over women. This, of course, was intolerable, and thus one function of the law was to exclude those women from society who took up the role of the desirous female. There were few of them anyway: 'respectable' women tried to distance themselves from a female nature embodying excess and moral inferiority. Only this enabled them to claim equality with men.

Increasingly those who lived outside the household order were feared as masterless and thus desirous. They were the anti-image of 'chaste daughters', who were kept in the parental home until their wedding, or went into service in their home town, or were sent away to relatives. This marginalization process affected highly mobile maidservants, but even more strongly *Eigenbrödlerinnen*, whose labour power was particularly needed by the expanding textiles production. We know very little about the conditions of their work. But while in genre paintings sewing and spinning became a favourite topos to depict mother's and daughter's quiet, domestic diligence, the work of these professional seamstresses and spinners was never related to any virtues, no matter how much their fingers would bleed and their eyes sting. Laws against fornication generally grew harsher during the seventeenth century. Those who were suspected most easily and punished most relentlessly for 'crimes of the flesh' were precisely those mobile women: maidservants and *Eigenbrödlerinnen*. They were also the prime suspects for an even graver crime: infanticide.

5

Infanticide

WOMEN who had an illicit sexual relationship found themselves in a miserable situation if they became pregnant and the man would not marry them. Orphanages were rare, and child abandonment was illegal.[1] Those who committed infanticide regarded that as the only way of defending their dignity, marriage chances, and material safety. Most were quite poor maidservants, *Eigenbrödlerinnen*, or impoverished day-labourers, though some were daughters in better-off households who had become pregnant too early or got involved with the wrong man; others were already married and tried to extinguish the trace of an extramarital affair. 'Child-murderesses', as they were called, were aged 25 on average, and had hoped for a marriage when they had agreed to sex with a man of similar age and rank.[2] When this man refused to accept the responsibility of father-hood, or was too poor to support a child, or could no longer be traced, the task of surviving with an illegitimate child could easily seem unmanageable.[3] For the woman, being pregnant therefore

---

[1] A. Obermaier, 'Findel- und Waisenkinder: Zur Geschichte der Sozialfürsorge in der Reichsstadt Augsburg', *Zeitschrift des historischen Vereins für Schwaben*, 83 (1990), 113–28.

[2] For Württemberg cases preserved in the *Strafakten der Oberämter* there are the following broad groups: thirty-eight women were maidservants, thirteen citizens' daughters living at home, twelve day-labourers and seamstresses, thirteen married or widowed; twenty-four men were servants, fifteen soldiers, eleven citizens' sons, six apprentices, nine married men. C. Zimmermann provides a detailed study of infanticide cases in several Württemberg districts (Altenstieg—Calw): '"Behörigs Orthen angezeigt": Kindsmörderinnen in der ländlichen Gesellschaft Württembergs, 1581–1792', *MedGG* 10 (1991), 67–102. For a highly differentiated analysis of the social background of women who committed infanticide see O. Ulbricht, *Kindsmord und Aufklärung in Deutschland* (Munich, 1990).

[3] In some cases the partner stayed and forced the woman to kill the child, as did a miller's servant in 1692, who told Anna Schuof to 'kill the child, otherwise he would do it and kill her as well'. A castle servant said to Sophia Pulka that 'if it was a boy, he wanted him to be alive, but if it was a girl she should give him the bastard and it would have to die', HStASt, A 209, Bü. 109; UAT, 84/26, 1673. Frequently it was the mutual mobility of both partners which made women carry the cost of 'uncertain unions'. Eva Rohrer's case is typical of a young woman whose life was highly

confronted her with the memory of a relationship she could not or did not trust in. Furthermore, an illegitimately pregnant maidservant or labourer usually had to quit her service, was banished from her place of residence, and had to go begging while her child was small. As we have seen, a strong sense of *social* shame was attached to being illegitimately pregnant. Not surprisingly, some women decided to hide their pregnancy. Once their belly attracted attention they would change their place of service. Even so, people at the new place would usually become suspicious and warn the woman not to kill the child and risk her own life. Typically, the woman would then vehemently deny her pregnancy, only to experience loneliness and despair in turn. About a quarter of all women suspected of infanticide tried to terminate the pregnancy.[4] It was largely for this reason that babies were often stillborn; in most cases, however, they were born alive and then killed. Women who were suspected of infanticide generally reconstructed their memory of the birth in the following way. They said that the birth had happened suddenly and that the baby had fallen onto the floor. The baby had either been born dead, or the umbilical cord had been broken through the fall; the child had bled to death because they did not know that it had to be bandaged. Few confessed immediately that they had not cared for the child, but suffocated or wounded it. After its death the baby was often wrapped in cloth, hidden, and sometimes buried. Bloodstains, a corpse, a smaller belly, or other signs led to detection. If there was proof that the child had been born healthy its mother was usually beheaded. If a natural stillbirth seemed to have taken place, or if the murder could not be proven, she would be banished from the territory for life. Most women tried to maintain that they had delivered a stillborn child. Trials were mainly aimed to test the truth of this statement by interrogation and torture.

If we look back at the development of the prosecution of infanticide it is clear that late medieval infanticide seldom came before the

mobile. Her innkeeper parents had died during the Thirty Years War, and she had grown up at her sister's house, but had been sent into service with an Esslingen innkeeper when she was aged 10. Three years later she worked at a Stuttgart inn, then served a shoemaker, worked as a day-labourer at the harvest, and went back into service with an innkeeper. The child's father was someone she had met while working in Esslingen, HStASt, A 209, Bü. 318, 1649.

[4] This was an important reason why, in their case, stillbirths occurred more frequently; see my article 'The Public Body: Policing Abortion in Early Modern Germany', in L. Abrams and E. Harvey (eds.), *Gender Relations in German History: Power, Agency and Experience from the Sixteenth to the Twentieth Century* (London, 1996).

courts.[5] Prosecutions then increased during the first half of the sixteenth century, but generous mitigations of punishment were still common. Only when the authorities began to systematize their legal policy during the second half of the century were harsh exemplary punishments such as drowning or burying alive abandoned; but so was mercy for those who had killed a living child. Infanticide had become a totally unforgivable crime, and women were almost certain to be beheaded for having killed a living child. Places like Nuremberg and Württemberg, which intensified their prosecution of infanticide during the seventeenth century and in turn convicted more offenders, reintroduced harsher punishments to increase the deterrent effect of executions.[6] Some women were tortured with hot pliers before being beheaded; others had their heads stuck on a post afterwards.

Although it was God's command that a murderer with blood on his hands had to atone with his own blood, it is striking that retribution for infanticide was much more likely than it was for unpremeditated manslaughter, which typically resulted from everyday male violence. Executions for manslaughter were rare;[7] for infanticide they were common. The meanings ascribed to killing were thus culturally constructed and variable. The fact that the killing of a living child was increasingly treated as an unforgivable crime expresses how much motherly aggression now went against the construction of good motherhood as a natural and stable female characteristic. The prosecution of infanticide thus served to naturalize motherly love, and it sought to draw clear boundaries between the civilized and the unnatural: women were expected to protect and raise their offspring regardless of how useful they were to themselves.

This call for the protection of each child stood of course in stark contrast to the stigmatization of single mothers and their 'whoreish

[5] H. Bode, 'Die Kindstötung und ihre Bestrafung im Nürnberg des Mittelalters', *Archiv für Strafrecht und Strafprozess*, 61 (1914), 430–81; A. Felber, *Unzucht und Kindsmord in der Rechtsprechung der freien Reichsstadt Nördlingen vom 15. bis 18. Jahrhundert* (Bonn, 1961), esp. 95 f.

[6] R. v. Dülmen, *Frauen vor Gericht: Kindsmord in der frühen Neuzeit* (Frankfurt on Main, 1991), 25 f.

[7] In Memmingen between 1551 and 1689 there were only two criminal trials for homicide as a single offence. One Ravensburg man was sentenced to the galleys in 1566, and in 1627 a Memmingen citizen was beheaded, but he had already been quarrelsome and threatening to others: StAMM, A 44 c, e. In Constance not a single citizen was executed for murder or homicide between 1570 and 1700, see *Adreßkalender für die Stadt Konstanz auf das Jahr 1852* (Constance, 1852), 7–12.

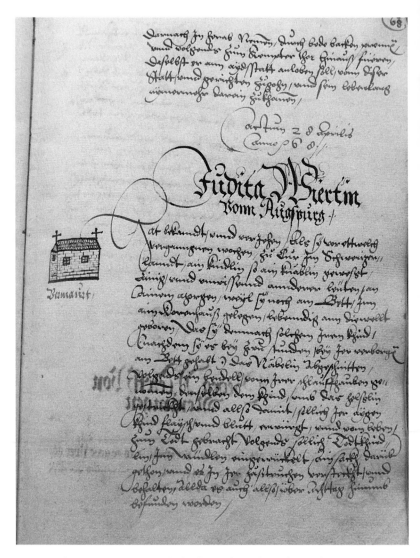

FIG. 9. Judita Wiertin is accused of infanticide and condemned to imprisonment for life

children'. Theologically it was difficult to represent them as a sign of God's blessing on a relationship between man and woman. On the contrary, they were taken to be God's punishment for lewd women despising the state of marriage. As Tübingen lawyers put it in 1689, one Magdalena Kropp should have known that 'fornication creates an innocent witness, who usually publicly accuses his frivolous parents before the world and causes them great shame about the misdeeds they have carried out in darkness'.[8] Such revealing commentaries were rarely made. For they showed unwillingly that it was paradoxical to expect a woman's motherly love for a socially despised and stigmatized child. Women who had committed infanticide could thus only serve as a foil to talk about ideals of motherhood if the conditions of their pregnancy were excluded from the discussion. After a discussion of the different meanings of manslaughter and infanticide in early modern culture, the chapter will thus look at the lives of women who committed infanticide, and examine popular responses to their punishment.

THE CULTURAL MEANING OF MURDER: MANSLAUGHTER AND INFANTICIDE

Early modern killings were almost always committed by men. Murder was a planned killing, manslaughter an unpremeditated killing resulting from self-defence, carelessness, or uncontrollable emotions. Murder was usually associated with robbery; when committed by social outsiders it was relentlessly punished by execution. Manslaughter however, typically followed a fight in the streets or a quarrel in an inn among citizens, peasants, or apprentices. This was more lightly punished. Offenders had to compensate the family of the deceased financially, pray for his soul, and repent.[9] Pilgrimages and masses were common means of repentance in Catholic areas; church prayers and the erection of stone crosses to commemorate the victim were characteristic of Protestant areas.[10] Like church penance, these rituals served to purify an

---

[8] HStASt, A 209, Bü. 701, 12 Apr. 1698.
[9] R. His, *Das Strafrecht des deutschen Mittelalters* (Weimar, 1935), ii. 296–341. For Swabia see H. Jänichen, 'Schwäbische Totschlagssühnen im 15. und 16. Jahrhundert', *ZfWLG* 19 (1960), 128–40. Interesting examples can be found in G. A. Stenzel (ed.), *Samuel Benjamin Kloses Darstellung der inneren Verhältnisse der Stadt Breslau vom Jahre 1458 bis zum Jahr 1526* (Breslau, 1847), 104–10.
[10] B. Losch, *Sühne und Gedenken in Baden-Württemberg: Ein Inventar* (Stuttgart, 1981).

offender. He was temporarily excluded from the community whose laws he had transgressed; then followed reconciliation with God and the family, until finally he was reintegrated in both the religious and the secular community. Composition could be arranged informally between the offender's and the victim's families. But during the sixteenth century, secular authorities insisted that agreements between families had to be controlled by judges. Moreover, they demanded some form of public punishment for the offender, such as temporary banishment into his home or from the town, usually for one year. Punishment, however, continued to be mitigated to a remarkable extent during the sixteenth and seventeenth centuries. Families could easily ensure that an offender was spared a criminal trial.

There was thus a great deal of tolerance when the aggression was between two (usually male) adults. Manslaughter was mainly interpreted as an unhappy change of fate. The social consequences of harsh punishment were considered, and it was understood that an execution or lifelong banishment might satisfy the victim's family's quest for revenge, but not their financial needs, while the offender's family would lose their means of existence, or a dear son, too. Material compensation seemed a more sensible solution. Its extent depended on the offender's and victim's wealth, but the minimum extent which would be demanded was likely to make such payments impossible for poorer citizens. Compensation thus protected honourable citizens from the consequences of uncontrolled violence. Even when those who had committed manslaughter claimed to be truly repentant, we should not overlook the fact that negotiations about the value of financial compensations could become a form of bargaining about the value of a person's life.

The Dead Seamstress

This is demonstrated by a 1698 Memmingen compensation contract.[11] It is particularly interesting because the victim was an innocent Swiss seamstress. The story was a sad one. One Sunday in April the son of a butcher, Georg Kleiber, aged 19, went to serve the period of his watch. Since his father's gun was not functioning, he borrowed the gun of the neighbouring cooper, who had told him that it was loaded. He removed gunpowder from the fuse cap to render it safe. After Georg had finished the watch, he returned to the

[11] StAMM, A 147/9, 6 May 1698.

cooper's house, where the cooper's wife sat with three Swiss sisters, presumably employed as seamstresses. The cooper's wife teased the lad about his manhood, doubting his ability to shoot a bird from afar. Georg pointed the gun at the cooper's wife and declared that he would shoot her. She warned him to be careful; he allegedly replied that the gun was safe. Then he pointed the gun at one of the Swiss sisters, Barbara Baldaussin, pulled the trigger, the gunpowder exploded, and she died within minutes. According to the later contract, he shouted 'Oh Jesus, what have I done!', and ran away, until neighbours caught him and took him to the hospital, where he remained. This representation of the scene was meant to demonstrate his innocence. Detaining him in the hospital set him apart from society without making him a criminal.

At the start of the negotiations for compensation, the surviving sisters claimed that Barbara's work had helped to maintain their old mother in the Tyrol. Informed that the offender was worth 400 florins, they demanded 200 florins compensation. Kleiber's father replied that Georg had not inherited more than seventy-five florins from his mother, and that all he could eventually inherit from him would be divided by so many children that his share would never amount to 400 florins. He emphasized that the act had not been premeditated, and that the cooper had led Georg to believe that the gun had been rendered safe. Kleiber had obviously sought legal advice and argued that Saxon law would require only the payment of a fine of fifteen florins (*halbes Wehrgeld*). He offered a compromise payment of thirty florins (*ganzes Wehrgeld*). The Swiss sisters insisted on 100 florins. Finally the hospital master mediated the compromise sum of sixty florins plus the funeral expenses. The butcher's son paid cash, and Barbara's family freed him of any further responsibility and guilt for the crime.

In such a case, then, the value of a life was determined by class and, possibly, gender.[12] A single seamstress without a significant dowry and with a poor, widowed mother at home was not worth much. The extinction of her life was equated only with a material loss—the ending of her support for the mother. The contract described Barbara's death as quiet. It mentioned neither the blood

---

[12] More research on this subject is needed; but class certainly mattered more than gender. In 1602, for example, a butcher's wife had to pay 100 florins as compensation to a baker's wife's family, even though the latter had died of a heart attack during a quarrel and the butcher's wife was clearly innocent: StAMM, A 135/5, 8 Jan., 11 Jan., 15 Jan. 1602.

nor the pain, nor her family's sadness and bereavement. It devoted little space to Barbara herself, and much to the offender's confused state. It was as if he had simply been unlucky; his plight provoked pity. The contrast with infanticide cases could not have been greater. The latter ignored the question of a child's 'social value', and emphasized that a God-given child had been lost. They described the details of the murder and the condition of the corpse, and they condemned violence against a helpless victim. Such a representation stimulated feelings of revenge against the offender. Even though Barbara had died young and wholly innocent, and had had no means to defend herself, her person was marginalized in ensuing negotiations. In the case of newborn babies, however, it was precisely their innocence which turned the killing into a grave offence. Finally and decisively, the murder of kin weighed heavy; the destruction of a family from inside was a highly threatening image in a society dependent on strong kinship ties.[13] The intensified prosecution of infanticide expressed the concern to naturalize the concept of limitless motherly love. Executing 'murdering mothers' generated the strongest possible statement about women's natural duty to protect their children from death, to love them, and to raise them regardless of the poverty, shame, and suffering they caused their mothers. The value of peaceful citizenship was not similarly endorsed. To understand this concern with motherhood we have to explore the fears aroused by infanticide more fully.

MOTHERHOOD

Swiss, aged 27, and apparently suffering from dropsy, Elisabetha Eggenmann in 1688 had been taken to the Constance hospital by her master. There one night a blind woman was angry that Elisabetha occupied the privy for too long. The woman told Elisabetha not to leave anything dirty behind which might infect her. Her nagging brought Elisabetha out in a hurry. In the privy, the blind woman felt some matter wrapped in a handkerchief. She thought it was a 'flux', or menstrual blood. When she brought it out, other women saw that it was a child's head. Except for the head and limbs,

---

[13] The broadsheet literature was obsessed with the theme of kinship-murder and the destruction of households; see J. Wiltenburg, *Disorderly Women and Female Power in the Street Literature of Early Modern England and Germany* (Charlottesville, Va., 1992), ch. 9.

the baby's body was found inside the privy. When the judges later asked Elisabetha whether she knew the reason for her conviction, she replied: 'She knew it, sadly enough, because she had carved it up like this.'[14]

Secret births often took place in what was called the 'secret chamber'. This equation of the child with excrement intensified the horror of the crime. Dismemberment, however, was rare. More commonly, a child was carried out of the house instead of being received by the civilized institutions of household, family, and friends. It would be killed or its corpse decomposed by animals and natural elements. In 1683, for example, a day-labourer took her baby to the forest, where it died unprotected and was later ferreted out by a dog.[15] Another woman, in Stuttgart, confessed that she had left her child in the woods. When it could not be found it was assumed that it had been consumed by foxes and wolves.[16] Thrown into water, infant corpses were quickly decomposed by fish and insects. In 1680, a piper found a rotted child hanging on a willow branch near a mill. 'Many fish and midges' covered the corpse.[17] In 1699, Esslingen men looked for floating timber at the Neckar and found a maidservant's baby instead. They immediately buried it in the ground, for it already 'smelt badly and was full of mites'.[18] Some babies were drowned like kittens in a bucket. Anna Maria Hamberger's mother did this with the baby of her daughter, who had afterwards kept it in a box for a year, allegedly to protect it from insects. It had 'finally, through God's fair justice, . . . been found in a cellar', though 'completely dried out'.[19] The manual treatment of a baby like an animal was deeply disturbing, too. In 1683, the Hall maidservant Margaretha Lebenzin, impregnated by a Glücksstadt apprentice, was reported to have 'picked up' her little boy 'from the ground like a dog at his throat'. The lawyer recommended that 'she should be pulled once or twice with pliers, so that she should cry before her life ended, just like her poor child'.[20] To prevent a child's crying, its throat was often twisted, like a chicken's. The suffocated and stabbed little corpses were usually wrapped and hidden. They

---

[14] StAKN, K 64, 9 July 1688.
[15] HStASt, A 209, Bü. 2003, 27 Nov. 1683, Johanna Lurger.
[16] HStASt, A 210, Abt. III, Bü. 28, 5 May 1683, Agnes Fried.
[17] It turned out that a Neckarembs maidservant had thrown the baby into the Neckar: HStASt, A 209, Bü. 2058, 12 Oct. 1680, Catharina Kluppert.
[18] HStASt, A 210, Abt. II, Bü. 125, 22 Feb. 1699, Maria Dorothea Sauer.
[19] HStASt, A 209, Bü. 1690, 1673.   [20] StAH, K 11, F. 44.

were rarely buried. This, too, not only subverted the laws of Christianity but of civilization: only animals did not bury each other. In these cases the border between bestial and human behaviour was blurred. Infanticide was therefore stigmatized as an extreme, a thoroughly 'unnatural' act. All beings created by God, theologians and lawyers agreed, were unable to kill their offspring. A 1678 legal accusation stated that God had 'planted into human nature' a mother's instinct not only to nurture her offspring but also to 'conserve' it even at the cost of her own life, if necessary. Not only Christians behaved like this, he believed, but barbaric and pagan people—even animals, who did not possess reason.[21] While Ursula Fugger still subjected one of her maidservants to several exorcisms in the 1570s because she claimed that the devil had induced her to commit infanticide,[22] the overwhelming majority of Protestant and Catholic lawyers refused to believe that the devil could defeat true motherly love. Motherliness was naturalized as a feeling dissociated from culture, religion, social status, and everyday love and violence. Similar comments were made in the 1652 verdict to execute Margaretha Weiß. She had thrown her unbaptized child onto the street at night, where it had been exposed to 'wolves, pigs, or dogs'. The famous Tübingen lawyer Harprecht was convinced that even 'barbaric Persians' despised infanticide. Likewise, no one had ever heard of an 'Indian maidservant' who had killed her child, 'for even in utmost poverty they love their children more than all the treasures of the world'. The baby's blood had disgraced the country, and Harprecht concluded practicably that only the offender's blood could expunge the disgrace.[23]

The Ambiguous Body

But the problem ran deeper. Once again the female body was the site of contradictory images. On the one hand, it was 'God's workshop' for the development of a natural child. On the other hand, instead of a child, strange growths could develop inside it. Female physiological processes therefore partly belonged to a nature which was created by God and served mankind, but they were also part of a nature which manifested itself unforeseeably, inexplicably, and

---

[21] HStASt, A 309, Bü. 14, Angelika Tilhausen.
[22] M. Schad, *Die Frauen des Hauses Fugger von der Lilie (15.–17. Jahrhundert): Augsburg—Ortenburg—Trient* (Tübingen, 1989), 52 f.; L. Roper, *Oedipus and the Devil: Witchcraft, Sexuality and Religion in Early Modern Europe* (London, 1994), ch. 8.
[23] HStASt, A 209, Bü. 587, 27 Oct. 1657.

destructively. Only by investigating such perceptions can we see the threatening realities which doctors, lawyers, and theologians tried to defy.

As we have already seen, the difference between animals and humans could be blurred by the analogous treatments of their bodies. Abortion, for example, could be induced with the same potions as were given to sick animals. In 1691 a seamstress declared that she needed a 'purgative like a horse',[24] and one man and an 'experienced surgeon' judged in 1667 that they would use the concoction a woman had taken to expel a filly from a mare.[25] It was commonly said that a woman had to be 'milked' at her breasts in order to prove that she was pregnant;[26] a midwife pulled 'a glass of milk' from a woman's breast as if it were an udder.[27] The female production of milk had been described as a link between humans and animals since Aristotle; female genitals were often described as animal-like as well.[28] Analogies between newborn babies and cats also came to people's minds: in 1627 a midwife reported that the child of a Constance maidservant looked like a dead cat.[29]

Whereas these comparisons might have seemed normal, the transgression of the sexual barriers between humans and animals was more deeply unsettling. A Württemberg parson's maidservant, for example, declared in 1583 that she had been impregnated by his dog, whereupon he had to pay for her lost virginity.[30] Male sodomy was a capital crime eagerly prosecuted in Württemberg. It exposed the horrifying desire mainly of unmarried men in rural occupations to copulate with cows and other animals. Women, however, were believed to be even able to nurture animals or monsters in their own body and give birth to them. When an English maidservant gave birth to a wild cat in 1569, she gave several explanations, but no one doubted the birth.[31] A Schleswig-Holstein woman likewise said that she had been delivered of a cat instead of a child.[32] When, in 1715, a woman in the south-west German village of Onstmettingen pretended that she had given birth to eight frogs, the Balingen doctor

[24] StAKN, K 4, 28 July 1691, Elisabetha Löffler.
[25] HStASt, A 209, Bü. 1923, 22 July, 30 Aug. 1667, Margaretha Schmollinger.
[26] G. Radbruch (ed.), *Die Peinliche Gerichtsordnung Kaiser Karls V. von 1532 (Carolina)* (4th edn. Stuttgart, 1991 edn.), 48.   [27] HStASt, A 210, Abt. II, Bü. 28, Agnes Fried.
[28] L. Schiebinger, *Nature's Body: Gender in the Making of Modern Science* (Boston, 1993), 55.   [29] StAKN, HIX, F. 46, 17 Sept. 1627, Anna Schander.
[30] HStASt, A 209, Bü. 352, Margaretha Abt.
[31] D. Cressy, 'De la fiction dans les archives? ou le monstre de 1569', *Annales ESC* 48 (1993), 1309–29.   [32] Ulbricht, *Kindsmord in Deutschland*, 156.

seriously inspected the frogs, and the pharmacists put them in brandy.[33] A clearly defined biological border between animals and human beings did not exist. All the more urgent, as well as difficult, then, the task of stabilizing the image of a distinct, superior human nature.

The ambiguities of female bodily processes were brought out particularly clearly by infanticide cases. Many women argued that they had not recognized the signs of pregnancy, but thought that they were suffering from dropsy, a 'flux', stuck blood, 'heart-blood', a 'growth', the 'wandering of the mother', or even flatulence.[34] The notion that a mother might ignore or misinterpret the signs of pregnancy was terrifying—'against nature and the common way of the world', as a legal reference put it in 1649.[35] This comment implied that the beginning of human life could be objectively defined, by the woman's instinct as it were. The contrary was the case, we must now see.

DIAGNOSING A PREGANCY

Let us return to the case of Elisabetha Eggenmann, who 'carved up' her child in that Constance hospital. According to her testimony, the birth had come as a complete surprise to her. She had believed herself ill, not pregnant. Illness had started while she had been working for the Constance merchant Salier. A 'growth' had 'overcome' her; her stomach and feet had swollen; and strong headaches troubled her. Her belly had not been very big, but it had sometimes felt 'as if a sponge had blown up' and contracted again. She was uncertain whether a child or the uterus had moved in her belly, and therefore sent a urine sample to the former executioner, Master Däubler. Like many of his profession, Däubler was a healer, an ability which had long been ascribed to executioners because of their first-hand knowledge of human anatomy. The council had prohibited Däubler from prescribing medicine, but people still consulted him for diagnoses.

Until Däubler's results came, Elisabetha told herself that missing her period could not mean that she was pregnant, even though she had been having an affair with an officer for the past year. She had

---

[33] Rublack, 'The Public Body', 69–74.
[34] HStASt, A 209, Bü. 2093, 19 Feb. 1694, Judith Zeller.
[35] HStASt, A 209, Bü. 1909, 1649, Sabina Caskarten.

missed it during previous illnesses. Besides, some women 'had a man for two, three, or more years without becoming pregnant'.

Coitus interruptus and anticipatus were common practice in premarital sexual relations, women telling courts vividly how the semen was ejaculated outside their body or how men ejaculated early.[36] Däubler's diagnosis confirmed Elisabetha's expectations. He told her sister that Elisabetha suffered from dropsy and that her 'stomach was full of mucus which had to be expelled'. She drank a powder soaked in (stolen) wine. It helped little and so she searched for other recipes against dropsy. One woman recommended berries, which Elisabetha soaked in wine too. Only the merchant Salier and his wife thought that this woman's illness was suspicious; her 'whole body' was swollen and she could only work at the spinning wheel. The mistress urged Elisabetha to 'give birth to the child properly' in case she was pregnant. But they remained uncertain about her condition. Finally, Elisabetha consulted the civic doctor. He tested her urine twice and prescribed a 'purgative drink' and then pills for her headache. After this she awoke at night, her stomach aching painfully. She soon gave birth to the child, and in a state of shock tried to push it down the privy.[37]

Elisabetha's interpretation of her pain had been reinforced by specialists. A missed period was typically seen as symptom of a checked flow of blood inside the female body out of which growths might develop. Numerous herbal mixtures were used to 'restore the flow'. Even a combination of symptoms, for example a missed period and a hard, swollen belly, could be interpreted as an impeded blood-flow. The criminalization of 'hidden pregnancies' therefore tried to impose a unified meaning upon a deeply ambiguous situation, in which subjective interpretation could apprehend a physical change as either the beginning of human life or a growth which had to be expelled from the body.[38]

[36] One Constance seamstress had not thought she was pregnant, because the man who had harassed her 'had done the thing, but without entering her body, leaving the semen between her legs before he had come to the place'; StAKN, K 4, 28 July 1691, Elisabetha Löffler. [37] StAKN, K 64, 1688.
[38] B. Duden, *Geschichte unter der Haut: Ein Eisenacher Arzt und seine Patientinnen um 1730* (Stuttgart, 1987), esp. 183–5, and ead., 'Die "Geheimnisse der Schwangeren" und das Öffentlichkeitsinteresse der Medizin: Zur sozialen Bedeutung der Kindsregung', in K. Hausen and H. Wunder (eds.), *Frauengeschichte/Geschlechtergeschichte* (Frankfurt on Main, 1992); M. Lorenz, ' "... als ob ihr ein Stein aus dem Leibe kollerte ..." ': Schwangerschaftswahrnehmungen und Geburtserfahrungen von Frauen im 18. Jahrhundert', in R. v. Dülmen (ed.), *Körper-Geschichten* (Frankfurt on Main, 1996).

The legal dilemma, however, remained, because even though most women who committed infanticide eventually realized that they were pregnant, their public denial of their state could not be refuted by biological evidence. Of course there were outwardly physical signs which people usually took as sufficient proof of pregnancy. These were loss of appetite, a craving for particular foods, missed menstruation, and, later, milk in the breasts, a swollen belly, swollen feet, and immobility which led to a reduced work ability. Social knowledge signified, too. Whereas married women (who led a normal married life) were hardly ever suspected of hiding a pregnancy, people were suspicious of single women, especially if they were said to have had an affair. People around such a woman therefore often firmly believed in her pregnancy and foresaw the danger of her committing infanticide.

But the ambiguity of all these signs made early convictions rare. The *Carolina*, for example, cautioned judges that milk in a woman's breasts could not prove pregnancy because 'several doctors say that for many natural reasons a woman who has not carried a child can sometimes have milk'.[39] The mother of a Stuttgart woman convicted of infanticide in 1699 argued that her daughter had 'been sucked by spirits in such a manner that she had given milk from her youth onwards'.[40] One midwife who extracted a whole glass of milk out of the breasts of a 20-year-old woman of good reputation could not decide whether she was pregnant either. The fact that she found her heart was swollen, too, suggested a different diagnosis.[41] Foetal movements were never officially tested, even though women were privately sensitive to them.[42] A midwife and the women assisting her would mainly test how hard and big a belly was. But a fat belly could, of course, be nothing more than a sign of corpulence. In 1674 the sworn women of Stuttgart were unable to decide about a maid-servant's pregnancy because she was a 'big, corpulent person'.[43] Maria Sauer defended herself by saying that she had 'always dressed in front of her parents', who had never suspected her of being pregnant. She had believed she suffered from a *Brand*—a feeling to do with dried and clogged-up blood.[44] In 1689, Magdalena Kopp

[39] Radbruch (ed.), *Peinliche Gerichtsordnung*, 48.
[40] HStASt, A 210, Abt. II, Bü. 125, 22 Feb. 1699.
[41] HStASt, A 210, Abt. II, Bü. 28, Agnes Fried, 5 May 1683.
[42] HStASt, A 209, Bü. 1634, 8 May 1655, Walburga Raiser, whose lover put his hands on her body and felt 'the living fruit lying under her heart'.
[43] HStASt, A 210, Abt. I, Bü. 447, 2 Mar. 1674, Anna Catharina Mann.
[44] HStASt, A 210, Abt. I, Bü. 125, 24 Apr. 1699.

likewise told people that her belly 'was burning badly', and later
assured the judges that she had not tied her belly and always dressed
and undressed in front of her parents.[45] A belly could be hard for
many reasons. One midwife wanted to swear that Catharina Kluppert was pregnant, but she maintained that her belly was always
hard and swollen when she missed her period.[46] Maria Vischer told a
woman that whenever she did not get her period, her belly was 'thin
in the morning, and thick and heavy in the evening'.[47] Barbara
Schönmann in Hall always felt that her body was voluminous and
defended herself by saying that 'she had simply been full and round,
and so she had not thought anything other than that she was fat'. She
believed that she had had her period between one and three times
during the past months, though 'not really properly'. But this had
happened before, and she attributed it to drinking cider. Other
women explained that they had missed their period after eating a
'grain soup' or wild dancing.[48] Menstruation could follow seasonal
rhythms; it was often assumed that if it stopped during winter it
would return in spring or summer.[49]

Bloody sheets were expected to appear regularly on clothes-
lines, but if a woman was not known to have had an affair, she
could convince people close to her that she had only missed her
period temporarily and had to take purging remedies to free her
blood. In 1680, a mother in Erdmannshausen near Marbach therefore denied that her daughter Barbara had kept her pregnancy
secret and claimed that she was as 'innocent as a child in its
mother's womb'. She had worried whether everything was
'clogged up' in Barbara's belly and whether she might have to
'die from it, like Kappen's daughter'. Barbara had not had her
period for four years. After the mayor's son had raped her, Barbara's belly had become big, but her breasts remained small. The
mayor's wife had touched her belly, but did not think she was
pregnant. So Barbara and her mother had gathered purgative herbs
in the forest, but after having taken them Barbara suddenly gave
birth to a child, and it soon died.[50] When in 1698 a maidservant in

[45] HStASt, A 209, Bü. 701, 12 Feb. 1689.
[46] HStASt, A 209, Bü. 2058, 12 Oct. 1680.   [47] StAH, K 11, F. 39.
[48] HStASt, A 209, Bü. 1690, 1673, Anna Maria Hamberger.
[49] HStASt, A 210, Abt. II, Bü. 128, 28 Jan. 1700, Maria Magdalena Fröhlich; A 209, Bü.
1024, 29 Feb. 1688, Christina Sophia Class.
[50] HStASt, A 209, Bü. 1559, Barbara Kleinknecht.

Upfingen missed her period, some women advised her to consult 'the man in Langenesslingen' for purgatives.[51] Healers, however, only rarely prescribed remedies to terminate pregnancies.[52] They were sceptical about single women's requests for purgatives, and would ask them why they had missed their periods and either tell them not to take purgatives if they thought they might be pregnant, or deny treatment altogether.[53] Licensed healers were cautious not to risk their living by inducing an abortion. One female Constance healer thus gave purgatives to a lying-in woman, so that she would resume her periods. She also gave them to a married woman, who assured her that she had not given birth to children for some time. But she refused to give them to a single woman, who was taken to the civic doctor instead.[54] Doctors had no better means of diagnosing a pregnancy, but they were protected from accusations of deliberately furthering terminations. In the case of a Memmingen woman in 1622, a female healer obtained the advice of the two city doctors. They agreed that their patient was not pregnant but suffered from 'an impure womb'. Unexpectedly she gave birth eight weeks later.[55] Such examples underline the point that people were usually suspicious if a single woman said she missed her period and wanted to restore it, but were either convinced by her subjective interpretation of her physical condition or unable to disprove it.

Things were different if a woman confessed to having had intercourse. In response to such a confession, the Hall midwife asked Barbara Schönmann indignantly: 'how can it be that a woman lies with a man all night and does not know whether she is likely to be pregnant or not?'[56] In regard to Swiss maidservants and spinning women who were reputably lewd anyway, mere suspicion sufficed for some women to form their judgements. Gröningen maidservants thus queried the spinner Barbara Dollinger in 1686, because her belly had grown big and she pulled it in, writhing with pain. Barbara

---

[51] HStASt, A 209, Bü. 2013, 21 Mar. 1698, Anna Munderich.

[52] Rublack, 'The Public Body', 61–6.

[53] A Leonberg barber's widow trusted a maidservant's assurance that she was not pregnant, and mixed the herbs which her husband used to give women who had 'missed their monthlies': HStASt, A 309, Bü. 127, Regina Kapphan. The Kleinasbach executioner warned a maidservant in 1699 not to take the powder he gave her if she was pregnant; HStASt, A 209, Bü. 558, 3 Feb. 1699, Anna Sailer.

[54] StAKN, K 72, 30 July 1697, Maria Hippenmayer.

[55] StAMM, A 140/5, 21 Oct. 1622, Magdalena Winter.

[56] StAH, 4/479, Sonntag nach Trinitatis, 1554, fo. 187[r–v].

said it was 'cutting hard' in her belly because her period was return-
ing strongly. 'Then she would be carrying a child,' the maidservants
replied promptly. Barbara insisted that she had had her period
regularly. They let her off, but when she was lying down once on
her bed they followed her suspiciously. Soon the midwife attacked
her: 'you lewd whore, you have a child, show it immediately,
otherwise I will do this.'[57] The Leonberg midwife told a Swiss maidservant whose diminished belly caused suspicion that she was convinced that she had given birth to a child and had 'the same
reputation as Swiss maids are generally said to have'.[58] In 1654 the
duke of Württemberg announced that he wanted to banish illegitimately pregnant Swiss maidservants from his country. The 1658
infanticide ordinance required Württemberg inhabitants to report
every woman suspected of hiding a pregnancy to the authorities.
The impossibility of being certain about a woman's true state
ensured that both ordinances were seldom observed.

THE DRAMA OF INTERPRETATIONS

Exhortations

Especially in the last weeks before birth, when people began to be
certain that all evidence pointed to a pregnancy, which the woman
herself denied, the drama of interpretations unfolded. In the last
third of the seventeenth century, Württemberg church consistories
provided a new institutional stage for it. The parson would read out
the 1658 infanticide mandate to the suspect, and warn her about
what temporal and eternal punishments God held in store for
women killing their offspring. This was important, for it was commonly believed that repentant poor sinners could enter heaven.
Orthodox ministers knew that hell awaited murderers.[59] During
the trial, women were once more interrogated about their knowledge of secular and divine punishments. In 1681 a Weinsheim
woman who had committed infanticide was asked whether she
knew how women who hid their pregnancy and birth were punished, if the child was dead. She thought a while. Then she
answered, 'eternal punishment', then: 'temporal punishment'. The

---

[57] HStASt, A 209, Bü. 1023, 3 May 1686.

[58] HStASt, A 209, Bü. 1471, 12 Mar. 1664, Barbara Sticker.

[59] S. Holtz, 'Der Fürst dieser Welt: Die Bedrohung der Lebenswelt aus lutherisch-
orthodoxer Perspektive', *Zeitschrift für Kirchengeschichte*, 107 (1996), 29–49.

district bailiff asked her what temporal punishment such wenches deserved. She thought again for some time, and was admonished to speak several times. Eternal punishment, she answered, was the pain of hell; temporal punishment was imprisonment. But soon she confessed that the parson had of course told her that the secular punishment was death by execution.[60] Clerical admonitious never seemed to prevent women from committing infanticide, but they made it possible to accuse 'child-murderesses' of having acted in full consciousness of the gravity of the crime and its punishment.

A woman strongly suspected of hiding her pregnancy would not only be interrogated by the parson; she would also be examined by midwives and 'sworn women'.[61] Once more this was not threatening because it might prove the pregnancy. The moral pressure midwives put on women mattered more. Midwives had access to women when they were at their weakest, lying partly naked on a bed, surrounded by older women who had given birth themselves and had firm opinions about the signs of pregnancy. Midwifery was a public office, and its respectability rested on the fact that midwives were increasingly the supervisors of deviant women and mothers.[62]

Again, earlier in the seventeenth century, we can still see traces of a view that Christian mercy should overrule harshness. Thus in February 1609, a very pregnant young woman was sitting in a field near a road. A passer-by asked her what was wrong with her. She said she was in labour, and that she had been dismissed and banished from

---

[60] HStASt. A 209, Bü. 1594, 14 May 1681.

[61] Midwives belonged to the middling sort and were mostly artisans' wives or widows of good reputation. Groups of four women, called the 'sworn' or 'honourable women', would voluntarily supervise and assist them. Sworn women also enjoyed high status. In cities they were usually patricians', merchants', or richer artisans' wives; in small towns commonly mayors' and pastors' wives. On midwives' 'increased public role in the handling of cases of abortion and infanticide' see M. E. Wiesner, 'The Midwives of South Germany and the Public/Private Dichotomy', in H. Marland (ed.), *The Art of Midwifery: Early Modern Midwives in Europe* (London, 1993), 86–8.

[62] U. Gleixner, 'Die "Gute" und die "Böse": Hebammen als Amtsfrauen auf dem Land (Altmark/Brandenburg, 18 Jahrhundert)', in C. Vanja and H. Wunder (eds.), *Weiber, Menscher, Frauenzimmer: Frauen in der ländlichen Gesellschaft, 1500–1800* (Göttingen, 1996). Midwives and sworn women had to exhort women rather than induce miscarriages to undergo their labour properly: U. Rublack, 'Pregnancy, Childbirth and the Female Body in Early Modern Germany', *P & P* 150 (1996), 84–110. They interrogated single women about the identity of their children's fathers before offering any physical or moral help during birth. In some places, midwives were even required to examine whether a couple's first child was born nine months after the marriage so as to see whether its parents were punishable for premarital fornication: Wiesner, 'Midwives and the Public/Private Dichotomy', 87. And they examined and had to report those suspected of hiding pregnancy or attempting abortion.

the town of Helffenberg. He comforted the freezing woman, and told her to 'have a good heart, he would fetch women for her'. When they arrived from Beilstein she had already given birth and the baby was dead. No one could tell whether it had been born alive. Even the judges later acknowledged that it had been 'unchristian' to dismiss her in winter.[63] But such charitable views were soon outmoded.

The 1658 infanticide ordinance, read aloud from pulpits once a year, explicitly emphasized the masters' and mistresses' duty to police their maidservants' and labourers' pregnancies. In some upper-class households honour mattered more than empathy. In 1666, the Stuttgart court pharmacist and his wife lost patience when everyone gossiped about their maidservant's presumed pregnancy. The 24-year-old woman was dismissed for having 'turned her master's home into a whore house'.[64] In 1678, an orphaned day-labourer from Alsace, who had moved to Stuttgart when she realized her pregnancy, was accused of having been 'insolent' in choosing the ducal estate-servant as her master. The dead baby had been found in a sledge in his garden shed: the lowest instincts had thus contaminated a noble household.[65]

Women's Admonitions

The 1658 infanticide ordinance moreover told masters and mistresses to watch out for suspicious signs, and either to report them to the authorities or warn women about 'the danger and grave punishment' they risked.[66] Most people, however, preferred to put pressure on women privately first and tell them not to bloody their hands. In 1665, for example, Anna Laistler's new mistress, a jug-maker's wife, warned her that 'there were many examples of wenches who had denied being pregnant and had borne children secretly and let them die, who had lost their head for it; and therefore she should bring it out in the open if it was so'.

[63] She was banished from Württemberg, HStASt, A 209, Bü. 544, 1609, Katharina Bachtan.　　[64] HStASt, A 209, Bü. 1345, 5 July 1666, Anna Maria Vischer.
[65] HStASt, A 210, Abt. I, Bü. 448, 27 Oct. 1678, Dorothea Hippert. 'Honourable' maidservants internalized such notions. In 1622, a Memmingen maidservant swore that she would herself have left her service had she known about her pregnancy. It would have been the 'worst for her' to 'dishonour' the *Junker* and his wife: StAMM, A 140/5, 21 Oct. 1622, Magdalena Winter; HStASt, A 209, Bü. 1144, 9 Aug. 1688, Anna Margaretha Mugler.
[66] A. L. Reyscher (ed.), *Vollständige, historisch und kritisch bearbeitete Sammlung der württembergischen Gesetze* (19 vols., Stuttgart and Tübingen, 1828–51), vi. 11 f.

She added pragmatically that Anna 'was not the first and surely not the last one who had been impregnated'. But Anna did not want to confess, and had 'shown her belly in her shirt only: "there she should see whether she was pregnant"'. The mistress reported the incident to the parson, and the midwife and sworn women were ordered to examine Anna. When Anna saw them coming, she feared that 'she would have to leave the house immediately'.[67]

Mature women knew about unhappy stories that could lead to an illegitimate pregnancy and the hardships of life with a bastard. Even so they would not tolerate the murder of a living child. Thus neighbouring women could regard it as their natural duty to warn seemingly pregnant single women about their possible punishment. One woman 'preached' to Katharina Heinrich in 1679 about the 'harsh sentence of the heavenly judges' and said she would be eternally damned.[68] 'Oh fat one', an old woman cried in Urach in 1630, 'you have had a child', as she opened Maria Späth's shirt and pulled at her breasts. Then she repeated that 'Maria had killed the child, and surely her head would be cut off'.[69] Forceful hints about the imminence of a death sentence were common. Anna Maurer was told by her stepmother to confess her pregnancy; otherwise she would 'fall under the hangman's hands'. She begged neighbours to talk to Anna. But Anna only shouted at her: 'she was just as bad as every other stepmother' and merely 'wanted to bring public shame upon her'.[70] A woman with whom Anna Fritz cut grass in 1664 likewise told her to confess her pregnancy and in no case to kill the child. She pointed towards 'the Besigheim gallows which they could see from there, at which two women had been executed for infanticide' as many as fifteen years earlier, in 1648 and 1649. Despite the war, the first woman had unsuccessfully claimed that a soldier had raped her; the other woman had been a cook in the 'Crown' and had hidden her baby in a flour barrel.[71] Fifteen years later a maidservant like Anna Fritz would still be warned with their example. The story of her pregnancy was, as in most cases, simple enough: a mason's daughter, she had gone into service at a bricklayer's and grown to like the bricklayer's servant. Some time after they had made love he went to fight in the Turkish wars. She was dismissed as soon as her

---

[67] HStASt, A 210, Abt. I, Bü. 424, 4 Oct. 1665.   [68] HStASt, A 210, Bü. 1359.
[69] HStASt, A 209, Bü. 1986, 14 Aug. 1630.
[70] HStASt, A 209, Bü. 1928, 24 Nov. 1671.
[71] HStASt, A 209, Bü. 382, 18 Oct. 1664; HStASt, A 209, Bü. 317, Barbara Bürckhler, Bü. 318, Eva Rohrer.

pregnancy was suspected, and went into service at a butcher's. Even Anna's stepmother, who lived 11 miles away in Brackenheim, heard rumours concerning the pregnancy. Three weeks before the delivery she visited Anna. Anna denied being pregnant. When she finally gave birth the butcher accidently entered her chamber. He grabbed the baby and took it to the bath that had just been prepared for his own children. Thus he saved the child's and Anna's life.[72]

To a pregnant girl, concrete offers of support were more important than moral warnings, and sometimes she received such support. In 1660, for example, a Swiss woman serving at her sister's in Stuttgart was vehemently offered every support and care she needed to give birth by that sister and a miller's wife.[73] But nothing removed the fact that she would be banished as a single mother, so little could be done.[74]

Soldiers' Whores

Women who became pregnant by a soldier found themselves in an even worse situation: they were immediately stigmatized as 'soldiers' whores' and had no prospect of marrying the child's father. Such women had to pay the price for a structural problem: standing armies were created and households were forced to take in quartered soldiers, but soldiers were almost never allowed to marry. Additionally soldiers could not be sued before civic courts to pay for illegitimate children. Württemberg laws demonstrate that councillors clearly recognized the problem of false promises of marriage. A mandate from 1691 declared angrily that soldiers behaved as if they were no longer bound to order like other subjects but could behave 'as they wished in matters of marriage'.[75] In 1700 a mandate commented on petitions the ducal chancellery received daily from women and their parents begging that the women could marry soldiers who had promised this. The duke proclaimed that it was well known that soldiers were allowed to

---

[72] HStASt, A 209, Bü. 382, 18 Oct. 1664, Anna Maria Fritz.
[73] UAT, 84/14, 10 Oct. 1660, fos. 424^r–433^r, Margaretha Brommer.
[74] See the discussion in Ch. 2. In a small Württemberg town a schoolmaster's wife in 1679 similarly offered to be a godparent to the pastor's maidservant's illegitimate child (in case she was pregnant). She wanted to give her 'flour and milk'. The girl was a soldier's daughter, aged 20. She imagined that the servant with whom she had slept three times would have stayed and married her if she had had a reasonable dowry, shouting at her stepfather and mother 'why they cared whether or not she was pregnant', because they 'gave her nothing'. Her stepfather was so shocked by the fact that she seemed to be planning a murder that he offered to raise the child for her. But she still denied her pregnancy, HStASt, A 209, Bü. 1359; A 309, Bü. 17, Katharina Heinrich.   [75] Reyscher, Gesetze, xix. 296f.

marry only by permission of their *Offizier*. Impregnated women who begged to be allowed marriage had always been turned away as examples to others. None the less the 'daughters of our countrymen's subjects' who disobeyed the law and 'hung onto' soldiers were promised marriage but then only impregnated. All future petitions were also going to be answered negatively and the soldiers would receive military punishment and the 'lusty wenches' would receive ordinary punishment. Parental order was called for: subjects were not to allow any flirtation between daughters or maids and soldiers to avoid burdening 'the country. . .with bastards'.[76]

The fact that soldiers used violence more commonly than other men did to conquer a woman was ignored. The responsibility for a relationship with a soldier was primarily ascribed to the woman herself, and to her parents and master. An impregnated daughter or maidservant was immediately stigmatized as a 'lusty wench' who had to suffer for her self-inflicted pain. Such reasoning elegantly relieved territorial and civic authorities from the cost of their own policy: they did not have to pay soldiers higher wages to allow them to keep wives and children and they avoided having to raise illegitimate children on civic alms. Even women who claimed to have been raped and impregnated by soldiers were distrusted: in 1646 a Württemberg mandate declared that most women falsely claimed to have been raped in order to hide other illegitimate liaisons and to receive alms. It announced that such a woman had to inform a parson or a respectable person she trusted about the rape within a month. This person then had to inform the bailiff. If a month had already gone by the woman would be sentenced for fornication.[77] The mandate did not therefore acknowledge what every chronicle of the Thirty Years War lamented, that is how commonly soldiers raped women when taking possession of town and country, not only to relieve desire but also to dishonour the men who could not protect their women. Later mandates, however, acknowledged that soldiers frequently made false promises of marriage to single women in order to persuade them to agree to have sex.[78] A mandate in 1700 noted that the supreme council had never granted such couples

---

[76] Ibid. 573.

[77] Reyscher, *Gesetze*, xix. 57f., 'General=Rescript, die angebliche Nothzüchtigung durch Soldaten betreffend', 3 June 1646.

[78] Reyscher, *Gesetze*, xix. 296f., 'General=Rescript, betreffend die Verehelichung der Militär=Personen', May 1691.

permission to marry, but imposed military punishment on the soldier and banished the 'lewd whores'. It told bailiffs to stop any liaison they heard of so that the country would not be burdened with illegitimate children.[79] This policy aimed to force soldiers to stay in the army and avoid the burden of possible families. Since it was unlikely that soldiers would abstain from sexual relationships, the policy produced illegitimate children, but enforced shaming punishments on their mothers in order to deter other women from any involvement with soldiers.

Shame

Not surprisingly, some of the women impregnated by a soldier tried to avoid such shame and such a fate. In 1693, for example, a Swiss maidservant was reported to have drowned 'in a bucket' a child fathered by a soldier, for the 'usual reason of such wenches and women who commit infanticide, namely to get rid of the shame before people'.[80] The judgement about the Swiss maidservant Anna Schuhler in 1686 ran similarly that she had tried to 'hide her immodesty' and not be 'subjected to shame'. But did she deserve such shame? Anna served at an inn just below the Württemberg fortress Hohentwiel. But she had clearly taken care not to get involved with soldiers and all those moving through the place. A Swiss smith's journeyman, working one and a half hours' walk away, seemed a more reliable choice. But once he had impregnated her, he refused to believe this was true.[81]

In the case of those living at home or those working close to home, the family could demand the killing of a shaming bastard. One spinner, who was illegitimately pregnant for the second time in 1686, killed the baby because of her father's and sibling's threats: 'if she

---

[79] Reyscher, *Gesetze*, xix. 324–6, 'General=Rescript, die Verhütung des Ausreissens der Soldaten, die Beifahung und Bestrafung der sie zu diesem und andern Vergehen verleitenden fremden Dirnen, die ehelichen Verbindungen derselben (betreffend)', 15 Dec. 1700.
[80] HStASt, A 209, Bü. 943, 10 Feb. 1693, Anna Barbara Sturzenacker. In most cases, the dowry was the key point, for only a marriage could restore the woman's honour. In 1679, Anna Gröninger's stepfather was finally prepared to give her a dowry out of his own property so that she could marry the soldier who had impregnated her. Anna's mother denied her every penny. First, both had been hostile to a marriage. The soldier could write what he wanted, they had told the parson, 'he only wanted their money'. Anna had confessed her pregnancy to two women, clearly worried 'what her parents were going to say if they knew she was pregnant'. Even her stepfather's final offer did not give her the courage to admit her pregnancy openly, HStASt, A 209, Bü. 2010, 10 Oct. 1679.   [81] HStASt, A 209, Bü. 1975, 4 Oct. 1687.

had a bastard again they would beat her.' She should go away forever. Her father needed all his property to survive, and the sum she had inherited from her mother amounted to no more than thirty-three florins.[82] Another maidservant had been threatened by her brother: 'he would beat her if she was pregnant', and: 'if he had to experience such shame he would run away' and leave all the work to his old father. Again the shame had nothing to do with the fact that she had lost her virginity. An illegitimate nephew disturbed a sense of kinship cohesion and ordered lines of inheritance, and would therefore have worsened his chances to find a good wife and a suitable brother-in-law with whom he could maintain the inherited land. For his parents an illegitimate grandchild and his escape would have been the end of a respectable life.[83] Sometimes there had been earlier conflicts about a daughter's indecent conduct. Maria Sauer, for example, to her father's great dismay, fell in love with an Irish soldier in Stuttgart, who did not understand a word of German (let alone Swabian). Her father finally consented to a marriage under the condition that Maria would remain Lutheran. The soldier pretended that he had already raised the matter with a parson. Maria's father still warned her not to get too close to the soldier. But instead of obeying his command, she slept in different places for a couple of nights with the soldier. When she returned home, he protected Maria from her father's punches. Soon, however, the soldier, who presumably had improved his language skills, heard that Maria was an 'immodest whore' and had made herself 'common' with other men. It transpired that she had been imprisoned for fornication and had moved away from Stuttgart for almost a year afterwards. After the Irish soldier had heard all this, he did not want pregnant Maria any longer. She gave birth secretly. Her father was furious. When the French had burned Calw, he had escaped to Stuttgart and rebuilt his life. Three of his children were in good places, one daughter served the upper council's secretary, his younger children worked in the duke's kitchen, and from the food they brought home, his wife cooked meals for boarders. Only Maria brought disorder to their household and shame upon them. This was why the father agreed that the dead baby's corpse should be dumped in the river Neckar, once it rotted and stank in the house.[84]

[82] HStASt, A 209, Bü. 1023, 13 Apr. 1686, Barbara Dollinger.
[83] HStASt, A 209, Bü. 1479, 9 Feb. 1681, Catharina Guldenmann.
[84] HStASt, A 210, Abt. II, Bü. 125, 24 Apr. 1699.

FIG. 10. Merian's View of Stuttgart

After a further, even more extreme family tragedy, a mother and her two daughters were beheaded for infanticide in Liebenzell in 1676. One daughter, Barbara, had been impregnated by a soldier. The family kept the birth secret. Barbara's sister baptized the child in the name of their deceased father. But because their mother suffered shame from gossip, they strangled the boy after a week and Barbara's brother buried him.[85] It was a sign of the times that by 1673 the dishonour not just of fornication with a soldier but even of premarital sex could be so feared that murder seemed to be the only way to secure respectability. Widows could see themselves under particular pressure to defend their own and their daughters' honour against the more likely charges of sexual immorality. Anna Hamberger's mother therefore drowned her grandchild on the day of her Anna's mother-in-law's first visit. Anna and her groom had served in wealthy households, and their parents were not poor. When the marriage had been agreed to they had had sex. Anna's mother seemed to expect that her daughter would be accused of having seduced her groom into sinful behaviour and bringing shame upon her new family.[86]

Cases such as the ones I have just described demonstrate that poor maidservants and spinners were not the only women who tried to kill unwanted babies. Women's social backgrounds, and the circumstances which turned the child into a threat, could be diverse. Take, for instance, the difficult situation of deserted wives who were pregnant by another man. Margaretha Schmollinger had been left by her husband five years ago and had been punished for adultery already once since then. She had been in 'such shame' that she now denied being pregnant 'to avoid further scorn'. She knew that otherwise things 'would get bad with her'.[87]

Poverty and Begging

Women who named poverty instead of shame as their main motive usually had no dowry or inheritance to look forward to and lived independently. One maidservant with poor parents who had been

[85] HStASt, A 209, Bü. 1511, Barbara Weiland, 1676.
[86] HStASt, A 209, Bü. 1690, 1673, Anna Hamberger; HStASt, A 209, Bü. 701, 12 Apr. 1698, Magdalena Kopp.
[87] HStASt, A 209, Bü. 1923, 30 Aug. 1667. Fornication could likewise be seen as grave if the woman did not marry the child's father and became pregnant soon after the wedding. Katharina Ruotweiß, who had been impregnated by a soldier and quickly married another man, feared that this man would 'cut her head off'. She and her mother had discussed 'about a hundred times' whether to abort or kill the child, HStASt, A 209, Bü. 1564, 24 Mar. 1690.

impregnated by a soldier in 1697 thus simply knew that there was 'no place where she would be welcome with a child'.[88] Anna Weilandt had been impregnated by a traveller in 1624 and had tried to terminate her pregnancy. She served in an inn and did not know where 'to go with a child during the present dearth', adding that she and the child's father were too poor to support a child.[89] In 1657, a woman who was working in Tübingen likewise confessed that she had thrown the child into the river Ammer because 'as an extremely poor person she would be unable to pay for the baptism soup and even less [able] to support the child or feed it'.[90] Of course it was not impossible to survive begging with an illegitimate child. But it comes as no surprise that women might feel unable to face this prospect. And they could make up their own minds about what were tolerable living conditions. In 1667, a 21-year-old maidservant, Wiperta, told the Stuttgart court her story. At the age of 19 she had moved from her village to the district town of Urach, where her brother was a miller. For a year she served a page at the castle, then a butcher in town. She and Mathes, a smith's servant, then laid eyes on each other, and one day at the market they arranged to meet at ten o'clock at night in the master's barn. Things went fast, maybe too fast for her: he would not let her go until she had 'lived his will' i.e. they had sex. He had promised to marry her, but had not given her a ring, wine, or even his hand to seal the promise. When she insisted on knowing what would happen if she got pregnant, he had firmly replied that he would restore her honour. During the next week he had come twice to her chamber at night, and they had lain naked in her bed. After that they had met three more times. Two months later, Wiperta decided to leave Urach to earn money at the harvest. Mathes accompanied her out of town, and assured her that if she was pregnant he would take her home to his village near Urach. After the harvest, Wiperta went into service with a butcher near Stuttgart, but at Christmas she wanted to return to Mathes, since their child would be born soon afterwards. She could trust Mathes, but not the fact that they could live independently. The child came a month early. It was alive. She confessed to having killed it, and was herself beheaded in Stuttgart one day in March in the year 1668.[91]

---

[88] Her father died when she was young, and her mother married a miller, HStASt, A 209, Bü. 2011, 2 Aug. 1697, Anna Holder.   [89] HStASt, A 209, Bü. 854, 5 Apr. 1624.
[90] HStASt, A 209, Bü. 1918, Martinodin.
[91] HStASt, A 210, Abt. II, Bü. 445, 3 Dec. 1667; 28 Feb. 1668, Wiperta Ruder.

Infanticide can therefore be interpreted to a large degree as a protest against the moral imperative of those who could afford to impose it upon others and against the worsening of a life that was already harsh enough. Stories like that of Angelika Tilhausen support this interpretation. In 1677 she moved from Catholic Westphalia to Kirchheim am Neckar. Aged 20, she had not heard from her parents and siblings for nine years. Working as a spinner and knitter she had earned 'her own bread' since the age of 11. Otherwise she 'owned nothing'. During the winter of 1667 a Polish captain was billeted with the peasant for whom she spun. They celebrated carnival together and he told his tales from foreign lands, promising to take her with him to war. Angelika entrusted her body to him, but four days later he had marched on. One October night, while she worked in a spinning-bee, her labour-pains started. After midnight, when everyone had left, she went into a field, gave birth, and killed the child quickly.[92]

Barbara Seyfried likewise defended herself in 1679 by saying that the child's father had told her to go away and that she had 'no means at all' to feed a child. The judges argued that she could have survived with a child through 'manual work'.[93] Was this true? How could the young widow and laundress Ursula Steiner have managed? The child's father was a journeyman who had told her that he was going to move away even if she put the child on his doorstep. Where could she have left her baby when she was at work during winter and how could she have got through her load when the child was screaming?[94] Who would employ a single mother with a small child? Begging was the only possibility for such women while the children were small. Banishment forced them onto the streets anyway. Of course it was not impossible to survive by begging, but it is hardly surprising that many women shunned the prospects of vagrancy.

Elisabetha Eggenmann's mistress, a merchant's wife, foresaw her fate and told her: 'give birth to the child properly and take it on your arm and search for your piece of bread, for God will not leave you.'[95] But reality could easily defeat trust in God's help. Anna Franz, for example, went begging with her newborn illegitimate child in 1690. A dragoon had impregnated her and later died in Mainz without leaving money for the child. On her way through villages she

---

[92] HStASt, A 209, Bü. 1355, 22 Oct. 1677.   [93] HStASt, A 209, Bü. 1353.
[94] HStASt, A 209, Bü. 261, 1625.   [95] StAKN, K 64, 18 May 1688.

was twice heard to declare that it would be no wonder if she killed herself and the child. 'Good-hearted people' let her stay at their house for two nights. Then soldiers took up the quarters and refused to tolerate a screaming baby in the house. Anna had to move to the stable. When the child did not stop crying she hit it twice. When it got dark, Anna went to the house to ask for a candle, but they would not give her one. Back in the stable the child was lying quietly in the hay. She felt that it was cold and stiff. She had not only hit it but kicked it earlier, so that it would die 'and she would be rid of the suffering'.[96]

CONTESTED PUNISHMENTS

The total denial of a child's existence was about as rare as care for its soul by burying the corpse.[97] Most women were neither cold-blooded nor heart broken, but above all determined not to lose all honour, marriage chances, and prospects of a minimally safe existence through an unwanted child. People around these women often saw the social background of the crime. Even though the murder of a living child was abhorred, there was no consensus about the question of whether or not the young woman's beheading was the right measure of revenge.

It is possible that different attitudes towards the death sentence generated two contrasting developments in the second half of the seventeenth century. On the one hand there was an intensification of prosecution of infanticide related to law enforcement against fornication; on the other hand there was an almost complete decline of infanticide trials. The first development can be seen in Württemberg and Hall, the second in Memmingen, Constance, and Esslingen. The Württemberg upper council, for example, began seriously to worry about these offences after at least nine infanticide cases were uncovered in the nine years after the end of the Thirty Years War: it responded in 1658 with the first Württemberg ordinance against infanticide.[98] Far from preventing the crime, however, the ordinance led to increased prosecution: only fourteen

---

[96] HStASt, A 209, Bü. 2068, 2 Jan. 1690; StAMM, A 44d, 6 June 1572, Anna Schweitzer.

[97] Contrary to Regina Schulte's claim that women were likely to defend themselves by ignoring their pregnancy; cf. her *The Village in Court: Arson, Infanticide and Poaching in the Court Records of Upper Bavaria, 1848–1910*, trans. B. Selman (Cambridge, 1994), ch. 4. I found seven examples of women burying the dead infant.

[98] Published on 1 Mar. 1658, see Reyscher, *Gesetze*, vi. 11.

infanticide cases can be traced for the whole sixteenth century, but at least fifty-five cases are known between 1600 and 1659, and a further 127 up to 1700.[99] By contrast, only four infanticide cases were tried in Memmingen during the seventeenth century, two in Esslingen, and seven in Constance. In Constance, six death sentences were announced between 1600 and 1644 and no further trial followed until the end of the century. The last two death sentences for infanticide in Memmingen were executed in 1630 and 1632. In Esslingen one woman was executed in 1676, against strong public opposition, as we shall see in a moment. Such differences cannot be explained with reference to population sizes in towns and territories. It furthermore seems unlikely that in Memmingen, Constance, and Esslingen civic policies to banish illegitimately pregnant women effectively diminished the numbers of women who gave secret birth. Rather, councillors may have been less sensitive towards the crime, thus putting less pressure on the population to accuse suspects. This low sensitivity may have been deliberate, in which case it would indicate reluctance to impose the death sentence for infanticide. Either way, it needs to be pointed out that the criminalization of infanticide was a significant development in several towns and territories, but not a geographically or confessionally uniform process.[100]

The ambivalence which judges could demonstrate is revealed by the example of Hall. During the seventeenth century seven women were sentenced to death for infanticide in Hall. Five of them were beheaded between 1671 and 1690, that is the years of the intensified campaign against sexual immorality. In seven further cases, however, punishments were mitigated, even if it was clear that the baby had been alive when killed. Such decisions were unthinkable in Württemberg by that time. In 1676 the final verdict that a maidservant from Altdorf in the Hall territory should die had already been read out, when such strong petitions came in for her that the judges decided to banish her for ever instead.[101] One year later ten communities in the Hall territory put together a petition for a woman who had committed infanticide, her mother, and the child's father, who had known about the murder.[102] In 1680 the people of Altdorf mobilized support for another petition. Maria Laidig, an orphan, had

---

[99] Figures for the 17th century are based on the results of the *Arbeitsgruppe Kindsmord in Württemberg*, University of Stuttgart, supervised by Dr P. D. Andreas Gestrich.

[100] For Nuremberg and Danzig see v. Dülmen, *Frauen vor Gericht*, 61, table 3.

[101] StAH 4/79, Margaretha Weiß.   [102] StAH, B4/284, RP 1677, 367^r, 394^r.

got herself into an affair with a village lad. The liaison ended with his escape and her imprisonment for killing their baby. She was to be beheaded. The council received a 'long and nicely written petition' from her brothers, brothers-in-law, friends, and three communities. Since she had always had a good reputation, they argued, and also promised to better herself, the council was asked to practise mildness instead of severity. The parson supported her, too, for she had 'always behaved in a good and Christian manner'.[103] The situation of another maidservant in the Hall territory in 1680 was worse. She had taken abortifacients and had wounded the baby's corpse seven times. Because of this cruelty the Hall councillor Schragmüller voted for a stronger sentence, namely to tweak her with hot pincers before she was beheaded. The woman's father herded animals in two territorial communities and asked the advocate to plead on his behalf. The council was divided about the matter, but nevertheless decided to decapitate her and to stick her head on a post. On the day of the execution people pleading for her life assembled in front of the town hall. The advocate read out the petitions of her parents, siblings, three communities, and the Michelfeld parson. The council decided not to pinch her breasts, but to stick up her head, though without telling her before she died.[104]

These examples therefore demonstrate once more that compassion was higher towards citizens. People were used to the fact that social *others* came under the hangman's hand. Beheading for infanticide was the only punishment which also threatened women who were known as ordinary community members. And thus it is perhaps not surprising that in such cases, as in those of male citizens accused of homicide, the legitimacy of the death sentence could be doubted and sometimes openly questioned.

Moreover, in the Esslingen council minutes we find a case in 1676 revealing the explosive atmosphere surrounding even the execution of a woman who was not local and had been involved with a soldier. Margaretha Münzinger was the only woman in seventeenth-century Esslingen charged with killing a living child; she had committed adultery with a soldier and become pregnant.[105] On the day set for her execution the hangman found 'suspicious objects' on the prison staircase. These caused him 'troubled thoughts and frightened

---

[103] When the child's father was finally arrested, three parsons instantly petitioned for him, StAH, B4/287, RP 1680, 421ʳ, 423ᵛ, 546ʳ.   [104] Ibid. 529ᵛ–530ʳ.
[105] StAL, B 169, Bü. 119, II, fos. 183ʳ–184ᵛ, 6 June 1676.

him'. It turned out that several soldiers planned to free Margaretha from the hangman's rope, or even to shoot her instead of seeing her die under his hands.[106] Her execution was delayed and the mayor demanded further information from the soldiers' commander. He told the mayor that a Lorraine civil servant had come into their camp bringing the message that the duke of Lorraine did not want Münzinger to die and thought her sentence ought to be mitigated. But the commander was not sure whether the message was true, since the duke of Lorraine was known to 'execute justice eagerly', and the commander thought the crime grave enough to merit a death sentence.[107] The mayor did not agree and asked for mitigation. When the council had to decide about the case three months later, the mayor lamented that it was the most painful act he had encountered during his office. In the meantime it had become clear that the duke favoured mitigation. Margaretha's execution, the mayor argued, would therefore disgrace Esslingen, and the whole town would have to suffer for it. Moreover there were other crimes, such as blasphemy, which the Bible and the *Carolina* defined as capital crimes, but which were never punished with death in practice. The mayor further argued that Margaretha had experienced the fear of death during her long imprisonment and this was worse than the actual death. Finally he mentioned a recent Württemberg case in which a 'cavalier' from Phillipsburg had threatened to wreak damage upon the whole country if they beheaded a woman for infanticide. She had been banished instead, and Esslingen should take an example from it. The mayor was overruled by his colleagues—and Margaretha was executed.[108]

TRADITION AND DISSENT

People's involvement through petitioning helped to generate criticism of the death sentence for infanticide which was to deepen in the late eighteenth century.[109] More generally, it demonstrated that early modern legal justice was not just passively received by subjects but contested. Harsher policies could not be enforced without hindrance. This seems to have been particularly true in Imperial

---

[106] StAE, RP, 1676, fo. 191ᵛ, 7 Apr. 1676.   [107] Ibid., fo. 202ʳ.
[108] Ibid., fos. 232ʳ–233ᵛ. For similarly polarized votes see, for example, StAK, RP 1600, BI 81, 37ʳ⁻ᵛ, Barbara Widmer, and Ch. 2.
[109] Ulbricht, *Kindsmord in Deutschland*, chs. 3 and 4.

cities, and in regard to offenders with whose fate people could identify, because they were seen as ordinary folk. In Württemberg, by contrast, we hear little about petitions for women who had committed infanticide. But the reason does not seem to have been a shared morality of officials and 'peasants'.[110] Rather, citizens had probably learnt that they could not shift the government's determination to enforce laws against infanticide. Moreover, the distance between those who in effect judged about offenders' lives and their communities mattered: Tübingen lawyers and Stuttgart ducal councillors were spatially and culturally remote from people in the localities. Territorial lawyers and councillors themselves were never faced with the sight of the family of a young woman who had been beheaded or the aggravation of, in some cases, whole communities. The warnings which mature women directed at those concealing their pregnancy thus perhaps not surprisingly reflected a deep knowledge that their beheading was unavoidable if their crime was detected.

Infanticide and the offical prosecution which followed the discovery of a corpse were thus, as Laura Gowing writes, very often a 'collective trauma which communities, and particularly women in communities, had to work hard to deal with'. This might have been not least because it involved 'imagining the emotions of maternal commitment and remorse', familiar to mothers anxious about a troubled relationship with their expected, living, or dead children.[111]

Firm laws against 'crimes of the flesh' in the seventeenth century clearly strengthened illegitimately pregnant women's anxieties about their future and their feeling of shame. Harsh punishment therefore did not prevent infanticide. It was the shame of a dishonoured woman and the prospect of poverty, aggravated by the policy of banishing single mothers rigorously, and sending them begging, which mainly caused pregnant women's anxiety and, finally, the murder of a child which would have grown up being called a bastard and a whore's son or daughter. In 1657, the daughter of a vine-dresser who had terminated her pregnancy with laurel said that she had always hoped that the one who had 'made her this child and promised to marry her would

---

[110] Zimmermann, '"Behörigs Orthen angezeigt"', 69; 'Peasants' are not a very visible group in the surviving cases anyway. Most cases were uncovered in district towns, not in villages.
[111] Cf. L. Gowing, 'Secret Births and Infanticide in Seventeenth-Century England', *Past and Present*, 156 (1997), 115.

come, marry her, and go to church with her, and thus make her pure again'.[112] Only by marriage could women who had left their family re-enter a stable order of purity and male control. This, at least, was the ideal.

[112] 'Allso sie wieder sauber machen': UAT, 84/11, fos. 309–10ʳ, 16 May 1657, Anna Maria Erstlerin.

6

Married Life

Grimmelshausen's fictional character, Courasche, was famously quick-witted in quarrels with her husband:

My dearest! (and with this I gave him an affectionate kiss) I thought we had already settled this argument. Never once did I mean to wear your breeches. Far from it. I know that Woman was taken from Man's side, not from his head. I hoped that, knowing this, my Sweetheart would not treat me as if I had been taken from the soles of his feet; I want to be regarded as his spouse, not as his door-mat. . . . 'Ha, ha!' he replied, 'such womanly wiles! She takes control before I realise it.'[1]

The metaphors embedded in this passage were embedded in real life too. In 1597, a Constance wife accused her husband of treating her not 'as a wife but as a door-mat'.[2] And in 1627 a Memmingen silk embroiderer petitioned to the council: 'if the wife wants to be master and Lord, and wants the husband to be her servant and door-mat, despised by her, defamed and persecuted . . . how can this please God?'[3]

Such sources suggest that 'ordered equality' was not always easily achieved in early modern marriages.[4] At the heart of the concept of marriage there was a chronic tension between companionate ideals on the one hand and patriarchal ideals on the other. It was always maintained that the husband's predominance was natural; but the humanist tradition stressed equally that a wife was to be valued as a

---

[1] Translation based in part on Johann von Grimmelshausen, *Mother Courage*, trans. W. Wallich (London, 1965), 51 f. Courasche is a sexually lustful woman wanting to be male in order to satisfy her greed for wealth, power, and military prowess. The story is set in the Thirty Years War and was first published in 1670: see W. Bender (ed.), *Lebensbeschreibungen der Ertzbetrügerin und Landstörtzerin Courasche* (Tübingen, 1967).

[2] StAKN, HIX, F. 41, 10 June 1597, Daniel Labhart; H. Fischer, *Schwäbisches Wörterbuch* (5 vols., Tübingen, 1908f–36), ii, col. 1897, 'Fußhader'.

[3] StAMM, A 144/1, 9 Jan. 1627, Hans Friedrich Raidel.

[4] S. Ozment, *When Fathers Ruled: Family Life in Reformation Europe* (Cambridge, Mass., 1983), 99.

companion and protected from maltreatment. This brought home to the wealthy and educated what common sense and necessity had taught peasants and artisans for centuries. With the 'familiarisation of work and life',[5] marriage had become the precondition of household formation, since agrarian and workshop economies were principally based on the labour of couples. 'Companionship' in the sense of joint work, mutual care, and respect had to stand its test in everyday life; economic survival depended on mutual cooperation.

The Reformation accentuated this development by insisting that marriage was a key element in the social order.[6] It dissolved monasteries and introduced priestly marriage; it closed civic brothels and prohibited prostitution; it prosecuted the secret exchange of marriage vows and stressed the importance of church weddings. As we have already seen, pre- and extramarital sex was condemned harshly, as were single women who lived and worked independently.[7] Marriage and a shared household were to be the typical form of life for more people than hitherto. Not passion (which burnt off quickly), but maturing affection and friendship were thought to unite husband and wife and help them master the vicissitudes of life. Inside the household, children and servants were to be educated as Christians. Naturally, the husband was expected to govern the household without force, just as the good prince was to bring his subjects peace and prosperity by governing justly, wisely, and rigorously; love was to be 'the virtue of sovereignty'.[8]

In marriage as in political theory, the main problem was posed by tyranny and 'bad government'. A husband's infidelity was akin to treachery; his violence threatened the life of others in the household; his feckless spending meant that food, protection, and peace were withheld. Could such government be termed legitimate? Since the household had become the 'crystallizing point of the social constitution', it is hardly surprising that Lutherans' answer to the question

[5] H. Wunder, '*Er ist die Sonn', sie ist der Mond': Frauen in der Ffrühen Neuzeit* (Munich, 1992), 88, 96 and ead., ' "Jede Arbeit ist ihres Lohnes wert": Zur geschlechtsspezifischen Teilung und Bewertung von Arbeit in der frühen Neuzeit', in K. Hausen (ed.), *Geschlechterhierarchie und Arbeitsteilung: Zur Geschichte ungleicher Erwerbschancen von Männern und Frauen* (Göttingen, 1993).

[6] Wunder, '*Er ist die Sonn*', *sie ist der Mond*', 88; J. Harrington, *Reordering Marriage and Society in Reformation Germany* (Cambridge, 1995), 14.   [7] See Chs. 4 and 5.

[8] Rainer Beck describes this as the theological position in regard to marriage in Catholic areas: 'Frauen in Krise: Eheleben und Ehescheidung in der ländlichen Gesellschaft Bayerns während des Ancien Régime', in R. v. Dülmen (ed.), *Dynamik der Tradition* (Frankfurt on Main, 1992).

was analogous to their theory of political resistance.[9] Although the Reformation sanctioned divorce (and sometimes allowed divorced couples to remarry),[10] Lutheran marriage courts were no different from their Catholic counterparts in insisting that men should put asunder those whom God had joined only in extreme cases.[11] For Lutherans as for Calvinists, the only legally acceptable grounds for divorce were long-term desertion or, surprisingly, adultery.[12] This expressed the Protestant contention that faithful sex formed the basis of marriage.[13] No matter how unbearable married life might be, a Christian's duty was to suffer and remain obedient to God's order.[14] Thus, although the Reformation had established that marriage was not a sacrament but a 'secular thing', an escape from a bad marriage and marital cruelty was immensely difficult. The believer might be consoled that in her sufferings she need not remain faithful to a tyrannical sovereign (husband) so much as to God, who had created this order and who would punish justly at the right time. In the eyes of the authorities, therefore, any woman's quest for separation or divorce on grounds of marital problems questioned the social order and faith in God's providence. Enduring marital disharmony challenged the notion that household and marriage were the natural basis of good political order. Couples who did not cohabit peacefully were therefore punished, and confessional differences in marital policies hardly existed.[15] We have to assume that for most partners

[9] C. Link, *Herrschaftsordnung und bürgerliche Freiheit: Grenzen der Staatsgewalt in der älteren deutschen Staatslehre* (Vienna, 1979), 28, 194, 226; E. Wolgast, *Die Religionsfrage als Problem des Widerstandsrechts im 16. Jahrhundert* (Heidelberg, 1980), 15–18.

[10] Instead of a separation from bed and board or annulment.

[11] Moreover, a divorce suit was expensive, so that among the common people only deeply unhappy couples with grown-up children would contemplate one. Thus divorce cases were seldom brought before marriage courts. Marriage courts were basically 'premarital' courts, in that they mainly dealt with broken promises of marriage.

[12] If a husband was impotent, the marriage would be annulled, G. Erbe, 'Das Ehescheidungsrecht im Herzogtum Württemberg seit der Reformation', *ZfWLG* 14 (1955), 95–144; T. M. Safley, Let No Man Put Asunder: The Control of Marriage in the German Southwest: A Comparative Study, *1550–1600* (Kirksville, Mo., 1984); R. Phillips, *Putting Asunder: A History of Divorce in Western Society* (Cambridge, 1988), 50; J. R. Watt, *The Making of Modern Marriage: Matrimonial Control and the Rise of Sentiment in Neuchâtel, 1550–1800* (Ithaca, NY, 1992); R. M. Kingdon, *Adultery and Divorce in Calvin's Geneva* (Cambridge, Mass., 1995). On Constance, U. Rublack, *Geordnete Verhältnisse? Ehealltag und Ehepolitik im frühneuzeitlichen Konstanz* (Constance, 1997).

[13] Philips, *Putting Asunder,* 86.

[14] In Geneva cruelty was accepted as a reason for divorce, but only a few women whose lives were manifestly endangered were granted a divorce: J. R. Watt, 'Women and the Consistory in Calvin's Geneva', *SCJ* 24/2 (1993), 429–39.

[15] Harrington, *Reordering Marriage,* 273–8.

who sought separation, a secret desertion remained the only escape route until the nineteenth century.[16] Desertion, however, usually seems to have been the male choice; women tended to stay, presumably because they could neither imagine leaving their children and family, nor believe they had reliable economic options elsewhere. Instead, wives used courts more intensely to achieve a disciplining of misbehaving husbands, for they knew how seriously magistrates and councillors wanted to fight men who neglected their duties, wasted money, and impoverished private and public revenues. But to assume an alliance of wives and judges in such cases is inappropriate;[17] women were frequently urged to behave better in future themselves and always forced to continue cohabitation.

Historians have long argued that early modern marriage was a pragmatic, emotionless union brought about by parental and economic interests. Although recent research has refuted this notion,[18] we still know little about the experiences of women whose married life was neither narrated in a chronicle, nor honoured in a printed funeral sermon, nor represented in a painting.[19] Hence the marital quarrels reflected in court records open an important window onto common people's attitudes towards married life. Admittedly they do not allow us to say whether happy marriages were more common than unhappy ones, or how far patriarchal ideals were diluted by companionate ideals. None the less these sources can still shift our understanding of some of the most hidden aspects of communal history by taking us into the lived textures of marriages in crisis, and the despair of couples who knew that only death could part them.

LIKE CAT AND DOG: QUARRELLING COUPLES

In 1517 the court of Hall dealt with one Hans Stadmann. Some years before, he had been allowed to remarry [*sic*] after his wife had deserted him. But now he had driven away his second wife as

---

[16] On the resulting 'wild marriages' see L. Abrams, 'Concubinage, Cohabitation and the Law: Class and Gender Relations in Nineteenth-Century Germany', *Gender & History*, 5 (1993), 81–100.

[17] H. R. Schmidt, *Dorf und Religion: Reformierte Sittenzucht in Berner Landgemeinden der frühen Neuzeit* (Stuttgart, 1995), 249.

[18] Ozment, *Family Life*: Beck, 'Frauen in der Krise' on Germany; on Europe see, for example, B. Gottlieb, *The Family in the Western World: From the Black Death to the Industrial Age* (New York, 1993), ch. 5.

[19] L. Roper's, *The Holy Household: Women and Morals in Reformation Augsburg* (Oxford, 1989), and Beck, 'Frauen in Krise', are important exceptions.

well. The court told Stadmann to 'cohabit with her, supply her with food and drink, cold and warm, and with clothes and other necessities, and not push or beat her, but honour her as befits a *Bidermann*'.[20] Arising within the late medieval civic artisan culture, this view of a husband's marital duties, and the State's obligation to ensure that he observed them, thus preceded the Reformation. The Reformation, however, helped to institutionalize it more broadly and widely. Industriousness, modesty, and moral integrity were to form the basis of economic success and companionship. Violent, drunk, and spendthrift husbands were to be punished with short imprisonment in Protestant Augsburg as much as in Counter-Reformation Constance.

Artisans were the citizens who most frequently used the council to restore domestic order, and this fact needs to be explained first. It suggests that artisans felt that the council represented them and their values in ways which day-labourers could not share. The pressure to maintain a functioning marriage was particularly high among artisans, partly because the survival of the workshop depended on it, and partly because so much time was spent collectively within the household. In artisan families, moreover, there was money enough to permit hard drinking, which could lead to repeated abuse. Finally, complaints about a bad marriage could be expensive if one partner had to pay a fine, or was imprisoned or temporarily banished because of it; labourers could not afford the risk.

This social profile of suitors put councils into an awkward position. As Lyndal Roper has shown, their quarrels made public the deep conflicts in the marriages of 'orderly citizens'. They demonstrated that gender did not 'naturally' dictate a wife's obedience or the husband's ability to lead the household.[21] Marriages were complicated. The following section traces the senses in which this was so. I am not concerned with the authorities' response to bad marriages,[22] the symbolism of insults and gender-specific means of violence,[23] or women's representation of their problems in court.[24] My main concern is to reconstruct neighbours' views of marital problems. Neighbours knew how they had developed and why, and their judgements were not self-interested. Their observations

[20] StAH, 4/477, fos. 39ᵛ-40ʳ, Stadmann was a Sieder.
[21] Roper, *Holy Household*, 165, 173.   [22] Ibid., ch. 5.
[23] D. W. Sabean, *Property, Production, and Family in Neckarhausen, 1700–1870* (Cambridge, 1990), ch. 4.   [24] Beck, 'Frauen in Krise'.

provide extremely valuable insights into how early modern marriages were experienced.

'The Worst Devil is the Marriage-Devil'

In 1578 the Constance table-maker Caspar Kiesser wept when he confessed to a neighbour that he could not and did not know how to continue living with his wife, because she dishonoured him daily. When a messenger had come from his home region (he reported), he had told his wife to prepare some soup. After the men had drunk three measures of wine together, Kiesser had accompanied his guest to the city gate. The moment he returned home his wife had shouted in anger that 'if he would not beat her, she would beat him'. He begged the neighbour to ask his wife why she did not want to live with him any more. Meanwhile she had told another man that her husband treated her badly. She admitted insulting him, but only because he had defamed her parents: 'you and your old monsters (*Unholden*) are just the same', he had said. Neighbours knew that he had beaten her at least twice, and that she had once thrown a tool in his face. Two witnesses described her as a 'lewd woman', but they also remembered the humiliations she had been subjected to. One reported that Kiesser had once sent his wife to buy pears; finding those she bought too expensive, he had thrown them at her head. She had had to pick them up from the floor and take them back to the market.[25] All reports about bad marriages were dominated by tales of violence, mockery, humiliation, selfishness, disgust, suspicion, or dislike of a partner's family. When council deputies collected information about quarrelsome couples, it was neighbours they consulted. Neighbours tended to offer several different diagnoses of marital quarrels; I discuss them in turn.

Women (first) who were defined as the guilty party were said to give their husbands 'bad words'—dishonouring them publicly—and give them little to eat. These were the shrews, whose verbal power men could not stop even through violence. In Memmingen, for example, a woman called Menhauserin not only quarrelled with neighbouring women, but swore and cursed throughout the year. When angry, she was like a 'wild beast'. Moreover, she wanted to 'govern' the journeymen, while her husband 'walked about the house like a sheep and was deemed worth less than a boy'.[26] The wife of a Constance glazier served drinks to several men in the

---

[25] StAKN, HIX, F. 62, 2 Feb. 1578. [26] StAMM, A 140/5, 14 Aug. 1622.

evening, and drank, sang, and danced with journeymen. She led a 'wild life', and unabashedly told neighbours that 'she had to send away her fool now, meaning her husband, so that she could have some good life (*ein gutleben*)'.[27] A cooper, considered by neighbours to be a 'virtuous fellow', was never given a 'good word' by his wife. She publicly called him 'fool and thief', and locked him out of the house one Sunday; she never gave him breakfast. She had been just as bad with her first husband, telling another cooper frankly that her husband 'would not see the day she would do him good; she wanted to destroy him; she wanted him to hang on the gallows'.[28] A Constance artisan's wife forced her husband and journeymen to work hard, and neighbours remarked that if he had worked as much while married to his first wife, he would have become rich. But his second wife went out in the morning and returned home drunk at night.[29] Thebus Behringer's case was the most tragic: he hanged himself in 1603. He was the victim of one of the many quiet, unofficial separations from bed and board. His wife had not slept with him for five years and had not fed him either. She had looked for other men, and one female neighbour knew that Thebus 'had been quite sad and lonely, and his wife had loved him little'. She had 'gone for the good life', while he had suffered hunger and want: 'when he had gone over the fields and returned home hungry and pale she had done nothing for him, had neither given him drink nor food', so that he had had to become indebted to the baker.[30]

The wife's guilt was even more obvious if her husband was not only well-meaning but *hauslich* too. For artisans this meant that he was always seen at work and hardly ever in taverns. The Constance butcher Ulrich Frey, for example, worked 'early and late'. But even so his household was in a deplorable condition. For years his wife 'did not listen quietly to what he said; everything was commented upon with the words you dog-fiddle, Bavarian, fool, thief, murderer of souls, adulterer'. She admitted that she wanted 'to do everything to drive him away'. This woman was also known to have treated her first husband badly; she had 'once attempted to attack him with a sword, so that he had to retreat into a chamber'.[31] The fact that these were second marriages, in which the wives might have been more experienced, wealthy, and less obedient, was not perceived to be

---

[27] StAKN, HIX, F. 33, 19 Jan. 1569, Simon Muntzen's wife.
[28] StAKN, HIX, F. 33, n.d., *c.* May 1571.
[29] StAKN, HIX, F. 46, 15 Jan. 1633, Jacob Keller and his wife.
[30] StAKN, HIX, F. 43, 11 Dec. 1603. [31] StAKN, HIX, F. 46, 1 July 1625.

part of the problem. The neighbours assumed that it simply lay in these women's nature to strive for control and to wear their husbands' breeches.

A husband's diligence weighed so strongly with artisan neighbours that they usually found it difficult to imagine him capable of bad behaviour otherwise. Their wives received little sympathy when they reported marital violence. Everyone saw that Hans Haller, for example, 'worked hard and did not go out to drink wine'. Shouts could often be heard in their house late at night; but when Haller's wife went to a neighbour on one such night, having been beaten by her husband, he advised her to 'return home and be quiet; he would, God grant it, not do more [harm] to her until tomorrow, and maybe it would get better'. Hans Haller himself had to endure his wife's scolding, and confessed to a female neighbour that his wife 'was a pain to him and he would have to leave her'.[32]

Guilt was even more readily ascribed to a wife if she herself was *unhauslich*—drinking, neglecting children, or keeping the household badly. In 1671, a Hall woman was lucky not to be punished with having to sweep the market (a shaming punishment for drunkards), as her husband was on his deathbed. The mayor ordered her to be chained at home, because she got drunk daily and then scolded her husband instead of consoling him.[33] In 1688, a salt-worker reported to the lower court that Caspar Blinzig's wife was often seen drunk, and now had a 'black and blue face' from her husband's thrashing. Blinzig explained that he had given her eleven *Kreuzer*, which she had wasted. She got him into debt, because she pawned clothes, furniture, and household goods. She often drank herself 'voll und doll' and 'kept herself and her bed so dirty that he could hardly stay with her anymore'.[34] Such physical disgust was not uncommon. It could be caused by slowly healing wounds. Margaretha Trinkler, for example, suffered from swollen thighs after an accident in 1530; herbal remedies would not heal them. Her husband refused to let her sleep in their matrimonial bed, declaring that 'she was so smelly that she was leprous like her brother'. He told the servant-maid he wanted her instead of his wife, who was 'full of ointments . . . up to her bum'.[35] When Kunigunde Clainer accused her husband before the Rothenburg peasants' court for not having sex with her, he

[32] StAKN, HIX, F. 33, n.d., *c.* 1571.
[33] StAH, 4/549, fos. 42^v, 44^r, 13 July 1671, Nicolaus Bauren's wife.
[34] StAH, 4/554, fos. 397^{v}-398^{r-v}, 27 Aug. 1688.   [35] HStASt, A 43, Bü. 9.

likewise argued that she was 'filthy and not clean or nice'.[36] Cleanliness therefore mattered. But otherwise 'good householding' meant the ability to work well and to be economical. Neighbouring women thought that a Constance tailor had every reason for beating his wife. He had 'flirted' with one of the maidservants, but only because 'she kept the house well' and was diligent: 'this was why the master had loved her.'[37] 'Love' was linked to the appreciation of a woman's work; how work was done said everything important about character. One had to be able to trust these qualities. When Sebastian Studer defended himself before the Constance council in 1577, he affirmed that he wanted to live with his wife 'as was fitting for an honest man'. But when he returned home at night for something to eat, 'she ran out of the house'. A week ago she had been supposed to prepare dough and take it to the bakehouse; but when he returned home from the watch he saw that she had stayed away overnight; 'he himself had had to knead and take the dough to the bakers.'[38]

If each partner hoped to feel certain about the other's ability to fulfil his or her duties, these duties were invariably assigned by the husband. Most of them did not need to be spelled out. It went without saying that if a household did not employ a maidservant, the wife got up first in the morning to light the fire, so that the husband entered a warm chamber and washed in warm water. It was equally natural that a woman should spin or knit in the evening, while the man took his leisure with friends. Women had to look after guests properly. Frequently, subtle sensitivities had to be tended to. One Memmingen woman put a fresh handkerchief for her husband on a bench instead of giving it to him directly before he went to a wedding in 1603: this made him feel justified in beating her with a rope. When he brought home a friend after the wedding, she baked 'cakes for them and thought she had done well, but even though Denzel [the friend] had eaten lots of them' her husband had spilt a measure of beer and told her to get out of his sight.[39] A husband's orders, moreover, were final and authoritative. Michael Perg took a light from his wife in the stable and declared that 'if she caused a fire, he as a *Hausvater* would be responsible'.[40]

[36] H. J. Grembowietz, *Das Bauerngericht der freien Reichsstadt Rothenburg ob der Tauber vom späten Mittelalter bis zu seinem Niedergang (1403–1678): Eine rechtshistorische Untersuchung an Hand der Gerichtsbücher und anderer Quellen* (Würzburg, 1974), 31.
[37] StAKN, HIX, F. 41, 25 Apr. 1595, Steiss.   [38] StAKN, HIX, F. 51, 10 Nov. 1577.
[39] StAMM, A 135/8, 13 Dec. 1603.   [40] StAKN, RP, BI 144, 1664, fo. 620ʳ.

Usually we hear of these rules presupposing a wife's obedience only when wives resisted them. This happened when Daniel Labhart, a wealthy Constance citizen, returned home in great excitement in 1597, to tell his wife to prepare the house for the visit of Archduke Mathias and his entourage: he himself would get wine, and she should get enough hay, in case the guests lodged with them. Labhart only received a sulky look in return. He began: this was 'his Lord's order and command, and did she want to resist it?' She answered defiantly by asking 'why she should care about his Lord's order'; throwing down her spoon she went into the kitchen. Other incidents added to Labhart's unhappiness. He had once told her to go to the baker's, but she had refused the order. He also suspected that she was having an affair with a man with whom she had on three occasions played music (he the lute, she the harp). Labhart had shown their matrimonial bed to a friend: he thought it was suspiciously muddy, as if people had lain on it with their shoes on. The family attempted a private reconciliation and restaged the marriage vow: the couple shook hands and took a sip of wine. But Labhart's wife later commented that 'no good would come until they were free of each other'.[41]

In all these situations neighbours thought the wife the guiltier party. A second set of neighbourly perceptions was that 'neither partner was better than the other'.[42] Two Hall couples who 'quarrelled all the time' and 'attacked each other viciously' were punished with two days' and seven nights' imprisonment in the fool's house before they were required to shake hands and swear forgiveness.[43] The usual background of such verdicts was that both partners were often drunk, and that they kept their household badly, were slanderous, and refused neighbours' interventions; neighbours would report the couple to the council after a particularly noisy quarrel. Thus in 1606 a Constance organ-player and his wife were accused of keeping their children 'meagrely' and leaving a sick child alone while going out to drink. Neighbours who warned the couple were scolded with 'immodest talk'.[44] Sometimes neighbours would be alarmed by crying toddlers who had been left alone. On the mother's part this was regarded as serious neglect, especially if she was visiting an inn rather than going to market, to the fields, or to

---

[41] StAKN, HIX, F. 41, 10 June 1597.
[42] StAKN, HIX, F. 46, 15 June 1633, Jacob Keller and his wife.
[43] StAH, 4/482, fo. 64ʳ, 24 June 1630.   [44] StAKN, HIX, F. 43, 24 Jan. 1606, Kerner.

friends. In 1609, after four years, the neighbours of Friedle Sauter and his wife finally had enough of their quarrels. Drunk almost daily, she hit him 'so shamefully that he had to be bandaged'; they lived 'in great disharmony and contrariness, hitting, insulting, and dishonouring each other, and not sparing their neighbours either'.[45] In 1617, a rope-maker's wife had 'ridiculed and mocked her husband', and once she scolded him down the street. Both drank heavily day after day, and a former maidservant affirmed that it was a 'miserable household'.[46] Wine was also sent home by husbands. In 1610 Felix Zimmermann of Memmingen had drunk one measure of wine and sent another home to his wife, but by then 'she was already drunk', and when he returned home at night she 'made such a noise, calling him a fool and a thief'. Only then (he claimed) had he slapped her face; he thought he was imprisoned unjustifiably.[47]

Neighbours dreaded these disorderly couples. They often framed their complaints by alluding to their fear of fire. This expressed anxiety about the real danger of drunken people's carelessness; on a symbolic level it spoke also for their fear of the glowing hatred which could destroy communities. Authorities thought God's punishment might be collectively suffered: 'it would be no wonder', the council remarked about a Memmingen woman in 1605, 'if she and the whole community were punished because of her'.[48] Therefore these couples were often banished from a town or territory altogether, if they did not improve their behaviour after repeated attempts to punish and reconcile them. In 1667, two Constance men asked the council to tell a tailor and a pastry cook and their wives to 'live together more peacefully', otherwise 'they would lose their citizens' rights and be sent away'.[49] The loss of one's work, home, and citizenship was a disaster. It can be safely assumed that threats like this induced even the most antagonistic of couples to douse their hostilities.

A third perception might be that quarrels resulted chiefly from a couple's unhappy economic situation. What determined this judgement was whether or not a couple had done well in times of better trade. The marital work relationship was crucial because about a third to a half of all workshops could not afford to employ a journeyman,

---

[45] StAKN, HIX, F. 44, 2 June 1609.
[46] StAKN, HIX, F. 45, 23 Sept. 1617, Jacob Straub and his wife.
[47] StAMM, A 138/2, 17 Oct. 1617, Schleebuzen.
[48] StAMM, A 135/8, 15 May 1605.
[49] StAKN, RP, BI 147, fo. 536^r, 17 Sept. 1667.

and depended on a wife's labour.[50] In 1597, a Constance cooper and his wife were said to be quarrelling all the time, because they had little work to do. Hitherto, a carpenter reported, they had always been peaceful; 'when one brought them work, they were always friendly and did the work well.'[51] Furious at his wife's secret debts, the cartwright Georg Gamel forced her to help him in the workshop, from which she repeatedly escaped. 'He could not live together with her any longer,' he exhaustedly told a neighbour: only their cooperation ensured survival.

In a fourth group of conflicts, alcohol was understood to have caused the problem. Some men were respected as good householders and 'dear neighbours'—except when they were drunk. This was what people said about the Constance mason Hans Borck in 1607: normally he would 'not insult a child', but when drunk he roamed about at home, violently. When once he brought a painter home, his wife had to forbid his fetching another measure of wine.[52] 'He was hardly like himself,' a Memmingen woman described her husband's behaviour when drunk. In 1617, he drank spirits in the morning, and beer and wine in the afternoon. Neighbours thought he was a 'good man'. Only alcohol was to blame for the fact that the couple 'lived together like cat and dog'.[53]

Finally, there was the group of notoriously drunk, violent, monstrous men, condemned by everyone. Their wives feared for their lives, and although physical cruelty was the only accepted reason for a legal separation, their claims that they lived in terror were not necessarily pretended. Over many years neighbours could usually see how little a husband worked and how much he drank, and that he could so little provide for the family that his wife and children were starving. Violence was rarely blind. Children were hardly ever attacked; it was the wife who bore the brunt. Jo Mangerstan, for example, came home with a 'drawn sword' and thrashed about with it; neighbours thought 'he was an old witch and worse than Betele, who had been decapitated'.[54] Jacob Zwaig, a cutler, 'always led a useless drunken life'. Although he had enough orders, his workshop was in bad shape, he did not look after servants and journeymen properly, and neither went himself to church nor told them to do so.

[50] Wunder, '"*Er ist die Sonn', sie ist der Mond*', 100.
[51] StAKN, HIX, F. 41, 9 Dec. 1597.   [52] StAKN, HIX, F. 44, 11 June 1607.
[53] StAMM, A 138/2, 17 Oct. 1617, Schleebuzen.
[54] This comment refered to Elsbetha Zeller, who had been decapitated two years previously for theft and infanticide, StAKN, HIX, F. 46, 10 Nov. 1629.

They suffered great want, as did his wife, whom he 'treated badly'.[55] Such violence did not lack poignancy. Erasmus Rauscher wanted to burn the marital bed, but then broke it in two, symbolically destroying the emblem of their union. Neighbours tried to calm the drunken man and offered his wife shelter. For years they had lent her bread, and listened when she told how he had put a knife at her heart and said he wanted to give her poison. The preparation and eating of food formed the main bond between husband and wife; his duty was to work for the resources, and he would expect a rewarding meal in return. Put on the table when he returned home at night and as fatty as possible, the meal would express her appreciation of his labour and give him strength.[56] The symbolism of poisoned food was correspondingly high.[57] Neighbours assured a woman like Rauscher's wife that they witnessed what went on between the couple and advised her to 'tell the authorities about it'. But this was not easy if you had a violent husband, and Rauscherin had obviously considered it already. 'Yes,' she replied, 'she would do so if he were then to be exiled from the town, but if he was only going to be imprisoned her life would be at risk.' So she never went to the authorities; a neighbour brought the whole misery into the open only when he accused Rauscher after a row.[58] Wives had to be cautious: one year later a shoemaker furiously locked up his wife in the pig stable. He accused her of being responsible for his two days' imprisonment even though she drank more than he did.[59]

Official punishment was a two-edged sword for women. A violent husband would be punished with short imprisonment and forbidden any drinking, a humiliation bound to increase his fury. The fact that communes were not prepared to subsidize children put women in a difficult position. In 1668, the bailiff and parson of Cannstatt wrote to the Württemberg supreme council for advice how to deal with a notoriously drunken shoemaker who coolly replied to their admonitions that 'he had already been driven into the suburb, and now they wanted to expel him altogether', and who threatened to desert his six children and go away. The Cannstatt authorities did not know how to solve such a situation, and the supreme council's reply was unhelpful: such men were to be imprisoned if they did not improve their behaviour.[60]

[55] StAKN, HIX, F. 41, n.d., c. 1595/6.   [56] See Beck, 'Frauen in Krise', 164f.
[57] See the murder cases later in this chapter.
[58] StAKN, HIX, F. 45, 14 Jan. 1617.   [59] StAKN, HIX, F. 45, 20 July 1618.
[60] HStASt, A 206, Bü. 1504.

One of the best solutions women could hope for was to obtain the council's permission to control family income and accounts. In 1685 a Hall goldsmith supported the wife of another smith when she complained to the lower court that her husband spent much money on wine and other things and that no food was good enough for him. During the past year she had 'lost all money'; 'she and her children had to . . . drag themselves along like poor worms; *addendo*, she wanted control over the incoming money'. It was decided that she should buy her husband one measure of wine daily and whatever else he needed, and herself pay the journeymen's salary. Two curators were told to monitor the case, while the smith was urged to 'work hard'.[61] This solution was better than banishment. Banishment merely created new financial worries; it was only a temporary solution, and had to be followed by reconciliation. Thus in Memmingen a written reconciliation contract was drawn up when Joachim Diendorff returned home from banishment in 1610. He promised to behave in future as was fitting for a 'Christian *Haus- und Biedermann*', while his wife declared her willingness to 'try it again with him, to accept him back home again, and to behave as befitted a God-loving Christian wife, as well as she could, and also not to seek revenge for his former behaviour'.[62] But only a few months later she wanted him banished again.[63]

When marital problems were brought before the council, the ways in which they were represented tended to change. Usually a couple was cautioned and told to seek reconciliation, but punishment was always possible. Cautioning might be formulaic but verdicts could also hurt. So each one of a couple would accuse the other, and apologies would be faint. Narratives would focus on the issues which according to the authorities determined the quality of married life: cohabitation in 'bed and board' (i.e. the mutual supply of food and sex), and the extent of physical violence, wastefulness, laziness, drunkenness, and blasphemy. Each partner stressed his or her sufferings. Clearly, then, the rifts between couples who appeared before the magistrates, already deep, were likely to be worsened by the accusation. Hence if reconciliation was ever achieved, it was usually achieved informally. The family or more commonly neighbours would simply tell a couple to pull themselves together.[64]

---

[61] StAH, 4/553, fos. 8ᵛ-9ʳ.   [62] StAMM, RP, 26 Apr. 1609–6 Aug. 1613, fo. 96ʳ⁻ᵛ.
[63] See below, p. 211.
[64] On the functions of neighbourhood see D. Garrioch, *Neighbourhood and Community in Paris, 1740–1790* (Cambridge, 1986); on the protection of wives see p. 19f.

Neighbours were the only listeners and witnesses with no interest in settling the conflict other than that of restoring neighbourhood peace.[65]

Neighbourliness was a fundamental bond. A Constance woman for example hosted a 'farewell drink' for neighbours before her husband left for the Turkish war. The couple made an oral will according to which the one who died first would inherit the other's property.[66] Feasts were attended 'for the neighbourhood's sake'.[67] Whenever the season made it possible, the women would knit or spin together on the street or in a courtyard during the evening, and meet in houses during autumn and winter nights. What everyone did was visible—and audible. Houses were built close to each other and with thin walls: neighbours overheard every row. Through low windows and open workshop doors one could see how people worked.[68] People popped in for visits, met at local shops, wells, or the market, went to the bath together, lent or exchanged goods, helped each other build things, had an eye on each other's children, and an open ear for noise and violence. When possible, people tried to stop quarrels. In 1567, for example, a cook said that she had run into a quarrelling couple's house 'to separate them and make peace', but the husband had thrown her out; a neighbour sitting in the street with women in the summertime remembered the wife's cries.[69] A baker's wife leaned out of the window and cried for help when her drunken husband threatened to kill her: immediately, neighbours trooped to the house with ladders, aware that thanks to his threats she had already had to spend several nights in other people's houses.[70] In 1597, Salome Ehrhard recalled sitting in front of her house breastfeeding her baby and hearing 'great uproar and shouting' between her brother-in-law Felix and her sister. A woman spinning in front of her house tried to make peace. Soon, Felix's wife ran across to Salome's house screaming and without her headdress; but the drunken husband followed her and 'knocked down the door and pillars'. Salome furiously shouted at him that 'he was full of dirt, and should destroy his own door'; neighbours stopped him beating

---

[65] In 1610, for example, Memmingen citizens complained about a man who shouted so noisily at night that he could be heard at Jörg Gryffen's house and no one could sleep: StAMM, RP, 26 Apr. 1609–6 Aug. 1613, fo. 96^{r-v}.
[66] StAKN, HIX, F. 53, 2 July 1566, Wendel Schlöch's wife.
[67] StAKN, HIX, F. 41, 9 Nov. 1598, Galli Schomüle.
[68] StAMM, A 138/6, 22 March 1619.
[69] StAKN, HIX, F. 53, Donnerstag nach Judion, 1567.
[70] StAKN, HIX, F. 43, 7 Aug. 1602, Galli Schomüle.

her.[71] Neighbours also supported each other during illness: one Memmingen woman said she would have died had not neighbours helped her when her husband made her carry heavy water-tubs and do other hard labour while she was ill. A male neighbour had lost patience and asked him 'whether he wanted to kill his wife'.[72]

Yet although unjustified violence against a wife ensured neighbourhood support, it was by no means invariably the case that women supported wives and men the husbands. People usually took the side of the partner who was treated unfairly. It was known that hierarchies of power could be inverted. One Constance woman, for example, often kept her husband outside in the street while she entertained her sister and mother. When he had slapped her face before bedtime she had not 'lain with him for a fortnight', neighbouring women reported.[73] Michael Perg's wife formed an alliance with her son: she took her meals with him and would only serve her husband his meals in the upper chamber. Perg lamented that she 'did not trust him in regard to any household and workshop matters'.[74] Alliances with children or relatives often changed the distribution of power, two standing against one.[75]

Servants were equally important in this context. If maidservants supported a wife, a useless, violent man could gradually be marginalized in the household. Anna Maria Vogler, Johann Diendorffer's wife, had already once been imprisoned in Memmingen, the council admonishing her to lead a peaceful marriage henceforth. Her husband, likewise once banished, had now returned. However, as she wrote in her 1610 petition, the situation now worsened every day. One evening her husband had returned drunk from the merchants' guild and shouted that 'by a thousand sacraments, he wanted to be master in this house, and you sacramental bag, don't you want to give me something to eat?' Margaretha (the maid) had summoned the beadle and his assistant. The beadle reminded her husband that he was not allowed to drink much. Aggression and despair were intertwined: during the next days her husband announced that he wanted to kill himself or her and the maidservant. As Anna wrote in her petition, this was tyranny; but if so, it was born of weakness. She had taken over all work and even went to Mundelsheim herself to finish off some work. She wanted to keep the earnings for herself.

[71] StAKN, HIX, F. 41, n.d., c. July 1597.   [72] StAMM, A 139/4.
[73] StAKN, HIX, F. 39, 26 Feb. 1587, Spyter.   [74] StAKN, RP, BI 144, 1664, fo. 620ʳ.
[75] StAKN, HIX, F. 41, 6 May 1598, is an example of how the husband's mother supported him against his wife.

She also expected 'peace and quiet' when she returned home with servants at night, being 'tired and exhausted, and sometimes wet, hungry and thirsty'. She had struggled hard, and wanted her husband banished 'so that she would not have to burden her body and soul with him any longer'. Otherwise, she added, she would have to leave him, hoping that he would earn his own bread since he could not keep his family. Anna Maria's children were no longer at home, so she would be all right. If the authorities did not permit the separation, she would no longer obey them.[76]

It was not uncommon for people to separate informally from 'bed and board' while staying in the same town. A 1529 Constance ordinance insisted that all such couples (except for if one partner had committed adultery) should immediately move together again or report their case to the council so that the guilty partner could be punished or banished.[77] In 1639, someone likewise told the Memmingen council that 'several marriages had separated themselves' in this way.[78] Although in Hall and Wildberg, several couples were ordered to live together again on pain of banishment,[79] most neighbours probably tolerated these informal separations. To wait for God's help sometimes seemed pointless. One woman told the Memmingen councillors that the chronically drunk Felix Kharer and his wife 'were so embittered with each other that there was no hope of improvement'. Felix himself had realized that their quarrels had changed their relationship forever: 'there was no worse devil', he said, 'than the marriage-devil.'[80]

BIGAMY AND ADULTERY

In 1536 Margaretha Trinkler was drowned for bigamy, a fate which demonstrated that Protestant Württemberg knew no mercy for women who took so extreme a step. Margaretha had given the court her excuses. Her husband, the Cannstatt city-scribe, had been notoriously unfaithful and violent; and after she had finally run off with the parson, the Zurich marriage court had allowed her to remarry. But back in Württemberg the marriage was deemed illegal. Margaretha

---

[76] StAMM, A 136/2, 9 Nov. 1610.

[77] O. Feger (ed.), *Die Statutensammlung des Stadtschreibers Jörg Vögeli* (Constance, 1951), 68, 'Ordnung der ußtriber der frömbden lüt', 22 Feb. 1529.

[78] StAMM, RP, 31 Oct. 1638–30 Dec. 1640, fos. 122^v-125^r, 9 Dec. 1639.

[79] StAMM, RP, 3 Oct. 1569–9 July 1572, fo. 179^v, Matthis Gayser and his wife.

[80] StAMM, A 136/1, 2 Nov. 1610.

died at Tübingen, in the Neckar—three years before Luther and
Melanchthon famously allowed Philip of Hesse to enter into a second marriage while his first wife still lived.[81]

Women who were accused of bigamy were usually less rebellious
than Margaretha.[82] They remarried because their first husband had
deserted them or was presumed to have died during war. If the
marriage had been brief and the husband an outsider, or if it was
clear that he had deserted his wife, local authorities would sometimes unofficially allow a second marriage.[83] An *official* permission to
remarry either required a death certificate or proof that the husband
had been absent for several years and that his wife had remained
chaste. This partly reflected confusion about how property and
inheritance rights were affected by a desertion.[84] The long wait for
a husband's return, however, was hard for women with small children. The case of Anna Beck is typical. She had lived in Ernstfelden
with her husband for two years and given birth to two children.
Then, after joining a Hungarian regiment, he left her 'in poverty and
without a goodbye', neither writing to her nor sending money for the
children. After a year Anna left the community, pretended to be a
widow, and married a miller. After his death in 1682 she returned to
Ernstfelden. There she was imprisoned, and forbidden to join 'honest company' again.[85]

From 1624 onwards, parsons were explicitly cautioned not to issue
death certificates for missing husbands on the basis of 'mere pretence or forged documents', since the first husband's reappearance
repeatedly caused problems.[86] Women who had forged documents
were likely to be punished harshly, especially if they knew that their
husband was still alive. Adultery was often similarly caused by a
husband's desertion. Anna Reich explained that she had committed
adultery only after her husband had left her for a vagrant woman
upon whom, she claimed, he fathered eleven children.[87]

---

[81] HStASt, A 43, Bü. 9. On theological and legal attitudes to bigamy see P. Migat, *Die
Polygamiefrage in der frühen Neuzeit* (Opladen, 1988).

[82] Though in 1615, for example, a Hall woman simply took some of her husband's
belongings and ran off with a market crier: StAH, 4/481, fo. 174ʳ, 6 Oct. 1615, Apolonia
Fürkornin.   [83] HStASt, A 209, Bü. 1006, 13 Aug. 1646.

[84] In a Memmingen case in 1592 a husband who had deserted his wife was told to
draw up an inventory of his property and the wife was told not to take away his
property: StAMM, RP 1 July 1590–10 Mar. 1595, fo. 73ᵛ, 7 June 1592.

[85] HStASt, A 209, Bü. 1512, 13 Oct. 1682.

[86] Reyscher, *Gesetze*, v. 198, 'General=Rescript, Ehesachen betreffend', 18 Apr. 1624;
for cases see StAH, 4/483, 17 Oct. 1670, Anna Maria Mair; HStASt, A 309, Bü. 167; A 209,
Bü. 1462, Anna Maria Schnell.   [87] HStASt, A 209, Bü. 886, 19 Aug. 1606.

Men either deserted their wives to start a new life, or to escape punishment for other offences. Anna Kohler, for example, had been married for four years before her husband left her after committing a theft. He several times asked her to follow him to Milan; when letters ceased she gave him up for dead. She and her two children moved to her parents' in Bodelshausen; she worked as a stocking-knitter and at harvests. After two years, Anna started an affair with a married man. After giving birth to an illegitimate child, she was imprisoned and had to do penance in church.[88]

Deserted women depended on their family's help and were probably tolerated in small towns or villages if they withdrew from close contact with men. As they were available and yet bound they attracted male desires and aggression and were easily stigmatized as whores. The same could happen to widows (who were also accused of adultery if they had affairs with married men). In 1527 the Protestant reformer Johannes Brenz analysed just how such defamation worked in his statement about Elsa Sommer's affair. This Hall widow was accused of having sex with a man nicknamed 'Tall George'. Brenz showed that each witness was either Sommer's personal enemy, or had only second-hand knowledge about the allegation. As a result the trial was abandoned.[89] Brenz's statement contributed to the virulent fight for an impartial administration of justice whose landmark, the *Carolina*, was published five years later. But educated men's efforts to intercede on behalf of women of humbler status were rare.

Single mothers who managed to stay in their community were in a similarly difficult position. One crime could lead to another. Anna Andri lived with a bastard in Winnenden. Once when she was cutting grass a man waved at her and pointed to his private parts. She did not react, and he went away, but came to her house on another day and said that he would give her tools and a linen sheet if she had sex with him. Only the child's crying deterred him. Eight days later he turned up again, locked the door, took his clothes off and tore hers, and even though she threatened to cut off his member with a sickle, he raped her.[90]

If a single woman knew that her lover was married and committed

---

[88] She was pilloried, whipped, and banished, HStASt, A 209, Bü. 1252, 15 July 1699.
[89] M. Brecht et al. (eds.), *Johannes Brenz: Frühschriften*, vol. ii (Tübingen, 1974), 322–30.
[90] UAT, 84/26, fos. 4ʳ-6ʳ, Anna Helena Andriß, 1673.

repeated adultery, she could be punished relentlessly.[91] In 1698, 35-year-old Barbara Heinrich, already once punished for adultery, and now convicted for an affair with a married tailor, was decapitated. An orphan, one of her brothers was said to have died after a dissolute life, another had been executed for sodomy, and two of her sisters were known whores. Barbara's decapitation further depleted the infamous family in the village of Burstall.[92] Abba Wiedman, a Sontheim seamstress, was decapitated in the same year. Her story was different: a smith and father of four children had twice had sex with her 'in a corner near her house' as she returned home from work at eight in the evening, and then a third time during spring when she returned from the field. When she told him that she was pregnant he replied that 'she should go away with him; he would find a place where they could marry so that they could live together'. She had not wanted this, so both had stayed, and endured imprisonment and church penance. Soon they made love again. They escaped, because this time they had to fear for their lives. They pretended to be married, and he found work as a cart driver in Stuttgart. It was probably the birth of their child that exposed their plot; it was still an infant when the mother was decapitated.[93]

The stories behind adulterous attraction mattered little to the authorities, except that when a wife denied intercourse the husband's adultery was deemed acceptable. In 1655 Georg Ringele had begun an affair with an orphaned seamstress in Gerlingen with whom he had moved to Heilbronn when she became pregnant. Ringele's wife claimed that she, a 'poor, weak woman', had been betrayed. Ringele's response was that he had married her when he was aged 21, and that 'whenever he had sought intercourse, she had started to cry and told him to let go of her, keeping her illness secret'. He maintained that she had allowed him to sleep with other women. Ringele and the seamstress were punished with church penance and banished from the district for as long as his wife lived.[94]

Such verdicts demonstrate that a wife's sexual fidelity was thought to be more fundamental to the functioning of a marriage than love and respect. Protestants partly regarded sex as important because it was a spiritual experience of becoming one flesh. However, more

---

[91] One maidservant was terrified to find that the servant she had slept with had 'shamefully deserted his wife and children'. She did not have to undergo church penance but was imprisoned: HStASt, A 209, Bü. 771, 9 Jan. 1667.
[92] HStASt, A 209, Bü. 1801.   [93] HStASt, A 209, Bü. 2014, 3 Sept. 1698.
[94] HStASt, A 309, Bü. 174.

important was the pragmatic consideration that sexual lust had to be satisfied inside a marriage in order to prevent sinful behaviour. Men *and* women could sue their partner if she or he refused intercourse. Sex had become a Christian duty, a medicine to be taken regularly in order to fight off lust. In an eighteenth-century incest case one woman was therefore asked 'how her husband had behaved towards her in the matrimonial bed'. Her answer was that 'he had shown himself in these matters as was Christian and proper; he had last cohabited with her a fortnight ago'.[95] In view of the fact that theologians only emphasized a wife's duty to serve her husband,[96] it is hardly surprising that wives felt guilty if their husbands went astray. The answer of a 54-year-old woman whose husband had slept with her daughter is sad to read. She told the court that 'he had performed his marital duties with her, and she had done everything so that he would not walk away from her'. While ill, she had repeatedly had to sleep with him 'to prevent him from becoming unfaithful'.[97]

If a husband had become impotent during a marriage, on the other hand, this was regarded as a 'calamity' a wife had to put up with. A husband's abstinence was not readily accepted as an excuse either.[98] Nor was female adultery excused if the emotional basis for sex in a marriage had disappeared. In 1649 Sabina Werlim had endured a difficult marriage for years and been endangered by her violent husband. 'Human weakness' had finally tempted her into an affair, and she had probably killed the child which resulted from it. Did her miserable marriage justify mitigation? The lawyers agreed it did not, because

even though this woman has endured much pain during her marriage, she knew what her husband was like and chose to marry him. Also the *debitum*

---

[95] HStASt, A 309, Bü. 147, 5 Dec. 1765.

[96] The Zurich reformer Bullinger, for example, warned women not to deny husbands sex 'disobediently and boldly, because such hostility often causes adultery', cited in A. Völker, 'Bilderpaare—Paarbilder: Die Ehe in Autobiographien des 16. Jahrhunderts', (D.Phil. thesis, Freiburg im Breisgau, 1990), 307.

[97] HStASt, A 309, Bü. 270, 22 March 1770, Elisabeth Metsch.

[98] A miller's wife in Bergfelden, who was promiscuous and had behaved 'nastily', taking her clothes off near a highway and exposing her private parts, said that her husband had neither changed his clothes for weeks nor been able to fulfil the *debitum conjugale* for her. But this, the Tübingen lawyers decided, was only an *abstinentia temporalis* and did not justify mitigation: HStASt, A 209, Bü. 1765, 10 July 1696, Jung Hans Jacob Fischer's wife.

conjugale consists not only in love but also in pain; and one has to endure the bad with patience and wait for God's help.[99]

The infanticide, of course, weighed heavily, but it also becomes apparent how little sympathy lawyers showed for a woman's search for an easier life. Until the third Württemberg marriage ordinance in 1687, a woman like Sabina Werlim heard from the pulpit four times a year that couples who had developed 'great hostility, envy, hatred, grudge, and unfriendliness' and did not cohabit were to be punished 'to protect the holy marriage and bond'. This ordinance had been law for 134 years. Its paragraph on marital disharmony ended with the demand that a husband should remember that his wife had been given to him by God as a helpmate, while the wife was to remember that her husband was her 'head and Lord'. Both were told to 'love the other as one loved one's own body'.[100]

A wife's adultery was therefore always an attack on her 'lord', a betrayal of her duty to be obedient, and directed against household order as such. Although since the sixteenth century male and female adultery had been treated equally in law, a wife's adultery was regarded as more serious.[101] Adultery with servants showed this. Men who impregnated maidservants were fined only slightly more than they were fined for adultery with a single women or widow. On the other hand, a mistress who merely drank wine with a journeyman while her husband was away risked her reputation, even if she did not sleep with him. If a married man fathered an illegitimate child, arrangements were quickly made; not so, however, when a wife conceived a bastard.

Socially, a wife's adultery was less alarming because of her sexual sin than because she undermined her husband's authority. The fact that the most common insult among married women was to call the other a whore is not without obvious meaning either. This says less about early modern sexual morality than about a wife's expected virtues: a prostitute was a sterile, independent, money-earning, and wasteful woman, and thus the antitype of a good housewife.[102] An

---

[99] God would punish the judges if she was not decapitated, because they would have failed to avenge the child's death, HStASt, A 209, Bü. 1908.

[100] Reyscher, *Gesetze*, iv. 90, 'Zweite Ehe=Ordnung', 1 Jan. 1553.

[101] Roper, *Holy Household*, 199.

[102] M. Dinges, '"Weiblichkeit" in "Männlichkeitsritualen"': Zu weiblichen Taktiken im Ehrenhandel im Paris des 18. Jahrhunderts', *Francia*, 18 (1991), 71–98; L. Gowing, *Domestic Dangers: Women, Words, and Sex in Early Modern London* (Oxford, 1996) ch. 3.

impressive case from the 1629 Wildberg district court shows how accusations of sexual infidelity could be located in this context. Wildberg was a small proto-industrial town in the Nagold valley. Pietist norms had gained ground quickly there, and misbehaviour was closely monitored. Until the introduction of church consistories in 1648, moral transgressors were accused before the district court. Women hardly ever brought charges themselves; male relatives did this for them. In August 1629, however, a married woman did bring her own accusation. It concerned the deep hatred which divided a group of female neighbours. Ursula, wife of the jug-maker Hans Bremen, told the court how eight days earlier a boy had beaten her cow as she drove it from the stable. She had said: 'you great devil, let the cow pass. You always beat my pig as well. I cannot drive them in or out when you are here.' As she returned to the house a neighbouring widow insulted her as a 'toad and dogfoot', and said that it would do no harm for the cow to be beaten, since no one had cut its leg off. Ursula replied that if anyone had cut a leg off, they would be too poor to pay for it. The exchange became heated as the widow's daughter joined in, declaring that she and her mother could certainly pay because they were richer than Ursula: 'we are rich in our souls, and even if she, Ursula, were rich in property, at least the devil had never tried to ensnare them, as he had the jug-maker's wife.' Ursula asked when exactly they thought the devil had tried to ensnare her. Four years ago, was the prompt reply: she should ask Caspar Harrich's wife. Ursula said that if they wanted to defame her, they should at least go away from her house. The neighbours retorted that they were sitting in front of their own house; if Ursula did not want to see them, she should go and sit under the gallows, where she belonged. They added she should go to the town hall; there she would find in the minutes that she was known as a whore. The main defamation then followed: 'you have taken in more than a hundred masons and journeymen and whored with them and afterwards stolen their money; that is why you have become so rich.' On the next day, stones were thrown at Ursula, and at night her windows were broken. Ursula accused the neighbour of owing her five florins and three *Batzen*, but the neighbour replied that she only owed Ursula the gallows. Ursula's report of the case to the bailiff further infuriated her neighbours. One of them attacked her so vehemently that her husband had to restrain her, whereupon she shouted that 'now he supported the whore; presumably he had also lain with her'. The court fined Ursula and her neighbour and cautioned the other women.[103]

Ursula was attacked because she had used her property as an instrument of power against others. Animals were commonly injured as a form of protesting against their owners.[104] The accusation 'whore' expressed the feeling that Ursula had capitalized on her main property, her body, to achieve material profit. This violated the laws of fertility, which required that a woman 'economized' on her sexual partners and only accepted the material provision her husband gave in return. Ursula's husband seemed to have lost control over her sexuality and their money. Others had become indebted to her, and thus she had gained power. The fictive number of more than a 'hundred journeymen' shows that sexual allegations were likely to glide into fantasy, once women were faced with the social behaviour of a dominating wife. In this case, female neighbours clearly 'authored' a fantasy in which they expressed their own anxieties and repressed desires to do with sexuality and power in the home.[105]

The inevitable socio-political dimension of all cases of female adultery also explains why women were more often accused of adultery as a capital offence than men. In Memmingen, in fact, only women were capitally accused of adultery. Two women were even decapitated. In 1574, the Memmingen citizen Agathe Menzler had to stand on the 'burdening-stone' and was expelled through the *Niedergasse* for having copulated 'several times with many men'. Her husband seemed to tolerate her working as a prostitute.[106] In 1606, another citizen was banished for adultery,[107] while in the same month Elsa Bayrin, nicknamed 'goatbelly', was decapitated for repeated adultery.[108] Christina Klein was decapitated for adultery with 'many married as well as single men' in 1629.[109] The 1630 Memmingen discipline ordinance set this out as official policy: a single adultery between a married and a single person was punished with fourteen days' imprisonment for a single person and eighteen days and the loss of all offices for a married person. The punishment

---

[103] HStASt, A 582, Bü. 86, 3 Aug. 1629.

[104] HStASt, A 44, U 2167, 27 March 1527, Barbara Handel, who had maltreated and cut a donkey's leg which belonged to Junker Klaus von Baldeck.

[105] See D. Purkiss, *The Witch in History: Early Modern and Twentieth-Century Representations* (London, 1996), ch. 4.   [106] StAMM, A 44d, 17 May 1574.

[107] StAMM, A 44d, 15 Oct. 1606, Anna Salben.   [108] StAMM, A 44d, 17 Oct. 1606.

[109] StAMM, A 44e, 23 Jan. 1629.

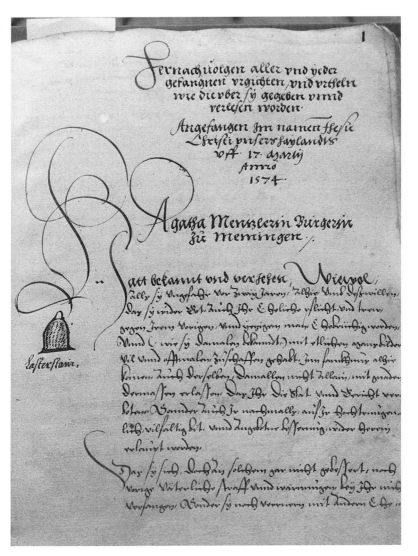

FIG. 11. The shaming punishment of a citizen found guilty of adultery

doubled if the couple had intercourse twice. Three or more times resulted in a punishment of 'life and limb'. If both adulterers were married both were imprisoned for a month on a diet of water and bread. If a wronged partner refused to accept the adulterer back, he or she was banished. Two married persons who had committed adultery twice were punished in 'life and limb'.[110] The 1532 Memmingen discipline ordinance, by contrast, prescribed only twentyfour days' imprisonment or banishment as the gravest punishment for adultery.[111] In Esslingen, on the other hand, even severe cases of adultery and prostitution were punished only with the pillory, whipping, and banishment. In Constance and Hall likewise nobody was executed for adultery or prostitution.[112] The 1556 Constance discipline ordinance stipulated that two married persons who had twice committed adultery were to be punished with twelve days' imprisonment, while those who had committed adultery three times or more would have their cases debated by the council.[113] Throughout the seventeenth century sentences for adultery continued to be commuted into fines in Constance, Hall, and Freiburg. In Hall, however, fines were considerably increased. Ordinances in 1671 and 1684 set a fifty-florin fine as punishment for adultery which had been committed twice.[114]

Only in Württemberg were laws harsher than in Memmingen. From 1586 onwards, adultery between a single and a married person was to be punished relentlessly with four weeks' imprisonment (raised to six weeks in 1642),[115] with church penance, and with the loss of all offices. If adultery had been committed twice, the man was to be decapitated and the woman drowned. All petitions had to be sent to the supreme council.[116] These measures reflect the extremely rigid Württemberg policy on marital order. Church penance for adulterers, too, was a carefully crafted Protestant ritual

---

[110] StAMM, A 265/2, *Zuchtordnung*, 26 Nov. 1630.

[111] StAMM, A 265/1, *Zuchtordnung*, 27 Mar. 1532.

[112] On the legal debate about the execution of women for adultery see A. Felber, *Unzucht und Kindsmord in der Rechtsprechung der freien Reichsstadt Nördlingen vom 15. bis 18. Jahrhundert* (Bonn, 1961), 68–78.

[113] StAKN, CI 203/241, 'New Pollecey vnnd Zucht Ordnung'.

[114] StAH, 4/495, 'Poena et taxa Criminum', 14 Jan. 1684. The sum was raised for people of higher rank. The council disliked the mitigation into fines, but the pressure from relatives and friends ensured that petitions had to be granted.

[115] Reyscher, *Gesetze*, v. 424, 'General=Rescript, die Bestrafung der Gottes-Lästerung und der Fleisches-Verbrechen betreffend', 29 July 1642.

[116] Reyscher, *Gesetze*, iv. 447, 'Mandat, die Bestrafung der Fleischesverbrechen betreffend', 21 May 1586.

which offenders could hardly take lightly. Württemberg theologians had designed a Protestant rite of reconciliation with little in common with Catholic equivalents. Catholic adulterers stood before the church on three Sundays, holding a candle, and dressed in a cloth of penitence (*Büßerhemd*)—which they might have been able to accept as we do parking fines today.[117] From 1564 onwards, adulterers convicted in Württemberg had to sit close to the altar on three subsequent Sundays. After the sermon they had to occupy both sides of the altar. On the first Sunday, the parson announced from the pulpit that their sins had angered God and aroused scandal in the community. Even though they had already been subjected to worldly punishment, they had to beg for God's mercy and forgiveness. They had to demonstrate penitence. On the second Sunday, the quest for reconciliation was repeated. The community was asked to pity the sinners. 'Fallen' people should be strengthened by the community's 'tender-hearted spirit'. On the third Sunday, the parson declared that the penitents were now forgiven their sins. The community was told to take an example from their punishment: what had happened to them might have 'happened to us, or even worse sins, if we do not live in permanent fear of God'. The adulterers had to kneel for absolution, and the community's prayer then emphasized that God had come into this world to make sinners repent and to bless them.[118] Although this ritual founded forgiveness on a sinner's spiritual conversion, individual penance and improvement depended on the community's support. The community was told not to stigmatize adulterers as sinners. Their weakness was human, their punishment a warning to retain faith.

The sources do not clearly indicate how common adultery was or how commonly it occupied early modern people's minds. The Württemberg penal policy (if implemented) could hardly fail to deter people. All authorities pursued a policy of punishment, repentance, and reconciliation up to the very end of our period. Banishment and corporal punishment were used only if no repentance was to be expected and God's fury loomed. The reservation was that in the

---

[117] W. Behringer, 'Mörder, Diebe, Ehebrecher: Verbrechen und Strafen in Kurbayern vom 16. bis 18. Jahrhundert', in R. v. Dülmen, *Verbrechen, Strafen und soziale Kontrolle* (Frankfurt on Main, 1990), 121. There is, however, ample evidence to the contrary, see G. Schindler, *Verbrechen und Strafen im Recht der Stadt Freiburg im Breisgau von der Einführung des neuen Stadtrechts bis zum Übergang an Baden* (1520–1806) (Freiburg im Breisgau, 1937), 140–7.

[118] Reyscher, *Gesetze*, viii. 288–90, 'Formel der öffentlichen Kirchenbuße für die Ehebrecher'.

case of married people such punishment effectively destroyed the family and household economy one was trying to protect.[119]

MURDER

Murder resulted from either the wish to marry a lover or insoluble marital problems. Murderesses sought a radical solution, the new beginning which Church and State denied them. The knowledge that a divorce was unlikely caused despair, especially if the marriage had been arranged, whereas the affair was linked to passionate love. In Erlenbach a young woman, long in love with the city-scribe's son, had to marry an old clothier, Johann Hunn, for whom she felt no 'marital love or affection'. Hunn was blasphemous and lazy, and suffered from falling sickness, whereas the city-scribe's son was 'young and fresh'. He often defamed Hunn and asked her what she 'did with this sick man'. Their love was deep; he had 'sucked milk from her breasts several times' and 'even drunk *s.v. [salva venia]* her chamber-water' for a bet. Unhappily Frau Hunn had told another woman that she would rather 'sit on the market square and have her head cut off than return to her husband'. A divorce was unlikely and would mean that the inheritance was lost. They therefore commissioned a murderer. Hunn died, and the couple was accused. Frau Hunn's life did indeed end under the hangman's sword.[120]

In cases of adultery, murder often paved the way for the establishment of a new household. Sexual dissatisfaction was usually linked to the feeling that a husband was a bad householder and his profession replaceable by the lover. Servants or journeymen were therefore favoured lovers. They had already proved their qualities, and were looking for a marriage and household. A Freiburg tanner's wife killed her husband in 1564 after she had slept several times with the servant,[121] and another woman made her husband drink mercury while he was ill, while the servant put sand and wax in his food.[122] A shepherd's wife, who had an affair with a servant in 1591, stabbed her sleeping husband. She said he was a 'loose man' who wasted

---

[119] Jerg Operwirdt described how after his wife had been banished for adultery he had lived with their child for five years and was 'not only helpless and unconsoled, but also suffered many disadvantages in his trade': StAMM, A 344, F. 1, 29 Jan. 1553.

[120] HStASt, A 209, Bü. 1557, 20 May 1677.

[121] StAFr, A 1 XIf, 1 Mar. 1564, Barbara Manz.

[122] HStASt, A 209, Bü. 573, Barbara Lehr, Kirchheim 1604/5.

their money and would soon have made her go begging.[123] Artisans' wives could run workshops with an apprentice after husbands' deaths.[124] It is not accidental that it was invariably artisans' wives who were suspected of adultery and murder. Such a wife along with a journeyman could replace all a husband's functions—and this was fearsome to the artisan community.

The second main motive for murder of a husband was women's determination to end a destructive marriage. Let us follow the story of the tanner's wife Maria Dreher, who planned to kill her husband. One July morning in 1688, Maria borrowed one florin from the mayor of Güglingen and then walked 5 miles to Brackenheim, where she entered the pharmacy. Telling the apprentice there that she came from Michelbach, she demanded 'the strongest poison' and that it should be 'unpounded'. When the apprentice asked why she needed the poison, Maria replied that 'she wanted it for mice', but then added that 'he should just give it to her; she could do with it what she liked'. When he refused to serve her, she grumbled that she would 'get it elsewhere, from the Italians'. The pharmacist's wife overheard this strange conversation. She called Maria back and offered her white lead, because she did not want her to buy poison elsewhere. Maria refused. She wanted the strongest poison and was willing to pay 'a ducat, a *Taler*, or a whole florin for it'. And so Maria gave the pharmacist's wife a florin for poison which only cost two *Kreuzer* and told her not to tell anyone that she had bought it. In the evening the pharmacist's wife reported the incident to her husband. He recognized Maria from the description and immediately sent the apprentice to Güglingen to warn Maria's husband. Shocked, the husband instantly demanded a divorce. This couple, too, had nearly separated from 'bed and board' quietly: Maria often slept at her sister's.

Maria confessed that she had bought the poison for her husband. But, she explained tellingly, she had not meant to kill him with it, 'only to weaken him, so that he would not be so strong and fat and rule her with such power and give her a hard time'. Maria had to defend herself in a criminal trial and the *Malefizglöckchen* was rung, indicating that her life was at risk. The bailiff reported her case to the supreme council. She was the daughter of a former judge and had cared for her parents until their death. They had thought she could

[123] HStASt, A 209, Bü. 2033, Barbara Ulmer; she was executed.
[124] StAFr, A 1 XIf, 4 Mar. 1586, Jacobea Löhslerin: 10 Sept. 1597, Ursula Gatterin.

not be married to anyone, because her arms were crippled. But people thought of her as intelligent, understanding, pious, and fit to lead a household. By the time she was 50 she was angry, melancholic, mistrustful, and diagnosed as sexually starved: it was felt that she 'avidly wanted a husband, lest otherwise she commit worse sins'. Friends had advised her to marry Hans the tanner; he had lived an honourable life. And so they were married in February 1679.[125] But little luck came of it. In the following spring, Maria accused her husband before the church consistory of insulting and beating her. He himself complained about the 'painful torture' he endured day and night, because she always mistrusted him and accused him of sleeping with other women. Unable to put up with further allegations, he had beaten her badly. Since both had obviously contributed to the misery, the judges tried to reconcile them, but a year later Maria accused Hans again.

During an argument on the open street she had escaped from Hans into a house. He promised to leave her in peace if she returned home with him. But there he had beaten her so badly that the wounds and bruises still showed. How could he be allowed to inflict more pain on a disabled woman? Hans was briefly imprisoned. Their relationship never recovered. They had last been ordered before the church consistory a year ago, to ensure that they should not receive communion with 'unreconciled hearts'. But Maria had refused reconciliation. She had written to Stuttgart, but the supreme councillors (who functioned as a ducal marriage court) had only advised reconciliation. So, because of her husband's 'great tyranny' and 'out of desperation' the 60-year-old woman had gone to the Brackenheim pharmacy that fatal morning.

It had not been a lonely decision. Her maidservants knew how ill-humoured Hans was. One of them had said that she would know how to deal with such a husband: she would mix something in his salad; one *Kreuzer*'s worth would suffice to weaken him. Moreover the whole village knew that Hans often wished Maria dead, beat her severely, and had once smashed everything in the house. 'With hot tears' Maria begged the court to spare her harsh punishment. She succeeded. Apart from lengthy confinement during the trial, she got away with a fine of twenty *Reichstaler.*

This seems surprising in view of the pharmacist's testimony, which pointed to a premeditated murder. But Maria had not executed her

---

[125] HStASt, A 209, Bü. 1064, 1 Aug. 1688.

plan; and failed attempts to murder a husband were punished with mild sentences of the pillory, whipping, and banishment for life, which separated the couple forever. Maria had also won the judges' understanding that her husband's violence had intensified over the years. Marital problems had appeared soon after the wedding, to which the authorities had responded only by advising reconciliation. A year before Maria planned to poison Hans, the third Württemberg marriage ordinance had come into force. The maximum concession in cases of permanent disaffection between couples was that they be separated for a year (during which they had to be celibate), and then 'reconciled in a Christian manner'. Before and during the separation the 'guilty and disobedient party' would be pressed to alter his or her behaviour through imprisonment, public labour, or banishment.[126] Again it is clear that Protestant authorities aimed to hold marriages together at all costs.

Women therefore fantasized about ways of murdering husbands. In 1546, Hans Klopfer reported how he had heard a group of women discussing the treatment they had endured from their husbands. One said to another that if she had a husband like that woman's she would mix into his meal one or two spiders, white flour, and a plant which grew on top of dung heaps. Another woman passed on a recipe which she had already tested on dogs and wild boars: menstrual blood mixed with flour and honey.[127]

Murder techniques were diverse. Women were considered to be strong enough to strangle or beat their husbands to death: the *Carolina* deemed it possible that 'a cruel wife can force a soft man to self-defence, especially if she has better weapons and he worse'.[128] In 1562 the Zurich councillor Johann Jacob Wick added to his chronicle a drawing of an artisan's wife who with bare hands had strangled her husband eight days after their wedding. In the same year he depicted a blacksmith's wife who had beaten her husband dead with an iron hammer. She was buried alive with a stake through her heart.[129] Husbands were usually stabbed or beaten to death in their sleep: Christina Röhslin, for example, had first run away repeatedly from her husband. Then in 1558 she had 'stabbed

---

[126] Reyscher, *Gesetze*, vi. 121.   [127] HStASt, A 43, Bü. 25.

[128] G. Radbruch (ed.), *Die Peinliche Gerichtsordnung Kaiser Karls V. von 1532 (Carolina)* (4th edn. Stuttgart, 1991), 95, *Artikel* 144.

[129] Central Library Zurich, Johann Jacobus Wick, *Ein kurze beschrybung was sich in diesem LXII Jahr verloffen,* Wick'sche Chronik, book III, part I, fos. 5ª, 6ª. The first woman was drowned.

him so severely with a knife that he had been seriously wounded'
and died soon afterwards.[130] Sooner or later such deeds were likely
to be exposed as murders. In Hallbach, Margaretha Craft had killed
her second husband in bed with an axe 'shortly after their union'.
She had buried his bones in the cellar and other parts of his body in
manure. After three years, during which time many had wondered at
his sudden disappearance, especially since the best horse was still in
the stable and his clothes in the wardrobe, people started to search
the cellar and discovered the remains.[131] Poison was much favoured,
though its purchase posed a problem, because pharmacists had to
scrutinize their customers. On the other hand, travelling hawkers
also sold poison, and asked fewer questions. In 1695 a widowed
hawker had tempted a woman in the Neuenburg district to poison
her husband's soup. 'She did not feel any affection' for him and had
had an affair with a servant.[132] The hawker herself was known in
Württemberg as the 'rat catcher'. Two years earlier she had sold the
Tübingen bailiff's wife enough poison to kill a large rat. The woman
had killed the bailiff with it instead and had since been nicknamed the
'poison bailiff's wife' (*Giftvögtin*). An autopsy revealed the murder.[133]

Seemingly unbridgeable voids commonly opened up between
couples after their weddings. Marriage was, of course, a matter of
luck for those who did not know each other well. Some were lucky,
and others grew together slowly; but some might not be patient
enough for this if unexpected characteristics of their partner
offended them. Five weeks after her wedding a Tübingen woman
had first slept with her husband, and shortly afterwards planned to
kill him with mercury in little cakes.[134] The husband of 22-year-old
Maria Bestlin had 'asked too much of her in marital matters': 'excessive sex' had confused her. Three times she had put rat poison into
his soup, which he ate while she went to prayer lessons. Her husband and his little sister had vomited repeatedly and finally fed a pig
with the soup which had died shortly afterwards.[135] In 1679, a

---

[130] StAFr, A1 XIf, 21 July 1559.

[131] HStASt, A 209, Bü. 758, 12 Nov. 1658, she was pulled with hot pincers and then
decapitated. See also HStASt, A 44, U 454, 15 June 1555, a woman who was banished
because she was suspected of killing her husband.

[132] HStASt, A 209, Bü. 1674, 27 July 1695, Anna Maria Kaur.

[133] HStASt, A 209, Bü. 19191.

[134] Since she had then told him to vomit she was only banished: HStASt, A 209, Bü.
1898, 1601, Dorothea Stirlin.

[135] She had to stand at the pillory, was whipped and banished from Württemberg,
HStASt, A 209, Bü. 1863, 30 Apr. 1679.

locksmith's wife had tried to kill her husband with poisoned cheese after they had been married eight weeks. One Sunday Eva fed her husband with goat cheese and rat poison which she had bought for a *Kreuzer*. In the evening his belly had swollen so much that a button popped off his trousers. Medicine had saved his life. Eva had her own grievances, however. She lamented that her husband had taken 'everything to eat', including the usual wedding gifts, eggs, flour, and fat, to his mother's house, where she had 'made cakes and other things'. Mother and son had lived well, while Eva had 'suffered starvation'. Moreover, he had repeatedly taken away grain. When she had reprimanded him, he had called her 'an old witch and fool'. She concluded bitterly that she had been talked into the marriage just because of her dowry of 600 florins.[136] In all these cases no dependent children seemed to live in the household. Older women knew that they lived best by themselves, and young wives felt that with a husband conveniently disposed of they could make a new start. Their decision sometimes reflected the fact that they had not wholeheartedly agreed to a marriage, or the fact that the husband had transgressed important barriers too quickly, so that they felt exploited or abused. The main issues were excessive sexual demands, disrespect of the family origin, differing opinions, and divisions of property. Murder did not express a lust for cruelty, but a wish for self-determination.

MARRIAGE TROUBLE

Franz Hals's wedding portrait of Isaac Massa and Beatrix von der Laen is often referred to by those who believe that the humanist emphasis on companionship increased equality and happiness in early modern marriages. However, full cheeks and luxurious dress convey how much of a couple's bloom rested on wealth; a good deal of life's hardships were passed on to servants and employees. The mass of early modern couples had to struggle with material problems and were more likely to quarrel in turn. Survival depended on hard daily labour and careful household management. Quite simply, one sex needed the other, and therefore women had ample scope in which to assert themselves. They retained a feudal-contractual understanding of marriage: if a husband failed to provide

---

[136] She also had to stand in the pillory, was whipped, and was banished from Württemberg, HStASt, A 209, Bü. 1301, 21 Aug. 1679.

protection, peace, and nourishment, a wife would no longer feel obliged to remain faithful and obedient. Contrary to this, Christian morals held that fidelity had to be maintained because God had created marriage as the basis of social order. Lutheran and Catholic legal practices therefore only differed marginally in cases of separation or divorce. Marriage was fundamental to political order. Civic councillors of both confessions showed similar interest in admonishing and punishing bad householders, quarrelsome couples, and unfaithful wives. The principle that marriage was an unshakeable pillar of social and religious order was insisted upon despite the paradoxes authorities encountered when they reconciled hopelessly divided couples. This chapter has therefore highlighted the stories of those who suffered from this policy and who were kept together at all costs. Neighbours' descriptions of marital conflicts make it clear that both husband and wife could hurt the other's dignity forever. Personal respect was closely though not exclusively tied to a partner's qualities as a householder, and spontaneous affection and individual personality structures had their bearing on the experience of everyday life. If people shared their concern about married life with neighbours, it was not merely to ensure the functioning of an economic unit. It was also because marriages entailed the deepest experience of the possibilities and limits of human life together.

Marital disputes thus present us with plenty of material which demonstrates women's agency within the household and their ability to challenge male authority. But they also remind us of a reality of male violence and forced silences within the home.[137] Such experiences not only affected a significant proportion of married women, but other relatives, too. Narratives of incest reveal this disturbingly.

[137] M. Hohkamp, 'Häusliche Gewalt: Beispiele aus einer ländlichen Region des mittleren Schwarzwaldes im 18. Jahrhundert', in T. Lindenberger and A. Lüdtke (eds.), *Physische Gewalt: Studien zur Geschichte der Neuzeit* (Frankfurt on Main, 1995).

7

Incest

One summer day in 1688, a vineyard labourer named Michel Pfeiffer and his 20-year-old stepdaughter Maria fled secretly from their home in Esslingen. We learn from the story she later told the court that they fled with good cause: she was pregnant by him. Pfeiffer had started to embrace her around Easter, she reported; he said that he wanted 'to do dishonourable things with her'. She had replied that 'it would lead to no good'. Later, after clearing hay together in their garret, he lifted her up and turned her around, telling her she 'wasn't worth a goat'; as he tried to kiss her she managed to free herself. Then one night Pfeiffer came home drunk. He crept into Maria's room, took off his coat and shoes, opened his trousers, and entered the bed. He pulled her back as she tried to jump out of bed, warning her to be quiet. He would do her no harm, he said (meaning that he would use coitus interruptus); but if the worst came about, he would look after her for the rest of his life. He threatened to kill her should she shout to awaken her mother.

Pfeiffer maintained that Maria resisted only slightly, and then only at first. Had she defended herself properly he could not have entered her. He claimed that he had intercourse with her only once that night; she said twice. Either way, the encounter lasted no longer than a quarter of an hour. Afterwards he went into the matrimonial bedchamber. Further assaults followed in the daytime, on the *Lotterbett*, in vineyards, in a meadow, and once after she had deloused him. One day, when they were together in a field, Maria told him in tears that she was pregnant. He wanted nothing of this, repeated that he could have done her no harm, and told her to be quiet. It was only when her pregnancy could no longer be ignored that he made her come away with him.

This chapter is a revised version of my article '"Viehisch, frech vnd onverschämpt": Inzest in Südwestdeutschland, ca. 1530–1700', in O. Ulbricht (ed.), *Von Huren und Rabenmüttern: Weibliche Kriminalität in der frühen Neuzeit* (Cologne, 1995).

They reached Marbach at midday, and Kaltenwesten by nightfall. Sharing a bed, he had sex with her. Arriving in the Palatinate town of Schlierbach, they pretended to be married. He found work as a woodcutter while she harvested morello cherries. Again they shared a bed, and he demanded intercourse several times. When the arrival of French troops in the Palatinate stopped people working, they moved to Heidelberg. There Pfeifer enlisted, and Maria returned to Esslingen. When her mother saw her, she said she wished 'she had drowned her with her first bath'. A beadle arrested Maria next day. She was put in the pillory and then banished from her home town for life.[1]

This chapter is based on 169 trials from Württemberg, Esslingen, and Hall in which women were themselves accused of incest. Their stories open a window on to complex feelings of dependency, aggression, and desire within families. They shed light on the emotional dynamics of particular kinship positions, for example that of brothers-in-law *vis-à-vis* the wives of brothers, and of stepfathers and stepdaughters. These relationships were common to early modern kinship systems, for spousal death and remarriage were ubiquitous. But they are usually ignored in a historiography of the family which still focuses on experiences within a parent–child triad familiar to us moderns.

Maria's story conveys several elements which were common to most experiences of incest. She was, for a start, one of those many daughters in early modern communities who were not sent into service because their labour was needed at home. Her work was taken for granted and wages were never paid in cash. She could not save for her dowry, it had to be given to her. Legally a stepfather had no right to determine a girl's dowry: children's inheritances had to be fixed before widows remarried. But presumably a stepfather could still have his say about a dowry—whether or not a stepdaughter was worth a cow, if so, how old a cow, or a goat, or not even a goat. A sense of dependence could be enforced.

A woman like Maria would have spent a lot of time with her stepfather. She worked with him in fields and vineyards, the mother remaining at home. There was nothing suspicious about this. There were also, unavoidably, moments of intimacy, as when a girl

---

[1] StAE, AII, Reichsstadt, F. 48 B II. Pfeiffer returned to Esslingen at Christmas and was imprisoned. The Tübingen legal reference pleaded for the death sentence, while Esslingen lawyers advised to sentence him to the pillory and banish him, because of his age and because he had been drunk the first time.

deloused her father or stepfather during a break at work in the warmth of early summer. This closeness might become ambiguous and threatening. The spatial and emotional experience of the house could change, too. Illegitimate domestic intercourse usually took place either in stables or on the *Lotterbett*, the last being part of the basic furnishing of every south-west German household and consisting of a linen bag filled with chaff placed on the oven-bench in the main chamber (*Stube*). In wealthier households the linen bag was replaced by a leather bag and cushions were added for comfort. Curtains made the space dark and private.[2] The *Lotterbett* seems to have been mainly used by men during the day to doze during breaks or after work, or at night to sober up. It was thus associated with a dream-state. It was the most comfortable domestic place available for illegitimate sex, and it lacked the symbolic weight of the matrimonial bed. The use of the *Lotterbett* was finally connected to a specific time rhythm. In the daytime it was used in between work and after meals, for a short time only. The intercourse was meant to be just as transitional and limited in time. A female bedchamber with a door which could not be shut, a cellar, stable, or garret, the *Lotterbett*—all became dangerous spaces for women threatened by abuse.[3]

CONTEMPORARY UNDERSTANDINGS OF INCEST

Before we look more closely at women's experiences, let us first describe how contemporary élites understood incest as crime. Incest appeared in German law codes only after the absorption of Roman Law in the fifteenth century; even so, the *Carolina* still defined the crime very broadly in 1532, merely mentioning stepdaughters, sisters-in-law, and stepmothers as illicit sexual partners. Protestant reformers were already arguing that 'the Churche's prohibitions against incest were intolerably lax,[4] and they debated what

---

[2] U. Meiners, 'Wohnkultur in süddeutschen Kleinstädten vom 17. Jahrhundert bis zum 19. Jahrhundert: Soziale Unterschiede und Wertestrukturen', in G. Wiegelmann (ed.), *Nord-Südunterschiede in der städtischen und ländlichen Kultur Mitteleuropas* (Munich, 1985).

[3] G. Bachelard, *The Poetics of Space: The Classic Look at How We Experience Intimate Places*, trans. M. Jolas (Boston, 1994), ignores this deeply gendered nature of experiences of intimacy within the home.

[4] In 1537, for example, the Nuremberg reformer Andreas Osiander argued that women's 'modesty, honour and chastity' were to be protected within the family. As things stood, he said, it was in the family that their chastity was most endangered; see his 'Von den verbotenen Heiraten', in G. Müller and G. Seebaß (eds.), *Andreas Osiander d. Ä., Schriften und Briefe 1535 bis 1538* (Gütersloh, 1985).

proper incest laws should be.[5] Some Protestant towns and territories, which had taken over jurisdiction in such matters from church courts, condemned and prosecuted incest with new vigour. In 1534, the first Württemberg marriage ordinance condemned offenders up to the third degree of kinship as 'animals, cheeky and insolent'. Incest was mostly interpreted as the outcome of a mindless quest for sexual satisfaction within the family.[6] Reformers therefore tried to construct the family as a territory in which 'natural modesty' rendered sexual desire unthinkable, as it was not among animals and savages. Like bestiality, incest came to stand on the boundary between the civilised and the uncivilised. Nuremberg Protestants who wanted tougher marriage laws accordingly lamented that the 'town allowed its citizens to marry like dogs, without distinctions and choice'.[7] As Keith Thomas has shown, early modern élites' understanding of the lower animals was invariably negative, 'helping to define, by contrast, what was supposedly distinctive and admirable about the human species'.[8]

The accused in court also made sense of incest through this concept, or at least reproduced it in their trial roles. When Barbara Reiser was accused of incest with her father in 1655, she justified herself by saying that 'she didn't think it was unchaste; that they had been brought up like animals; if she had known better, she would have resisted more strongly'.[9] And the wife of a man who escaped after being accused of incest with his brother's wife justified his act by alluding to the Thirty Years War, saying that 'it had happened in times, when people had to live in deserted lands and woods like animals'.[10] The absence of education or of households was thus assumed to induce social disorder, and to dissolve the normal barriers of shame. Actual incidents of incest accordingly indicated a fragile moral order. In 1553, the Esslingen chronicler Dreytwein noted of the case of an elderly citizen who had impregnated his

[5] On reformer's views see M. Jónson, 'Incest and the Word of God: Early Sixteenth Century Protestant Disputes', *ARG* 85(1994), 96–118.

[6] It signified shamelessness and the absence of civilization. Still in this tradition, Freud expected the 'primitives' he discussed in 1912–'poor, naked cannibals', he wrote—to be innocent of modesty, to follow instincts instead of laws, and hence to practise incest as a matter of course; see S. Freud, *Totem und Tabu: Einige Übereinstimmungen im Seelenleben der Wilden und der Neurotiker* (Frankfurt on Main, 1991), 48.

[7] Cited in S. Ozment, *When Fathers Ruled: Family Life in Reformation Europe* (Cambridge, Mass., 1983), 201 n. 209.

[8] K. Thomas, *Man and the Natural World: Changing Attitudes in England, 1500–1800* (Harmondsworth, 1984), 40.   [9] HStASt, A 209, Bü. 1912.

[10] HStASt, A 209, Bü. 90.

stepdaughter that 'all shame had been done away with' in the world.[11] Similarly, a judge impatiently ended a long discussion as to whether or not Barbara Reiser might have been too simple to know that intercourse with her father was sinful by saying that 'it should anyway be dictated not only by reason but by *nature*, that this was sin—and shameful, which is why many a people abhor ignorant animals'.[12] Incest was perceived as a unnatural, monstrous crime, a shameless sexual experience. It was not perceived as one of abuse within the family. Punishments varied according to the degree of kinship and whether or not the parties had committed related offences like adultery (if one or both partners were married), or infanticide. Relatives in the first degree were punished with death. In the most commonly reported cases of incest, involving stepfathers and stepdaughters and brothers- and sisters-in-law, sentences were much more varied. Most offenders in these categories were sentenced to the pillory, public whipping, and banishment to 10 or more miles' distance.

DISPLACED RELATIONSHIPS

As in Maria's case, incest was nearly always discovered only because the woman got pregnant. This fact implies that there was an extraordinarily high dark figure. It also means that most accused women were over 18 years old, since on average early modern women became fertile only when they were aged 16 or 17.[13] Judges took it for granted that both parties' desire had led to incest, excepting only girls aged below 14. Women tried to maintain that they had been coerced or seduced, while men claimed that they had been drunk when committing the crime, or that they had been seduced, or that their wives had not lately fulfilled their conjugal duties. The court assessed the credibility of these arguments in the light of the accused's reputation, but generally dismissed them as excuses. Frequently evidence was sought which might show that the woman had been impregnated by some other man.

Although the German term for incest was *Blutschande* (blood

---

[11] A. Diehl (ed.), *Dionysius Dreytweins Esslingische Chronik (1548–1564)* (Tübingen, 1901), 133 f. For another entry on an incest case see p. 179.
[12] HStASt, A 309, Bü. 90b.
[13] This means that it is impossible to say much about the abuse of boys and girls. The Stuttgart records contain only one case involving an abused son, HStASt, A 209, Bü. 862, Hans Martin Bronnen.

shame), the incestuous relationships most frequently reported involved a woman and her stepfather, brother-in-law, or uncle, and not relatives by blood.[14] There are some clues which may explain the frequency of those relationships. These relatives often stepped into the places of dead fathers or husbands, for example. A stepfather might decide to look after the woman; a brother-in-law might provide her with legal and material support, as well as a male-headed household to which a widow might publicly belong; an uncle might replace the father while a girl served in his household. Women depended on these relatives' acceptance and had to entrust themselves to their protection and care. But this acceptance was not always automatic. A woman might have to pay a price, especially if she seemed useless in the household or was in some way disturbed. In relationships between uncles and non-affinal nieces, the man might demand sexual rewards, exploiting her dependency and the protective silence within families. Sometimes men experienced their relatedness as ambivalent, because they held power in someone else's place. A man's sexual claim on a relative could indicate a wish to influence the balance of power within a family. Finally, another constellation could arise from a younger, less wealthy man's marriage to an older widow with daughters who were nearly his age. The response could be sexual aggression to prove masculinity.[15]

DEPENDENCE AND DESIRE

The family provided a secure frame for sexual abuse because it so often achieved a conspiracy of silence. Outsiders were usually only suspicious about the most extreme kinds of intimacy between fathers and daughters. In 1538, for example, the Stuttgart mintmaster Boßweyl and his daughter were reported by neighbours because her belly had 'swollen' twice. Each time, she was sent away and returned 'much smaller'. One witness said that father and daughter had been 'friendly with each other', sometimes having 'fun' together for hours in the main chamber. One maidservant had seen them 'on

---

[14] The whole sample of 169 cases involves 43 stepfathers, 26 brothers-in-law, 21 uncles, 15 unnamed relatives, 14 husbands of deceased sisters, 13 fathers and 3 suspected fathers, 7 fathers-in-law, 6 cousins, 4 brothers, 2 stepsons, and 2 sons; also 13 punishments according to Mosaic law, e.g. where a woman had had intercourse with two brothers.

[15] A revealing 18th-cent. case in this context is HStASt, A 309, Bü. 147, 20 Nov. 1765, Johannes Bauer.

top of each other', another reported that things in that house were outrageous. Maria was asked in court whether it was true that she had 'opened his trousers and closed them again, which had all been observed by honourable people through the windows'.[16] In fact it had only been Maria's repeated pregnancies that had led to the report.

Much more typical was the way in which Barbara Reiser was detected. She gave birth to an illegitimate child in 1655, with six women watching her: in her extremity she had shouted out that her father 'was also the child's father'.[17] Both were duly hauled before the church-court, and after trial were banished from Württemberg. Barbara was aged 29 and had managed domestic affairs for her 60-year-old father. She said that sometimes 'when he had been drunk, he lay on her and had his way with her'. Before she had died, Barbara's mother had told her that 'it would do her no harm'. Barbara understood that 'harm' meant that her father's semen would enter her and that she could get pregnant. She described how her father had intercourse with her one night, but how 'it hadn't done her any harm'. He had always been drunk, and, compared to young Merklin from Christnau, with whom Barbara had slept four times after the harvest and before the church-ale, her father had never 'completed' his 'thing'. She was nevertheless sure that her periods had ceased before she slept with Merklin. Barbara's father denied the charge, by referring sometimes to his age and ailments ('he was merely half a man'), sometimes to his drunkenness. He also argued that she had seduced him when he was drunk, saying 'Father, I want to lie with you': in short, 'she had asked for it'. Barbara reported that they usually had intercourse in the early morning hours, between one and two o'clock, except that last time he had got at her when he returned from the inn. It had happened five times altogether, twice while her mother was still alive. Her father had 'cruelly loved her', she thought: 'he had her in bed and got her below and himself on top of her and he had done with her as it pleased him.' 'He told her when he was coming and she had likewise told him when she came.' She confessed having had intercourse twice with a soldier in the mayor's barn, seven years before. The district official, disgusted, reported that she was nothing more than 'boy's fodder'; Merklin's father said likewise that she 'craved men'; and her own father thought of her as a 'useless, bad person'. Thus was created an image of a woman driven by passions, her alleged lust for her father increasingly plausible.

It was typically held that the only 'harm' awaiting an abused woman was pregnancy. When in 1657 a tanner was accused of thrice abusing his 11-year-old stepdaughter, the mother pleaded for leniency because the daughter had not been 'injured or harmed'.[18] Only a pregnancy made manifest the fact that both relationships and inheritance rights were in disorder. Moreover this view connived in the fact that if a male relative practised coitus interruptus a woman had to put up with his demands. Accepting abuse at least forestalled the disruption of families. A Leonberg case shows how deeply internalized this view of having to put up with sexual claims could be. In 1630, a woman looked for her cow in her neighbour's stables and saw him and his step-granddaughter together. Later the step-granddaughter told her that 'she had come just in time': 'you have been my saviour, I would have had to put up with it otherwise.'[19] The Hall councillor Schragmüller suggested in a 1683 legal reference on an incest case that the daughter might have thought that she had to 'obey her father in every way'.[20]

Ultimately, however, lawyers gave next to no weight to such arguments. Women's references to their own simple-mindedness carried little weight either. Ursula Specht is a case in point.[21] Her brother had taken her into his home after his wife had died. Ursula looked after him and his two children. One night she had taken an ill child to sleep with her on the *Lotterbett* in the kitchen, when her brother came in drunk and lay next to her. Ursula told him not to do it. He replied that 'nothing bad would happen to her and it was not going to do her harm'. When in 1698 he realized that she was pregnant,

he became very ill-tempered and did not want her in his house any longer, but demanded that she go into service elsewhere, and promised to give her money, clothes, and other things, and said he did not wish her to go to church, she should rather creep into a mousehole [sic!] than go to church with that big belly.[22]

When interrogated in court for the first time, he said he was as innocent 'as a baby in its cradle'. Then he escaped from prison.

---

[18] HStASt, A 209, Bü. 755, 23 Sept. 1657.
[19] HStASt, A 309, Bü. 145, 2 July 1630, Katharina Lonhardt.
[20] StAH, A 11, Bü. 41; see also HStASt, A 309, Bü. 268, 2 Dec. 1758, Katharina Ehelin.
[21] HStASt, A 209, Bü. 1619.   [22] HStASt, A 209, Bü. 1619, 5 June 1689.

Everyone thought of Ursula as simple-minded. Village lads always shouted at her, 'you're a donkey'. A former mistress asserted that it was quite possible that Ursula had been 'pushed into such a sinful life'.[23] Such a statement could have alleviated her guilt. Truly simple-minded people were thought of as having no moral sense. But in a 'civilized' world, lawyers agreed, only children and mentally handicapped people could count as witless. So in Ursula's case it was clear to the lawyers that though she might have been stupid, she was not simple-minded. She had after all told her brother to abstain from sex with her and obviously knew it was sinful.[24]

To assess evidence of coercion, lawyers applied the same rules in incest cases as in rape cases. Legal descriptions of how a rape charge could be proved were extremely visual. From medieval law onwards, they had built up to what we can call a semiology of rape. A woman had to shout her protests while she was raped, to cry while she returned home, to show her torn clothes, wounded hands, and dishevelled hair to everyone she met, and to urge them to follow the rapist.[25] These expectations were based on the notion that rape usually occurred unexpectedly outside the home, in forests and fields, and was committed by an alien man. They assumed the guilt of women who remained silent. Again, family and home were conceived as places of protection.

When judges thus assessed an incest case even concerning a woman of good reputation, they would usually assume that her silence proved her collaboration or increasing pleasure in her sexual encounters. In 1590, in Margaretha Müller's case, Tübingen lawyers acknowledged that as a young girl she had been 'forced to do it' by her father, and that she had tried to resist the first time. They were certain, however, that she could have avoided further sex with her father had she 'told her mother or other people she trusted and asked for help and advice'. But since she had let such 'shame

---

[23] HStASt, A 209, Bü. 1619, 5 June 1689.

[24] The decision taken in the case of one Barbara Stampfer in 1660 was therefore exceptional: 'the accused is a simple woman and a peasant who has probably never in her life heard what incest is and even less of the laws regarding it, so that she must be treated more leniently.' It was admitted here that sexual shame was not implanted naturally, but learnt. The judgement can mainly be explained by the fact that the Dettingen widow had slept with a father and his son and that the upper council was interested in weakening the influence of Mosaic law, HStASt, A 209, Bü. 1988, 8 Jan. 1660.

[25] R. His, *Das Strafrecht des deutschen Mittelalters in 2 Teilen* (Weimar, 1935), ii. 151 f.; E. Osenbrüggen, *Das alemannische Strafrecht im deutschen Mittelalter* (Schaffhausen, 1860), 237.

happen to her even when her mother was at home', the lawyers decided that she could not have been taken by force. Besides, she was old enough to defend herself by shouting and physical resisting. Also they thought that she would not have become pregnant had she not 'indulged in it'.[26] Margaretha Müller was drowned for committing incest and adultery.[27]

In these ways it was many times reasserted that a woman who did not immediately resist sex must desire it. In Margaretha Schäfer's case the supreme ducal council in 1658 referred to the Old Testament principle that an incestuous man and woman ought to be stoned: the woman because she had not shouted her protests, the man because he had ravished his 'brother's' wife. Dutiful governors, they pointed out, should follow divine law. Although Margaretha claimed that she had resisted her husband's brother, the lawyers thought there was insufficient proof of her shouting and concluded that 'she did not do much against it'.[28]

Ultimately, the fact that a man was able to enter a woman's body was in itself taken as a sign of consent. A 1627 Tübingen reference discussing a rape case pointed out that you could not put a sword into a sheath if the sheath was not already large and firm enough to receive it.[29] However, there was a more popular male saying in this context which stated exactly the reverse: even the hardest nut could be cracked.[30]

Women who did not have a good reputation were often judged guilty at the very beginning of their trials. In 1668, in the case of a 20-year-old peasant girl who had been abused by her stepfather, it was agreed that her 'immodest spirit' was obvious. The excuse that they were forced to have intercourse was 'common to all wenches', the judges agreed.[31] Margaretha Schwarz, pregnant by her father-in-law, told the jury that she had shouted several times until he put a handkerchief into her mouth and raped her in the stables. No one could hear her. Aged 21, her husband had died young: now she lived

---

[26] For, according to certain medical writers, only women who experienced pleasure and an orgasm could become pregnant, see J. Cadden, *Meanings of Sex Difference in the Middle Ages: Medicine, Science and Culture* (Cambridge, 1993), ch. 3; T. Laqueur, *Making Sex: Body and Gender from the Greeks to Freud* (Cambridge, Mass., 1990), ch. 3.

[27] HStASt, A 209, Bü. 567, 25 May 1590.   [28] HStASt, A 209 Bü. 1702, 15 Dec. 1657.

[29] HStASt, A 209, Bü. 47, 30 Jan. 1627, 10 Feb. 1627, Michel Thumb. The use of these metaphors is discussed in J. Müller, *Schwert und Scheide: Der sexuelle und skatologische Wortschatz im Nürnberger Fastnachtsspiel des 15. Jahrhunderts* (Frankfurt on Main, 1988).

[30] Cf. W. Lahne, *Magdeburgs Zerstörung in der zeitgenössischen Publizistik* (Magdeburg, 1931), 70.   [31] HStASt, A 209, Bü. 1348, 17 Jan. 1668, Margaretha Reiser.

at his father's and managed the household. On her wedding day she had already been pregnant by her husband and was thus not permitted to wear her wreath of honour. As a married woman, she had led a 'pious, quiet, and religious' life for one and a half years—a fact that was taken positively into account, along with her youth. But her earlier offence of premarital sex proved how easily she was tempted into sin.[32]

Such assessments of guilt and coercion ignored the difficulties of resisting abuse and of getting support from families. Margaretha Schäffer is a case in point. She had signalled to her family that she was being harassed and had even told her husband that his brother wanted intercourse with her. But her husband told her to be quiet and not get his brother into trouble. His connivance had a good reason. In Württemberg the practice of partible inheritance meant that one brother could inherit (say) the front part of a cart and the other its rear.[33] So brothers and brothers-in-law had to live in some peace if they were to sustain their livelihoods. Hence, despite the fact in this case that the whole village regarded Schäffer's brother as disreputable, Schaffer wanted to protect him. Then during the harvest Margaretha was sent home by her husband to fetch a bottle of wine for the cutters. Her brother-in-law seized his chance, called her into his house, and raped her.[34]

In 1688 22-year-old Anna Vöhringer had a similar experience. After their wedding she and her husband lived at his parents'. Soon her father-in-law told Anna that he wanted sex with her. He threatened that 'it was not much of a sin, and if she did not do what he told her to do, she wouldn't have one good hour left; but if she did it she would enjoy it'.[35] Two weeks later he locked her up and had intercourse with her. His wife had refused to have sex with him ever since a stillbirth three years earlier, he said. She slept in the children's

---

[32] She had to stand in the pillory and was banished 10 miles away, HStASt, A 209, Bü. 1554.

[33] D. W. Sabean, '"Junge Immen im leeren Korb": Beziehungen zwischen Schwägern in einem schwäbischen Dorf', in id. and H. Medick (eds.), *Emotionen und materielle Interessen: Sozialanthropologische und historische Beiträge zur Familienforschung* (Göttingen, 1984).

[34] The process of her sentencing was complicated: first, the junior bailiff and parson decided to punish her with church penance and a secular shaming punishment. In response to this her husband announced that he would not take her back into his household afterwards, because of the shame caused. Only now did the junior bailiff ask the upper council for advice how to treat the case. The councillors ordered the opening of a criminal trial, HStASt, A 209, Bü. 1702, 15 Jan. 1658.

[35] HStASt, A 209, Bü. 2008, 30 June 1688.

bed or joined him only after he was asleep. If he sought 'marital cohabitation' in the morning she would refuse him angrily.[36] Her father-in-law was wealthy and had been mayor in his time. While away at markets he often got drunk and then 'acted without shame and strangely with women'. The son knew his father was like this, too. When Anna suggested to him that 'his father was so strange that he would assault her when he got drunk', he merely replied that that was probable.[37] When Anna finally broke down crying at her uncle's house in a nearby village, she told them that she could no longer live in Bernloch because 'her husband hated her and she had no peace from her father-in-law who had made her a whore'. Her uncle, himself a mayor, confronted her father-in-law. The only consequence was that he was so angered by the 'gossip' that he hit Anna.[38]

This case shows what it could mean for women to transfer to their husbands' families. Houses were 'made by men', as Christiane Klapisch-Zuber writes. Men were not only the 'natural' heads of households, they also actually built them; they passed them on more often to sons than to daughters, and filled them with children and relatives of their own name.[39] Married women often found themselves wholly dependent on their acceptance by their husband's relatives; they had to be on good terms with them, especially if they lived with their parents-in-law. If difficulties arose, only their husbands could help. The husband's support made quarrels likely. Moreover, since the death rate of women in their first childbirth was very high, newly married women were not always regarded as permanent family members.[40] A husband, on the other hand, was bonded to his family forever. Proverbially blood was thicker than water.[41] So women were caught up in the dilemma of familial dependencies, often not understanding why their husband failed to protect them from his relatives' abuse. Husbands, however, avoided confrontations because family

---

[36] HStASt, A 209, Bü. 2008, 27 July 1688.
[37] HStASt, A 209, Bü. 2008, 30 June 1688.   [38] Ibid.
[39] C. Klapisch-Zuber, *Women, Family, and Ritual in Renaissance Italy* (Chicago, 1985), 117f. This situation was particularly marked in Florence, because women were prohibited from inheriting houses.
[40] For an overview of demographic research on the subject see H. Wunder, '*Er ist die Sonn', sie ist der Mond': Frauen in der frühen Neuzeit* (Munich 1992), 158.
[41] Cf. R. Beck, 'Frauen in Krise: Eheleben und Ehescheidung in der ländlichen Gesellschaft Bayerns während des Ancien Régime', in R. v. Dülmen (ed.), *Dynamik der Tradition* (Frankfurt on Main, 1992).

alliances were too important to them, or because they did not realize that their wives were not just 'touched' or wooed, but raped.

BELONGING

How far a woman could feel that she 'belonged' to a family was thus highly variable. Single women typically experienced their dependency on acceptance through their exposure to promises and threats. Aged only 35, Johann Schliere had been married three times already. His last wife, a councillor's daughter, had died recently, leaving him with a 19-year-old stepdaughter named Susanna. Her chances of finding work or a husband were small: she was a 'bent, poor, pretty stupid *Mensch*', and she was forced to sleep on the *Lotterbett* behind the oven. On St Stephen's Day, shortly after Christmas, Schliere returned home drunk and wanted sex with her. Susanna pushed him away and threatened to shout. He replied that if she resisted 'she would have to leave the house straight away; but if she obeyed him he would never leave her, and would look after her as if she were his own child'.[42]

Maria Faulhaber, aged 25, experienced this link between care and sexual demand differently—from the perspective of a married woman with three children, whose brother-in-law managed to take up the role of her unsatisfactory husband, a Böblingen carpenter. Her husband often worked away, even when she was in childbed, and never brought her enough to eat. Her 'marital affection' had diminished. Her sister's husband, a miller, had started to send her cabbage and meat two years ago. Although gifts of food and care were normal among relatives, gifts between a woman and a relative by marriage were ambivalent. She owed him something, but was unable to pay back by similar means; so she might pay with other means. One day when Maria entered her brother-in-law's mill he carried her into the back room. On another day he put two pieces of meat on her doorstep and then came in person for his payment at three o'clock in the morning. Maria later justified herself by saying that she thought she 'had to love him'. Her closeness to the brother-in-law made it possible for her to show her husband that if he failed in his marital duties she would, too. For which lesson, Maria Faulhaber and her brother-in-law were decapitated.[43]

---

[42] He had raped her; now she was pregnant, he had escaped, HStASt, A 209, Bü. 1275, 13 July 1691.   [43] HStASt, A 209, Bü. 473.

Because of the complex feelings incest created, relatives usually offered help only if they witnessed abuse at its very beginning. In 1672, for example, an ill woman in Hedelfingen swopped beds with her 16-year-old daughter. Later she heard the daughter screaming. She shouted out to ask her daughter what was happening, and the answer was that 'father hurt her so much': her husband had tried to have sex with the girl while she slept. Again, little could to be done against a husband, so the mother decided that it would be best for her daughter to leave the house.[44]

Other women had to tolerate abuse also. Katharina Lohnhardt's case in Leonberg demonstrates how a whole family might have to turn a blind eye because the only alternative was to prosecute. Katharina was abused by her grandfather Severin Stahl from the age of 14.[45] Aged 50, Stahl was a saddler. He had first been married to the daughter of a wealthy local artisan and councillor,[46] and then on her death married in 1621 a widow who came from one of the best Leonberg families. But she was sixteen years older than Stahl.[47] When his granddaughter was aged 18 Stahl got her married because she was pregnant by him. He promised her long-time suitor, Lonhardt, a good dowry, a house, and money. At first he had jealously disliked Lonhardt. Once he had cut his hat in half when he had entered the house to see Katharina, announcing that he would throw him downstairs if he came again. Stahl did not give up on Katharina after the wedding, and four years later she was again pregnant by him. He had forced his wife to get Katharina into a room with him. Otherwise, Stahl said, he would make sure there was 'no worse marriage in town'. The threat worked. Margaretha asked her grandchild to go to bed with him. Stahl said to her: 'Katharina, if you are going to leave me, I shall leave you too.' His second wife's death was imminent. He told Katharina to get away from 'her husband and all other guys' and marry him.[48] Stahl escaped when the trial started. Margaretha had just died, and Katharina was banished from Württemberg.

[44] HStASt, A 209, Bü. 790, Dorothea Paguet, 1674.

[45] Stahl was regarded as step-grandfather, but Katharina was in fact a child of his first wife's daughter.

[46] Through this marriage Stahl could enter the council seven years later. In 1616 he became a judge in the town court. He left the court in 1626.

[47] V. Trugenberger, *Zwischen Schloß und Vorstadt: Sozialgeschichte der Stadt Leonberg im 16. Jahrhundert* (Vaihingen, 1984), appendix: Prosopography of Leonberg citizens 1560–1580, Father: Heinrich Stahel, No. 334; First Marriage: Barbara Beltzner, No. 25; Second Marriage: Margaretha Schmid, née Beutelsbacher.

[48] HStASt, A 309, Bü. 145, 31 Aug. 1630, Bü. 90e, 27 July 1630.

Incest thus brought abused and betrayed women into complicated tangles. They could say little against their husbands; and because they depended on them, they would routinely plead for lenient sentences. Often they were still not quite sure about what had happened, since abused women normally did not talk much about the pressure and threats they had experienced. Others had to cope with the fact that their daughters or sisters had got a child by their husbands. 'She understood it [the baby] was from her husband', one woman denounced her sister: the sister had 'lain next to her husband when she herself had been in childbed, and had tried it so long until once, when he had been drunk, he sadly had given in'.[49]

The shock of revelation increased the longer the story was kept secret. In Esslingen, it took a shoemaker's wife two years to realize that her second husband had abused her daughter from her first marriage. She had wondered what the two of them were doing when they stayed in rooms together for a long time, but the truth came out only after a bitter quarrel between daughter and stepfather. At a wedding he had forbidden her to dance with someone who fancied her. She shouted angrily at him: 'Fool! Debt-maker! Whore's bird! Pig! Yes! If I only did what you wanted it would please you, and you wouldn't treat me like this!' She exploded against her mother, too: 'at last she wanted to talk, even if her head was cut off tomorrow!' (People were aware of punishments for incest: usually they cemented the silence.) Her mother replied: 'you loose wench, what do you know? What do you want to say? Why haven't you told me about it? I would have prevented it!' The daughter replied that the mother had known about it all along! Her mother denied this and said that the girl had paid her brother ten pence not to tell the mother that she had lain with her stepfather.

Both of them were right. Her mother had already tried to confront her husband, but he had cursed her so passionately that she was not sure what to believe. This male response was typical and could be much more violent. One man beat his wife 'blue' for accusing him of sleeping with her daughter.[50] Women had to remain silent if they wanted to avoid that kind of retribution. The daughter's silence in turn resulted from her insecurity about whether the mother would understand and trust her. For half a year Meyer had been waking up his stepdaughter in the mornings, sitting on her bed and gliding his

[49] HStASt, A 209, Bü. 90, Catharina Rommel, 9 Mar. 1654.
[50] HStASt, A 209, Bü. 332, 9 Nov. 1683, Wilhelm Hartmann.

hands under the bedcover. She had tried to push them away, 'so that he would not get at her naked body'. The brother slept in the same bed and had seen everything. One morning he wanted to run downstairs and tell his mother: that was when Maria gave him ten pence to stay quiet.

Meyer still slept with his wife. He was not deprived of sex. He thought that by having sex with her he expended his fertile semen. Hence he would tell his stepdaughter that 'he was just coming from mother and had had to do with her: sex now should do her no harm'. Meyer tried to tempt her with his sexual experience: 'he was not a rough man; he knew what to do with her; he was not as plump and piggish as others; he wanted to do it with her in a clean way.' She had no peace from him and never felt safe. He was an artisan, so his workshop was in their home. When she did the washing-up, he held her breasts from behind, and when she knelt down to light the fire he tried to catch her arms and force her on his lap. Even after the quarrel the situation remained the same, except for some fragile trust building up between her and her mother. The two women agreed that the mother should not leave the home for long, so that she could protect her daughter. But one day, Meyer sent his wife away with a long shopping list. The daughter was in her room reading a love-letter from one of her suitors. Her father entered the room and locked the door. She shouted that she was going to jump out of the window. The mother returned early. She found the two of them in a state of great shock, saw the untidy bed, heard his excuses, and her daughter's sigh: 'God had sent her, otherwise it would have happened.' Once more the mother did not know what to think.

The situation was insoluble. She could not have her husband prosecuted. The household's honour would be damaged forever, and the daughter would be handed over to the judges and possibly the hangman as well. Abuse in the family had to be lived with. To a large extent this was a consequence of the authorities' view of this crime.[51] And thus, as in so many other cases, the Meyer family did nothing until the stepdaughter became pregnant and was accused of incest. In court she had to pretend that she suffered from a skin disease for long periods, so as to hide that the abuse had lasted for

---

[51] When in 1703 one woman finally went to a parson to accuse her stepson of abusing her, his siblings mobilized a number of partial witnesses so that in the end the Tübingen lawyers recommended that she should be beheaded.

two years. But it did not help her or them: neighbours testified that incestuous, 'indecent impositions' had happened for a long time.[52] Interestingly, Meyer's position had changed in the same way the Leonberg saddler Stahl's had. Their ability to abuse depended on their being heads of households who were able to enforce obedience and silence. At the same time, their endless obsession with the woman in the case, the stepdaughter or the step-granddaughter, demonstrated a kind of helplessness. Neither could come to terms with the fact that the girls had young suitors and were mature enough to marry. Each claimed the girl as his possession, despite the fact that he had no proper parental rights. The possessiveness of each became more and more obvious to the family. Meyer's wife found one solution in walking to nearby Plochingen to get her father-in-law's (that is, Meyer's father's) opinion. He sent his other son back with her to Esslingen, where he beat Meyer with a stick. Afterwards Meyer stood there 'like a poor sinner', and was only 'able to say that he did not want to do it again'. The brother then played on Meyer's jealousy: when he pretended to give the daughter a kiss, Meyer turned white.[53] Nothing exhibited his helpless possessiveness more clearly.

Other cases also confirm that abuse reflected not only men's violence within the family but also their weakness. Strikingly, some abusive men were nearly or fully sterile or impotent. It is not surprising that they so often convinced themselves that intercourse did no 'harm'. Sometimes it did harm, however: pregnancy ensued.[54] Then other excuses came into play. In 1699, Hans Stoll told the court that he had only wanted to see whether it 'worked better' with his daughter than with his wife. He had crawled across the bed to his daughter twice, just wearing his shirt, but had been turned away. The third time he forced her; but on that occasion he still missed his 'manly powers' (*männliche Kräfte*); his '*membrum virile* had collapsed without the desired effect'. He had then rubbed his penis until 'semen flowed'. Stoll had also exposed his member to a 14-year-old girl, to an old widow, and to his own stepmother, demanding intercourse with her, too, so that she could see what was wrong with him, because he had heard once that she had 'cured someone else who had lost his manly power'. Stoll's problems, his 'incapacity

---

[52] Tobias Meyer was banished for six years, his stepdaughter escaped from prison, StAE, Reichsstadt, A 43B, 12 Mar. 1691.   [53] Ibid.
[54] For a particularly interesting case see HStASt, A 309, Bü.265, 22 June 1723, Hans Jakob Hofmeister.

for marital action', as the lawyers put it, began after a horse injured his penis. The barber had treated him, but even with his first wife things had never been 'right'. Stoll admitted that he did not know whether 'their' child was his or another man's. A medical inspection revealed nothing wrong with his penis, but one testicle was bean-sized and the other one appeared to be diminishing.[55] So rape and harassment were the results of Stoll's struggle for 'manly powers'; his abuse exposed his weakness and power equally.

POTENCY

Potency measured status and masculinity, even in the family. A telling proof of this is how women sometimes wanted to destroy a relative's penis. In 1655, a Hall butcher's wife went to her daughter's husband in the middle of the night, tore his shirt off, and began to strike him in his 'secret place'. If neighbours had not been alarmed by the noise and stopped her, she would have 'damaged' him.[56] Likewise, the unhappily married wife of Jacob Mever told her stepson that she wanted to cut off her husband's penis (the record puts it: 'this old fool his p. p. : meaning the *membrum virile*) and 'put it into the chimney and into the smoke so that he would not make her another child'.[57] The man's ability to give a woman children was the foundation of marriage, and she wanted to destroy it. By the same token, loss of potency symbolized the decline of virility and fertility. For men, virility meant power over people, and went hand in hand with attractiveness, command, control, and satisfaction.[58] In the early modern period, verbs expressing command were nearly always used to describe intercourse: a woman succumbed to his 'will' or did 'his will' (*ihm zum Willen werden*).

There were some men, it was thought, whose power no woman could resist. In 1695 Angelika Schaut explained that her uncle must have bewitched her. It was no secret that he could 'get women to do his will as he wants them to'.[59] Her stepson was a sorcerer, one woman reported in 1703: 'he had brought many women to his will and blinded another one'.[60] Those who did not achieve such effects

[55] HStASt, A 209, Bü. 1632, 20 Feb. 1699.
[56] StAH, 4/482, fo. 208ʳ, 2 Aug. 1655, Veronica Bootzen.
[57] StAH, 4/484, fo. 67ʳ⁻ᵛ, 3 May 1678.
[58] L. Roper, *Oedipus and the Devil: Witchcraft, Sexuality and Religion in Early Modern Europe* (London, 1994), ch. 6.   [59] HStASt, A 209, Bü. 179.
[60] HStASt, A 209, Bü. 1500, 8 Feb. 1703.

naturally had to use other means: one old man was said to have seduced his son's lover through love-magic.[61]

While age might reduce men to being 'half a man' (this is how Georg Reiser put it), 'youth' and 'freshness' characterized in one phrase the phase of greatest potency. Middle-aged men could try to resist the natural order by demonstrating their sexual experience to younger women. Meyer told his stepdaughter that he could give her more pleasure than young lads: they would be raw and dirty and ignorant of what to do with a woman. There was pride in the ability to control ejaculation and to use coitus interruptus. He had always given his niece money for intercourse, the Bohingen mayor Fuchs said in 1655, and had also 'done it in such a manner that she would not get pregnant by him'—thus continuing even after she married.[62] With old age, potency and power within the family declined. Sons and sons-in-law increasingly took over the business, and fathers had less say. They could ensure their closest kin's respect for some time by giving away property slowly and carefully. But there came a point when the ability to manipulate dependency and affection receded; then they had to rely only on sympathy.[63] Such generational change had to be accepted. However, a sexual life could seemingly slow down the surrender of power. The Bohingen mayor Vöhringer demonstrated to his son through his sexual demands on his wife that she did not belong to her husband solely, and that he still held power over his son's life. Sexual aggression was one way of expressing who had the most 'manly powers' and potential to manipulate.

It was doubtless in this context that we should understand why so many incestuous men turned anxieties about the loss of power into sexual aggression. The ways they described the women they abused confirmed this. The women were described either as useless and simple-minded, or as whores, who had gained complete control over men's desires. Such depictions were meant to serve them well in court: sex with a simple woman could seem unimportant, sex with a lewd woman as the expression of *her* abuse. But these descriptions also reveal how the men's desire for control and experience of a loss of control were worked through and repeated. Femininity, as constructed in the experience of abuse, stood for extremes: women were

[61] HStASt, A 209, Bü. 1231, 1 Oct. 1658.
[62] HStASt, A 209, Bü. 1720 (2), 15 July 1655.
[63] Sabean, 'Junge Immen im leeren Korb'.

either simple and to be overpowered, or desirous and overpowering. Abusive men, it seems, split off their own feelings of desire for power and disrespect for themselves and projected them onto the woman. One man, aged 67, said about his 41-year-old daughter that she was simple, bad, and addicted to men. She had told him 'father, lie down' (whereas she reported that he had forced her to sleep in his room after her mother's death and had one night attacked her).[64] Men's description of the women's character of course tied in with the concept that all women were desirous. Rudolph Wacker, a carpenter, argued in 1684 that his stepdaughter had tried to seduce him and that he 'had finally succumbed to her will'.[65] She had been more wicked than his wife, he said: she had put her hands in his breeches and pulled his 'lad' out. The junior bailiff and parson believed him since the stepdaughter and her three sisters had already all been punished for premarital sex and were therefore 'lewd whores'.[66]

The Hall councillor Schragmüller confidently held that even a man's age-related potency problems could be eased by an 'active and desirous' woman. In 1683 he wrote a legal reference about a 70-year-old carpenter who had impregnated his daughter. Schragmüller thought that there were 'many and especially [*sic*!] male persons who in their sixties, seventies, eighties, and even older age have [sexual] ability, [and] that even in their nineties they have had children by women'. A medical examination of Roth's penis and the fact that the daughter had been punished for fornication three times settled the question of his possible paternity to everyone's satisfaction.[67]

The theological concept of ever-present temptation to sin was equally relevant. Protestant popular literature was inhabited by devils who whored and danced. Desire for pleasure and extravagance were thus split off from the self and projected onto an omnipotent figure of evil. This was one way of dealing with anxieties about fantasies of desire. Men's descriptions of their seduction by women therefore bore no trace of internalized guilt. Michel Eytinger, for example, related how he had been 'tempted into whoredom', like other men: she had 'opened his breeches and lifted his shirt and taken his penis'. Every man was likely to be sympathetic when he

[64] HStASt, A 209, Bü. 1442, 9 July 1675, Margaretha Erbacher.
[65] Roper, *Oedipus and the Devil*, ch. 2.
[66] She was beheaded, HStASt, A 209, Bü. 1937, 10 Jan. 1684.
[67] She was a child from his second marriage and managed his household. He was beheaded, she was banished after their child had been born, StAH, 11, 41/1683.

said he could not stop her.[68] At the same time, devil and woman, the two principal figures embodying seductive evil, could raise fears of an absolute loss of control. For once the devil or desirous woman gained permanent power over man and reason, the boundaries between the self and the other broke down.[69] Wilhelm Hartmann from Besigheim experienced this state as equally pleasurable and painful, and sought liberation. He had married an older, 54-year-old widow. Her daughter Margaretha, aged 18, had seen how she could master men through seduction. Hartmann was soon given advice to get 'rid of his shameful daughter'. She not only had sex with him and soldiers, but with the junior bailiff, too, who therefore tried to forge the trial record. Margaretha drank too much. It was from this, the Tübingen lawyers wrote with reference to the Epistles, that desire and shamelessness followed. This view was affirmed by the evidence of a former apprentice. He remembered how once a man had come from Liebenzell trading salt and spices. Margaretha and her stepfather had drunk wine with him, and he had played the fiddle. The moon shone. Later Margaretha and Hartmann quietly disappeared. The apprentice claimed to have seen them lying on top of each other, with Hartmann moving vigorously. At another time they had lain together in the *Lotterbett*; its curtains had been drawn. Hartmann did not deny this, but defended himself by saying that in no case could he have impregnated Margaretha, for he had rarely emitted semen, and if he did it was into his shirt. Margaretha had often scolded him that he was 'no use: she had felt nothing from him'. It was a widespread assumption that women felt the men's semen upon ejaculation: this enabled them to check male potency and control contraception. In this case, both had felt the semen 'come'; the stepfather described how he then 'held back and got out'. Likewise, when Margaretha felt his ejaculation, she 'pushed him away with his member'. She still ridiculed him for not having done it as well as the junior bailiff, Weinmann. She had thought everyone did it like him. Weinmann was a 'fresh, strong man', she said, whereas with her stepfather it had been 'no good'; she had no idea 'where he had put his semen'. She confessed that she had approached him on the *Lotterbett* when he had been drunk; there she had 'kissed' and 'tickled' him, 'taken his member and teased it'

---

[68] HStASt, A 209, Bü. 35.
[69] E. Bronfen, *Over her Dead Body: Death, Femininity and the Aesthetic* (Manchester, 1992), 181f.

until he did 'what pleased her'. He had often been angry with her afterwards, but she just laughed. Hartmann said that she had not let him get away until 'he had served her will'.[70] Margaretha teased him and hurt him, while he controlled neither his reason nor his member. A woman's control over a stepfather's desire was never described as powerfully as this in any other cases.

In trial narratives, the simple-minded woman occupied the opposite position to this one. She was beyond lust or desire. Sex happened to her, and she endured it without feeling. This description was contrasted with extreme male desire. Barbara Stampfer, who was treated leniently because she was a simple peasant woman, described her abuse as follows. In 1660, her uncle, the Urach junior bailiff Georg König, told her to come out of the fields. He made her 'lean forward, and bend with her head towards the earth below her, in which position he had not only entered her from behind, but had also . . . done her harm'. Later he had demanded it in 'his chamber at the door which she had held shut with one hand, while he warned her to take care that his wife did not enter from the kitchen; he had done it with her from behind'. He had also done it 'when she had been kneeling on a bench and looked out of the window and he had seen her behind'. Then he did it on the *Lotterbett*, and 'she had had to lift her thighs and put them onto his shoulders'.[71] König could do with her what he wanted and she obeyed, but she felt nothing except pain. Sabinam Scherer, aged 33, suffered from epilepsy and was described as a 'crippled, thin, little, and shy woman', 'naive and simple'. On a visit to her mother and stepfather she decided to stay overnight. It was winter, and so cold that they all slept in one bed. In the morning her mother rose early to light the fire and feed the cattle: then her stepfather raped her. He held her mouth shut, saying that if she told anyone, her head would be cut off. He would take a horse and ride away. The threat worked, and Sabina told her mother in tears after he had escaped.[72]

MALE HONOUR AND ABUSE

As several previous examples have shown, abusive men frequently escaped when detention was imminent and a possible death sentence

[70] She was beheaded, HStASt, A 209, Bü. 332, 9 Nov. 1684.
[71] HStASt, A 209, Bü. 1988, 29 Mar. 1660.
[72] HStASt, A 209, Bü. 1011, 30 June 1663.

loomed. An escape was a form of self-banishment, but men could at least hope to find work as soldiers or day-labourers, whereas pregnant women had no such hopes. Even so, it was a remarkable decision to leave family, property, trade, and home behind, especially because it was often easier for men to plead for mercy in court. A woman's reputation was solely determined by her modesty, her 'withdrawn' (*eingezogenes*) behaviour. Male honour, on the other hand, was defined by mixtures of military, communal, and professional achievement, all of which could be weighed against moral misbehaviour. At Rudolph Wackernagel's trial none of the witnesses could believe that he forced his stepdaughter to have sex with him. The whole community petitioned that they would not like to lose him; he was their village carpenter and 'had always worked from early till late'.[73] Agnes Seering's stepfather confidently claimed that he had 'a good reputation for having fought in the Palatinate wars' and for being respectable. So the Tübingen lawyers decided not to execute him, provided his wife, children, and family petitioned on his behalf.[74] Similarly, Hanns Legeder asserted that his niece, who served in his house, had seduced him when he had been drunk and his wife was ill. Moreover, he had been a mayor, 'a member of council and court for fifteen years and been sent to the estate assemblies'. He enjoyed such a high reputation that even in neighbouring communities everyone was sorry for him. Moreover his wife was pregnant and they already had four small children.[75] For Georg Fuchs, likewise, there was a petition from all master smiths in the town and district of Nürtingen, as well as from the Oberbohingen parson, citizens, judges. They pleaded that he be allowed to 'follow his trade, for the great benefit of the whole place, so that they would not need to go to other places and be unable to get on with their own work'.[76]

However, the frequent self-exiles, flights, and escapes can be explained by noting that reported abuse predominantly involved respectable citizens, artisans, and men who had held office.[77] The

---

[73] HStASt, A 209, Bü. 1937, 22 Jan. 1685.   [74] HStASt, A 209, Bü. 373.
[75] HStASt, A 209, Bü. 845.   [76] HStASt, A 209, Bü. 1720 (2), 28 Sept. 1655.
[77] The profession is, of course, only given for a small number of cases, but the distribution nevertheless stands out in comparison to other crimes. We find: two parsons, one schoolmaster, two former bailiffs, two former mayors, one former official, one civic officer, one member of the *Ehrbarkeit*, one landlord, five citizens who are identifiable as wealthy, two innkeepers, three carpenters, two tailors, two smiths, one shoemaker, one mintmaster, one tanner, one watchmaker, one unspecified artisan, one miller, one knife-sharpener, one vine-dresser, one pigherd, one shepherd, two day-labourers.

threat of losing honour through trial and public punishment presumably seemed as bad as death to many of them. The wife and children of the former mayor Vöhringer wrote that 'if he were to die from the hangman's hand' it would leave 'an inextinguishable stain' on the family.[78] Until then, these men would have been thought of as good, respectable citizens, *unbescholtene Biedermänner*. Nobody, the mayor and judges of Ditzingen wrote to the Württemberg supreme council, had thought Siglin Laux was 'capable of doing any such thing'.[79] The Neuenstatt envoy similarly had led a good life—at least until soldiers heard his stepdaughter's shouts in an inn and in the morning found the sheets stained with semen.[80] Melchior Rebion, imprisoned for having sex with his niece while his wife was ill, lamented that 'he had brought shame upon his kin (*Geschlecht*)'.[81] Such a loss of honour sealed these men's lost battle for appreciation and standing. They had dishonoured their family, and even the children of their grandchildren would be told that one of their ancestors had been touched by the hangman. Their fear of losing authority had become real.

---

[78] HStASt, A 209, Bü. 2008, 27 July 1668.   [79] HStASt, A 309, Bü. 151, 4 Jan. 1611.
[80] HStASt, A 309, Bü. 268, 2 Dec. 1758, Samuel Bayer.
[81] HStASt, A 309, Bü. 90b.

Conclusion

THE aim of this study has been to show how sixteenth- and seventeenth-century élites in the south-west of Germany used the law to enforce their notions of moral and sexual order, and how this affected ordinary women. Trial records have illuminated the family histories, material conditions, life experiences, and social practices of women who are not often written about: the thieves and maidservants, day-labourers, artisan wives, and single mothers of early modern Germany. Such documents fix on a moment in history and on one kind of question: did the jug-maker's wife insult her husband, the maidservant drown her baby, or the vagrant steal a silver spoon? Obviously, the historian's interests are different from the judge's: whereas judges wanted to establish the evidence, we want to know about social conflicts behind the crime. The conditions which enabled a woman to trust in a relationship matter more to us than whether her baby was killed or stillborn. Women's defences in criminal trials reflect how they felt they should behave to receive mercy. To trace the cultural and personal significance of transgressions and their punishment we have to read depositions carefully. These in turn open a window onto a community's moral values. In the end, we may not know the 'truth' about the jug-maker's responsibility for his wife's unhappiness, but we may have recovered their neighbours' views of marital duties. Furthermore, we are left with an intense sense of what was needed to avoid misery in marriages, master–servant relationships, or love affairs of the young. Court records thus reveal the ties that bind as much as moments of rupture.[1] They illuminate the dynamics of social relations in early modern society, revealing how order was contested in households and conflicts worked out in society.

What do court records tell us about the changes in women's social position in these centuries? They mainly point to a seventeenth-century tightening of patriarchal values through the enforced prosecution of illegitimate sexual relations, bastard-bearing, and infanticide.

[1] E. Muir and G. Ruggiero, 'Afterword', in id. (eds.), *History from Crime* (Baltimore, 1994), 226.

This was linked to efforts to naturalize maternal love and praise chastity and marriage as women's sole avenues towards respectability. The message to single women was clear: no matter whether they could afford to marry at 20 or had to wait until they were 30, chastity was expected from them. One night of dancing on New Year's Eve or a small carnival feast with three other servants could result in a fine (which made savings dwindle) and the accusation that, like most women, they had an immoderate nature and lewd character, which tempted men into sin. A new sense of shame attached to premarital sex if wedding celebrations were forbidden. Skills in negotiation and money were needed to mitigate ever-mounting prison sentences. For those who were imprisoned lengthily for fornication the shame could be so intense that they moved away afterwards. In the whole of south-west Germany illegitimately pregnant women were banished and condemned to begging and vagrancy while their children were small. Increasingly, the offers of others to raise the child were rejected, and the return to one's home town made impossible even years later. Women who were accused of fornication with soldiers faced the same fate, and repentance gained them little.

Moreover, all areas of a specifically female work-culture, from spinning to sewing and service, and washing to wet-nursing, became associated with immorality. Single women's independence was suspicious. It was interpreted as indicating disobedience and a desire for sexual freedom. This points to a crucial dilemma in south-west society in the seventeenth century, which was based on state corporatism, strict guild rules, and household morality. Spinning was a labour no man wanted to do, and the expansion of large-scale textile manufacturing depended on large supplies of yarn. It needed the labour force of single women. They had to move to the places of production, accept poor wages, and rent themselves rooms. The places of production and of domestic residence were separated, pay was largely monetary, and the master–servant bond was upset. The demand for such labour and the conditions of production that went with it were difficult to reconcile with the desire to protect the ordered hierarchies of the community, based on household rule. The desire to keep the number of independent single female workers as low as possible might thus have reinforced economic stagnation, because the output was expensive, limited, and inflexible. Likewise, the mobility of servants was needed during harvest time, when they became seasonal day-labourers and thus helped to secure agricultural wealth. But masters and mistresses deplored mobility which undermined loyalty to them. Pamphlets, mandates, and sermons disseminated a highly negative image of the maidservant. This probably reinforced the shortage in the labour market. Respectable families preferred to keep their daughters at home until marriage. Service (if ever it was) was no longer a life-cycle employment for every girl, but became highly class-specific. Poor maidservants had to work until their late twenties, and were more likely to stake out their claims for just rewards and self-determination as they grew older. Seventeenth-century households could no longer be seen as schools of good government which ensured social harmony, but became an area where hierarchies of rank were contested. And yet the answer to demographic, economic, and social change was a reinforced moralism which attempted to strengthen basic social institutions, such as the family, household, school, guild, and church. This depended on an increasing state force and social exclusion mechanisms to deal with those stepping outside this order.

The second half of the seventeenth century thus emerges as a period when the search for post-war order led to a more rigid defence of resources and hierarchies of rank as well as reinforced defences of marriage and the family. Yet we must not assume that there was a straight development towards greater state control. Rather, the State remained highly dependent on communal cooperation in the prosecution of crime and deviance throughout the sixteenth and seventeenth centuries and had to adapt its moral goals largely to those of the population. The population in turn tended to accuse those who violated key norms, were social outsiders, or notoriously broke the common peace. Prosecution patterns are thus very much an expression of diverse interplays of socio-economic, administrative, political, institutional, and confessional structures, and of change which was often localized and never linear.[2] This study has demonstrated that isolated factors such as confession explain little in themselves: infanticide accusations declined in Constance as much as in Esslingen and Memmingen; evidence for the harsh prosecution of premarital sexuality and fornication exists for Hall but not for other towns, whereas strict measures against single mothers, soldiers' whores, and vagrants became

---

[2] Cf. K. Wrightson, 'The Politics of the Parish in Early Modern England', in P. Griffiths, A. Fox and S. Hindle (eds.), *The Experience of Authority in Early Modern England* (London, 1996).

common everywhere. By the second half of the sixteenth century, household morality was being enforced in Catholic as much as Protestant towns, and the concern with secret marriages, prostitutes, the poor, and unruly youth was a shared one. Lutheran divorce policies kept unhappy couples tied together as much as Catholic policies did. It is impossible to discern in this practice important confessional differences in understandings of human sin. Looking at two other Catholic countries, we find that in seventeenth-century France the State also became more disciplinarian and orientated towards the harsher prosecution of sexual crimes,[3] whereas in Italy, Nicholas Davidson claims, sexuality was understood as natural and God-given, and sexual sin therefore treated with greater leniency.[4] In contrast to German Catholic territories more efforts were made in Italy to prevent crime, for example by dowering poor women and reforming, rather than merely physically punishing, prostitutes.[5] Thus, two points emerge: 'the Reformation' did not create a specifically 'Protestant' social order and mentality in Germany,[6] and confessional change did not have similar effects in the whole of Europe. The success of church and state attempts to discipline subjects' behaviour needs to be assessed cautiously.

In this study, we have been concerned with women's experiences of and resistance to the rigidity of social and moral policies. We have witnessed how artisans' wives could cleverly appropriate the political language of tyrannical rule to claim that they had the right to resist bad husbands. Likewise, unmarried women sometimes appropriated the role of the seductress to show how little men— even powerful men—could control their sexual desire. Women who committed infanticide did not accept that they should bear all the shame and hardship attached to life with a bastard. Maidservants and cooks stole meat, wine, and cloth to undermine unequal pay structures. Female thieves abandoned all respect for punishments when they stole sheets from prison beds and slid out of the window. What

---

[3] J. Farr, *Authority and Sexuality in Early Modern Burgundy (1550–1730)* (New York, 1995).

[4] N. Davidson, 'Theology, Nature and the Law: Sexual Sin and Sexual Crime in Italy from the Fourteenth to the Seventeenth Century', in T. Dean and K. J. P. Lowe (eds.), *Crime, Society and the Law in Renaissance Italy* (Cambridge, 1994), 96 f.

[5] O. Hufton, *The Prospect before Her: A History of Women in Western Europe*, i: 1500–1800 (London, 1995), 68; by the 18th-century, Rome endowed 2,000 girls a year; cf. pp. 320 f. on institutions for penitent prostitutes.

[6] As, for example, L. Roper, *The Holy Household: Women and Morals in Reformation Augsburg* (Oxford, 1989), still suggested.

I have tried to recapture is women's alertness, unruliness, and participation in early modern culture which was all too obvious for people then, and often asserted their negative images of femininity, but has been made difficult for us to imagine today. This has to do with a major shift in western history which has not yet been adequately explained. It is that from the late eighteenth century women were no longer believed *collectively* to embody desirousness and danger, but rather embodied sexual passivity, softness, and sensitivity. Men were increasingly seen as the sexual villains, seducers, and abusers. Male sexual energy came to be defined as the prime source of social disorder. Chastity, which used to be something a woman had to yearn and struggle for, was increasingly regarded as her 'natural' self. In many if not all parts of Europe, this had important consequences for women's judicial treatment. Murdering mothers, whom early modern lawyers described as bestial, were more likely to be seen as victims of irresponsible males and sentenced to imprisonment. Witches became unheard of. The notion of female sensitivity certainly connected with older notions of female feebleness, and continued to naturalize women's subordination by ruling out their right to political participation. But within the home it was linked to characteristics which now seemed desirable: sensibility, tenderness, and feeling. Women were set up for their roles as domesticated, caring wives and mothers—though, whether most women accepted 'domestication' as their destiny is an issue of current debate.[7]

This new view of womanhood was nevertheless applied not sweepingly, but selectively. It encoded a respectability upper- and middle-class women had striven for and which established their separateness from aristocrats and working classes. It stressed bourgeois women's capacity for education and some 'reasonable' behaviour. But women *below* these social strata tended still to be characterized in old terms: arguably, little had changed here. What did change was the level of stigmatization these women experienced. For, whereas the State explicitly began to protect the privacy of people inside the family order, that is, all those who were heterosexual, married, and procreative within marriage, it enforced the

---

[7] A.-C. Trepp, *Sanfte Männlichkeit und selbstständige Weiblichkeit: Frauen und Männer im Hamburger Bürgertum zwischen 1770 und 1840* (Göttingen, 1996); ead., 'The Emotional Side of Men in Late Eighteenth-Century Germany', *Central European History*, 27 (1994), 127–52.

criminalization of those who were deemed too poor to be fit to participate in it.[8]

An impressive manifestation of this was the widespread introduction of marriage restrictions for people below certain incomes in the nineteenth century: their desire to marry was deemed 'immodest', their prospective children could only be seen as a burden to the country. They were allowed neither to marry, nor to have sex or reproduce. In Württemberg, these restrictions remained intact until unification in 1871, and went hand-in-hand with the harsh prosecution of single mothers and of women accused of fornication or a bad reputation. These women were largely migrant factory workers, who were generally associated with sexual lewdness and moral irresponsibility. Between 1853 and 1862 as many as 2,634 persons were banished from Württemberg towns and villages on these grounds, 613 for fornication, 153 for prostitution, 98 for concubinage, and 619 for a bad reputation.[9] The notion of a female depravity based on female licentiousness was thus never eradicated in these centuries; rather it became a way of explicitly characterizing differences by class.

[8] I. Hull, *Sex, State, and Civil Society in Germany, 1700–1815* (Ithaca, NY, 1996).
[9] C. Lipp, 'Die Innenseite der Arbeiterkultur: Sexualität im Arbeitermilieu des 19. und frühen 20. Jahrhunderts', in R. v. Dülmen (ed.), *Arbeit, Frömmigkeit und Eigensinn* (Frankfurt on Main, 1990), 219.

APPENDIX
A Note on Sources and on Quantitative Methods

MY sources for Württemberg are found in the Hauptstaatsarchiv
Stuttgart. Here the recognizances (Urfehden) and trial records from
the Württemberg districts are collected. Recognizances were a flexible legal instrument mainly used against poachers, politically disobedient men, and drunkards during the first half of the sixteenth
century: these had to swear not to take revenge against their punishment, which was usually imprisonment and a fine or temporary
banishment. Out of 7,000 such documents surviving, only 335 were
sworn by women. Records of criminal trials mostly date from the
seventeenth century and seem to be better preserved for some
districts than others. Minutes of the weekly work of the supreme
council which dealt with criminal justice in the duchy, and legal
references housed in the Tübingen university archives and relating
to Württemberg criminal cases, also suggest that the sources are
incomplete.[1] However, we find a body of 252 relatively complete
trial records in which women were accused of crimes other than
witchcraft. Usually these contain communications between the ducal
junior bailiff and supreme council, minutes of the interrogation of
the accused and witnesses, a legal reference commissioned from the
Tübingen law faculty, the verdict, and sometimes petitions. Similarly,
well-kept court books survive for Leonberg, a wine-growing town
with 800–1,000 inhabitants near Stuttgart. They cover the period 1528–
1683. Verdicts and confessions were written down in separate books
which do not always overlap, but this source nevertheless give us an
impression of the goals of criminal justice in a Württemberg district
town. Information on how lesser crimes in Württemberg were treated from the second half of the century onwards is revealed only by
a few surviving minutes of annual district court sessions held by
junior bailiffs, as well as court books from quarterly district court

---

[1] I began to work on the Tübingen sources only after the completion of the
manuscript. I have therefore chosen not to integrate much of the material, especially
since it seems to support rather than change the picture gathered from the Stuttgart
sources.

sessions in the pietist, proto-industrial town of Wildberg, with a population of 1,700 (1621–31). Outside Württemberg my main criterion for the choice of towns was the quality of their records. Even so, the feeling that a patchwork of sources needs to be sewn together is unavoidable. *Urfehdbücher*, volumes which briefly describe the misdeeds and sentences of bail-bound offenders, survive in a rare series in Hall from 1523 to 1700. They contain over 2,000 sentences on women, but an *Urgichtbuch* is lacking, which would describe the sentences of those tried for capital offences.[2] In Memmingen, on the other hand, we find well-kept *Urgichtbücher* for 1551–1689, but the *Urfehdbücher* are lost. In Esslingen so-called 'blood-books', recording the confessions of tried offenders, are preserved for both centuries, but almost all trial records (with the minutes of interrogations etc.) are missing, while the collection of *Urfehden* is incomplete. To get a more balanced view of how crime was prosecuted in each town, therefore, I have additionally worked on council minutes. These record the petitioning process and the passing of sentences for serious and (often) lesser offences. For Memmingen and Constance, furthermore, I have examined the pre-trial minutes of interrogations conducted by councillors investigating evidence which could lead to the detention of offenders (*Kundschaften und Verhöre*). These are particularly well preserved in Constance, supplementing trial records and *Urgichten*. The Freiburg sources I consulted were the *Urgichtbuch* for 1550 to 1618, and an extensive collection of Urfehden from 1500–1700. Finally I use the prescriptive literature of mandates—abundant and edited for Württemberg, preserved in bound volumes for Hall, though largely lost in Memmingen, Constance, and Esslingen.

My method is qualitative, except when the documentation permits a reliable picture of rising prosecution rates. The Memmingen court books, for example, have been analysed quantitatively and the figures widely used, but R. v. Dülmen who first publicized them gave no indication that the last court book is not well kept and figures therefore unreliable. The second Esslingen court-book also has obvious gaps, and the Stuttgart collection of trial records is certainly highly incomplete. I hope that I have nevertheless managed to give readers a sense of the most important trends in the

---

[2] Criminal trials in Hall can be reconstructed only through an early 18th-century register of former sentences (the *Fraisch- and Malefizrepertorium*), some remaining trial records, council minutes, and chronicles.

prosecution of offences, which, however, as I point out in Chapters 4 and 5, were never uniform, and thus have to be interpreted carefully.[3]

[3] On the problems of quantitative methods see J. Innes and J. Styles, 'The Crime Wave: Recent Writing on Crime and Criminal Justice in Eighteenth-Century England', in A. Wilson (ed.), *Rethinking Social History: English Society 1570–1920 and its Interpretation* (Manchester, 1993).

BIBLIOGRAPHY

UNPRINTED SOURCES

Württembergisches Hauptstaatsarchiv Stuttgart

A 43 Urgichten
A 44 Urfehden
A 206 Oberrat Ältere Ämterakten
A 209 Oberrat Malefizakten
A 210 Amt Stuttgart
A 214 Oberrat Kommissionen
A 238a Ehegericht
A 309 Kriminalakten der Ämter
A 573 Stadt und Amt Wildberg
    Vogt- und Rüggerichtsbücher
    Peinliches Gerichtsbuch
    Rechtstagprotkolle

Schwäbisch Hall, Stadtarchiv

Bestand 2 Kirchenbücher
    Todtenbuch St. Michael
Bestand 4 Amtsbücher
    Urfehdbücher
    Ratsprotokollbücher
    Einungergerichtsbücher
Bestand 11 Kriminaluntersuchungen

Constance, Stadtarchiv

A Selecta
    Franz-Bickel-Chronik
B Städtische Kanzlei
    Ratsprotokollbücher
H Gerichtswesen
K Strafrechtspflege
L Rechnungs- und Steuerwesen
    Einnahmbücher

Memmingen, Stadtarchiv

A Reichsstadt
    Ratsprotokollbücher
A 44 Peinliche Gerichtsbücher

A 81–131 Kundschaften und Verhöre
A 265 Zuchtordnungen
D 169 Bettelordnungen

Ludwigsburg, Staatsarchiv

B 169, Bü. 119 I, II: Blut- oder Peinliches Urtelbuech Esslingen

Esslingen, Stadtarchiv

A II Reichsstadt
F. 68 Urfehden
F. 43b Gerichtsprotokolle
F. 43c Stadtammansprotokolle
F. 42 Beschreibung Diebsbande
Ratsprotokolle

Freiburg im Breisgau, Stadtarchiv

A 1 XI f Urfehden
B 5 III c 4 No. 7 Urgichtbuch
B 5 III c 8 Straf- und Frevelbücher

Tübingen, Universitätsarchiv

84/1–27 Strafrechtsgutachten der juristischen Fakultät

Besigheim, Stadtarchiv

01–10 Gerichtsbücher

Bad Mergentheim, Stadtarchiv

K III, No. 344, Handschriftliche Aufzeichnungen des Bürgermeisters
Gassenfaydt über Klagen und Strafen

Rottweil, Stadtarchiv

Lade III, Prothocollum aller Urgichten anno 1588
Lade IV, Prothocollum aller Urfehden anno 1588

Riedlingen, Stadtarchiv

Kopialbuch, Verzaichnus Aller Beschribner Vrgichten vnd Bekandtnusen,
der Malefizischen Personen, so alhie in Riedlingen, nach vnd nach ger-
ichtet, mit Ruoten aussgeschwungen, an Pranger gestelt, vnd der Statt
Zwing vnd Pänn verwisen worden.

PRINTED SOURCES

ADAM, A. E., *Württembergische Landtagsakten unter Herzog Friedrich I, 1599–1608*
(Stuttgart, 1911).
Adreßkalender für die Stadt Konstanz auf das Jahr 1852 (Constance, 1852).
BOSSERT, G. (ed.), *Quellen zur Geschichte der Wiedertäufer* (2 vols., Leipzig,
1930).

266 *Bibliography*

BRECHT, M. (ed.), *Johannes Brenz: Frühschriften*, vol. ii (Tübingen, 1974).

Die Chroniken der deutschen Städte vom 14. bis ins 16. Jahrhundert (36 vols., Leipzig, 1862–1931).

Die Wickiana: Johann Jakob Wicks Nachrichtensammlung aus dem 16. Jahrhundert. Texte und Bilder zu den Jahren 1560 bis 1571, ed. M. Senn (Zurich, 1975).

DIEHL, A. (ed.), *Dionysius Dreytweins Esslingische Chronik* (1548–1564) (Tübingen, 1901).

DÖPLER, J., *Theatrum poenarum . . . Oder Schau-platz derer Leibes- und Lebens-Strafen* (2 vols., Sondershausen, 1693).

FEGER, O. (ed.), *Die Statutensammlung des Stadtschreibers Jörg Vögeli* (Constance, 1951).

FISCHER, H., *Schwäbisches Wörterbuch* (5 vols., Tübingen, 1904–36).

GRIMM, J., *Deutsche Rechtsalterthümer* (2 vols., Leipzig, 1899).

GRIMMELSHAUSEN, J. v., *Lebensbeschreibungen der Ertzbetrügerin und Landstörtzerin Courasche*, ed. W. Bender (Tübingen, 1967).

—— *Mother Courage*, trans. W. Wallich (London, 1965).

HARMS, W. (ed.), *Deutsche illustrierte Flugblätter des 16. und 17. Jahrhunderts* (Tübingen, 1987).

LEIBNIZ, G. W., 'Ermahnung an die Teutsche, ihren Verstand und Sprache beβer zu üben, sammt beygefügten vorschlag einer Teutsch gesinnten Gesellschaft', in O. Klopp (ed.), *Die Werke von Leibniz. Erste Reihe: Historisch-politische und staatswissenschaftliche Schriften* (Hanover, 1872).

LIPSIUS, J., *Sixe Bookes of Politickes or Civil Doctrine*, trans. W. Iones (London, 1594, repr. Amsterdam, 1970).

MONTAIGNE, M. de, *The Complete Essays*, trans. M. A. Screech (Harmondsworth, 1991).

MÜLLER, G., and SEEBAβ, G., (eds.), *Andreas Osiander d. Ä., Schriften und Briefe 1535 bis 1538* (Gütersloh, 1985).

Neweröffnete Hebammen-Schul. Anfangs auf vieler Begehren In Druck gegeben, von Christoph Völtern, Hochfürstlich. Durchl. zu Württemberg Leibchirurgen (Stuttgart, 1687).

PALLAS, K. (ed.), *Die Registraturen der Kirchenvisitationen im ehemals sächsischen Kurkreise* (6 vols., Halle, 1906).

PETERS, J. (ed.), *Ein Söldnerleben im Dreißigjährigen Krieg: Eine Quelle zur Sozialgeschichte* (Berlin, 1993).

PUFENDORF, S., *On the Duty of Man and Citizen According to Natural Law*, ed. J. Tully, trans. M. Silverthorne (Cambridge, 1991).

RADBRUCH, G. (ed.), *Die Peinliche Gerichtsordnung Kaiser Karls V. von 1532 (Carolina)* (4th edn. Stuttgart, 1991).

REYSCHER, A. L., *Vollständige, historisch und kritisch bearbeitete Sammlung der württembergischen Gesetze* (19 vols., Stuttgart and Tübingen, 1828–51).

RODER, C. (ed.), *Heinrich Hugs Villinger Chronik von 1495 bis 1533* (Tübingen, 1883).

SCHUMM, K., and Schumm, M. (eds.), *Hohenlohische Dorfordnungen* (Stuttgart, 1985).

STENZEL, G. A. (ed.), *Samuel Benjamin Kloses Darstellung der inneren Verhältnisse der Stadt Breslau vom Jahre 1458 bis zum Jahr 1526* (Breslau, 1847).

WAGNER, T., *Siebenfältiger Ehehalten-Teuffel / Das ist, Ein ernsthaffter Sermon / von uberhandnemmender Boßheit der Ehehalten und Dienstbotten jetziger Zeit* (Esslingen, 1651).

WINTTERLIN, F. (ed.), *Württembergische ländliche Rechtsquellen* (6 vols., Stuttgart, 1910–55).

SELECTED SECONDARY WORKS

ABEGG, V., 'Beiträge zur Geschichte der Strafrechtspflege in Schlesien, insbesondere im fünfzehnten und sechzehnten Jahrhundert', *ZRG* 18 (1858), 447 ff.

ABRAMS, L., 'Concubinage, Cohabitation and the Law: Class and Gender Relations in Nineteenth-Century Germany', *Gender & History*, 5 (1993), 81–100.

AMUSSEN, S. D., *An Ordered Society: Gender and Class in Early Modern England* (Oxford, 1988).

ANGSTMANN, E., *Der Henker in der Volksmeinung: Seine Namen und sein Vorkommen in der mündlichen Volksüberlieferung* (Bonn, 1928).

ARON, J.-P., 'The Art of Using Leftovers: Paris, 1850–1900', in R. Forster and O. Ranum (eds.), *Food and Drink in History*, trans. E. Forster and P. M. Ranum (Baltimore, 1979).

BACHELARD, G., *The Poetics of Space: The Classic Look at How We Experience Intimate Places*, trans. M. Jolas (Boston, 1994).

BADER, K. S., *Die Zimmersche Chronik als Quelle der rechtlichen Volkskunde* (Freiburg im Breisgau, 1942).

BÀTORI, I., 'Frauen in Handel und Handwerk der Reichsstadt Nördlingen im 15. und 16. Jahrhundert', in U. Weckel and B. Vogel (eds.), *Frauen in der Ständegesellschaft: Leben und Arbeiten in der Stadt vom späten Mittelalter zur Neuzeit* (Hamburg, 1991).

BECK, R., 'Illegitimität und voreheliche Sexualität auf dem Land: Unterfinning, 1671–1770', in R. v. Dülmen (ed.), *Kultur der einfachen Leute: Bayerisches Volksleben vom 16. bis 19. Jahrhundert* (Frankfurt on Main, 1983).

—— *Naturale Ökonomie: Unterfinning. Bäuerliche Wirtschaft in einem oberbayerischen Dorf des frühen 18. Jahrhunderts* (Munich, 1986).

—— 'Frauen in Krise: Eheleben und Ehescheidung in der ländlichen Gesellschaft Bayerns während des Ancien Régime', in R. v. Dülmen (ed.), *Dynamik der Tradition* (Frankfurt on Main, 1992).

BECKER, P., *Leben und Lieben in einem kalten Land: Sexualität im Spannungsfeld von Ökonomie und Demographie. Das Beispiel St. Lambrecht* (Frankfurt on Main, 1990).

BEHRINGER, W., 'Erträge und Perspektiven der Hexenforschung', *HZ* 249 (1989), 619–40.

BEHRINGER, W., 'Mörder, Diebe, Ehebrecher: Verbrechen und Strafen in Kurbayern vom 16. bis 18. Jahrhundert', in R. v. Dülmen (ed.), *Verbrechen, Strafen und soziale Kontrolle* (Frankfurt on Main, 1990).

BENECKE, G., *Germany in the Thirty Years War* (London, 1978).

BISKOP, M., 'Die Einwohnerverzeichnisse der Stadt Mergentheim aus dem 16. Jahrhundert', *ZfWLG* 44 (1985), 143–63.

BLASIUS, D., *Kriminalität und Alltag: Zur Konfliktgeschichte des Alltagslebens im 19. Jahrhundert* (Göttingen, 1978).

BLAUERT, A., *Sackgreifer und Beutelschneider: Die Diebesbande der Alten Lisel, ihre Streifzüge um den Bodensee und ihr Prozeß 1732* (Constance, 1993).

—— 'Kriminaljustiz und Sittenreform als Krisenmanagement? Das Hochstift Speyer im 16. und 17. Jahrhundert', in id. and G. Schwerhoff (eds.), *Mit den Waffen der Justiz: Zur Kriminalitätsgeschichte des Spätmittelalters und der frühen Neuzeit* (Frankfurt on Main, 1993).

BLICKLE, P., 'Wem gehört der Wald? Konflikte zwischen Bauern und Obrigkeiten um Nutzungs- und Eigentumsansprüche', *ZfWLG* 45 (1986), 167–78.

BODE, H., 'Die Kindstötung und ihre Bestrafung im Nürnberg des Mittelalters', *Archiv für Strafrecht und Strafprozess*, 61 (1914), 430–81.

BONNEKAMP, C. G., *Die Zimmersche Chronik als Quelle des Strafrechts, der Strafgerichtsbarkeit und des Strafverfahrens in Schwaben am Ausgang des Mittelalters* (Bonn, 1940).

BRACKETT, J. K., *Criminal Justice and Crime in Late Renaissance Florence, 1537–1609* (Cambridge, 1992).

BRADY, T. A., Jr. et al. (eds.), *Handbook of European History, 1400–1600: Late Middle Ages, Renaissance and Reformation* (2 vols., Leiden, 1994–5).

BRÄUER, H., *Gesellen im sächsischen Zunfthandwerk des 15. und 16. Jahrhunderts* (Weimar, 1989).

BRECHT, M., *Kirchenordnung und Kirchenzucht in Württemberg vom 16. bis zum 18. Jahrhundert* (Stuttgart, 1967).

BREIT, S., *'Leichtfertigkeit' und ländliche Gesellschaft: Voreheliche Sexualität in der frühen Neuzeit* (Munich, 1991).

BRIGGS, R., *Witches and Neighbours: The Social and Cultural Context of European Witchcraft* (London, 1996).

BRONFEN, E., *Over her Dead Body: Death, Femininity and the Aesthetic* (Manchester, 1992).

BRUNDAGE, J. A., *Law, Sex, and Christian Society in Medieval Europe* (Chicago, 1987).

BULL, K.-O., 'Wirtschafts- und Sozialgeschichte der württembergischen Amtsstadt Vaihingen an der Enz bis zum Dreissigjährigen Krieg', *ZfWLG* 38 (1980), 97–140.

BULST, N., 'Kleidung als sozialer Konfliktstoff: Probleme kleidergesetzlicher Normierungen im sozialen Gefüge', *Saeculum*, 44 (1993), 32–46.

BURCKHARDT, M., Dobras, W., and ZIMMERMANN, W., *Konstanz in der frühen Neuzeit* (Constance, 1991).

BURGHARTZ, S., 'Disziplinierung oder Konfliktregelung? Zur Funktion städtischer Gerichte im Spätmittelalter: Das Zürcher Ratsgericht', *ZHF* 16 (1989), 385–406.

—— *Leib, Ehre und Gut: Delinquenz in Zürich am Ende des 14. Jahrhunderts* (Zurich, 1990).

—— 'Kein Ort für Frauen? Städtische Gerichte im Spätmittelalter', in B. Lundt (ed.), *Auf der Suche nach der Frau im Mittelalter: Fragen, Quellen, Antworten* (Munich, 1991).

—— 'Jungfräulichkeit oder Reinheit? Zur Änderung von Argumentationsmustern vor dem Basler Ehegericht im 16. und 17. Jahrhundert', in R. v. Dülmen (ed.), *Dynamik der Tradition* (Frankfurt on Main, 1992).

—— 'Geschlecht—Körper—Ehre: Überlegungen zur weiblichen Ehre in der frühen Neuzeit am Beispiel der Basler Ehegerichtsprotokolle', in K. Schreiner and G. Schwerhoff (eds.), *Verletzte Elire: Ehrkonflikte in Gesellschaften des Mittelalters und der frühen Neuzeit* (Cologne, 1995).

BURKE, P., *The Historical Anthropology of Early Modern Italy* (Cambridge, 1987).

CADDEN, J., *Meanings of Sex Difference in the Middle Ages: Medicine, Science and Culture* (Cambridge, 1993).

CAMPORESI, P., *Juice of Life: The Symbolic and Magic Significance of Blood*, trans. R. R. Barr (New York, 1995).

CASTAN, N., 'The Arbitration of Disputes under the Ancien Régime', in J. Bossy (ed.), *Disputes and Settlements: Law and Human Relations in the West* (Cambridge, 1983).

CATTELONA, G., 'Control and Collaboration: The Role of Women in Regulating Female Sexual Behaviour in Early Modern Marseille', *French Historical Studies*, 18 (1993), 13–35.

CAVALLO, S., and CERRUTI, S., 'Female Honour and the Social Control of Reproduction in Piedmont between 1600 and 1800', in E. Muir and G. Ruggiero (eds.), *Sex and Gender in Historical Perspective* (Baltimore, 1990).

CHAYTOR, M., 'Husband(ry): Narratives of Rape in the Seventeenth Century', *Gender & History*, 7 (1995), 378–407.

CLANCHY, M., 'Law and Love in the Middle Ages', in J. Bossy (ed.), *Disputes and Settlements: Law and Human Relationships in the West* (Cambridge, 1983).

COBB, R., *A Sense of Place* (London, 1975).

COHEN, T. V., and COHEN, E. S., *Words and Deeds in Renaissance Rome: Trials before the Papal Magistrates* (Toronto, 1993).

COLLINSON, P., *The Birthpangs of Protestant England: Religious and Cultural Change in the Sixteenth and Seventeenth Centuries* (London, 1988).

CRESSY, D., 'De la fiction dans les archives? ou le monstre de 1569', *Annales ESC* 48 (1993), 1309–29.

DANKER, U., *Räuberbanden im Alten Reich um 1700: Ein Beitrag zur Geschichte von Herrschaft und Kriminalität in der frühen Neuzeit* (2 vols., Frankfurt on Main, 1988).

DAVIDSON, N., 'Theology, Nature and the Law: Sexual Sin and Sexual Crime in Italy from the Fourteenth to the Seventeenth Century', in T. Dean and K. J. P. Lowe (eds.), *Crime, Society and the Law in Renaissance Italy* (Cambridge, 1994).

DAVIS, N. Z., *Society and Culture in Early Modern France* (Stanford, Calif., 1975).

—— 'Women in the Crafts in Sixteenth-Century Lyon', *Feminist Studies*, 8 (1982), 47–80.

—— *Fiction in the Archives: Pardon Tales and their Tellers in Sixteenth-Century France* (Princeton, 1988).

—— *Women on the Margins: Three Seventeenth-Century Lives* (Cambridge, Mass., 1995).

DAVIS, R. C., *The War of the Fists: Popular Culture and Public Violence in Late Renaissance Venice* (New York, 1994).

DECKER-HAUFF, H.-M., 'Die Entstehung der altwürttembergischen Ehrbarkeit, 1250–1534', (D.Phil. thesis, Vienna, 1946).

DEKKER, R. M., and POL, C. v. d., *The Tradition of Female Transvestism in Early Modern Europe* (Basingstoke, 1989).

DEUTSCH, A. (ed.), *Richter, Henker, Folterknechte: Strafjustiz im alten Hall* (Schwäbisch Hall, 1993).

DINGES, M., *Stadtarmut in Bordeaux, 1525–1675: Alltag, Politik, Mentalitäten* (Bonn, 1988).

—— '"Weiblichkeit" in "Männlichkeitsritualen"? Zu weiblichen Taktiken im Ehrhandel im Paris des 18. Jahrhunderts', *Francia*, 18 (1991), 71–98.

DOBRAS, W., *Ratsregiment, Sittenpolizei und Kirchenzucht in der Reichsstadt Konstanz 1531–1548: Ein Beitrag zur Geschichte der oberdeutsch-schweizerischen Reformation* (Gütersloh, 1993).

DÖHRING, E., *Geschichte der deutschen Rechtspflege seit 1500* (Berlin, 1953).

DOLAN, F. E., *Dangerous Familiars: Representations of Domestic Crime in England 1550–1700* (Ithaca, NY, 1994).

duBOIS, P., *Torture and Truth* (London, 1991).

DUDEN, B., *Geschichte unter der Haut: Ein Eisenacher Arzt und seiner Patientinnen um 1730* (Stuttgart, 1987); trans. as *The Woman beneath the Skin: A Doctor's Patients in Eighteenth-Century Germany*, trans. T. Dunlap (Cambridge, Mass., 1991).

—— 'Die "Geheimnisse der Schwangeren" und das Öffentlichkeitsinteresse der Medizin: Zur sozialen Bedeutung der Kindsregung', in K. Hausen and H. Wunder (eds.), *Frauengeschichte/Geschlechtergeschichte* (Frankfurt on Main, 1992).

DÜLMEN, R. v., *Theatre of Horror: Crime and Punishment in Early Modern Germany*, trans. E. Neu (Cambridge, 1990).

—— *Frauen vor Gericht: Kindsmord in der frühen Neuzeit* (Frankfurt on Main, 1991).

DÜNNINGER, J., 'Rügegerichte eines unterfränkischen Dorfes im 19. Jahrhundert', in P. Assion (ed.), *Ländliche Kulturformen im deutschen Südwesten: Festschrift für Heiner Heimberger* (Stuttgart, 1971).

Bibliography

Dürr, R., 'Ursula Gräfin: Der Lebensweg einer Haller Magd und ledigen Mutter im 17. Jahrhundert', *Württembergisch Franken*, 76 (1992), 169–76.

—— *Mägde in der Stadt: Das Beispiel Schwäbisch Hall in der frühen Neuzeit* (Frankfurt on Main, 1995).

Eckardt, H. W., *Herrschaftliche Jagd, bäuerliche Not und bürgerliche Kritik: Zur Geschichte der fürstlichen und adeligen Jagdprivilegien vornehmlich im süddeutschen Raum* (Stuttgart, 1958).

Egmond, F., *Underworlds: Organized Crime in the Netherlands, 1650–1800* (Oxford, 1993).

Eibach, J., 'Kriminalitätsgeschichte zwischen Sozialgeschichte und historischer Kulturforschung', *HZ* 263 (1996), 681–715.

Eirich, R., *Memmingens Wirtschaft und Patriziat von 1347 bis 1557: Eine wirtschafts- und sozialgeschichtliche Untersuchung über das Memminger Patriziat während der Zunftverfassung* (Ottobeuren, 1971).

Erbe, G., 'Das Ehescheidungsrecht im Herzogtum Württemberg seit der Reformation', *ZfWLG* 14 (1955), 95–144.

Evans, R. J., *Rituals of Retribution: Capital Punishment in Germany 1600–1987* (Oxford, 1996).

Farge, A., and Foucault, M., *Le Désordre des familles: Lettres de cachet des archives de la Bastille* (Paris, 1982).

Farr, J. R., 'The Pure and Disciplined Body: Hierarchy, Morality, and Symbolism in France during the Catholic Reformation', *JIH* 21 (1991), 391–414.

—— *Authority and Sexuality in Early Modern Burgundy (1550–1730)* (New York, 1995).

Felber, A., *Unzucht und Kindsmord in der Rechtsprechung der freien Reichsstadt Nördlingen vom 15. bis 18. Jahrhundert* (Bonn, 1961).

Feucht, D., *Grube und Pfahl: Ein Beitrag zu deutschen Hinrichtungsbräuchen* (Tübingen, 1967).

Fischer, T., *Städtische Armut und Armenfürsorge im 15. und 16. Jahrhundert: Sozialgeschichtliche Untersuchungen am Beispiel der Städte Basel, Freiburg im Breisgau und Straburg* (Göttingen, 1979).

Fischer-Homberger, E., *Medizin vor Gericht: Zur Sozialgeschichte der Gerichtsmedizin* (Darmstadt, 1988).

Fletcher, A., *Gender, Sex and Subordination in England 1500–1800* (New Haven, 1995).

Foucault, M., *Discipline and Punish: The Birth of the Prison*, trans. A. Sheridan (London, 1977).

—— (ed.), *I, Pierre Rivière, Having Slaughtered my Mother, my Sister and my Brother . . .: A Case of Parricide in the Nineteenth Century*, trans. A. Sheridan (Harmondsworth, 1978).

Frank, M., *Dörfliche Gesellschaft und Kriminalität: Das Fallbeispiel Lippe (1650–1800)* (Paderborn, 1995).

Freud, S., *Totem und Tabu: Einige Übereinstimmungen im Seelenleben der Wilden und der Neurotiker* (Frankfurt on Main, 1991).

FREVERT, U., *'Mann und Weib, und Weib und Mann'*: *Geschlechter-Differenzen in der Moderne* (Munich, 1995).

FRIEβ, P., *Die Außenpolitik der Reichsstadt Memmingen in der Reformationszeit 1517–1555* (Memmingen, 1993).

—— 'Die Steuerbücher der Reichsstadt Memmingen von 1450 und 1451', *Memminger Geschichtsblätter* (1989/90), 268 ff.

FRÖHLICH, K., *Mittelalterliche Bauwerke als Rechtsdenkmäler* (Tübingen, 1939).

—— *Alte Dorfplätze und andere Stätten mittelalterlicher Rechtspflege im niederdeutschen Recht* (Giessen, 1946).

FULBROOK, M., *Piety and Politics: Religion and the Rise of Absolutism in England, Württemberg and Prussia* (Cambridge, 1983).

GARRIOCH, D., *Neighbourhood and Community in Paris, 1740–1790* (Cambridge, 1986).

GATRELL, V. A. C., 'Crime, Authority and the Policeman State', in F. M. L. Thompson (ed.), *The Cambridge Social History of Britain, 1750–1950*, vol. iii (Cambridge, 1991).

—— *The Hanging Tree: Execution and the English People 1770–1868* (Oxford, 1994).

GAUVARD, C., *'De grâce especiale': crime, état et société en France à la fin du Moyen Âge* (2 vols., Paris, 1991).

GEREMEK, B., *The Margins of Society in Late Medieval Paris* (Cambridge, 1987).

GESTRICH, A., *Traditionelle Jugendkultur und Industrialisierung: Sozialgeschichte der Jugend in einer ländlichen Arbeitergemeinde Württembergs, 1800–1920* (Göttingen, 1986).

GIERL, I., *Bauernleben und Bauernwallfahrt in Altbayern: Eine kulturkundliche Studie auf Grund der Tuntenhausener Mirakelbücher* (Munich, 1960).

GILMORE, D. D., *Manhood in the Making: Cultural Concepts of Masculinity* (New Haven, 1990).

GINZBURG, G., *The Cheese and the Worms: The Cosmos of a Sixteenth-Century Miller*, trans. J. and A. Tedeschi (Harmondsworth, 1992).

—— *Il guidice e lo storico: Considerazioni in margine al processo Sofri* (Turin, 1991).

GLEIXNER, U., *'Das Mensch' und 'der Kerl': Die Konstruktion von Geschlecht in Unzuchtsverfahren der frühen Neuzeit (1700–1760)* (Frankfurt on Main, 1994).

—— 'Das Gesamtgericht der Herrschaft Schulenburg im 18. Jahrhundert: Funktionsweise und Zugang von Frauen und Männern', in J. Peters (ed.), *Gutsherrschaft als soziales Modell: Vergleichende Betrachtungen zur Funktionsweise frühneuzeitlicher Agrargesellschaften* (Munich, 1995).

—— 'Die 'Gute' und die 'Böse': Hebammen als Amtsfrauen auf dem Land (Altmark/Brandenburg, 18. Jahrhundert)', in C. Vanja and H. Wunder (eds.), *Weiber, Menscher, Frauenzimmer: Frauen in der ländlichen Gesellschaft, 1500–1800* (Göttingen, 1996).

GLUCKMAN, M., 'Gossip and Scandal', *Current Anthropology*, 4 (1963), 307–15.

GOTTLIEB, B., *The Family in the Western World: From the Black Death to the Industrial Age* (New York, 1993).

GÖTTSCH, S., '"Vielmahls aber hätte sie gewünscht, einen anderen Mann zu haben": Gattenmord im 18. Jahrhundert', in O. Ulbricht (ed.), *Von Huren und Rabenmüttern: Weibliche Kriminalität in der frühen Neuzeit* (Cologne, 1995).

GOWING, L., *Domestic Dangers: Women, Words, and Sex in Early Modern London* (Oxford, 1996).

—— 'Secret Births and Infanticide in Seventeenth-Century England,' *Past and Present*, 156 (1997), 87–115.

GREMBOWIETZ, H. J., *Das Bauerngericht der freien Reichsstadt Rothenburg ob der Tauber vom späten Mittelalter bis zu seinem Niedergang (1403–1678): Eine rechtshistorische Untersuchung an Hand der Gerichtsbücher und anderer Quellen* (Würzburg, 1974).

GRIFFITHS, P., *Youth and Authority: Formative Experiences in England, 1560–1640* (Oxford, 1996).

GROEBNER, V., *Ökonomie ohne Haus: Zum Wirtschaften armer Leute in Nürnberg am Ende des 15. Jahrhunderts* (Göttingen, 1993).

GRUBE, W., *Der Stuttgarter Landtag, 1457–1957: Von den Landständen zum demokratischen Parlament* (Stuttgart, 1957).

GÜTTNER, M., 'Unterklassenkriminalität in Hamburg: Güterberaubung im Hamburger Hafen, 1888–1923', in H. Reif (ed.), *Räuber, Volk und Obrigkeit: Studien zur Geschichte der Kriminalität in Deutschland seit dem 18. Jahrhundert* (Frankfurt on Main, 1984).

HANLEY, S., 'Engendering the State: Family Formation and State Building in Early Modern France', *French Historical Studies*, 16 (1989), 4–27.

HARRINGTON, J. F., *Reordering Marriage and Society in Reformation Germany* (Cambridge, 1995).

—— 'Singing for his Supper': The Reinvention of Juvenile Streetsinging in Early Modern Nuremberg, *Social History*, 22 (1997), 27–45.

HARRIS, R., *Murders and Madness: Medicine, Law, and Society in the Fin de Siècle* (Oxford, 1989).

HAVILAND, J. B., *Gossip, Reputation and Knowledge in Zinacantan* (Chicago, 1977).

HAY, D., et al. (eds.), *Albion's Fatal Tree: Crime and Society in Eighteenth-Century England* (London, 1975).

HELMHOLTZ, R. H., 'Infanticide in the Province of Canterbury during the Fifteenth Century', *History of Childhood Quarterly*, 2 (1973), 379–90.

HERRUP, C. B., *The Common Peace: Participation and the Criminal Law in Seventeenth-Century England* (Cambridge, 1987).

HINDLE, S., 'The Shaming of Margaret Knowsley: Gossip, Gender and the Experience of Authority in Early Modern England', *Continuity and Change*, 9 (1994), 391–419.

HIS, R., *Das Strafrecht des deutschen Mittelalters in 2 Teilen* (Weimar, 1935).

274 *Bibliography*

HOBSBAWM, E. J., and RUDÉ, G., *Captain Swing* (London, 1969).

HOFFMANN, T., 'Zaubersprüche aus dem 17. Jahrhundert', *Volkskunde = Blätter aus Württemberg und Hohenzollern*, 1 (1911), 6ff.

HOHKAMP, H., 'Häusliche Gewalt: Beispiele aus einer ländlichen Region des mittleren Schwarzwaldes im 18. Jahrhundert', in T. Lindenberger and A. Lüdtke (eds.), *Physische Gewalt: Studien zur Geschichte der Neuzeit* (Frankfurt on Main, 1995).

—— 'Macht, Herrschaft und Geschlecht: Ein Plädoyer zur Erforschung von Gewaltverhältnissen in der frühen Neuzeit', *L'Homme*, 7 (1996), 8–17.

HOLTZ, H., 'Der Fürst dieser Welt: Die Bedrohung der Lebenswelt aus lutherisch-orthodoxer Perspektive', *Zeitschrift für Kirchengeschichte*, 107 (1996), 29–49.

HUFTON, O. H., *The Poor of Eighteenth Century France, 1750–1789* (Oxford, 1974).

—— 'Attitudes towards Authority in Eighteenth-Century Languedoc', *JSH* 3 (1978), 281–302.

—— *The Prospect before Her: A History of Women in Western Europe*, i: 1500–1800 (London, 1995).

HUGGLE, U., *Johann Simler: Kupferschmid und Rat zu Freiburg im 17. Jahrhundert* (Freiburg im Breisgau, 1989).

HUGHES, D. O., 'Sumptuary Law and Social Relations in Renaissance Italy', in J. Bossy (ed.), *Disputes and Settlements: Law and Human Relations in the West* (Cambridge, 1983).

HULL, I., *Sex, State, and Civil Society in Germany, 1700–1815* (Ithaca, NY, 1996).

HUNT, L., 'The Many Bodies of Marie Antoinette: Political Pornography and the Problem of the Feminine in the French Revolution', in ead. (ed.), *Eroticism and the Body Politic* (Baltimore, 1991).

INGRAM, M., *Church Courts, Sex and Marriage in England, 1570–1640* (Cambridge, 1987).

INNES, J., and STYLES, J., 'The Crime Wave: Recent Writing on Crime and Criminal Justice in Eighteenth-Century England', in A. Wilson (ed.), *Rethinking Social History: English Society 1570–1920 and its Interpretation* (Manchester, 1993).

JÄNICHEN, H., 'Schwäbische Totschlagssühnen im 15. und 16. Jahrhundert', *ZfWLG* 19 (1960), 128–40.

JEROUSCHEK, G., '"Diabolus habitat in eis". Wo der Teufel zu Hause ist: Geschlechtlichkeit im rechtstheologischen Diskurs des ausgehenden Mittelalters und der frühen Neuzeit', in H.-J. Bachorski (ed.), *Ordnung und Lust: Bilder von Liebe, Ehe und Sexualität in Spätmittelalter und Früher Neuzeit* (Trier, 1989).

—— *Die Hexen und ihr Prozeß: Die Hexenverfolgung in der Reichsstadt Esslingen* (Esslingen, 1992).

JÓNSON, M., 'Incest and the Word of God: Early Sixteenth Century Protestant Disputes', *ARG* 85 (1994), 96–118.

JÜTTE, R., *Obrigkeitliche Armenfürsorge in Deutschen Reichsstädten der frühen*

Neuzeit: Städtisches Armenwesen in Frankfurt am Main und Köln (Cologne, 1984).

JÜTTE, R., 'Geschlechtsspezifische Kriminalität im Späten Mittelalter und in der frühen Neuzeit', *ZRG Germ. Abt.* 108 (1991), 86–116.

—— (ed.), *Geschichte der Abtreibung: Von der Antike bis zur Gegenwart* (Munich, 1993).

—— *Poverty and Deviance in Early Modern Europe* (Cambridge, 1994).

KAMEN, R. L., *Lucrecia's Dreams: Politics and Prophecy in Sixteenth-Century Spain* (Berkeley, 1990).

KAPPL, C., *Die Not der kleinen Leute: Der Alltag der Armen im 18. Jahrhundert im Spiegel der Bamberger Malefizakten* (Bamberg, 1984).

KELLER, A., *Der Scharfrichter in der deutschen Kulturgeschichte* (2nd edn. Hildesheim, 1968).

KERMODE, J., and WALKER, G. (eds.), *Women, Crime and the Courts in Early Modern England* (London, 1994).

KIENITZ, S., *Unterwegs—Frauen zwischen Not und Normen: Lebensweise und Mentalität vagierender Frauen um 1800 in Württemberg* (Tübingen, 1989).

KIEßLING, R., *Die Stadt und ihr Land: Umlandpolitik, Bürgerbesitz und Wirtschaftsgefüge in Oberschwaben vom 14. bis ins 16. Jahrhundert* (Cologne, 1989).

KING, P. J. R., 'Crime, Law and Society in Essex, 1740–1820', (Ph.D. thesis, Cambridge, 1984).

—— 'Gleaners and Farmers and the Failure of Legal Sanctions in England, 1750–1850', *P&P* 125 (1989), 116–50.

KINGDON, R. M., *Adultery and Divorce in Calvin's Geneva* (Cambridge, Mass., 1995).

KINTNER, P. L., 'Die Teuerungen von 1570/2 in Memmingen', *Memminger Geschichtsblätter* (1987/8), 27–76.

KLAPISCH-ZUBER, C., *Women, Family, and Ritual in Renaissance Italy*, trans. G. Cochrane (Chicago, 1985).

KOPF, R., 'Mitteilungen über volkstümliche Überlieferungen in Württemberg: Festbräuche', *Württembergisches Jahrbuch*, 2 (1906), 45–65.

KRAMER, K.-S., *Bauern und Bürger im nachmittelalterlichen Unterfranken: Eine Volkskunde auf Grund archivalischer Quellen* (Würzburg, 1951).

—— 'Problematik der rechtlichen Volkskunde', *Bayerisches Jahrbuch für Volkskunde* (1962), 50–66.

—— *Volksleben im Hochstift Bamberg und in Fürstenberg Coburg (1500–1800): Eine Volkskunde auf Grund archivalischer Quellen* (Würzburg, 1967).

—— *Grundriß einer rechtlichen Volkskunde* (Göttingen, 1974).

KROEMER, B., 'Die Einführung der Reformation in Memmingen: Die Bedeutung ihrer sozialen, wirtschaftlichen und politischen Faktoren', *Memminger Geschichtsblätter*, (1980).

KÜNßBERG, E., *Zur Strafe des Steintragens* (Berlin, 1926).

KÜTHER, C., 'Räuber, Volk und Obrigkeit. Zur Wirkungsweise staatlicher Strafverfolgung im 18. Jahrhundert', in H. Reif (ed.), *Räuber, Volk und*

Obrigkeit: Studien zur Geschichte der Kriminalität in Deutschland seit dem 18. Jahrhundert (Frankfurt on Main, 1984).

LABOUVIE, E., *Zauberei und Hexenwerk: Ländlicher Hexenglaube in der frühen Neuzeit* (Frankfurt on Main, 1991).

LAQUEUR, T., *Making Sex: Body and Gender from the Greeks to Freud* (Cambridge, Mass., 1990).

LAHNE, W., *Magdeburgs Zerstörung in der zeitgenössischen Publizistik* (Magdeburg, 1931).

LANGBEIN, J. H., *Prosecuting Crime in the Renaissance: England, Germany, France* (Cambridge, Mass., 1974).

—— *Torture and the Law of Proof: Europe and England in the Ancien Régime* (Chicago, 1972).

LEBOUTTE, R., 'Offence against Family Order: Infanticide in Belgium from the Fifteenth to the Early Twentieth Centuries', in J. C. Fout (ed.), *Forbidden History: The State, Society and the Regulation of Sexuality in Modern Europe* (Chicago, 1992).

LEE, W. R., 'Bastardy and the Socioeconomic Structure of South Germany', *JIH* 7 (1977), 403–25.

—— 'Bastardy in South Germany: A Reply', *JIH* 8 (1978), 471–6.

—— 'Women's Work and the Family: Some Demographic Implications of Gender-Specific Rural Work Patterns in Nineteenth-Century Germany', in id. and P. Hudson (eds.), *Women's Work and the Family Economy in Historical Perspective* (Manchester, 1990).

LINK, C., *Herrschaftsordnung und bürgerliche Freiheit: Grenzen der Staatsgewalt in der älteren deutschen Staatslehre* (Vienna, 1979).

LIPP, C., 'Die Innenseite der Arbeiterkultur: Sexualität im Arbeitermilieu des 19. und frühen 20. Jahrhunderts', in R. v. Dülmen (ed.), *Arbeit, Frömmigkeit und Eigensinn* (Frankfurt on Main, 1990).

—— 'Ledige Mutter, "Hüren" und "Lumpenhunde": Sexualmoral und Ehrenhändel im Arbeitermilieu des 19. Jahrhunderts', in U. Jeggle et al. (eds.), *Tübinger Beiträge zur Volkskunde* (Tübingen, 1986).

LIPPERT, E., *Glockenläuten als Rechtsbrauch* (Freiburg im Breisgau, 1939).

LORENZ, M., 'Da der anfängliche Schmerz in Liebeshitze übergehen kann: Das Delikt der "Nothzucht" im gerichtsmedizinischen Diskurs des 18. Jahrhunderts', *ÖZG* 3 (1994), 328–57.

—— '" . . . als ob ihr ein Stein aus dem Leibe kollerte . . . ": Schwangerschaftswahrnehmungen und Geburtserfahrungen von Frauen im 18. Jahrhundert', in R. v. Dülmen (ed.), *Körper-Geschichten* (Frankfurt on Main, 1996).

LOSCH, B., *Sühne und Gedenken in Baden-Württemberg: Ein Inventar* (Stuttgart, 1981).

LÜDTKE, A., *Police and State in Prussia, 1815–1850*, trans. P. Burgess (Cambridge, 1989).

MacCORMACK, C. P., 'Nature, Culture and Gender: A Critique', in ead. and M. Strathern (eds.), *Nature, Culture and Gender* (Cambridge, 1980).

McINTOSH, T., *Urban Decline in Early Modern Germany: Schwäbisch Hall and its Region, 1650–1750* (Chapel Hill, NC, 1997).

MAIER, K., *Das Strafrecht der Reichsstadt Esslingen im Spätmittelalter und zu Beginn der Neuzeit* (Tübingen, 1960).

MAISCH, A., *Notdürftiger Unterhalt und gehörige Schranken: Lebensbedingungen und Lebensstile in württembergischen Dörfern der frühen Neuzeit* (Stuttgart, 1992).

—— '"Wider die natürliche Pflicht und eingepflanzte Liebe": Illegitimität und Kindsmord in Württenberg im 17. und 18. Jahrhundert', *ZfWLG* 56 (1997), 65–104.

MARCUS, K., 'A Question of Corruption: The Case of Martin Nuttel, 1543–44', *German History*, 11 (1992), 127–40.

MAURER, H., *Geschichte der Stadt Konstanz im Mittelalter* (2 vols., Constance, 1989).

MEDICK, H., 'Village Spinning Bees: Sexual Culture and Free Time among Rural Youths in Early Modern Germany', in id. and D. W. Sabean (eds.), *Interest and Emotion: Essays on the Study of Family and Kinship* (Cambridge, 1984).

—— *Weben und Überleben in Laichingen 1650–1900: Lokalgeschichte als allgemeine Geschichte* (Göttingen, 1996).

MEIER, T., *Handwerk, Hauswerk, Heimarbeit: Nicht-agrarische Tätigkeiten und Erwerbsformen in einem traditionellen Ackerbaugebiet des 18. Jahrhunderts (Züricher Unterland)* (Zurich, 1986).

MEINERS, M., 'Wohnkultur in süddeutschen Kleinstädten vom 17. Jahrhundert bis zum 19. Jahrhundert: Soziale Unterschiede und Wertestrukturen', in G. Wiegelmann (ed.), *Nord-Südunterschiede in der städtischen und ländlichen Kultur Mitteleuropas* (Munich, 1985).

MIDELFORT, H. C. E., *Witch-Hunting in Southwestern Germany, 1562–1684: The Social and Intellectual Foundations* (Stanford, Calif., 1972).

MIGAT, P., *Die Polygamiefrage in der frühen Neuzeit* (Opladen, 1988).

MOMMERTZ, M., '"Hat ermeldetes Waib mich angefallen"—Gerichtsherrschaft und dörfliche Sozialkontrolle in Rechtshilfeanfragen an den Brandenburger Schöppenstuhl um 1600: Ein Werstattbericht', in J. Peters (ed.), *Gutsherrschaft als soziales Modell: Vergleichende Betrachtungen zur Funktionsweise frühneuzeitlicher Agrargesellschaften* (Munich, 1995).

—— '"Ich, Lisa Thielen": Text als Handlung und sprachliche Struktur—ein methodischer Vorschlag', *HA* 3 (1996), 303–29.

MOOSER, J., '"Furcht bewahrt das Holz": Holzdiebstahl und sozialer Konflikt in der ländlichen Gesellschaft 1800–1850 an westfälischen Beispielen', in H. Reif (ed.), *Räuber, Volk und Obrigkeit: Studien zur Geschichte der Kriminalität in Deutschland seit dem 18. Jahrhundert* (Frankfurt on Main, 1984).

MUIR, E., and Ruggiero, G. (eds.), *History from Crime*, trans. C. B. Curry et al. (Baltimore, 1994).

MÜLLER, J., *Schwert und Scheide: Der sexuelle und skatologische Wortschatz im Nürnberger Fastnachtsspiel des 15. Jahrhunderts* (Frankfurt on Main, 1988).

MÜNCH, P., 'The Growth of the Modern State', in B. Scribner (ed.), *Germany: A New Social and Economic History* (London, 1996).

NAUJOCKS, E., *Obrigkeitsgedanke, Zunftverfassung und Reformation: Studien zur Verfassungsgeschichte von Ulm, Esslingen und Schwäbisch Gmünd* (Stuttgart, 1958).

NOAK, F., 'Die französische Einwanderung in Freiburg im Breisgau 1677–1698', *VSWG* 23 (1930), 324–41.

NORDHOFF-BEHNE, H., *Gerichtsbarkeit und Strafrechtspflege in der Reichsstadt Schwäbisch-Hall seit dem 15. Jahrhundert* (Sigmaringen, 1971).

NOWOSADTKO, J., *Scharfrichter und Abdecker: Der Alltag zweier 'unehrlicher Berufe' in der frühen Neuzeit* (Paderborn, 1994).

OBERMAIER, A., 'Findel- und Waisenkinder: Zur Geschichte der Sozialfürsorge in der Reichsstadt Augsburg', *Zeitschrift des historischen Vereins für Schwaben*, 83 (1990), 113–28.

OESTREICH, G., *Neostoicism and the Early Modern State*, trans. D. McLintock (Cambridge, 1982).

—— and OESTREICH, B. (ed.), *Strukturprobleme der frühen Neuzeit: Ausgewählte Aufsätze* (Berlin, 1980).

OGILVIE, S. C., 'Coming of Age in a Corporate Society: Capitalism, Pietism and Family Authority in Rural Württemberg, 1590–1740', *Continuity and Change*, 1 (1986), 279–332.

—— 'Women and Proto-industrialisation in a Corporate Society: Württemberg Woollen Weaving, 1590–1760', in W. R. Lee and P. Hudson (eds.), *Women's Work and the Family Economy in Historical Perspective* (Manchester, 1990).

—— *State Corporatism and Proto-industry: The Württemberg Black Forest 1586–1797* (Cambridge, 1997).

O'NEIL, M., 'Magical Healing, Love Magic and the Inquisition in Late Sixteenth-Century Modena', in S. Haliczer (ed.), *Inquisition and Society in Early Modern Europe* (London, 1987).

ORTNER, S. B., 'Is Female to Male as Nature is to Culture?', in M. Z. Rosaldo and L. Lamphere (eds.), *Woman, Culture, and Society* (Stanford, Calif., 1974).

OSENBRÜGGEN, E., *Das alemannische Strafrecht im deutschen Mittelalter* (Schaffhausen, 1860).

OZMENT, S., *When Fathers Ruled: Family Life in Reformation Europe* (Cambridge, Mass., 1983).

PERRY, M. E., *Gender and Disorder in Early Modern Seville* (Princeton, 1990).

PFAFF, K., *Geschichte der Stadt Stuttgart nach Archival-Urkunden und anderen bewährten Quellen* (Stuttgart, 1846; repr. Frankfurt on Main, 1981).

PHILLIPS, R., *Putting Asunder: A History of Divorce in Western Society* (Cambridge, 1988).

PO-CHIA HSIA, R., *Social Discipline in the Reformation: Central Europe 1550–1750* (London, 1989).

PURKISS, D., *The Witch in History: Early Modern and Twentieth-Century Representations* (London, 1996).

REBEL, H., *Peasant Classes: The Bureaucratization of Property and Family Relations under Early Habsburg Absolutism, 1511–1636* (Princeton, 1983).

REILING, M., *Bevölkerung und Sozialtopographie Freiburgs im Breisgau im 17. und 18. Jahrhundert: Familien, Gewerbe und sozialer Status* (Freiburg im Breisgau, 1989).

RICHTER, G., *Das anatomische Theater* (Berlin, 1936).

ROBISHEAUX, T., *Rural Society and the Search for Order in Early Modern Germany* (Cambridge, 1989).

ROECK, B., *Eine Stadt in Krieg und Frieden: Studien zur Geschichte der Reichsstadt Augsburg zwischen Kalenderstreit und Parität* (2 vols., Göttingen, 1989).

ROPER, L., '"The Common Man", "the Common Good", "Common Women": Gender and Meaning in the German Reformation Commune', *Social History*, 12 (1987), 1–22.

—— *The Holy Household: Women and Morals in Reformation Augsburg* (Oxford, 1989).

—— *Oedipus and the Devil: Witchcraft, Sexuality and Religion in Early Modern Europe* (London, 1994).

ROWLANDS, A., 'To Wear a Virgin's Wreath: Gender and Problems of Conformity in Early Modern Germany', *European Review of History—Revue européenne d'histoire*, 1 (1994), 227–32.

—— 'Women, Gender and Power in Rothenburg ob der Tauber and its Rural Environs, 1500–c.1618', (Ph.D. thesis, Cambridge, 1995).

—— '"In Great Secrecy": The Crime of Infanticide in Rothenburg ob der Tauber, 1501–1618', *German History*, 2 (1997), 181–99.

RUBLACK, U., '"Viehisch, frech vnd onverschämpt": Inzest in Südwestdeutschland, ca. 1530–1700', in O. Ulbricht (ed.), *Von Huren und Rabenmüttern: Weibliche Kriminalität in der frühen Neuzeit* (Cologne, 1995).

—— 'Anschläge auf die Ehre: Schmähschriften und -zeichen in der städtischen Kultur des Ancien Régime', in K. Schreiner and G. Schwerhoff (eds.), *Verletzte Ehre: Ehrkonflikte in Gesellschaften des Mittelalters und der frühen Neuzeit* (Cologne, 1995).

—— 'Pregnancy, Childbirth and the Female Body in Early Modern Germany', *P&P* 150 (1996), 84–110.

—— 'The Public Body: Policing Abortion in Early Modern Germany', in L. Abrams and E. Harvey (eds.), *Gender Relations in German History: Power, Agency and Experience from the Sixteenth to the Twentieth Century* (London, 1996).

RUBLACK, U., 'Wench and Maiden: Women, War and the Pictorial Function of the Feminine in Early Modern German Towns', *HWJ* 44 (1997), 1–22.

—— *Geordnete Verhältnisse? Ehealltag und Ehepolitik im frühneuzeitlichen Konstanz* (Constance, 1997).

—— 'Frühneuzeitliche Staatlichkeit und lokale Herrschaftspraxis in Württemberg', *ZHF* 3 (1997), 347–376.

—— *Magd, Metz' oder Mörderin? Frauen vor frühneuzeitlichen Gerichten* (Frankfurt on Main, 1998).

RUGGIERO, G., *The Boundaries of Eros: Sex Crime and Sexuality in Renaissance Venice* (New York, 1995).

—— *Binding Passions: Tales of Magic, Marriage, and Power at the End of the Renaissance* (New York, 1993).

SABEAN, D. W., *Power in the Blood: Popular Culture and Village Discourse in Early Modern Germany* (Cambridge, 1984).

—— '"Junge Immen im leeren Korb": Beziehungen zwischen Schwägern in einem schwäbischen Dorf', in id. and H. Medick (eds.), *Emotionen und materielle Interessen: Sozialanthropologische und historische Beiträge zur Familienforschung* (Göttingen, 1984).

—— *Property, Production, and Family in Neckarhausen, 1700–1870* (Cambridge, 1990).

—— 'Soziale Distanzierungen: Ritualisierte Gestik in deutscher bürokratischer Prosa der frühen Neuzeit', *HA* 2 (1996), 216–33.

SAFLEY, T. M., *Let No Man Put Asunder: The Control of Marriage in the German Southwest: A Comparative Study, 1550–1600* (Kirksville, Mo., 1984).

—— 'Production, Transaction, and Proletarianization: The Textile Industry in Upper Swabia, 1580–1660', in id. and L. N. Rosenband (eds.), *The Workplace before the Factory: Artisans and Proletarians, 1500–1800* (Ithaca, NY, 1993).

SAHLINS, P., *Forest Rites: The War of the Demoiselles in Nineteenth-Century France* (Cambridge, Mass., 1994).

SÁNCHES ORTEGA, M. H., 'Sorcery and Eroticism in Love Magic', in M. E. Perry and A. J. Cruz (eds.), *Cultural Encounters: The Impact of the Inquisition in Spain and the New World* (Los Angeles, 1991).

SAUER, P., 'Not und Armut in den Dörfern des Mittleren Neckarraums in vorindustrieller Zeit', *ZfWLG* 41 (1982), 131–49.

—— *Im Namen des Königs: Strafgesetzgebung und Strafvollzug im Königreich Württemberg von 1806 bis 1871* (Stuttgart, 1984).

SCHAD, M., *Die Frauen des Hauses Fugger von der Lilie (15.–17. Jahrhundert): Augsburg—Ortenburg—Trient* (Tübingen, 1989).

SCHARFE, M., 'Zum Rügebrauch', *Hessische Blätter für Volkskunde*, 61 (1970), 45–68.

SCHIEBINGER, L., *Nature's Body: Gender in the Making of Modern Science* (Boston, 1993).

SCHILLING, H., '"History of Crime" or "History of Sin"? Some Reflections on the Social History of Early Modern Church Discipline', in E. Kouri and T. Scott (eds.), *Politics and Society in Reformation Europe* (London, 1987).

SCHILLING H., *Civic Calvinism in Northwestern Germany and the Netherlands: Sixteenth to Nineteenth Centuries* (Ann Arbor, 1991).

SCHINDLER, G., *Verbrechen und Strafen im Recht der Stadt Freiburg im Breisgau von der Einführung des neuen Strafrechts bis zum Übergang an Baden (1520–1806)* (Freiburg im Breisgau, 1937).

Schindler, N., and Holenstein, P., 'Geschwätzgeschichte(n): Ein kulturhistorisches Plädoyer für die Rehabilitierung der unkontrollierten Rede', in R. v. Dülmen (ed.), *Dynamik der Tradition* (Frankfurt on Main, 1992).

—— *Widerspenstige Leute: Studien zur Volkskultur in der frühen Neuzeit* (Frankfurt on Main, 1992).

SCHMIDT, H. R., *Dorf und Religion: Reformierte Sittenzucht in Berner Landgemeinden der frühen Neuzeit* (Stuttgart, 1995).

SCHNABEL-SCHÜLE, H., 'Calvinistische Kirchenzucht in Württemberg? Zur Theorie und Praxis der württembergischen Kirchenkonvente', *ZfWLG* 49 (1990), 169–223.

—— *Überwachen und Strafen im frühneuzeitlichen Württemberg* (Cologne, 1997).

SCHOTT, C., *Armenfürsorge, Bettelwesen und Vagantenbekämpfung in der Reichsabtei Salem* (Bühl, 1978).

SCHRÖDER, T., *Das Kirchenregiment der Reichsstadt Esslingen: Grundlagen—Geschichte—Organisation* (Esslingen, 1987).

SCHUBERT, E., *Arme Leute, Bettler und Gauner im Franken des 18. Jahrhunderts* (Neustadt, 1983).

SCHULTE, R., *The Village in Court: Arson, Infanticide and Poaching in the Court Records of Upper Bavaria, 1848–1910*, trans. B. Selman (Cambridge, 1994).

SCHULZE, W., 'Vom Gemeinnutz zum Eigennutz: Über den Normenwandel in der ständischen Gesellschaft der frühen Neuzeit', *HZ* 243 (1986), 591–626.

—— 'Gerhard Oestreichs Begriff "Sozialdisziplinierung" in der frühen Neuzeit', *ZHF* 14 (1987), 265–302.

SCHUSTER, B., *Die freien Frauen: Dirnen und Frauenhäuser im 15. und 16. Jahrhundert* (Frankfurt on Main, 1995).

SCHUSTER, P., *Das Frauenhaus: Städtische Bordelle in Deutschland 1350–1600* (Paderborn, 1992).

SCHWERHOFF, G., *Köln im Kreuzverhör: Kriminalität, Herrschaft und Gesellschaft in einer frühneuzeitlichen Stadt* (Bonn, 1991).

—— 'Devianz in der 'alteuropäischen Gesellschaft: Umrisse einer historischen Kriminalitätsforschung', *ZHF* 19 (1992), 385–414.

—— '"Mach, dass wir nicht in Schande geraten!"': Frauen in Kölner Kriminalfällen des 16. Jahrhunderts', *GWU* 44 (1993), 451–73.

—— 'Verordnete Schande? Spätmittelalterliche und frühneuzeitliche Ehrenstrafen zwischen Rechtsakt und sozialer Sanktion', in id. and A. Blauert (eds.), *Mit den Waffen der Justiz: Zur Kriminalitätsgeschichte des späten Mittelalters und der frühen Neuzeit* (Frankfurt on Main, 1993).

SCRIBNER, R. W., 'Police and the Territorial State in Sixteenth-Century Württemberg', in E. I. Kouri and T. Scott (eds.), *Politics and Society in Reformation Europe* (London, 1987).

—— 'Mobility: Voluntary or Enforced? Vagrants in Württemberg in the Sixteenth Century', in G. Jaritz and A. Müller (eds.), *Migration in der Feudalgesellschaft* (Frankfurt on Main, 1988).

—— 'The Mordbrenner Fear in Sixteenth-Century Germany: Political Paranoia or the Revenge of the Outcast?', in R. J. Evans (ed.), *The German Underworld: Deviants and Outcasts in German History* (London, 1988).

SHARPE, J. A., 'Enforcing the Law in the Seventeenth-Century Village', in V. A. C. Gatrell, B. Lenman and G. Parker (eds.), *Crime and the Law: The Social History of Crime in Western Europe since 1500* (London, 1980).

SHOEMAKER, R., *Prosecution and Punishment: Petty Crime and the Law in London and Rural Middlesex, c.1660–1725* (Cambridge, 1991).

SHORTER, E., 'Bastardy in South Germany: A Commentary', *JIH* 8 (1978), 459–69.

SIMON, C., *Untertanenverhalten und obrigkeitliche Moralpolitik: Studien zum Verhältnis zwischen Stadt und Land im ausgehenden 18. Jahrhundert am Beispiel Basel* (Basle, 1981).

SIMON-MUSCHEID, K., '"Und ob sie schon einen Dienst finden, so sind sie nit bekleidet dennoch": Die Kleidung städtischer Unterschichten zwischen Projektion und Realität im Spätmittelalter und in der frühen Neuzeit', *Saeculum*, 44 (1993), 47–64.

SMOLINSKY, H., 'Ehespiegel im Konfessionalisierungsprozeß', in W. Reinhard and H. Schilling (eds.), *Die katholische Konfessionalisierung* (Gütersloh, 1995).

SPICKER-BECK, M., *Räuber, Mordbrenner, umschweifendes Gesind: Zur Kriminalität im 16. Jahrhundert* (Freiburg im Breisgau, 1995).

SPIERENBURG, P., *The Prison Experience: Disciplinary Institutions and their Inmates in Early Modern Europe* (London, 1991).

STIASSNY, S., *Die Pfählung: Eine Form der Todesstrafe* (Vienna, 1903).

STONE, L., *Road to Divorce: England, 1530–1987* (Oxford, 1990).

SUMNER, C., *The Sociology of Deviance: An Obituary* (Cambridge, 1994).

THEIBAULT, J. C., *German Villages in Crisis: Rural Life in Hesse-Kassel and the Thirty Years' War, 1580–1720* (Atlantic Highlands, NJ, 1995).

THOMAS, K., *Man and the Natural World: Changing Attitudes in England, 1500–1800* (Harmondsworth, 1984).

THOMPSON, E. P., *Whigs and Hunters: The Origin of the Black Act* (London, 1975).

TOLLEY, B., *Pastors and Parishioners in Württemberg during the Late Reformation 1581–1621* (Stanford, Calif., 1995).

TREPP, A.-C., 'The Emotional Side of Men in Late Eighteenth-Century Germany', *Central European History*, 27 (1994), 127–52.

TREPP, A.-C., *Sanfte Männlichkeit und selbstständige Weiblichkeit: Frauen und Männer im Hamburger Bürgertum zwischen 1770 und 1840* (Göttingen, 1996).

TREXLER, R., 'Infanticide in Florence: New Sources and First Results', *History of Childhood Quarterly*, 1 (1973), 96–116.

TROβBACH, W., *Bauern 1648–1806* (Munich, 1993).

TRUGENBERGER, V., *Zwischen Schloβ und Vorstadt: Sozialgeschichte der Stadt Leonberg im 16. Jahrhundert* (Vaihingen, 1984).

ULBRICH, C. 'Unartige Weiber: Präsenz und Renitenz von Frauen im frühneuzeitlichen Deutschland', in R. v. Dülmen (ed.), *Arbeit, Frömmigkeit und Eigensinn* (Frankfurt on Main, 1990).

—— 'Frauenarmut in der frühen Neuzeit', *Zeitschrift für die Geschichte der Saargegend*, 40 (1992), 108–20.

ULBRICHT, O., *Kindsmord und Aufklärung in Deutschland* (Munich, 1990).

—— 'Kindsmörderinnen vor Gericht: Verteidigungstrategien von Frauen in Norddeutschland', in A. Blauert and G. Schwerhoff (eds.), *Mit den Waffen der Justiz: Zur Kriminalitätsgeschichte des Spätmittelalters und der frühen Neuzeit* (Frankfurt on Main, 1993).

—— 'Einleitung', in id. (ed.), *Von Huren und Rabenmüttern: Weibliche Kriminalität in der frühen Neuzeit* (Cologne, 1995).

—— 'Zwischen Vergeltung und Zukunftsplanung: Hausdiebstahl von Mägden in Schleswig-Holstein vom 16. bis zum 19. Jahrhundert', in id. (ed.), *Von Huren und Rabenmüttern: Weibliche Kriminalität in der frühen Neuzeit* (Cologne, 1995).

UNDERDOWN, D., *Fire from Heaven: Life in an English Town in the Seventeenth Century* (London, 1993).

UNHOLD, W., *Geschichte der Stadt Memmingen* (Memmingen, 1929).

VANJA, C., 'Frauen im Dorf: Ihre Stellung unter besonderer Berücksichtigung landgräflich-hessischer Quellen des späten Mittelalters', *Zeitschrift für Agrargeschichte und Agrarsoziologie*, 34 (1986), 147–59.

—— 'Das "Weibergericht" zu Breitenbach: Verkehrte Welt in einem hessischen Dorf des 17. Jahrhunderts', in ead. and H. Wunder (eds.), *Weiber, Menscher, Frauenzimmer: Frauen in der ländlichen Gesellschaft 1500–1800* (Göttingen, 1996).

VANN, J. A., *The Making of a State: Württemberg 1593–1793* (Ithaca, NY. 1984).

VÖLKER, A., 'Bilderpaare—Paarbilder: Die Ehe in Autobiographien des 16. Jahrhunderts', (D. Phil. thesis, Freiburg im Breisgau, 1990).

WAGNER, U., *Tauberbischofsheim und Bad Mergentheim: Eine Analyse der Raumbeziehungen zweier Städte in der frühen Neuzeit* (Heidelberg, 1985).

WALKER, G., 'Rereading Rape and Sexual Violence in Early Modern England', *Gender & History* 10, (1998), 1–25.

WALZ, R., *Hexenglaube und magische Kommunikation im Dorf der frühen Neuzeit: Die Verfolgung in der Grafschaft Lippe* (Paderborn, 1993).

—— 'Schimpfende Weiber: Frauen in lippischen Beleidigungsprozessen des 17. Jahrhunderts', in H. Wunder and C. Vanja (eds.), *Weiber, Menscher, Frauenzimmer: Frauen in der ländlichen Gesellschaft 1500–1800* (Göttingen, 1996).

WARNKE, M., *Politische Landschaft: Zur Kunstgeschichte der Natur* (Munich, 1992).

WATT, J. R., *The Making of Modern Marriage: Matrimonial Control and the Rise of Sentiment in Neuchâtel, 1550–1800* (Ithaca, NY, 1992).

—— 'Women and the Consistory in Calvin's Geneva', *SCJ* 24 (1993), 429–39.

WEBER, W., *Prudentia gubernatoria: Studien zur Herrschaftslehre in der deutschen politischen Wissenschaft des 17. Jahrhunderts* (Tübingen, 1992).

WEGERT, K., *Popular Culture, Crime, and Social Control in 18th Century Württemberg* (Stuttgart, 1994).

WETTMANN-JUNGBLUT, P., '"Stelen inn rechter hungersnott". Diebstahl, Eigentumsschutz und strafrechtliche Kontrolle im vorindustriellen Baden, 1600–1800', in R. v. Dülmen (ed.), *Verbrechen, Strafen und soziale Kontrolle* (Frankfurt on Main, 1990).

—— 'Vater–Mutter–Kind: Gefühlswelt und Moral einer Freiburger Familie im 18. Jahrhundert', in E. Labouvie (ed.), *Ungleiche Paare: Zur Kulturgeschichte menschlicher Beziehungen* (Munich, 1997).

WIESNER, M. E., *Working Women in Renaissance Germany* (New Brunswick, NY, 1986).

—— 'Spinsters and Seamstresses: Women in Cloth and Clothing Production', in M. W. Ferguson et al. (eds.), *Rewriting the Renaissance: The Discourses of Sexual Difference in Early Modern Europe* (Chicago, 1986).

—— 'The Midwives of South Germany and the Public/Private Dichotomy', in H. Marland (ed.), *The Art of Midwifery: Early Modern Midwives in Europe* (London, 1993).

—— *Women and Gender in Early Modern Europe* (Cambridge, 1993).

WILSON, P., *War, State and Society in Württemberg, 1677–1793* (Cambridge, 1995).

WILTENBURG, J., *Disorderly Women and Female Power in the Street Literature of Early Modern England and Germany* (Charlottesville, Va., 1992).

WOLF, T., *Reichsstädte in Kriegszeiten: Untersuchungen zur Verfassungs-, Wirtschafts- und Sozialgeschichte von Isny, Lindau, Memmingen und Ravensburg im 17. Jahrhundert* (Memmingen, 1991).

WOLFART, J. C., 'Political Culture and Religion in Lindau, 1520–1628', (Ph.D. thesis, Cambridge, 1993).

WOLGAST, E., *Die Religionsfrage als Problem des Widerstandsrechts im 16. Jahrhundert* (Heidelberg, 1980).

WRIGHTSON, K., 'Two Concepts of Order: Justices, Constables and Jurymen in Seventeenth-Century England', in J. Brewer and J. Styles (eds.), *An Ungovernable People: The English and their Law in the Seventeenth and Eighteenth Centuries* (London, 1980).

—— and LEVINE, D., *Poverty and Piety in an English Village: Terling, 1525–1700* (2nd edn. Oxford, 1995).

—— 'The Politics of the Parish in Early Modern England', in P. Griffiths, A. Fox and S. Hindle (eds.), *The Experience of Authority in Early Modern England* (London, 1996).

WUNDER, B., *Frankreich, Württemberg und der schwäbische Kreis während der*

Auseinandersetzungen über die Reunionen (1679–97): Ein Beitrag zur Deutschlandpolitik Ludwig XIV. (Stuttgart, 1971).

WUNDER, G., *Die Bürger von Hall: Sozialgeschichte einer Reichsstadt 1216–1802* (Sigmaringen, 1980).

—— 'Geschlechter und Gemeinde: Soziale Veränderungen in süddeutschen Reichsstädten zu Beginn der Neuzeit', in W. Rausch (ed.), *Die Stadt an der Schwelle zur Neuzeit: Beiträge zur Geschichte der Städte Mitteleuropas* (Linz, 1980).

WUNDER, H., *'Er ist die Sonn, sie ist der Mond': Frauen in der frühen Neuzeit* (Munich, 1992).

—— '"Jede Arbeit ist ihres Lohnes wert": Zur geschlechtsspezifischen Teilung und Bewertung von Arbeit in der frühen Neuzeit', in K. Hausen (ed.), *Geschlechterhierarchie und Arbeitsteilung: Zur Geschichte ungleicher Erwerbschancen von Männern und Frauen* (Göttingen, 1993).

—— '"Weibliche Kriminalität" in der frühen Neuzeit: Überlegungen aus der Sicht der Geschlechtergeschichte', in O. Ulbricht (ed.), *Von Huren und Rabenmüttern: Weibliche Kriminalität in der frühen Neuzeit* (Cologne, 1995).

—— 'Wie wird man ein Mann? Befunde am Beginn der Neuzeit (15.–17. Jahrhundert)', in C. Eifert et al. (eds.), *Was sind Männer? Was sind Frauen? Geschlechterkonstruktionen im historischen Wandel* (Frankfurt on Main, 1996).

—— 'Gender Norms and their Enforcement in Early Modern Germany', in L. Abrams and E. Harvey (eds.), *Gender Relations in German History: Power, Agency and Experience from the Sixteenth to the Twentieth Century* (London, 1996).

ZIMMERMANN, C., '"Behörigs Orthen angezeigt": Kindsmörderinnen in der ländlichen Gesellschaft Württembergs, 1581–1792', *MedGG* 10 (1991), 67–102.

ZIMMERMANN, W., *Rekatholisierung, Konfessionalisierung und Ratsregiment: Der Prozeß des politischen und religiösen Wandels in der österreichischen Stadt Konstanz 1548–1637* (Sigmaringen, 1994).

INDEX